ROUTLEDGE LIBRARY EDITIONS:
EDUCATION

EDUCABILITY AND GROUP
DIFFERENCES

EDUCABILITY AND GROUP DIFFERENCES

ARTHUR R. JENSEN

Volume 61

Routledge
Taylor & Francis Group

LONDON AND NEW YORK

First published in 1973

This edition first published in 2012
by Routledge
2 Park Square, Milton Park, Abingdon, Oxon, OX14 4RN

Simultaneously published in the USA and Canada
by Routledge
711 Third Avenue, New York, NY 10017

Routledge is an imprint of the Taylor & Francis Group, an informa business

British Library Cataloguing in Publication Data
A catalogue record for this book is available from the British Library

ISBN 13: 978-0-415-61517-4 (Set)
eISBN 13: 978-0-203-81617-2 (Set)
ISBN 13: 978-0-415-67856-8 (Volume 61)
eISBN 13: 978-0-203-80741-5 (Volume 61)

Publisher's Note
The publisher has gone to great lengths to ensure the quality of this reprint but
points out that some imperfections in the original copies may be apparent.

Disclaimer
The publisher has made every effort to trace copyright holders and would
welcome correspondence from those they have been unable to trace.

Educability and Group Differences

ARTHUR R. JENSEN

METHUEN & CO LTD
11 New Fetter Lane London EC4

First published in 1973
by Methuen & Co Ltd, 11 New Fetter Lane, London EC4P 4EE
First published as a University Paperback in 1976
© 1973 Arthur R. Jensen
Printed in Great Britain
by T. & A. Constable Ltd, Hopetoun Street, Edinburgh

ISBN 0 416 75780 4 (hardback edition)
ISBN 0 416 70460 3 (paperback edition)

To the memory of Sir Cyril Burt

Contents

List of Tables

List of Figures

Acknowledgements

The author gratefully acknowledges the kindness of the following in allowing him to reproduce material from their work: C. E. Noble and the University of Chicago Press for Figures 18.1 and 18.2; W. A. Kennedy, V. Van De Reit, J. C. White and The Society for Research in Child Development for Figure 8.2; N. Weyl and *Mankind Quarterly* for Table 12.2; Marjorie P. Honzik, Jean W. MacFarlane, L. Allen and the *Journal of Experimental Education* for Table 3.3; Julia R. Vane and *Psychology in the Schools* for Table 3.1; Marion M. DeLemos and the *International Journal of Psychology* for Table 17.1; G. H. Bracht, K. D. Hopkins, J. C. Stanley and Prentice-Hall, Inc. for Table 3.2; R. J. Havighurst and the American Psychological Association for permission to quote an extract from 'Minority subcultures and the law of effect', *American Psychologist*, 1926, Vol. 25, p. 313 (see p. 32); J. M. Thoday, J. B. Gibson and the American Association for the Advancement of Science for permission to quote an extract from 'Environmental and genetic contributions to class difference: a model experiment', *Science*, 1970, Vol. 167, p. 992 (see pp. 154-5).

Preface

Educability and Group Differences deals with the fact that various subpopulations (social classes and ethnic groups) in the United States and elsewhere show marked differences in the distributions of those mental abilities most importantly related to educability and its occupational and socioeconomic correlates. This book challenges some of the prevailing explanations of these differences, particularly those theories that involve exclusively social and psychological causative factors. The substantial genetic heritability of intelligence within European and North American Caucasian populations is now generally accepted by most scientists who have reviewed the evidence. Although one cannot formally generalize from *within*-group heritability to *between*-groups heritability, the evidence from studies of within-group heritability does, in fact, impose severe constraints on some of the most popular environmental theories of the existing racial and social class differences in educational performance. My review of this evidence, with its impressive consistency, does, I believe, cast serious doubt on the currently popular explanations in terms of environment. While the existing body of evidence has many gaps and may not compel definitive conclusions, it appears to me that, when viewed all together, it does point more strongly and consistently in the one direction than in the other. The gaps in knowledge suggest new methods, not yet tried, for testing genetic hypotheses of group differences, and these are described herein. Also, at this stage it still seems necessary to discuss some of the popular misconceptions and the non-scientific hindrances to the advancement of research in this field.

1

If population differences, whatever their causes might be, are not superficial or easily eliminated, as probably most behavioral scientists would now agree is the case, the major question that arises concerns the educational and occupational implications of such differences. What are the possibilities for capitalizing on individual differences in the pattern or profile of abilities in improving methods of instruction? What are the prospects for discovering aptitude × training interactions that will maximize overall achievement and minimize group differences? A growth model of scholastic achievement, along with the results of recent research on these questions, suggests that the prospects are poor for supposing that aptitude × training interactions will diminish achievement differences within the context of traditional schooling, in which, by and large, there is essentially no substitute for intelligence as psychologists generally use the term. Finally, it is proposed for consideration that perhaps radically altered and diversified forms of education, both as to methods and goals, might be able to utilize a broader spectrum of human abilities in order to increase the personal, social and occupational benefits of education to a wider segment of our population than is now truly served by the prevailing educational system. So much by way of summary.

The background of the problems treated in the present volume is provided in my 1969 article in the *Harvard Educational Review*, 'How much can we boost IQ and scholastic achievement?', and, more fully, in the collection of my subsequent related articles (including the *HER* article) in the recently published volume entitled *Genetics and Education* (Jensen, 1972). A third volume, soon to be published, brings together a number of my writings on a wide variety of more specific theoretical and applied topics in this field.

Since the greatest amount of discussion, and surely the most heated, following my *HER* article (Jensen, 1969a) centered on the topic of race differences in intelligence, and since this topic was treated only very briefly in that article (taking up less than one-tenth of the total number of pages), I saw the need to take it up more thoroughly and to present a more detailed account of the issues and evidence. A number of opportunities were presented for me to do this, more or less, in various scientific symposia following my *HER* article, and it was from these that the present volume gradually evolved. It began in 1970 as a paper prepared for a symposium held in London on social implications of human differences, in which I was invited to discuss the educational aspects. This paper was then greatly elaborated when I was invited to prepare an extensive paper as the basis for a symposium on cultural and genetic determinants of educability at the International Congress of Applied Psychology in Liège, Belgium, in the summer of 1971. Comments and criticisms by the several highly qualified discussants in the symposium, who had received copies of my paper for detailed study beforehand, led to still further additions and changes. Some twenty or so copies of the typescript, under the title 'Genetics, Educability, and Subpopulation Differences', were then sent out to colleagues in psychology and genetics, with an invitation to make critical comments. Many responded with most helpful criticisms, usually of selected portions which fell within each critic's own speciality. I am most grateful for all their comments and advice. There are several to whom I am most specially indebted for their great generosity and thoroughness in corresponding with me so willingly and patiently about many technical matters. They contributed much to the improvement of my first draft of this book and to my own education on matters in genetics. I take this opportunity to thank them again: Professors Everett Dempster, John Loehlin, Peter Workman, and the late Sir Cyril Burt. The book's overall shortcomings must be accounted to me alone.

Though I always heeded expert advice on purely factual and technical matters, I usually kept my own counsel on matters of interpretation and judgment, and in such cases my helpful critics may not always find themselves in agreement, either with me or with each other. There are always differences among investigators working on the frontiers of a field. They differ in their weighting of items of evidence, in the range of facts in which an underlying consistency is perceived, in the degree of caution with which they will try to avoid possible criticisms of their opinions, and in the thinness of the ice upon which they are willing to skate in hopes of glimpsing seemingly remote phenomena and relationships among lines of evidence which might otherwise go unnoticed as grist for new hypotheses and further investigations. On all these points we differ in varying degrees, and my own inclination is perhaps to be somewhat less conservative than would be some other students in dealing with the central topics of this book. My

own reading of the history of science, however, leads me to believe
that conservatism in generating hypotheses and in seeking means
for testing them has not made for progress as often as a more
adventurous approach.

The nature of scientific 'proof' is poorly understood by most
non-scientists. It is surely not an either-or affair, and in fact the
term 'proof' is actually inappropriate in the empirical sciences.
Proof exists in formal logic and pure mathematics, which, as
Bertrand Russell pointed out, are one vast tautology in which
certain consequences are formally derived from fundamental
definitions, axioms and postulates according to set rules, which,
when strictly followed, constitute the proof of the conclusion.
Empirical science operates quite differently. It aims to find the
best explanation of phenomena by ruling out other alternative
explanations on a probabilistic basis. Progress consists of weaken-
ing the explanatory power of one or more competing hypotheses
and strengthening that of another on the basis of objective evidence.
It is a most complex process into which enter consideration of the
basic assumptions underlying a given theory, the range of phenomena that can be comprehended by one theory as opposed to
another, and the number of *ad hoc* hypotheses (and the extent of
their mutual inconsistency) that must proliferate to take care of
each new failure of a theory's predictions as the evidence mounts.
On all these grounds, in my opinion, a largely genetic explanation
of the evidence on racial and social group differences in educational
performance is in a stronger position scientifically than those
explanations which postulate the absence of any genetic differences
in mental traits and ascribe all behavioral variation between groups
to cultural differences, social discrimination, and inequalities of
opportunity – a view that has long been orthodox in the social
sciences and in education.

Questioning this doctrine of egalitarian environmentalism is
often regarded as unrespectable and is therefore eschewed by some
researchers who may regard the key issues as improper or scientifically unrewarding territory for exploration. The exercise of
intellectual fastidiousness is an attraction to many who engage in
research, and indeed it is one of the virtues. But sheer respectability
when it becomes a motive or a goal in itself, in scientific research
is crippling and deadening. Preordained notions and inhibitions
concerning what is and what is not respectable grist for research

are intrinsically antithetical to scientific investigation. The existing research taboos concerning racial genetic differences and the design of studies that could lead to rejection of the null hypothesis are not in the main externally imposed; they are self-imposed restrictions of individual scientists who apparently fear the outcome of unrelenting research on the problem.

Scientific knowledge advances from lesser to greater levels of probability, and most complex subjects do not make this ascent in one leap. Statements such as 'Circumstantial evidence does not constitute scientific evidence', do, I believe, misrepresent the process of science. Though they indeed contain an element of truth, they permit the overly simple interpretation that there are two clear-cut categories of evidence – 'circumstantial' and 'scientific' – while in fact all we ever have as scientists is circumstantial evidence which varies along a probabilistic continuum in quality and quantity and theoretical consistency. What emerges finally as scientific truth is a preponderance of self-consistent evidence which points to one theory to the exclusion of others. In complex subjects this is a gradual process punctuated by ambiguities and doubts, gaps and inconsistencies, as the work progresses and a preponderance of evidence favors certain key hypotheses and leads to the abandonment of others. The future of research on the causes of individual and group differences in mental abilities may be likened scientifically more to the detective work of a Darwin, patiently collecting and sifting and fitting together the myriad pieces of the jigsaw puzzle bearing on his theory of evolution, than to Archimedes suddenly shouting 'Eureka!' in his bath when he discovered the explanation of floatation. The models of biology fit the behavioral sciences better than do those of classical physics.

This book was written with mainly behavioral scientists and educational researchers in mind. I have presupposed only a familiarity with basic statistical concepts that are common background in these fields. But it is these very concepts that create considerable difficulty in properly explaining the nature of the evidence and arguments to the man in the street. Secondary schools unfortunately do not ordinarily include in their science curricula the elementary concepts of probability and statistical inference, or the properties of the normal distribution, or the understanding of correlation and the differences between correlational and experimental methods, or even how to interpret graphs, all of which are fundamental tools for properly understanding research in the behavioral sciences. One always has some trepidation about the message conveyed to readers who are not at home with the tools. An admirable popular treatment of some of the main themes of the present work which presupposes no technical background whatever is the highly readable little book by Professor Eysenck (1971). It is a good example of popular science writing, avoiding the technical yet being accurate, and could well serve as a non-technical introduction to the present work and as a fair summary, albeit not in my own style, of some of the major issues treated herein for readers who might shy away from the more quantitative presentation of data and theoretical formulations in this book.

There are some major conceptions and misconceptions, however, that must be made clear for all readers of this book right from the outset. Some critics have unjustly linked these misconceptions to my name in their use of the term 'jensenism'. I think this must be righted lest the reader begin with quite erroneous preconceptions of the essential message of this book. Since I did not coin the word 'jensenism', I do not know all the meanings that it may have acquired in the popular press. To the best of my knowledge, 'jensenism' was coined by the *Wall Street Journal*, shortly after the publication of my *HER* article. It has since been used in the popular press and elsewhere (e.g., the *Bulletin of the Atomic Scientists*, March, May 1970) as a term intended to summarize the user's interpretation of one or another aspect of my article: the failure of large-scale compensatory education programs, the theory of the inheritance of mental abilities, the hypothesis that not only individual differences but social class and racial differences in intelligence involve genetic as well as environmental factors, and that mental abilities may be viewed in terms of two broad categories (called Level I and Level II) which are differentially correlated with social class and might have useful implications for instruction in scholastic skills. Some of my most vehement critics, however, have used the term pejoratively. Professor Lewontin, for example, likened 'jensenism' to Jansenism, named after Bishop Jansen in the seventeenth century for his 'pernicious heresy . . . of total depravity, irresistible grace, lack of free will, predestination and limited atonement' (Lewontin, 1970a, b; Jensen, 1970d).

If 'jensenism' has any valid meaning at all, from my own

standpoint, what it means is a biological and genetical view of human kind and of human differences – both individual differences and group differences. For me, 'jensenism' is the bringing to bear of this genetic viewpoint upon understanding some of the problems of education. The genetic view of man has often been badly misunderstood in this context, and 99 percent of the heated debate I have seen in the three years since the publication of my *Harvard Educational Review* article I believe reflects this misunderstanding. Much of the emotional reaction I attribute to the fact that a generation or more of social scientists and educators have been indoctrinated to ignore genetics, or to believe that genetic factors are of little or no importance in human behavior and human differences, or to think non-genetically or anti-genetically. Any attempt by anyone to introduce into this scene theory and research on genetics as it relates to vital educational and social problems was destined at first to meet hostility and rejection.

The modern genetic view of man calls for a revolution in our thinking, in our whole orientation. It demands on everyone's part an even more drastic reorientation of thinking than was required by other historical revolutions of thought, such as the Copernican, Darwinian, and Einsteinian revolutions. The Mendelian revolution (and Fisher's pioneering extensions of Mendelian genetics to polygenic systems) is already established in biological science, but it has not yet filtered into other domains. The Mendelian revolution, if it can be called that, has not yet influenced social scientists on any large scale; it has not characterized the thinking of our social policy makers, and it is totally foreign to the general public, which in terms of thinking genetically in the modern sense is surely at the flat earth stage of scientific sophistication. The educational task that is called for is awesome. Major revolutions of thought are generally absorbed most slowly and imperfectly.

The genetic view of man stands in sharp contrast to the prevailing views that dominate most people's thinking. One class of anti-genetic view can be characterized as social elitism and racism. These old-fashioned beliefs are quite out of touch with modern genetics; they are now more political and ideological than scientific. They are based on typological notions of genetics, and not on statistical and stochastic conceptions of continuous variation. They are apparently ignorant of the genetic facts of random segregation and recombination of genes, or of the fundamental principle that the properties of an individual depend upon the state in which he finds himself and not upon the state from which he is derived, or the fact that social classes and races are discrete systems of classification imposed upon what in nature are not at all discrete but rather continuous gene pools which vary statistically. This mistaken typological thinking proclaims 'like begets like' but ignores the other half of genetic fact – that 'like also begets unlike', due to segregation and recombination of genes in the creation of every individual. In a profound sense, social elitism and racism deny individuality, the very individuality that is in fact insured by genetic mechanisms.

There is another class of anti-genetic misconceptions which shares many characteristics in common with the first class of erroneous thinking I have just described. It can be called egalitarian environmentalism. Like social elitism and racism, it too ignores the facts of genetics, and it too denies individuality if you follow its reasoning all the way. And similarly, it is more political and ideological than scientific. It denies genetic variability, at least with respect to certain characteristics, usually behavioral, and insists that the environment alone – usually the social environment – makes the person and all the behavioral differences among persons. It may at times pay a kind of lip service to genetics, which is often seen as ceasing in importance after the moment of conception, but its conclusions invariably deny the importance of genetic factors in human behavioral differences. It may also wear the guise of 'interactionism', based on the truism that the individual is a product of the interaction of genetic and environmental factors, but always with the implication that the genetic factors are more or less totally submerged or obscured by environmental influences.

Much of the debate and fulmination surrounding my *HER* article, I submit, was a result of most persons knowing only these two mistaken views and feeling that their only choice was the one or the other. Most well-intentioned persons have deemed it necessary to put down the first view at all costs and to defend the second. Often it was viewed as the battle of the 'good guys' versus the 'bad guys'. I have been opposed to both these views. The antidote to both is to *think genetically*, that is to say, in the most fundamental sense to think about yourself, about other persons, and about groups (your own group and other groups, whatever they may be) in ways that are consistent with already well-established modern principles of genetics. In short, I am saying we should get abreast of the Mendelian revolution.

Just what does this mean? Let us get down to specific points. First and most important, it means that you and everyone else (except monozygotic twins) are genetically unique. The probability that even any two siblings (other than MZ twins) will inherit the same genotypes (i.e., the individual's total genetic 'blueprint') is less than 1 in 73 trillions! So if we are to think realistically in terms of what we know from genetics, we must recognize uniqueness and individuality. A genetic corollary of this is that *you* are not your *parents*. Parents do not transmit their own genotypes to their off-spring, but only their genes, and a random selection of only one half of them at that. Each offspring is a new assortment, a new combination of genetic material, and thus we see great variability among members of the same family, probably much greater variability than most persons would like to acknowledge. The average amount of genetic variability *within* families is only slightly less than the genetic variability *between* families. By the same token, nature has seen to it that your children will not be *you*. Perhaps here is the crux of the revolution called for by Mendelism in our thinking and in our attitudes. This is what must sink into our consciousness: the disassociation of our individuality, our genetic uniqueness, from our biological role as mere transmitters of randomly segregating and recombining genetic materials which indeed obey statistical laws but which are not 'us'. When you have children, you don't make what you want; you take what you get. Since genes obey statistical laws, it may be possible to predict probabilistically what you will get, and you can be statistically assured of the variance as well as the mean. These ideas are admittedly hard to grasp, especially when they come face to face with our long-conditioned proclivities toward personal possessiveness regarding our ancestry and our future descendants. But the first lesson of Mendelism, it seems to me, is the distinction between the individual *qua* individual and his quite separate biologic function as a mere transmitter of nature's (not his own) genetic material. The difficulties of thinking in these terms are often exemplified in the emotional attitudes expressed in discussions of artificial insemination.

This distinction between the individual and the particular gene pool from which the unique combination forming his genotype was derived extends beyond his family to the racial group with which he is identified and to the social status into which he is born. You are not your race; you are not your group. You are you. That is, if you are talking genetics. If you are talking sociology or politics, that may be another matter. You may be *psychologically* tied to and influenced by whatever groups you happen to identify with. If you are either elated or depressed about yourself because of such identification, don't attribute this to genetics. It in fact contradicts this kind of typology which compels so many persons to identify with various groups as if the statistical attributes of the group determined their own characteristics. Racism and social elitism fundamentally arise from identification of individuals with their genetic ancestry; they ignore individuality in favor of group characteristics; they emphasize pride in group characteristics, not individual accomplishment; they are more concerned with who belongs to what, and with head-counting and percentages and quotas than with respecting the characteristics of individuals in their own right. This kind of thinking is contradicted by genetics; it is anti-Mendelian. And even if you profess to abhor racism and social elitism and are joined in battle against them, you can only remain in a miserable quandary if at the same time you continue to think, explicitly or implicitly, in terms of non-genetic or anti-genetic theories of human differences. Wrong theories exact their own penalties from those who believe them. Unfortunately, among many of my critics and among many students I repeatedly encounter lines of argument which reveal disturbing thought-blocks to distinguishing individuals from statistical characteristics (usually the mean) of the groups with which they are historically or socially identified. I know professors, for example, who cannot bring themselves to discuss racial group differences when any persons from different racial groups are present, and the fact that I am able to do so perhaps makes me appear insensitive in their eyes. I was once bothered by this too. I got over it as I studied more genetics and came more and more to appreciate its real implications.

If one must think of individuals not in terms of their own characteristics but in typological terms according to the supposed or real *average* characteristics of whatever group one classifies them as a member of, then one will have to pay a price for one's erroneous thinking, which is often quite discomforting fear and embarrassment and feeling like a 'bad guy'. This is the guilt of racism; we have all known it at one time or another, at least if we are not identified with a minority group. The overt ideological racists, of course, feel no guilt; the anti-racists (or as Raymond Cattell calls them, the 'ignoracists'), whose thinking is fundamentally the same but is morally unacceptable to them, experience feelings of guilt. Racism shows up in blatant forms among avowed racists, who would deny equal civil rights and opportunities in education and employment and housing on the basis of racial origin. But racism also shows up in many more subtle forms; it leads the ignoracists unconsciously to attribute traits to *individuals* which they do not actually possess, and also dogmatically to deny certain *group* characteristics or differences which may in fact exist. Then there is counter-racism, which some ignoracists seem to condone, although it is nothing other than the racism and chauvinism of minority groups who have historically been victimized by the racism of the majority. And two wrongs, we know, only make a bigger wrong. The racists may be popularly perceived as the 'bad guys' and the ignoracists as the 'good guys', but in principle they are much the same: they are both equally wrong and in the long run probably equally harmful. The solution, I repeat, is to think more genetically. The problem on both sides is fundamentally a matter of ignorance, the cure for which is a proper education about genetics.

Since one picture is worth a thousand words, let me illustrate just one of the contrasts between popular misconception and genetic fact, with a couple of simple diagrams devised by geneticist Ching Chun Li (1971). The upper diagram shows the popular conception of the genetic relationship between two generations in a population which has been stratified in terms of some polygenic trait having this distribution of values in the population. To make the illustration even more cogent, imagine that the divisions of the trait are perfectly coincident with some extrinsic classification such as social class. Note the lines of direct descent, from the parent generation to the offspring generation. Now, something closely approximating this could actually occur if the trait in question had zero heritability, i.e., if none of the trait variance was attributable to variance in genotypes. Then, if the environments of these 'classes' differ sharply, and there are no genetic influences involved in the total variance, then we would see the realization of this non-genetic picture in which 'like begets like'.

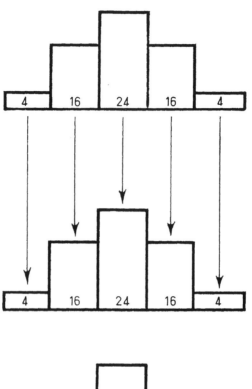

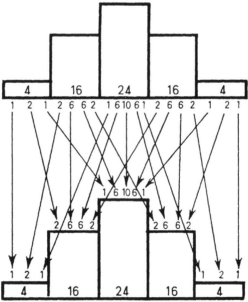

Figure P.1 Wrong and correct conceptions of intergenerational inheritance. (From Li, 1971.)

But to the extent that genetic factors play a part in the distribution of the trait, this is precisely what does not occur. What does occur, in fact, is shown in the lower diagram. Here we see that, genetically speaking, 'like begets like' but also 'like begets unlike'. Any individual in any group in the second generation could have had any origin in the first. There is some probabilistic correlation between the two generations, to be sure, but the important point to notice is that any given individual in the second generation is what he is, genetically speaking, because of what he actually *got*, and not because of *where* he got it. Has anyone ever pointed to a better argument for equality of opportunity? And, also, I must add, for equality of opportunity for a diversity of opportunities? This, more than anything else, is the essential meaning of 'jensenism'.

I find that those who do not think genetically are usually surprised, even shocked and often disbelieving, when they are informed that fewer than 60 percent of persons as adults are in the same social status that they were born into, or that more than two-thirds of Terman's gifted children, with IQs over 140, did not come from the highest socioeconomic group labeled 'professional and managerial'. Yet the vast majority of the gifted children themselves ended up in that top socioeconomic level. And their children? The lower diagram in Figure P.1 should give you a hint of the genetic prediction which is borne out in fact. While the Terman gifted were all above IQ 140 and averaged 152, their own children's IQs (with the exception of the 0·5 percent who are severely retarded) range from below 80 to over 180, with a mean of 132 and a standard deviation as large as that in the general population.

Thus the emphasis that I placed in my *HER* article upon the importance of distinguishing between individuals and populations bears repeating:

> The important distinction between the *individual* and the *population* must always be kept clearly in mind in any discussion of racial differences in mental abilities or any behavioral characteristics. Whenever we select a person for some special educational purpose, whether for special instruction in a grade-school class for children with learning problems, or for a 'gifted' class with an advanced curriculum, or for college attendance, or for admission to graduate training or a professional school, we are

selecting an *individual*, and we are selecting him and dealing with him as an individual for reasons of his individuality. Similarly, when we employ someone, or promote someone in his occupation, or give some special award or honor to someone for his accomplishments, we are doing this to an individual. The variables of social class, race, and national origin are correlated so imperfectly with any of the valid criteria on which the above decisions should depend, or, for that matter, with any behavioral characteristic, that these background factors are irrelevant as a basis for dealing with individuals – as students, as employees, as neighbors. Furthermore, since, as far as we know, the full range of human talents is represented in all the major races of man and in all socioeconomic levels, it is unjust to allow the mere fact of an individual's racial or social background to affect the treatment accorded to him. All persons rightfully must be regarded on the basis of their individual qualities and merits, and all social, educational, and economic institutions must have built into them the mechanisms for insuring and maximizing the treatment of persons according to their individual behavior.

If a society completely believed and practiced the ideal of treating every person as an individual, it would be hard to see why there should be any problems about 'race' *per se*. There might still be problems concerning poverty, unemployment, crime, and other social ills, and, given the will, they could be tackled just as any other problems that require rational methods for solution. But if this philosophy prevailed in practice, there would not need to be a 'race problem'.

The question of *race* differences in intelligence comes up not when we deal with individuals as individuals, but when certain identifiable *groups* or subcultures within the society are brought into comparison with one another *as groups or populations*. It is only when the groups are disproportionately represented in what are commonly perceived as the most desirable and the least desirable social and occupational roles in a society that the question arises concerning average differences among groups. Since much of the current thinking behind civil rights, fair employment, and equality of educational opportunity appeals to the fact that there is a disproportionate representation of different racial groups in the various levels of the educational, occupational, and socioeconomic hierarchy, we are forced to examine all the possible reasons for this inequality among racial groups in the attainments and rewards generally valued by all groups within our society. To what extent can such inequalities be attributed to unfairness in society's multiple selection processes? ('Unfair' meaning that selection is influenced by intrinsically irrelevant criteria, such as skin color, racial or national origin, etc.) And to what extent are these inequalities attributable to really relevant selection criteria which apply equally to all individuals but at the same time select disproportionately between some racial groups because there exist, in fact, real average differences among the groups – differences in the population distributions of those characteristics which are indisputably relevant to educational and occupational performance? This is certainly one of the most important questions confronting our nation today. The answer, which can be found only through unfettered research, has enormous consequences for the welfare of all, particularly of minorities whose plight is now in the foreground of public attention. A preordained, doctrinaire stance with regard to this issue hinders the achievement of a scientific understanding of the problem. To rule out of court, so to speak, any reasonable hypotheses on purely ideological grounds is to argue that static ignorance is preferable to increasing our knowledge of reality. I strongly disagree with those who believe in searching for the truth by scientific means only under certain circumstances and eschew this course in favor of ignorance under other circumstances, or who believe that the results of inquiry on some subjects cannot be entrusted to the public but should be kept the guarded possession of a scientific elite. Such attitudes, in my opinion, represent a danger to free inquiry and, consequently, in the long run, work to the disadvantage of society's general welfare. 'No holds barred' is the formula for scientific inquiry. One does not decree beforehand which phenomena cannot be studied or which questions cannot be answered.

The really fundamental and intrinsic problem in education, and in society in general, is not group differences, but individual differences in characteristics related to educability. But society creates group differences, which, once created, may be just as real as individual differences, and like many kinds of individual differences may involve genetic as well as experientially derived variation. A sharp dichotomy in our causal account of individual and group differences seems to me to be scientifically unwarranted, and to act as if such a dichotomy exists, when it is unlikely that it accords with the true state of nature, would seem to me to be undesirable. Groups are the result of classification, whether in terms of geographic origin of one's ancestors, visible physical characteristics, socioeconomic status, occupation, sex, or whatever – it can be quite arbitrary. Although average group differences in any characteristic are really just an average of individual differences classified by some particular rule, when viewed in this collective form they can appear quite troublesome if the behavioral characteristic in question is socially valued and differentially rewarded by the economic system, and especially if the mean differences between groups are large relative to individual differences within groups. The problems are magnified when group membership is rigidly imposed and the group identity of individuals is highly visible, as in the case of physical characteristics associated with racial classification.

Race differences and social class differences, therefore, are essentially more a social problem than a scientific one. But they are there, nevertheless, and society demands that they be dealt with in many spheres of public concern, and perhaps more in education than in anything else. If this is the case, then attempting to bring scientific knowledge and methods to bear upon understanding the nature of group differences would seem most appropriate. At the same time, we should not let the fact of group differences make us lose sight of the more fundamental fact of individual differences. The problem of the importance of intelligence in schools as they are presently constituted is not *primarily* a problem of any particular minority group within our population. Although the average IQ of the Negro population of the United States, for example, is about one standard deviation (i.e. 15 IQ points) below that of the white population, because of the disproportionate sizes of the Negro and white populations there are more whites with IQs below the Negro average than there are Negroes. It is only when society is ideologically, politically and economically sensitive to its classifications of persons into socially identifiable groups that unequal *percentages* of different groups in, say, special classes for the academically gifted and the educationally retarded become a matter of dissension. The causes of such inequalities of course need to be properly understood. If the variability in a socially valued trait such as intelligence were evenly or randomly spread throughout the total population, we would still have the educational problem of dealing with wide individual differences in aptitudes. But a whole other class of problems would disappear, the problems related to the fact that human variability is not spread homogeneously throughout the population. Mental retardation, for example, tends to become concentrated in particular families, neighbourhoods and communities, and a whole class of problems arises from the sheer fact of concentration itself, to blight such disproportionately handicapped segments of the society. In one large city, for example, it was reported that a neighbourhood comprising only 2 percent of the total population contributed over 30 percent of the children diagnosed as mentally retarded in the entire city's schools. Such social concentration of varying levels of intelligence must have marked environmental consequences, thereby creating a substantial source of population variance in IQ due to the covariance and mutual reinforcement of genetic and environmental factors.

The scientific task is to get at the facts and properly verifiable explanations. Recommendations for dealing with specific problems in educational practice, and in social action in general, are mainly a social problem. But would anyone argue that educational and social policies should ignore the actual nature of the problems with which they must deal? The real danger is ignorance, and not that further research will result eventually in one or another hypothesis becoming generally accepted by the scientific community. In the sphere of social action, any theory, true or false, can be twisted to serve bad intentions. But good intentions are impotent unless based on reality. Posing and testing alternative hypotheses are necessary stepping stones toward a knowledge of reality in the scientific sense. To liken this process to screaming 'FIRE . . . I think' in a crowded theatre (an analogy drawn by Scarr-Salapatek, 1971b, p. 1228) is thus quite mistaken, it seems to me. A much more subtle and complete expression of a similar attitude came to me by way of the comments of one of the several anonymous reviewers whose judgments on the draft of this book were solicited by the publishers. It summarizes so well the feelings of a good number of scientists that it deserves to be quoted at length.

The author tends to show marked impatience with those individuals who insist that in the race–IQ controversy genetic arguments for the difference must be conclusively demonstrated before the scientific community accords them standing. He points out that for any number of other questions the scientific community, when confronted by a body of what might be called substantial circumstantial or correlational evidence, would adopt the position that even though an hypothesis stood not conclusively proven it was most probably right. Furthermore, he indicates that this view, because it offers a convenient theoretical framework in which to fit observations and is congruent with the observations of racial differences in just about everything else, would also recommend itself to the scientific community. Emphasizing all these considerations, he suggests that the scientific community has failed to endorse the genetic hypothesis as the most likely explanation for difference in test performance by different racial populations merely because the area of race relations is a highly charged one. In several parts of the text he either directly or indirectly indicts the scientific community for showing such extreme caution in its reluctance to embrace the genetic hypothesis he so ably promulgates.

This is an indictment to which the community of scientists should plead guilty as charged. Unlike more esoteric and abstract questions an endorsement of the admittedly unproven, but in Professor Jensen's view highly plausible, genetic hypothesis will likely be picked up by those who make public policy and by the public they serve, and viewed as established truths rather than plausible hypotheses. It is not difficult to see such a public leaning toward the genetic hypothesis by the scientific community being used to justify all sorts of racially restrictive policies. It does not really matter that the legislature who passed such restrictive legislation did not really understand that the scientific community was only collectively betting on a hunch rather than handing down truth. The problem is that wherever science has a large and direct interface with the social policy one must always weigh the potential social effects of saying as a scientist that one subscribes to this or that unproven hypothesis. The scientific community has, I believe, rightly felt that subscription to one or the other presently competing hypothesis has implications that extend beyond science into areas of social concern.

It is likely that public policies based on the belief that differences in the environment account for the black–white difference would differ from policies based on the alternative genetic hypothesis. A plausible extension of the genetic hypothesis would suggest that the under-representation of blacks in many areas of society is, as one might expect, because the pool of able individuals is inherently proportionately lower in that population than in the white population and other racial populations. Subscription to the environmental view suggests that improvement of the environment, extension of opportunity and efforts to compensate for obvious educational and economic disadvantages if sufficiently massive and continuous will narrow and eliminate that gap. Whichever of these views is correct, the one adopted by the larger society could have an important effect on the direction and goals of public policies. Many who have examined the history of race relations in the United States and round the world feel that of the two hypotheses, neither of which stands proven, subscription to the genetic one carries considerable potential for mischief. It is for this reason such emphasis has been placed on exposing the difficulties of the work that must be done before the genetic view is raised from the level of hypothesis to the status of scientifically demonstrated fact.

I take little exception to this statement at its face value, and none at all to its spirit. The interesting point is that I have *not* urged acceptance of an hypothesis on the basis of insufficient evidence, but have tried to show that the evidence we have does not support the environmentalist theory which, until quite recently, had been clearly promulgated as scientifically established. By social scientists, at least, it was generally unquestioned, and most scientists in other fields gave silent assent. I have assembled evidence which, I believe, makes such complacent assent no longer possible and reveals the issue as an open question calling for much further scientific study. My critics cannot now say that this was always known to be the case anyway, for they were saying nothing of the kind prior to the appearance of my 1969 *Harvard Educational Review* article. It was just my questioning of orthodox environmental doctrine that set off such a furore in the social science world.

B

But my chief complaint with the attitudes expressed in the above quotation is that they do not indicate the full complexity of the options we face. Even the simplest formulation of the issue requires a 2×2 table of possible consequences, as follows:

	Reality	
Prevailing hypotheses	Genetic	Environmental
Genetic	True G	False G
Environmental	False E	True E

(It is understood that a genetic hypothesis does not exclude environmental variance, while the environmental hypothesis excludes a genetic difference.) The aim of science clearly is to rule out False G and False E, that is to say, it strives to determine which hypothesis accords with reality, so that the result of sufficient research would be either True G or True E. What the practical implications of True G or True E would be is another matter. But apparently, for some persons the crucial alternative is not between conditions True G and E, on the one hand, versus False G and E, on the other, which are the alternatives of interest to science, but between True G and False G (which are usually viewed as indistinguishable and equally bad), on the one hand, versus False E and True E on the other, which are seen as equally good. This amounts to saying that the hypothesis that prevails, whether true or false, is more important than the reality. Agreed, we would prefer the outcome True E to True G; but this wish has often led also to a preference for False E over True G. Since by subscription to the environmental hypothesis the two preferable conditions, False E and True E, prevail, there is no incentive to research that would decide between them. It is gratuitously assumed that False E is also good, or at worst harmless, while False G, to say nothing of True G, would give rise to incalculable 'mischief'. False E is made to appear a more benign falsehood than False G. This may be debatable. What seems to me to be much less debatable is the choice between True and False, whether E or G, even acknowledging the preference for True E. Is there less 'mischief' in False E than in True G? When the question is viewed in this way, it seems to me, it places the burden upon research rather than upon personal preference and prejudice, and that, to my way of thinking, is as it should be. Is the choice between False G and False E worthy of debate? When all the arguments are lined up so as to favor False E over False G (and sometimes even over True G), the importance of the scientific question seems moot. But is False E really all that much preferable to False G? Dwight Ingle (1967, p. 498) suggested that it may not be:

> When all Negroes are told that their problems are caused solely by racial discrimination and that none are inherent within themselves, the ensuing hatred, frustration behavior – largely negative and destructive – and reverse racism become forms of social malignancy. Is the dogma which has fostered it true or false?

False E could generate a kind of social paranoia, a belief that mysterious, hostile forces are operating to cause inequalities in educational and occupational performance, despite all apparent efforts to eliminate prejudice and discrimination – a fertile ground for the generation of frustrations, suspicions and hates. Added to this is the massive expenditure of limited resources on misguided, irrelevant and ineffective remedies based upon theories not in accord with reality, and the resultant shattering of false hopes. The scientific consequences of False E, if it is very strongly preferred to False G or True G, is the discouragement of scientific thinking and research on such problems. A penalty is attached to scientific skepticism and dissent, and there is a denigration and corruption of the very tools and methods that can lead to better studies of the problems, such as we are seeing presently in the ideological condemnation of psychometrics by persons with no demonstrated competence in this field and with no ideas for advancing this important branch of behavioral science.

Would True G really make for the social catastrophe that some persons seem to fear would ensue? Since this has been an unquestionable assumption underlying much of the opposition to investigation in this area, little, if any, serious sociological thought has been given to the possible problems that might be expected to arise when two or more visibly distinguishable populations, with different distributions of those abilities needed for competing in the performances most closely connected with the reward system of a society, are brought together to share in the same territory and culture. What arrangements would be most likely to make such a situation workable to everyone's satisfaction? It has often been assumed that such a combination of two or more disparate populations could not work; hence the fear of True G and the preference for False E rather than to take the risk of doing research that might result in True E but could also result in True G – a risk that many seem unwilling to take. There is indeed still much room for philosophic, ethical, sociological and political thought and discussion on these issues. It was with respect to the scientific investigation of such difficult human problems that Herbert Spencer remarked, '. . . the ultimate infidelity is the fear that the truth will be bad.'

Readers will find no dearth of published criticisms of my position. (An extensive bibliography is presented in *Genetics and Education* [Jensen, 1972].) Norman and Margaret Silberberg (1972) made a content analysis of the critical articles following publication of my *HER* article, and classified the criticisms into four major categories:

1. The definition of intelligence: questioning the 'g' theory of intelligence, problems surrounding the measurement of intelligence (including arguments concerning whether intelligence means capacity or functional level), and weaknesses found in Jensen's proposed Level I and Level II intelligence.
2. Genetics: pitfalls of genetic research and the measurement of heritability.
3. Compensatory education: arguments that IQ can be raised, the effects of social-environment on achievement, the question of whether compensatory education has received a fair trial, and prenatal and other physiological-environmental factors in school achievement.
4. Political: accusations that Jensen misused data, documentation that many blacks *are* intelligent, and the evaluation of possible furthering of racist prejudices as a result of the article.

Of course, I have studied all these criticisms, but I have found nothing to cause me to alter my original thesis in the 1969 *HER* article in any major respect. The present work greatly amplifies a limited aspect of it. I have not here dealt specifically with my formulation of mental abilities as Level I and Level II, nor have I said anything more about the failures of compensatory education, for these topics are taken up in *Genetics and Education* and in my forthcoming book on educational differences. The mounting evidence on the failures of an enormous variety of compensatory education programs to significantly raise the intelligence or scholastic performance of the classes of children they were intended to help, relative to the majority, would seem to constitute impressive evidence against the theory that environmental influences are paramount as a cause of differences in IQ and achievement. If certain factors are hypothesized to be causally predominant, then manipulation of such factors should produce marked effects. But the effects have in fact been practically nil. No efforts, reported in the research literature in such a way as to permit evaluation, have come to my attention which have shown any experimental techniques or programs that have raised group IQs more than the five points or so that regularly result from the practice effect of repeated testing on highly similar tests, and which also have stood the test of replication, either by the original investigator or by others. Without such replication, the few reports of marked effects of compensatory efforts in the literature, against the total background of the large number of studies reporting negative results, can be interpreted in terms of statistical expectations of sampling error – the so-called Type I error. How many such Type I errors have been reported at professional meetings and proclaimed in the popular press, never to be heard of again?

A thoughtful critique of one of the earlier versions of the present book was recently published by Biesheuvel (1972), a leading industrial psychologist in South Africa, whose article is more constructive than most criticisms, pointing to a number of important issues for further research. Biesheuvel makes at least one point which I have not commented on before. He writes: 'On evolutionary grounds, I can see no good reason why in the process of adapting, races should only have differentiated in the physical and not in the mental domain' (pp. 87-8). I agree. But this notion has also been used to argue that various races the world over have not become differentiated in mental abilities and, on the contrary, have become more alike because of the supposed common survival value of intelligence. This was argued in an editorial in *Nature* (1970):

> The outstanding truth about the human species is that half a dozen races have somehow managed to survive the climatic ups and downs of the Pleistocene. As many races and even genera may have disappeared without trace. What, after all, has become of the robust australopithecines (Leakey's *Zinganthropus*)? In circumstances in which it is plain that intelligence has been a crucial asset in survival, it is only reasonable to suppose that all of the races now extant are much of a muchness in intelligence.

I believe this is a mistaken inference. It equates intelligence with Darwinian fitness, that is, the ability to produce surviving progeny. This is a broadening of the concept of intelligence far beyond its meaning in psychology. All existing species have displayed Darwinian fitness, some much more impressively than homo sapiens, a relative newcomer. Intelligence cannot be equated with overall behavioral adaptability. It is but one aspect of the total spectrum of human abilities, albeit a uniquely important aspect in the industrialized world. Mental abilities, of which intelligence is one, we well know are differentiated in racially homogeneous groups and even among members of the same family. It is not at all unlikely that different environments and cultures could make differential genetically selective demands on various aspects of behavioral adaptability. Evolution and selection do not occur in a vacuum nor under ecologically homogeneous pressures. Europeans and Africans have been evolving in widely separated areas and cultures for at least a thousand generations, under different conditions of selection which could have affected their gene pools for behavioral traits just as for physical characteristics. The result is more or less uncorrelated differences in a wide variety of characteristics, not a simple monolithic continuum going from 'inferior' to 'superior' as some persons so wrongly imagine.

I have not tried to be comprehensive in my treatment of group differences but have considered only a few of the many facets of the topic. Critics will probably point out that one or another relevant type of problem or evidence was not brought into the picture. I would be the first to agree that the topic of racial differences has more aspects than could be adequately treated by one author in a single volume. No one knows better than the person with some scholarly expertise in a particular field how inadequate is one's technical judgment about other research specialities based on quite different methodologies. In evaluating and piecing together the published research in a given field, the scholar cannot simply take each investigator's word for the conclusions he has drawn from his own study. The nature of the data and the methods of analysis must be evaluated to determine whether the reported conclusions do in fact follow from the study in question. The popular science writer usually has no other choice but to take each investigator's findings and conclusions at their face value, if he wishes to cover the contributions of a number of different fields bearing on the same general topic. In order to maintain a critical and evaluative stance throughout, I have limited my consideration to the quantitative genetic and psychometric aspects of group differences in mental abilities and their relation to educability. I hope that in due course students in other disciplines will examine the other lines of relevant evidence.

For example, I have scarcely mentioned the bearing of evolutionary theory on this subject; this is a highly specialized branch of biology and genetics, and one which should be able to throw light on the subject of intraspecies variation. Closely related to this is physical anthropology and the study of the origin of races. How well supported and how relevant to our present concerns, for example, is Professor Carleton Coon's (1962) theory, which I am told is highly debatable, that the major races differ in evolutionary age, supposedly having crossed the homo erectus-homo sapiens threshold at different points in the evolutionary time scale? Even knowing where to look for all the relevant evidence, to say nothing of evaluating it, demands the attention of specialists in evolution and physical anthropology.

Then there is the intimate evolutionary relationship between function and structure which must have implications, to those who are qualified to discern them, for the study of anatomical and physiological differences and their connection with behavior. There are said to be average differences in cranial capacity and brain weight, in relation to overall body size, among races and even social classes. Are such data scientifically meaningful and, if so, what is their relevance, if any, to the questions we are here discussing only in terms of psychometrics and genetics? What is known of histological, architectonic and biochemical differences in the brain? Here again, a very different expertise is called upon to evaluate the evidence.

Finally, I have not touched upon the demographic aspects of group and individual differences in behavioral characteristics, particularly in relation to the troublesome question of possible dysgenic trends in the population – in intelligence and in mental health in general. These are questions that have long concerned geneticists and which, after some decades of apparent disinterest, are again coming up for public discussion. Population geneticist Carl J. Bajema (1971, pp. 71-2) has most cogently expressed this concern:

> The overall net effect of current American life styles in reproduction appears to be slightly dysgenic – to be favoring an increase in harmful genes which will genetically handicap a larger proportion of the next generation of Americans. . . .
> The proportion of the American population that already is genetically handicapped – that suffers a restriction of liberty or competence because of the genes they are carrying – is not small. Therefore the genetic component of the human population-environment equation must be taken into account as we attempt to establish an environment that has a high degree of ecological stability and that maximizes the number of opportunities for self-fulfilment available to each individual human being.

In dedicating this book to the memory of Sir Cyril Burt, I pay tribute to his genius as a leading pioneer in the study of the genetics of mental ability and in the implications of individual differences for education. I am personally indebted to him for the kindly interest he took in my own work, for the many enlightening conversations I was privileged to have with him, and for his detailed critical comments and helpful advice on the first draft of this book. He was always a great teacher as well as a great psychologist and researcher. In the light of the evidence I have reviewed regarding human differences and educability, Burt's own words, I believe, are at present most apt and wise:

The paramount need is not equality of educational opportunity, but diversity. According to his own innate potentialities, each child should, in an ideal system, be provided with the peculiar types of opportunity that can best minister to his needs. (Burt, 1969.)

June, 1972   Arthur R. Jensen

Institute of Human Learning
University of California
Berkeley, California

1 *Subpopulation differences in educability*

Many educators and social scientists have either shunned or denigrated questions and evidence pertaining to the genetic aspect of intelligence and educability, often from fear that such discussion would move out of the safe realm of *individual differences* and inevitably impinge on the sorely charged preeminent problem of the current education scene – *subpopulation differences* in educability. The purpose of this book is to face this issue as squarely as possible. What is the connection, if any, between the heritability of individual differences in intelligence and the heritability of subpopulation differences? And what is the connection between intelligence and educability? These are the key questions which underlie nearly all the serious discussions stimulated by my article 'How much can we boost IQ and scholastic achievement?' (Jensen, 1969a).

Before proceeding another step, some quick definitions are in order for those who are not yet familiar with the terminology of this debate.

The term *heritability*[1] refers to the proportion of the total variance[2] of a measurable characteristic (e.g. intelligence) in a population which is attributable to genetic factors.

Educability is the ability to learn the traditional scholastic subjects under conditions of ordinary classroom instruction. *Educability* is much narrower in scope than the more general term *learning ability*, and neither term is entirely synonymous with *intelligence*. It will pay to keep these distinctions clear; they are explicated later on.

Subpopulation has the advantage of being a theoretically neutral term. Unlike such terms as *social class* and *race*, a subpopulation does not connote more than its bare operational definition. Thus, the term *subpopulation* does not beg any questions. It can help to prevent us from mixing up the questions with the answers. And it can help to forestall fallacious thinking about social classes and races as Platonic categories. A subpopulation is simply any particular subdivision of the population which an investigator chooses to select for whatever purpose he may have. The only requirement is operational definition, that is to say, clearly specified objective criteria for the inclusion (and exclusion) of individuals. The reliability of the classification procedure is strictly an empirical question and not a matter for semantic debate. It can be answered in terms of a reliability coefficient, which can take any value from 0 (no reliability whatsoever) to 1 (perfect reliability). A subpopulation can consist of redheads, or females, or owners of a Rolls Royce, or persons with incomes under $4000 per annum, or whatever criterion or combination of multiple criteria one may choose. All other questions follow, their relevance depending on the purposes of the investigator.

The subpopulations we shall be most concerned with in the following discussion are Negroes and whites as they are ordinarily identified in our society. Studies of Negroes have at least the common criterion for inclusion in this subpopulation that they are those individuals (or their parents) who identify themselves as Negroes and are so identified by others. The degree to which this criterion has biological correlates is an empirical question. It undoubtedly does have a number of known biological correlates – skin color, hair texture, certain physical features, and distributions of blood groups, which distinguish the Negro from other subpopulations. Obviously, the introduction of other criteria would permit the further subdivision of this large subpopulation. The subpopulation of *whites* includes those who call themselves 'white', or Caucasian, and are usually of European ancestry; it usually does not include other subpopulations such as Orientals, Mexican-Americans, and American Indians.

IMPORTANCE OF THE QUESTION

Is the question of the causes of subpopulation differences in educational and occupational performance of any importance to educators or to society in general? Some persons disparage the question of whether genetic factors are implicated in subpopulation differences in educability. Lewontin (1970b, p. 25), for example, doubts that the question whether there is a genetic difference between Negroes and whites in IQ is an important social question and suggests that an interest in this question is simply a matter of 'vulgar curiosity'.[3] Whether the question is called 'vulgar curiosity' or 'scientific curiosity', the fact remains that many social scientists and educators have been discussing the causes of differences in scholastic performance between Negroes and whites for many years. They are propounding theories as to the causes of these differences, but usually they have not undertaken the kinds of research that would be needed to support their social-environmental theories or to disprove other causal hypotheses which include genetic factors. Those who are dedicated to investigating the causes of educational deficits among the disadvantaged, rather than exploiting them for ideological and political purposes, probably would agree with Dwight Ingle (1967, p. 498) that 'All possible causes of peoples' being disadvantaged should be investigated, and hopefully the application of knowledge to their advancement will be guided by moral principles.'

If genetic differences in mental abilities relevant to scholastic performance do, in fact, exist but are never openly recognized or are dogmatically denied within a context of scientific authority, one consequence, among many others, could be a destructive and perpetual condemnation of the schools for failure to produce equality of achievement among the various subpopulations they serve.

Those who hold up the fact of inequalities in educational performance as 'proof' of inequalities of educational opportunity, often seem bent on depicting public education as an instrument of the 'establishment' intended to suppress the disadvantaged. The focus of attention is thus diverted from seeking better means for insuring the proper goal of public education, viz., that all children should benefit from their schooling, to building up the impression that there exists a 'class conflict' between the 'privileged' and the 'disadvantaged' segments of our society. Those who insist that equality of educational performance should be the chief criterion of the existence of equality of educational opportunity are therefore not illogical in blaming the schools for any subpopulation differences that persist, even if there is no other objective evidence for the unequal treatment of 'privileged' and 'disadvantaged' children. The full flavor of this school of thought is found in the following statement by two educators:

> The disastrous effects of the schools on lower-class children are now finally becoming known. The 'compensatory' concept has gained some headway, but most educators are so overloaded with work and so traditional in outlook that the schools have become partners with the economic system in reinforcing a system of privilege that usually panders to the children of those in power and finds metaphysical excuses to make only minor gestures toward the less fortunate. The 'special programs for the gifted' would be more accurately labeled 'special programs for the privileged', for the gifted are primarily the children from socio-economic classes which provide the most opportunities. The less fortunate (usually lower-class children) are ordinarily neglected or convinced that they are innately inferior. Once they become convinced, the prophesy is soon realized. (Boyer & Walsh, 1968, p. 68)

Later on these authors say,

> It is not merely racism which bogs down American progress, but also the more pervasive belief in intellectual inequality. The failure to develop the abilities of people was useful to the early American aristocracy and to the power elite of an industrial-scarcity economy. . . . All institutions, including the schools, will either need to re-examine their self-consoling elitist beliefs and create real and equal opportunity, or else risk that violence and revolution will increasingly become the dominant instruments of social change. (p. 69)

When equality of educational performance is regarded as the only proof of equality of opportunity, and the failure to demonstrate such equality can have the social consequences predicted in the above quotation by Boyer and Walsh, then it would indeed seem important to question the basic assumption underlying this logic, viz., that the gene pools of all subpopulations, social-class and racial, are equal or equivalent for the characteristics involved in educability. It is merely assumed by some persons on the basis of very weak evidence that this is the case; yet although it is far from proved, some social scientists act as though genetic factors had already been investigated and ruled out by scientific evidence. This attitude was well expressed in a recent article by Robert J. Havighurst (1970, p. 313):

> As for the truly disadvantaged group of 15-20 percent of the population, there is disturbing evidence that this group is in danger of becoming a permanent 'underclass' characterized by absence of steady employment, low level of education and work skills, living on welfare payments, and social isolation from the remainder of society. The presence of this social and human problem cannot be passed off in any of the ways that might have been possible a century ago, or might be possible today in poor countries. It cannot be ascribed to inherited inferiority of the disadvantaged. It cannot be blamed on the country's poverty, since we are an affluent society. It cannot be passed off with the optimistic prediction that the current group of disadvantaged will soon become assimilated into the general society as most ethnic groups have done in the past – the Irish, Germans, Swedes, Poles, Italians, etc. The problem is brought to a head by the clearly established fact that the children of this group are *not* doing as well in school or in the world of juvenile work as did the children of poor people 50 and 100 years ago. Furthermore, most Americans believe that true democracy means equality of economic and educational opportunity. There is a growing conviction that the proof of the existence of equality of economic and educational *opportunity* is the achievement of economic and educational *equality* by the previously disadvantaged groups within a reasonable period of time, measured by decades and not by centuries or even by generations.

OBSTACLES TO CLEAR THINKING ON THIS TOPIC

Discussions of social class and racial differences in mental ability are often obscured by confusing the scientific and substantive aspects of the problem with moral, political, and ideological attitudes about it. Failure to keep these two realms quite separate can only hinder clear thinking. Unfortunately, this point still needs to be repeatedly emphasized in discussions of racial differences. In introducing their admirable discussion of behavioral differences between races, Spuhler and Lindzey (1967, p. 375) state:

Most important of all, we should like to state unequivocally the lack of any meaningful association between the existence, or lack of existence, of racial differences in behavior and political-legal decisions in regard to civil liberties, equal opportunities, or personal freedoms. The latter issues are rooted in moral, ethical, evaluative considerations that can never be derived from scientific fact and should not be confused with empirical questions. To blend the two issues is to risk the likelihood that both will suffer. The quality of research may suffer because certain findings are likely to assume an odious and ethically objectionable quality that makes it difficult for most investigators to work in the area or to report their findings bluntly. On the other hand, what may be a straightforward moral or ethical issue can become hopelessly confused if an attempt is made to demonstrate that it is somehow derivable from a set of scientific findings.

It will pay to give some examples of the more typical snares so as to help sensitize the reader to the forms of obfuscation that abound in this realm.

Perhaps the pitfall most difficult to avoid is the confusion of the empirical question of genetic racial differences and the deplorable historical discrimination against Negroes and other ethnic minorities. It is feared by many that admitting the possibility of genetic differences in behavioral characteristics will be equated with blindness or insensitivity to the mistreatment of minorities, particularly Negroes, that has existed in the past and still exists in varying degrees today. Justifiable moral indignation at such conditions and a natural sympathy for the plight of historically disadvantaged minorities reinforce our reluctance to examine possible causes of racial differences that cannot easily be blamed directly on persons or institutions that condone or perpetuate discrimination. Causality thus becomes equated with *blame*, and vicarious guilt often makes it all too easy to accept this simple formula. It lurks, thinly disguised, in numerous commentaries, as when Christopher Jencks (1969, p. 29), after noting that Negroes are at a disadvantage in dealings with the police and with landlords, goes on in the same context to say, 'Low IQs are not the cause of America's racial problems and higher IQs would not solve these problems. Any white reader who doubts this should simply ask himself whether he would trade the genes which make his skin white for genes which would raise his IQ 15 points.' This kind of statement not only sidetracks examination of the central question, but it also confuses the different meanings and implications that an IQ difference of, say, 15 points can have for an individual and for a subpopulation. This is a most important distinction.

For an individual, the addition or subtraction of 15 ('true score') IQ points from his potential mental development will have quite different consequences depending on the part of the range in which the resultant IQ falls. Fifteen points added to an IQ of 70 could mean the difference between institutionalization or social dependency and self-sufficiency in the world of work; 15 points added to an IQ of 100 could mean the difference between failing or succeeding in college. Since the standardized regression of income on IQ is probably between 0·3 and 0·4, we can predict, on the average, that along with a 15-point increase in IQ would come an increase in income amounting to 0·3 or 0·4 standard deviations on the scale of income. Also, the person with 15 points added to his IQ, assuming the heritability of IQ remained the same, would add, on the average, about 7 points to the IQs of his (or her) children. And there would be many other individual consequences of such a change in IQ. The reason we are not apt to be very impressed by the observable differences between individuals that result from a 15-point IQ difference is that we observe specific cases rather than averages, and the correlation between IQ and our various criteria of success is far from perfect. So we note the very bright youngster who becomes a mediocre adult, and his intellectually less favored classmate who becomes rich and famous. Many factors other than intelligence obviously must play an important part in a person's career and fortunes, but there is no reason to believe that on the average all these non-intellectual factors will add up more favorably for those who are intellectually less endowed than for those who are more endowed. If anything, slightly the reverse is the case. There is a small but real positive correlation between intelligence and other traits of personality and character which favor success in our society. This should not be too surprising. In an educational, occupational, and social system that tends to sort out people according to their abilities, it seems most likely that those traits of personality and temperament which most complement and reinforce the development of intellectual skills requiring persistent application, practice, freedom from emotional distraction, and resistance to mental fatigue and boredom in the absence of gross physical activity, should to some degree become genetically assorted and segregated, and thereby become correlated, with those mental abilities requiring the most education for their full development – those abilities most highly valued in a technological culture. Thus ability and personality traits will tend, on the whole, to work together in determining individuals' overall capability in such a society. In noting that certain personality variables, when factor-analyzed along with tests of mental abilities, were correlated to the extent of about 0·3 to 0·5 with a general ability factor, R. B. Cattell (1950, pp. 98-9) commented that '. . . there is a moderate tendency . . . for the person gifted with higher general ability, to acquire a more integrated character, somewhat more emotional stability, and a more conscientious outlook. He tends to become "morally intelligent" as well as "abstractly intelligent." '

But a difference of, say, 15 IQ points between two large groups or populations takes on still another dimension of implications from those found for an individual. If the distribution of intelligence (or IQs) in any large subpopulation approximates the normal or Gaussian curve, groups that have a mean difference will show an increasingly greater disparity in the proportions of the group that fall farther and farther above or below the mean. This can make for extremely conspicuous population differences in the proportions of each that fall above or below some given level of selection criteria. For example, schools with special curricula for the academically gifted typically find six to seven times as many white as Negro children who meet the usual criteria for admission to these programs, assuming equal numbers in the populations; while, conversely, the ratios are almost exactly reversed for the proportions of Negro and white children who qualify for placement in special classes for the educationally retarded. Thus, one school psychologist, pointing to what he regarded as a flagrant injustice, complained that '. . . although 27·8 percent of all students in the district are black, 47·4 percent of the students in educationally handicapped classes are black, and 53·8 percent in the district's mentally retarded classes are black. This is a most seriously disproportionate state of affairs' (*San Francisco Chronicle*, 6 May, 1970, p. 18). But actually, if there were a 15 IQ point difference between the Negro and white means, which is the best estimate of the national average, and if IQ below 75 was the chief criterion for inclusion in classes for the retarded, we should expect about 67 percent, rather than only 53·8 percent, of this district's mentally retarded classes to be composed of Negro children, assuming normality of the IQ distributions in the Negro and white populations of this district. If anything, therefore, there is evidence that Negro children are discriminated against by not being given the same special educational attention as is given white children with the same educational deficiencies and needs. Children with IQs below 75 can generally benefit more from the smaller classes and specially trained teachers provided in the programs for the educationally retarded than from placement in regular classes, at least when it comes to acquiring the traditional scholastic skills. I am not here arguing the issue of whether the special classes for the retarded as presently constituted are the best treatment we can accord to these children, or that Negro and white children with IQs below 75 are also the same in all other educationally relevant characteristics (I believe they are not). The question of whether the tests of intelligence on which such educational decisions are based are 'unfair' to Negro or other minority children is taken up in a later section.

Not only will there be disproportionate representation above (or below) some selection criterion on the IQ scale for subpopulations differing in mean IQ, but there will also be disproportionate representation of the two groups in all other selection criteria that are correlated with IQ, the degree of disproportion being directly related to the correlation between IQ and the particular selection criteria in question. If the correlation is relatively high, as is the case of admission criteria to selective colleges, the proportions of qualified Negro and white students who qualify will differ considerably; while in some other pursuits depending upon abilities only slightly correlated with intelligence the disproportion will be much less, assuming the absence of irrelevant discriminatory factors. Notable examples are seen in the world of entertainment and sports, where the prime requisites are special talents and capacities which have little correlation with intelligence and are probably distributed quite differently than intelligence in various subpopulations.

Another obstacle to examining the scientific question of genetic differences between subpopulations in its own right is the fear that the knowledge could be misused. This fear is often reinforced by imagining terrible abuses that might conceivably follow from pressing investigation too far, although these are usually fantastic *non sequiturs* which no responsible scientists have ever endorsed. Again, it amounts to beclouding a scientific issue by moral rhetoric, such as that displayed in Lewontin's (1970b, p. 25) bugaboo question: 'But suppose the difference between the black and white IQ distributions were completely genetic: What program for social action flows from that fact? Should all black children be given a different education from all white children, even the 11 percent who are better than the average white child? Should all black men be unskilled laborers and all black women clean other women's houses?' There seems to be a presumption that one's common sense, to say nothing of one's ethics, social philosophy, and humanity, hinge on the outcome of research that would establish the existence or non-existence of racial genetic differences in intelligence. Presumably, if the answer came out one way it would turn us all into 'bad guys' and if it came out the other way we would all have to be 'good guys'. This kind of argument reminds me of an eccentric preacher I once heard at London's famous speaker's corner at Marble Arch, who warned that if men became atheists, or even agnostics, they would inevitably take to gambling, fornicating, and beating their wives and children! The history of civilization, I believe, bears out the conclusion that scientific knowledge has had beneficent consequences for mankind far more often than evil consequences. True, knowledge can be misused, but so can ignorance and closed systems of belief. Historically, ignorance and dogma have wrought much more human suffering than ever resulted from any scientific advances. Moreover, even with the best of intentions, ignorance stands impotent when faced with problems that need to be solved, while knowledge, given the will, can lead to solutions.

Still another constellation of attitudes aligns the genetic study of intelligence with efforts to maintain the *status quo* in our educational practices. Evidence for the role of genetic factors in educability is equated with support for inadequate and antiquated educational practices, with opposition to improving schools and instructional techniques. There is, of course, no logical connection between the educator's obligation to seek ways of improving educational practices and the outcome of any research on the nature-nurture issue. There is no rational basis for supposing that an extreme 'hereditarian' view should lead to any less radical changes in educational practices than an extreme 'environmentalist' view, or that educational policies and techniques should be any more or any less humanitarian in one case than in the other. It may well be less humanitarian, however, to knowingly guide educational policies and practices by beliefs that categorically exclude certain kinds of knowledge about individual differences which may be highly germane to education.

Schools are blamed for achievement differences among individuals or subpopulations, usually without any consideration of evidence or even acknowledgement that evidence is relevant to the issue, on the assumption that differences in educability are either directly caused by the schools or are caused elsewhere but are so superficial that the schools should easily be able to eliminate the differences if they really wished to do so. No attention is paid to those schools in which large inequalities of achievement persist even though no inequalities of facilities, teaching practices, or opportunities can be shown to exist. The standard criticisms usually directed against schools do not hold up in these cases; this should not imply that examination and criticisms are not in order. But at least the criticism should not be totally misdirected. Schools, for example, might be legitimately criticized for interpreting 'equality of educational opportunity' so literally as to mean uniformity of instructional facilities and practices. They could be accused of not seeking a diversity of educational approaches for children of differing abilities so as to possibly maximize their benefits from schooling. Reluctance to blame the schools for the existence of individual and group differences should never be equated with exempting the schools from scrutiny and criticism, or with approving of the educational *status quo*. It could well be that individual differences have to be taken even more seriously than they have been, and that recognizing differences at all stages of the educational process is necessary for optimizing the benefits of schooling to all children. Many of those who call themselves 'environmentalists' have consistently ignored or minimized differences, seeing them as something to be eliminated rather than taken account of in the design of instruction. But, of course, the true source of the philosophy that says 'blame the schools' for the existing differences is the need to place *blame*, and to place the blame on *someone*. From a scientific standpoint, the attribution of blame, instead of the analysis of causality, is a form of primitive thinking. Its effectiveness in debate depends not only on its primitive simplicity, evoking images of the 'good guys' versus the 'bad guys', but on feelings of guilt and sympathy for the underdog. The argument goes that if one does not blame the schools, then one must find that the children themselves are to blame. And who could be so mean as to place the blame all on innocent little children?

Racism itself is a major hindrance and threat to the scientific study and understanding of racial differences.[4] An abhorrence of racism can understandably create in researchers a reluctance to pursue inquiries that might be ignorantly misconstrued as 'racist'. And if one should engage in such investigation, no matter how objective one's approach, there are those who would claim that curiosity along these lines is possible only in one whose abhorrence of racism is not strong enough. Such thinking can be countered best by distinguishing clearly between research on racial differences and racism. Racism usually implies hate or aversion and is aimed at the denial of equal rights and opportunities to persons on the basis of their racial origin. Racism should be attacked in the spheres in which it operates, by enacting and enforcing laws and arrangements that help to insure equality of civil and political rights and to guard against discrimination with respect to educational and occupational opportunities on the basis of racial membership. To fear research on genetic racial differences, or the discovery of evidence of a biological basis for differences in abilities, is, in a sense, to grant the racist's assumption – that if it should be established beyond reasonable doubt that there are biological or genetically conditioned differences in mental abilities among individuals or groups, then we are justified in oppressing or exploiting those who are most limited in genetic endowment. This is, of course, a perfect *non sequitur*.

In a free society, one which permits freedom of speech and of the press, both to express and to criticize diverse views, the social responsibility of the scientist is perfectly clear. It is simply to do his research as competently and carefully as he can, and to report his methods, results, and conclusions as fully and as accurately as possible. The scientist, when speaking as a scientist about his research, should not make it subordinate to his non-scientifically attained personal, social, religious, or political ideologies. We have seen clear examples of what happens when science is corrupted by servitude to political dogma – in the bizarre racist theories of the Nazis and the disastrous Lysenkoism of the Soviet Union under Stalin.

Serious consideration of the question whether the observed racial differences in mental abilities and scholastic performance involve genetic as well as environmental factors has been generally taboo in political, academic, scientific, and intellectual circles in the United States. Nevertheless, it remains a persistent question. My belief is that scientists in the appropriate disciplines must finally face the question squarely and not repeatedly sweep it under the rug. In the long run, the safest and sanest course we can urge is intensive, no-holds-barred inquiry in the best tradition of science. The obstructions to rational discussion, outlined above, probably will be increasingly overcome in future discussions the more widely and openly the subject is researched and discussed among scientists, scholars, and the general public. As some of the taboos and misconceptions that hinder open discussion of the topic fall away, the issues will become clarified on a rational basis. We will come to know better just what we do and do not yet know about the subject, and we will then be in a better position to deal with it objectively, humanely, and constructively for the good of all.

NOTES

1. Geneticists distinguish between *broad* and *narrow* heritability. Broad heritability is the proportion of variance attributable to *all* genetic components of the genotype; it is the *total* genetic variance. Narrow heritability refers to that part of the genetic variance which 'breeds true,' i.e., which accounts for the genetic resemblance between parents and offspring, and is called 'additive' genetic variance. It is primarily of interest to agriculturists and animal breeders. Psychologists, on the other hand, are primarily interested in broad heritability, i.e., all the genetic factors involved in individual differences in a given trait. Throughout this article, unless it is specified otherwise, the term heritability is used in the broad sense. Some geneticists reserve the term heritability only for the narrow sense, and for heritability in the broad sense they use the expression 'degree of genetic determination' (Haseman & Elston, 1970). The quantitative

genetic model for continuous characters, which is based on Mendelian algebra and probability theory, is most lucidly explicated by Burt (1971).

2. *Variance* (σ^2) is the average of the squared deviation of each individual in the population from the arithmetic mean of the population. The square root of the variance (σ) is called the standard deviation. The standard deviation of IQ in the white population of the United States is 15 IQ points.

3. One may wonder if Lewontin had in mind Webster's definition of *vulgar* as 'morally crude, undeveloped, or unregenerate', again suggesting moral opprobrium for curiosity about a scientifically legitimate question.

4. Webster's Unabridged Dictionary defines *racism* as 'Assumption of inherent racial superiority or the purity and superiority of certain races and consequent discrimination against other races; also any doctrine or program of racial domination and discrimination based on such an assumption. Also, less specifically, race hatred and discrimination.'

2 Current technical misconceptions and obfuscations

Readers who have kept up with the current literature in this field are apt to have encountered a number of issues which have created confusion. It will pay to clear up these misconceptions so they will not interfere with the understanding of the more fundamental problems to be discussed in the remainder of this book.

POPULATION V. INDIVIDUAL

One current misconception concerns the meaning of heritability (henceforth signified by h^2) in relation to individual measurements or test scores.* The fact that h^2 is derived from the concepts and methods of the branch of genetics called quantitative genetics and depends upon population samples for its estimation has led some writers to believe, or at least to create the impression, that h^2 has no relevance to individual scores. And there are some persons who apparently find some comfort in the notion that even though the estimation of h^2 might have some validity with respect to a population, it has no relevance to the individual. An implicit extension of this line of reasoning is that since h^2 is irrelevant for the individual and since populations are composed of individuals, h^2 must really not mean anything in populations either.

The fact is, h^2 pertains both to individual scores and to population variance. What it does *not* pertain to is the population mean.

* See Appendix on Heritability for an explanation of how h^2 values are empirically obtained.

If we understand the meaning of h^2, all this should be perfectly clear. What, then, is the cause of the confusion?

The first cause of confusion is the failure to distinguish clearly between genetic factors as (*a*) the *sine qua non* for the development of all traits, behavioral as well as physical, in all organisms, and as (*b*) the cause of differences (i.e., variance) among individuals in a population. It is axiomatic in biology that all organisms and their development have a genetic basis. Without the genes the organism would not have come into existence and *ipso facto* its various characteristics would not exist; in short, it would never be a datum in any scientific sense. Furthermore, no organism exists without an environment. Thus no observations of organisms or their characteristics can exist which do not depend upon genetic *and* environmental factors. In this fundamental sense, therefore, questions about 'heredity *or* environment' and 'heredity *versus* environment' are merely pseudo-questions without any scientific interest. It only makes sense to think in terms of heredity *and* environment.

But granted the truism that every organismic characteristic, including behavior, has a genetic and environmental basis, we can go on and ask, 'How much of the difference or variation among individuals in the population is attributable to (i.e. caused by) genetic differences and how much to environmental differences?' (The *interaction* of genetic and environmental factors, which is subject to still other misconceptions, is taken up in the next section.) This is the question that the estimation of h^2 is intended to answer. Like *all* measurement and quantification in science, without exception, the estimation of h^2 is based on a *model*, and, like every model, this implies certain assumptions. The basic assumption of the heritability model used by geneticists is *additivity*, that is, the conception of genetic and environmental effects as being additive. The value of the phenotype, P (some observable or measurable characteristic of the individual organisms, e.g., height, skin color, IQ, etc.), is conceived of as analyzable into two additive components, a genetic component, G, and an environmental component, E. Thus,

$$P = G + E \qquad (2.1)$$

But what are the units of measurement of P, G, and E? Failure to consider this crucial question leads to confusion. The only meaning that P has in terms of our model is that it is a *deviation score,* i.e., a measure of deviation from the mean of the population of which it is an individual member. It cannot be thought of as an *absolute amount* of something unless we can be sure that we have measured P on an absolute scale (sometimes called a ratio scale) with a true zero point (total absence of the characteristic in question) and with equal intervals (i.e., 0-1 is the same distance as 1-2 as 100-101, etc.). But an absolute scale, though preferable for certain purposes, is non-essential for heritability analysis so long as we think of the phenotype values merely as deviation scores. Nearly all psychological test scores are only deviation scores. The raw score (number of items got 'right') on a test is a meaningful measure only in relation to the mean score in some reference population.

Thus, when we are estimating heritability, we are dealing with *differences* among individuals and not with absolute amounts of some attribute. A quite simplified model which fits much data reasonably well represents each individual's P value as a deviation from the population mean ($\bar{P}$), which is analyzable into two components as follows:

$$\bar{P} = \bar{G} + \bar{E} \tag{2.2}$$

where P is the mean phenotypic value in the population, $\bar{G}$ is the mean value of the genetic component of the characteristic in the population, and $\bar{E}$ is the mean value of the environmental component in the population.[1] But note that without an absolute scale the mean values, $\bar{P}$, $\bar{G}$, and $\bar{E}$ are entirely arbitrary; we can add or subtract any constant we wish without altering them in any essential way. Usually, in psychometrics we arbitrarily give $\bar{P}$ a mean value which is simply convenient, such as 100 for the mean IQ in the population.

Similarly, the phenotypic variance (σ_P^2) in the population can be thought of in terms of our model as the sum of the variances of the genetic and environmental components and their covariance:

$$\sigma_P^2 = \sigma_G^2 + \sigma_E^2 + \sigma_{GE}^2 \tag{2.3}$$

And here is another place one can often go wrong: one should not think of σ_E^2 as the variance in *environments.* The value σ_E^2 refers to that portion of the phenotypic variance attributable to variation or differences in environments. Only if we assume (or empirically demonstrate) a perfect relationship between characteristics or measurements of the environment and the *effects* of these environmental differences upon the phenotype can we directly equate σ_E^2 with the variance of some independent measurement of environments. The model as presented here may assume or imply a one-to-one correspondence between the objective environment and the *effects* of the environment on the phenotype.

Heritability, then, is defined as the proportion of total phenotypic variance (individual differences) shown by a trait that can be attributed to genetic variation in the population:

$$h^2 = \frac{\sigma_G^2}{\sigma_G^2 + \sigma_E^2} = \frac{\sigma_G^2}{\sigma_P^2} \qquad (2.4)$$

What are the limitations of this h^2? First of all, since we usually cannot measure a trait in every member of the population, we have to be content with a *sample* from the population which provides us with an *estimate* of h^2. From the sample we get an approximation of the value of h^2 in the entire population, and the larger the sample, the better is the approximation. Conversely, the larger the sample, the smaller is the margin of error in our estimate. So we must be aware that estimates of h^2 all involve sampling error, more or less, depending upon the adequacy of the sample.

Secondly, since populations can change over time, the obtained estimate of h^2 pertains only to the population that was actually sampled. How much h^2 varies from time to time or from one population to another can only be answered empirically. It has often been noted, however, that much of the interest and value in heritability estimates derives from the fact that h^2 for a given characteristic is not a highly unstable statistic but under natural conditions generally remains very much in the same range across time and across a variety of populations. This, of course, means no more than the fact that the populations and conditions under which heritability estimates are generally made do not differ all that much. It is entirely possible, on the other hand, to find marked exceptions, and it is also possible experimentally to produce great changes in h^2 by radically increasing or decreasing the variation in environmental factors, or by increasing or decreasing the genetic variance through selective breeding. Since h^2 reflects a *ratio* of genetic to phenotypic variance, a change in either source of variance will alter the value of h^2. It is possible to go wrong by believing that when σ_G^2 is zero or close to zero that the trait itself is not genetic, when what it really means is that all individuals in the population are genetically the same or very nearly the same on the trait and that the phenotypic differences among individuals are mostly attributable to non-genetic or environmental factors. Similarly, when σ_E^2 is zero it does not mean that the environment is unimportant in the development of the trait; it only means that environmental factors do not contribute to individual *differences* in phenotypes.

We can sum up by emphasizing that h^2 is not to be thought of as a constant, like π or the speed of light, but as a population statistic like the birth rate or the mortality rate, which can differ from one time to another depending on a multitude of conditions.

But does this mean that h^2 is irrelevant to the individual member of a population in which h^2 has been estimated? Not at all, if we understand our model correctly. Formulas 1 and 3, above, tell us that individual differences in P are composed of individual differences in G plus individual differences in E. Since h^2 tells us the proportion of variance in P accounted for by variance in G, the correlation r_{GP}, between genetic value² and phenotype, will be the square root of h^2, i.e., h. This means that by knowing h^2 we can estimate an individual's genetic value, given his phenotype, and the standard error of the genetic value, SE_G, is

$$SE_G = \sigma_t\sqrt{1-h^2} \qquad (2.5)$$

where $\sigma_t = SD$ of obtained scores.

This means that approximately 68 percent of individuals will have true genotypic values (G) that lie within one SE_G of their estimated genotype; approximately 95 percent will have G within 2 SE_Gs of their estimated value, and approximately 99·7 percent estimated Gs will lie within 3 SE_Gs of their true G. In short, we can estimate an individual's genetic value from a knowledge of his phenotype and of h^2 of the trait in question in the population of which the individual is a member. If we take the estimate of h^2 for IQ of 0·80, and if IQ has a standard deviation of 15 points in the population, then the total variance of P, or σ_P^2, is $15^2 = 225$. The standard error of G for an individual, therefore, will be $\sqrt{225} \times \sqrt{1-0·80} = 6·75$ IQ points. This means that 68 percent of our estimates of individuals' genetic values will be less than about 7 points off, 95 percent will be less than 14 points (i.e.,

$2\,SE_G$s) off, and 99·7 percent will be less than 20 points $(3\,SE_G$s) off. The estimated genetic value $(\hat{G}_i)$ for an individual, according to this model is

$$\hat{G}_i = h^2\,(P_i - \bar{P}_p) + \bar{P}_p \qquad (2.6)$$

where h^2 is the heritability
P_i is the phenotypic value for the individual
$\bar{P}_p$ is the population mean of the phenotype.
For example, a person with an IQ of, say, 140 would have an estimated genetic value of approximately $0\cdot8\,(140-100)+100 = 132$ IQ; a person with an IQ of 70 would have a genetic value of approximately $0\cdot8\,(70-100)+100 = 76$.

For the sake of simplicity we have not considered test unreliability or measurement error. All measurements involve some amount of error, and consequently part of the total population variance is made up of variation due to errors of measurement. This variance is commonly included as part of E or the non-genetic variance, unless it is independently accounted for, as by estimating the reliability of the test. The effect of test error, is, of course, to lower the estimated heritability, since

$$h^2 = \frac{\sigma_G^2}{\sigma_G^2 + \sigma_E^2 + \sigma_e^2} \qquad (2.7)$$

where σ_e^2 is the error variance. Most tests of intelligence have reliabilities between $0\cdot90$ and $0\cdot95$, which means that errors of measurement constitute from 5 to 10 percent of the total phenotypic variance. When this error is removed from our estimate of h^2 it is said to be 'corrected for attenuation'; unless explicitly specified, no correction for measurement error is assumed and $1-h^2 = $ all non-genetic variance including error variance.

The reader who is familiar with psychometric theory will notice the parallel between regression of true score on obtained scores, which is the square root of the test's reliability, and the regression of genetic values on phenotypic values (i.e., obtained scores), which is the square root of the heritability.

Similarly, we can estimate the environmental value, E, from a given P for an individual. The correlation, r_{EP}, between environment and phenotype is $\sqrt{1-h^2}$, which for IQ would be about $0\cdot45$. The standard error of estimate (s_e) of the environmental value would then be approximately 6 IQ points, or exactly the same as the s_e for the genetic value. An individual's estimated environmental value, $\bar{E}_i$, would be

$$\bar{E}_i = r_{EP}^2 (P_i - \bar{P}_p) + \bar{P}_p \qquad (2.8)$$

so that a person with IQ 140, for example, would have an estimated environmental value of $0\cdot20\,(140 - 100) + 100 = 108$ IQ, and someone with an IQ of 70 would have an estimated environmental value of 94 IQ. An h^2 of $0\cdot80$ means that genetic factors outweigh environmental factors by 2 to 1, in determining individual differences in IQ, since the ratio of $\sqrt{h^2}$ to $\sqrt{1 - h^2}$ is $0\cdot894$ to $0\cdot447$ or 2 to 1. Note also that if we express an individual's values for P_i, G_i, and E_i all as deviations from the population mean $\bar{P}_p$, the estimated deviation values of $P_i = G_i + E_i$ are:

$$P_i - \bar{P}_p = (G_i - \bar{P}_p) + (E_i - \bar{P}_p) \qquad (2.9)$$

which in our hypothetical case of the person with an IQ of 140 are estimated as

$$140 - 100 = (132 - 100) + (108 - 100)$$
$$40 = 32 + 8.$$

And thus we are back to formula 1, with which we started, showing that the individual's phenotypic score (expressed as a deviation from the population mean) is equal to the sum of the individual's genetic value and his environmental value, i.e., $P_i = G_i + E_i$. This detailed exposition has made clear the relationship between heritability as a population parameter and heritability as a means of estimating an individual's genetic value. Only if heritability were complete ($h^2 = 1\cdot00$) would the phenotype be a perfect indicator of the genotype. The fact that h^2 for intelligence is less than $1\cdot00$ (being around $0\cdot70$ to $0\cdot80$), means that an individual's test score estimates his genetic value only with some margin of error, the magnitude of which is indicated by the standard error of estimate, SE_G.

THE MEANING AND NON-MEANING OF 'INTERACTION'

There are three main ways in which the term 'interaction' is used in discussions of heredity and environment. The meanings that make sense must be distinguished from the more commonly encountered abuse of the term, which only confuses discussion.

In some discussions 'interactionism' has become merely a substitute for extreme environmentalism. It is a self-deceptive attempt to pay lip service to genetics while in fact maintaining all the beliefs of extreme environmentalism. By 'extreme environmentalism' I mean the view which ignores or uncritically discounts all the evidence supporting the conclusion that genetic factors contribute a greater share than environmental factors in the causation of individual differences in intelligence. Persons who refer to themselves as 'environmentalists' view genetic differences as either non-existent or as so small as to be a negligible factor in the development of intelligence. Individual differences in IQ are attributed entirely to inequalities in environmental, cultural, and educational opportunities. When it became evident that geneticists found no support for this theory and marshalled much evidence that contradicted it, many 'environmentalists' began calling themselves 'interactionists', which meant they acknowledged genetic differences but believed that phenotypic differences were an unanalyzable amalgam of genetic and environmental effects, since these factors 'interacted' so inextricably in developing the phenotype (e.g., Deutsch, 1969). Thus the interactionist theory holds that although there may be significant genetic differences at the time of conception, the organism's development involves such complex interactions with the environment that the genetic blueprint, so to speak, becomes completely hidden or obscured beneath an impenetrable overlay of environmental influences. This view argues, therefore, that the relative influences of genetic and environmental factors cannot be disentangled. Consequently, it would be seen as impossible to speak meaningfully of estimating the correlation between genotypes and phenotypes or of estimating, albeit with some margin of error, an individual's genetic value from a knowledge of his phenotype. The whole notion of heritability is, in effect, dismissed. The question of the relative importance of heredity and environment in determining individual differences in the development of a characteristic is viewed as fundamentally unanswerable.

This position has arisen from a failure to understand the real meaning of the term 'interaction' as it is used in population genetics; but even more it is the result of failure to distinguish between (*a*) the *development* of the individual organism, on the one hand, and (*b*) *differences* among individuals in the population. To say that a growing organism, from the moment of conception, 'interacts' with its environment is a mere truism. It says no more than the fact that there are no organisms that have existed and grown without an environment. The interactionist position is merely tantamount to stating that the organism exists. But we already take this for granted, and repeating the assertion that the individual is the result of 'the complex interaction of genetic and environmental factors' is simply stating the obvious. What the population geneticist actually wishes to know is what proportion of the *variation* in a particular trait among individuals is attributable to their genetic differences and what proportion is attributable to differences in their environmental histories. For the answer to this question one must turn to the methods of quantitative-genetic analysis. The estimation of heritability is among these methods. If it were true that environmental factors so 'interacted' with the genetic factors, in the sense intended by the 'interactionists', as to completely obliterate any correlational or predictive connection between an individual's genotypes and phenotypes, the methods of quantitative genetics are quite capable of revealing this. If our phenotypic characteristics or measurements gave no clue as to the 'genetic value' of individuals, it would mean that h^2 would be zero, and, of course, the correlation between phenotype and genotype ($r_{PG} = h$) would also be zero. But in fact, for human intelligence in our present society, most estimates of h^2 fall in the range from 0·60 to 0·90, with an average close to 0·80 (Jensen, 1967, 1969a; Jinks & Fulker, 1970). So much, then, for the abuse of the term *interaction*.

But now a clear distinction must be made between two theoretically quite legitimate though quite different meanings of interaction. The popular confusion of the two among behavioral scientists is probably most due to a well-known and often reprinted article 'Heredity, environment and the question "How?" ' by Anastasi (1958). Anastasi points out that attempts to determine the proportional contribution of heredity and environment to observed individual differences in given traits (i.e., heritability estimation)

> . . . have usually been based upon the implicit assumption that hereditary and environmental factors combine in an additive fashion. Both geneticists and psychologists have repeatedly demonstrated, however, that a more tenable hypothesis is that of interaction [4 references]. In other words, the nature and

extent of the influence of each type of factor depends upon the contribution of the other. Thus the proportional contribution of heredity to the variance of a given trait, rather than being a constant, will vary under different environmental conditions. Similarly, under different hereditary conditions, the relative contribution of environment will differ. Studies designed to estimate the proportional contribution of heredity and environment, however, have rarely included measures of such interaction. (Anastasi, 1958, p. 197)

First, a few clarifying comments. The assumption of additivity is not, as Anastasi says, an *implicit* assumption, it is a very *explicit* feature of the model for phenotypic variance, viz., $P = G + E$ and $\sigma_P^2 = \sigma_G^2 + \sigma_E^2$. Furthermore, geneticists and psychologists, including those referred to by Anastasi, have not offered any demonstrations that the additive model does not fit the data or that any other models do a better job of prediction in agricultural genetics where the additive model can be tested directly in breeding experiments. What Anastasi is saying, essentially, is that the additive model $P = G + E$ is either wrong or inadequate and that in place of it should be substituted a *multiplicative* model, i.e., $P = G \times E$, or some more complex non-additive function which can be represented simply as $P = f(G, E)$. No one who understands the nature and role of models in science would deny that $P = G \times E$ or some form of $P = f(G, E)$, like all other possible models, are potentially valid.[3] The only question is, which model is simplest and the easiest to work with, and which has the closest fit to the data and explains most of the facts? Up to the present time there has been no demonstration that a multiplicative model, in terms of these criteria, has any advantage over the additive model which has continued to serve as the theoretical and methodological basis of all quantitative genetics. This is not to say that some better model might not be possible. But the fact remains that a demonstrably better model has not been put forward. Until someone can show that the multiplicative model (or any other model) better comprehends the existing data or makes better predictions of new data than the traditional additive model, the two models must be regarded as redundant. We should therefore stick to the additive model for its greater simplicity and convenience. In fact, if for any reason it was decided that genetic and environmental factors actually did

c

act multiplicatively or for some good reason should be represented as doing so, geneticists would probably stick to the additive model for its greater simplicity, merely by transforming phenotypic measurements to a logarithmic scale. Since adding the logarithms of quantities is the same as multiplying the quantities, $P = G \times E$ can be represented in an additive model as $\log P = \log G + \log E$. If taking the logarithm of IQs (or any other measurements) makes for a better fit of the data to the theoretical expectations called for by the model, then there is no objection to performing this logarithmic transformation (or any other transformation) of the original measurements.

For example, two statistically useful criteria commonly sought through transformation are normality of distribution of measurements in the population and the absence of a constant proportionality of the means and variances of population subgroups.

Transformation of the scale of measurement to achieve the simplest representation of the data is a standard practice in all branches of science, including genetics.[4]

The standard model of population genetics, which we have so far presented only in its simplest form, actually includes a provision for estimating non-additive or interaction effects of genetic and environmental factors, as indicated in the formulas:

$$P = G + E + GE \tag{2.10}$$

$$\sigma_P^2 = \sigma_G^2 + \sigma_E^2 + \sigma_{GE}^2 \tag{2.11}$$

where GE represents $G \times E$, i.e., the interactive or multiplicative effects of genetic and environmental factors. (Many other non-additive effects besides multiplicative effects may contribute to the non-additive variance, e.g., $\sqrt{G \times E}$, $\log (G+E)$, etc.) The model attempts to account for as much of the phenotypic variance as possible in terms of additive effects $(G+E)$ and the remainder of the variance that cannot be accounted for (and also cannot be accounted for as arising from epistasis,[5] assortative mating,[6] covariance of G and E,[7] and errors of measurement) is attributed to interaction, i.e., $G \times E$ (or GE). The interaction term, GE, reflects either the fact that a unit change in the environment does not produce the same amount of change in the phenotype of every genotype in the population or that a unit change in genetic value does not produce the same change in phenotype at different points on the environmental scale. When attempts are made to estimate the proportion of σ_P^2 attributable to genotype × environment interaction (σ_{GE}^2/σ_P^2) for intelligence test data in humans, it usually turns out to be so small as to be either negligible for any practical considerations or altogether undetectable through the 'noise' of measurement and sampling error. Analyses of appropriate data which should reveal the presence of genotype × environment interaction if it were present have failed to reveal any statistically significant interaction component (Jinks & Fulker, 1970; Jensen, 1970a). In speculating about the reasons for the absence of genotype × environment interaction effects (as well as variance due to the covariance or correlation of genetic and environmental factors) in intelligence test data, Jinks and Fulker (1970, p. 347) have this to say:

> The reasons why correlation effects are of little importance is not entirely clear to us, but may result from using tests having high test-retest reliability over long intervals. Such tests measure traits showing little dramatic change [in relative status] throughout long periods of the subject's life. However, these tests will, necessarily, measure aspects of subjects determined very early on, and may, therefore, reflect primarily genetic and prenatal and early postnatal influences. If this is so, many of the cultural factors, which would normally lead to correlated environments . . . will produce little or no effect. . . . The absence of important genotype-environment interaction may also result from the use of tests with a high genetic component showing stability over long periods of time. A further factor may result, however, from the practice in test construction of aiming at a constant reliability [or standard error of measurement] throughout the range of the trait.

They add that

> . . . an apparent lack of evidence of substantial genotype-environment interaction in intelligence-test scores strongly suggests that none of the range of environments provided by our society is likely uniformly to produce a high (or low) level of intelligence. The importance of trying to detect genotype-environment interaction in different societies, as a means of assessing their relative efficacy in achieving this end, is clearly indicated. (p. 324)

From their detailed and sophisticated re-analysis of relevant intelligence test data by the most advanced methods of biometrical genetics, Jinks and Fulker conclude that these data conform to a simple additive model with dominance[8] of intelligence-enhancing genes. The analyses detect a significant level of dominant gene action in the direction of dominance for high IQ, which, they state, is indicative of 'an evolutionary history of strong directional selection for this measure (IQ)'. (Jinks & Fulker, 1970, p. 347)

Genotype-environment correlation, r_{GE}, may contribute to phenotypic variance, but it may well be that much, if not most, of this effect should be included in the genetic variance, because, in part, r_{GE} is a result of the genotype's selective utilization of the environment. Many micro-environmental influences on the individual are a *result* of genetic differences as well as a *cause* of further phenotypic differences. For example, it would be practically impossible to create for, or impose upon, the average child as musically stimulating an environment as that experienced by, say, a Mozart. Jinks and Fulker recognize this problem with respect to intelligence, as follows:

> An innately intelligent person may well select his environment so as to produce positive r_{WHWE} [i.e., heredity-environment correlation within families], and likewise a dull person may produce the same correlation by selecting less stimulating features of his environment. But is not this a more or less inevitable result of genotype? To what extent could we ever get a dull person to select for himself an intellectually stimulating environment to the same extent as a bright person might? Even when these correlations exist because of the pressure of others on an individual, it is not clear to what extent the correlation can be manipulated. Perhaps it can to some extent by such drastic procedures as intensively coaching the dull, and drastically depriving the intelligent, but the effect on the correlation is still not entirely clear. (Jinks & Fulker, 1970, p. 323)

GENES AND DEVELOPMENT

A common misconception often arises in connection with standards such as the following from an article by Dreeben (1969): 'First, genetic forces and environmental forces operate on two distinct dimensions of time. Genetic effects are established when an ovum is fertilized – at one moment in time; environmental effects extend over time.' This is often erroneously believed to mean that although individuals may be endowed with different genotypes at the moment of conception, all change and differentiation that take place thereafter are the result of environmental forces. But this interpretation overlooks the fact that the genes exert a *continuing* influence on developmental processes. Many genetic effects are manifested phenotypically only in later stages of development. As an obvious example, patterns of baldness are genetically determined but do not show up until middle age. Behavioral characteristics associated with maturational processes, like mental development, variously manifest genetic effects increasingly as the individual grows from infant to adult. This is clearly seen in the gradually increasing degree of correlation between the mental abilities of parents and their biological children from infancy to late adolescence, which occurs even when the children have never had contact with their biological parents after infancy and have been reared by adoptive or foster parents (e.g., Honzik, 1957). Under a normal range of environmental conditions, an individual's phenotypic IQ, from infancy to maturity, converges toward its genotypic value.

TEACHABILITY AND HERITABILITY

On this issue we see more confusion and misunderstanding. Consider the following quotations.

Speaking of Jensen's (1969a) average estimate of the heritability of intelligence as 0·80, Benjamin Bloom (1969, p. 419) says, 'This is an old estimate which many of us have used, but we have used it to determine what could be done with the variance left for the environment.' In a similar vein, Torsten Husén (1963, p. 108) writes, 'I observed on the basis of previous studies . . . that the intra-class correlations for identical twins reared together are almost as high as the "reliability ceiling". That scarcely left any room for "environmental influences".' As Jerry Hirsch (1970, p. 100) has emphatically pointed out, statements such as the above seem to assume, fallaciously according to Hirsch, that there is an inverse relationship between heritability magnitude and the individual's improvability by training and teaching; that is to say, if heritability is high, little room is left for improvement by environmental modification, and, conversely, if heritability is low, much more improvement is possible. Hirsch is quite correct in noting a possible fallacy that may be implicit in this interpretation of heritability, and he points to a passage in one of my articles which appears to express much the same notion:

> The fact that scholastic achievement is considerably less heritable than intelligence also means that many other traits, habits, attitudes, and values enter into a child's performance in school besides just his intelligence, and these non-cognitive factors are largely environmentally determined, mainly through influences within the child's family. This means there is potentially much more we can do to improve school performance through environmental means than we can do to change intelligence *per se*. (Jensen, 1969a, p. 59)

The wording of this statement was unfortunately too imprecise, for although it occurs in a context dealing with reducing group differences in scholastic achievement through compensatory education, it is possible to read the passage without also reading into it the fact that it concerns altering group differences (i.e., improving the achievement of disadvantaged groups relative to the advantaged). In this sense, the message imparted by the passage is quite valid. A more precise wording of the second sentence would have been, 'This means there is potentially much more we can do to *improve the school performance of low achieving children relative to the majority of children* through environmental means than we can to raise their intelligence *per se*.' But Hirsch's essentially valid critique of this point has since become transformed (by Hirsch himself) into such sweeping and either meaningless or incorrect generalizations as '. . . there is no relationship at all between teachability and heritability' (Hirsch, in a talk at the Brain Research Conference, Cambridge, England, 17 July 1970) and the aphorism printed in bold face on the heading of the *Bulletin of the ERIC Information Retrieval Center on the Disadvantaged* (1969, 4, no. 4): 'Teachability is not a function of heritability.' The same confusion is seen when an individual child or a group of children show some response to training and this is held up as evidence against the heritability of intelligence or learning ability.

Let us now get these various notions sorted out.

First of all, the fact that learning ability has high heritability surely does *not* mean that individuals cannot learn much. Even if learning ability had 100 percent heritability it would not mean that individuals cannot learn, and therefore the demonstration of learning or the improvement of performance, with or without specific instruction or intervention by a teacher, says absolutely nothing about heritability. But knowing that learning ability has high heritability does tell us this: if a number of individuals are all given equal opportunity – the same background, the same conditions, and the same amount of time – for learning something, they will still differ from one another in their rates of learning and consequently in the amount they learn per unit of time spent in learning. That is the meaning of heritability. It does not say the individuals cannot learn or improve with instruction and practice. It says that given equal conditions, individuals will differ from one another, not because of differences in the external conditions but because of differences in the internal environment which is conditioned by genetic factors. 'Teachability' presumably means the ability to learn under conditions of instruction by a teacher. If this is the case, then it is true that heritability has nothing to do with teachability. But was this ever the question? And is not propounding it as an answer apt to be quite misleading? No one has questioned the fact that *all* school children are teachable. The important question has concerned *differences* in teachability – differences both among individuals and among subgroups of the population. And with reference to the question of *differences*, heritability is indeed a relevant concept.

But what, if anything, is wrong with the statements of Bloom and Husén, quoted above, and which Hirsch must have had in mind when he correctly criticized the notion that teachability is inversely related to heritability? It comes back again to the fact that heritability deals with differences. The degree to which equal conditions of teaching or instruction will diminish individual differences in achievement *is* inversely related to the heritability of the 'teachability' of the subject in question, and various school subjects probably differ considerably in heritability – a topic discussed in a later section.

But is it incorrect, as Hirsch asserts, to say that there is potentially more we can do environmentally to reduce individual or subgroup differences if we find that the heritability is low? No, it is not incorrect. It is precisely what the agricultural geneticist does with his heritability estimates of such traits as the egg-laying capacity of chickens, the milk production of cows, and the lardiness of pigs. If the geneticist wants to change the phenotypic value of the trait, his method will differ depending on the trait's heritability. If h^2 is very high, genetic selection rather than environmental manipulation is likely to yield the most rapid results. If h^2 is very low, the controlling environmental factors will be sought out and manipulated so as to change the phenotype in the desired direction. If h^2 has an intermediate value, both genetic selection and environmental manipulation will ordinarily be efficacious in improving the characteristic.

The fact that scholastic achievement shows lower heritability than IQ means that more of the variance in scholastic achievement is attributable to non-genetic factors than is the case for IQ. Consequently, we can hypothesize what the sources of the environmental variance in scholastic achievement are, and possibly we can manipulate them. For example, it might be hypothesized that one source of environmental variance in reading achievement is whether or not the child's parents read to him between the ages of 3 and 4, and we can obviously test this hypothesis experimentally. Much of the psychological research on the environmental correlates of scholastic achievement has been of this nature. The proportion of variance indicated by $1 - h^2$, if small, does in fact mean that the sources of environmental variance are skimpy under the conditions that prevailed in the population in which h^2 was estimated. It means that the *already existing* variations in environmental (or instructional) conditions are not a potent source of phenotypic variance, so that making the best variations available to everyone will do relatively little to reduce individual differences. This is not to say that as yet undiscovered (or possibly already discovered but as yet rarely used) environmental manipulations or forms of intervention in the learning or developmental process cannot, in principle, markedly reduce individual differences in a trait which under ordinary conditions has very high heritability. By the same token, low heritability does not guarantee that most of the non-genetic sources of variance can be manipulated systematically. A multitude of uncontrollable, fortuitous micro-environmental events may constitute the largest source of phenotypic variance in some traits, so that although they have low heritability, they are even much less potentially controllable than if the heritability were very high, at least permitting sure control through genetic selection.

THE FALLACY OF ASSUMING GENETIC HOMOGENEITY WITHIN RACIAL GROUPS

This fallacy probably originated in the belief that any suggestion of genetic behavioral differences between racial groups must be part of an attempt to 'put down' one racial group or to claim 'superiority' for one at the expense of another. Those with such a motive would presumably resist any suggestion of genetic differences among various subpopulations within their own 'superior' racial population. Thus, one noted psychologist argued that 'Professor Jensen has no more basis in evidence for his contention[9] that the academic retardation of minority-group children is genetically determined than he would have evidence in support of a contention that the academic retardation of lower-status white children is genetically determined'. Actually, of course, on the basis of the available evidence, a much stronger case can be made for genetic differences in intelligence and educability among social classes *within* the white population than for genetic differences between Negroes and whites. In fact, there is virtually no longer any fundamental disagreement among scientists who have viewed the evidence that the probability of genetic differences in intelligence between groups of high and low socioeconomic status in the white population is extremely high. Even those who are most dubious or hesitant about entertaining a genetic hypothesis about racial differences in IQ do not take exception to the evidence for genetic social class differences within the white population (e.g., Eckland, 1967; Bodmer & Cavalli-Sforza, 1970).

Another example of this fallacy, which raises an additional point worth considering, is seen in an article by Jencks:

Jensen makes a great deal of the fact that black children do worse on IQ and achievement tests, and are six times more likely to be mentally retarded, than white children at the same socioeconomic level. But what does this prove? . . . Jewish children also do better on IQ tests than Christians at the same socioeconomic level, but very few people conclude that

c*

Jews are genetically superior[10] to Christians. (Jencks, 1969, p. 28)

The fact that very few people might suggest a genetic factor in the Jewish *v.* non-Jewish IQ difference (which averages about 8 to 10 points), however, does not make it an unreasonable hypothesis that genetic factors are involved in this subpopulation difference as well as in many others. The reason this particular question is not regarded as very important socially, educationally, or scientifically, is that no one believes that the Jewish minority as a group suffers any disadvantages due to an inability to compete intellectually, educationally, or occupationally in our society. Any social disadvantages that Jews may suffer as a result of their minority status is clearly not associated with their intelligence or educability, except possibly through the resentment of those who envy their conspicuous success in this realm. It is quite likely that genetic as well as cultural factors are involved in the average intellectual superiority of Jews, but in terms of social priorities it hardly seems a point worth researching. The same thing is probably true of the Oriental population of the United States as well.

A peculiar manifestation of the fallacious belief in racial genetic homogeneity is the notion that regional differences in IQ among whites must be entirely environmental and therefore, if they are of considerable magnitude, can be pointed to as evidence that racial differences must also be entirely environmental. The fallacy of this argument, of course, is that no sophisticated person today would insist that regional differences in IQ *within* the white (or Negro) population are entirely due to cultural and educational differences. The argument from regional differences among whites as entirely environmental to differences between racial groups as entirely environmental might be called the Klineberg fallacy, since it was Otto Klineberg (1935, 1944) who first popularized the comparison of Army Alpha test scores of whites in four Southern states, where the white Alpha medians were lowest in the nation for whites, with the test scores of Negroes in four Northern states, where the Negro Alpha medians were the highest in the nation for Negroes. (The four highest Negro medians were all above the four lowest white medians. Comparison of Negro and white medians within the same state, on the other hand, showed about the same difference as for the average Negro-white difference in the nation as a whole.) As evidence for an environmental explanation of racial differences, Klineberg (1963, p. 200) also points to an isolated group of impoverished white children living in the hollows of the Blue Ridge Mountains of Appalachia who had an average IQ lower than the Negro national mean. But of course genetic differences in intelligence among subgroups of the white population are no less improbable than differences among racial groups, and this would seem especially true of relatively isolated groups in the 'hollows' of Appalachia. The fact that the Army Alpha is highly loaded with scholastic knowledge, correlating close to 0·70 with number of years of schooling, means that it probably reflects regional differences in mean level of education to some degree, independently of intelligence, especially in the period of World War I, when there was much greater regional variance in the quality and the number of years of schooling than exists at the present time.

Since a much greater degree of equality of educational opportunity, school facilities, and curricula has come about nationwide in the half-century since World War I, it should be interesting to bring up to date the point that Klineberg made with World War I Army Alpha scores by looking at the most recently available Selective Service Test results.

Under the system of Selective Service virtually all American male youths, on becoming eighteen years of age, are required to take the Armed Forces Qualification Test (AFQT), a rather typical self-administered paper-and-pencil test of general intelligence. Specifically, the AFQT was designed (1) to 'measure a person's ability to absorb military training within reasonable limits of time, in order to eliminate those who do not have such ability', and (2) 'to provide a uniform measure of general usefulness in the services of those who qualified on the test' (Kárpinos, 1962, p. 10). The test consists of 100 questions equally distributed in four areas: vocabulary (ability to handle words and understand verbal concepts), arithmetic (ability to reason with numbers and solve simple mathematical problems), spatial relations (ability to distinguish forms and patterns), and mechanical ability (ability to interrelate tools and equipment). On the basis of AFQT scores, examinees are classified into five groups ranging in mental ability from very rapid learners (mental group I) to very slow learners (mental group V), according to the following percentiles:

Mental Group	Percentile Score	Equivalent Correct Answers*
I	93-100	89-100
II	65-92	74-88
III	31-64	53-73
IV	10-30	25-52
V	9 and below	1-24

* The number of equivalent correct answers is computed by subtracting from the number of questions answered correctly one-third of the questions answered incorrectly

A percentile score of 10 was fixed by Congress as a minimum passing score, intended to eliminate the 10 percent of the total draft-age population within the lowest aptitude range of the distribution of mental test scores (designated as mental group V). Those in mental group V are disqualified from entering the armed forces. According to a report from the Office of the Surgeon General:

> The Army has found . . . that an appreciable number of those in mental group IV (10th to 30th percentile), though they had met the required minimum requirement on the AFQT, did not possess sufficient aptitude to assimilate training in even the most basic military skills. Many of them had to be discharged later from the Army as inapt or unsuitable. (Kárpinos, 1962, p. 11)

The last year for which complete statistics on the AFQT have been published is 1968 (Office of the Surgeon General, 1969). They are based on the AFQT scores of 1,009,381 whites and 155,531 Negroes from every state of the continental United States who were eligible for the draft. (These statistics do not include Alaska, Hawaii, Guam, and Puerto Rico.)

The percent of each population group with AFQT scores below the tenth percentile in 1968 were 5·2 percent of whites and 26·8 percent of Negroes. This corresponds to a difference of 1·01 sigma (σ) or standard deviation units. If we put AFQT scores on a scale with the same standard deviation as the IQ scale in the white population ($\sigma = 15$), the difference of 1·01σ would equal 15·15 points. The distributions of whites and Negroes in mental groups I to IV was as follows:

Mental Group	White	Negro	Ratio: $W\%/N\%$
I	7·3	0·4	18·25
II	36·1	6·6	5·47
III	38·3	30·7	1·25
IV	18·0	59·5	0·30
Administrative Acceptees*	0·3	2·8	0·11

* Draftees who failed the mental tests but who were declared administratively acceptable on the basis of personal interviews

From the above figures, and assuming normality of the distribution of AFQT scores and equal sigmas for whites and Negroes, one may infer from the table of areas under the normal curve that there was $0·99\sigma$ mean difference on the AFQT scale between the whites and the Negroes who were recruited into the armed forces in 1968.

While the AFQT is not strictly an IQ test, its correlation with various standard IQ tests is probably as high as the correlations among various IQ tests. It is not inappropriate, therefore, to transform the AFQT score to a scale having the same mean (100) and sigma (15) as the IQ scale in the white population. If we put the white mean IQ at 100, and $\sigma = 15$, and if 5·2 percent of whites fail the test, we can infer from the tables of the normal curve that the failure cut-off is equivalent to an IQ of 76. If 26·8 percent of Negroes fall below this point, as the 1968 AFQT results indicate, it would put the mean of the Negro distribution (assuming normality) at 84·85 or approximately 85.[11]

Coming back now to the point made by Klineberg, that there are regional differences in test scores among both racial populations, we can view the current situation by comparing the results obtained in various states.

Highest percent of failures in any state:
   White = 9·7 percent (Tennessee)
   Negro = 46·7 percent (Mississippi)
   Sigma difference = $1·12\sigma \simeq 16·8$ IQ points.

Second-highest percent of failures in any state:
   White = 9·4 percent (Kentucky)
   Negro = 42·7 percent (Tennessee)
   Sigma difference = $1·13\sigma \simeq 16·9$ IQ points.

Lowest percent of failures in any state:
  White = 0·6 percent (Rhode Island)
  Negro = 7·4 percent (Wisconsin)
  Sigma difference = $1·06\sigma \simeq 15·9$ IQ points.

Second-lowest percent of failures in any state:
  White = 0·9 percent (Minnesota)
  Negro = 11·1 percent (California)
  Sigma difference = $1·29\sigma \simeq 19·4$ IQ points.

Comparison of highest *white and* lowest *Negro failure rates:*
  Highest white = 9·7 percent (Tennessee)
  Lowest Negro = 7·4 percent (Wisconsin)
  Sigma difference = $0·15\sigma \simeq 2·25$ IQ points (in favor of Negroes).

Comparison of lowest *white and* highest *Negro failure rates:*
  Lowest white = 0·6 percent (Rhode Island)
  Highest Negro = 46·7 percent (Mississippi)
  Sigma difference = $2·43\sigma \simeq 36·45$ IQ points.

Comparison of second-highest *white and* second-lowest *Negro failure rates:*
  Second-highest white = 9·4 percent (Kentucky)
  Second-lowest Negro = 11·1 percent (California)
  Sigma difference = $0·11\sigma \simeq 1·65$ IQ points (in favor of whites).

Thus, we see that in contrast to the data noted by Klineberg from World War I, when the Negro medians of four Northern states exceeded the white median of four Southern states, in 1968 there are only two pairs of states (Tennessee and Wisconsin, and Kentucky and Wisconsin) in which Negroes obtain higher AFQT scores, on the average, than whites. In this 1968 sample, the mean score of white males in Tennessee would correspond to 95, i.e., 5 points below the whites' national average, on an IQ scale, while the mean score of Negro males in Wisconsin would be 97·25, i.e., nearly 13 points above the Negroes' national average.

Since the AFQT is clearly predictive of individuals' capabilities in learning and performance in the armed forces, the above figures must give pause concerning the capabilities of Negroes, on the average, for competing with other subpopulations educationally and occupationally outside the armed forces. Whatever the causes, the facts themselves cannot be taken lightly. Reviews of the evidence on the predictive validity of IQ and aptitude tests indicate that such tests have the same validity for Negroes and whites for predicting educational performance (Stanley, 1971; Sattler, 1972).

Why has the number of Northern states with Negro means higher than white means in Southern states decreased from World War I to the present time – a period marked by educational and economic advances for the whole population and especially for Negroes? The increasing migration of Negroes from the rural South to the urban North is the most likely explanation. Generally the first migrants are selected for superior abilities and physical characteristics which is not the case with later migrants. Negroes who migrated North prior to World War I probably represent a different selection of Southern Negroes from those who migrated North after World War II. In World War II, the percentage of Southern Negroes who failed the Army General Classification Test was consistently greater than for Northern Negroes, even when matched for amount of formal education, from less than five years of schooling up to the college level. Northern Negroes constituted nearly one-third of all Negroes accepted into the armed forces in World War II, although they constituted less than a fourth of all Negro registrants (Stouffer *et al.*, 1965, pp. 493-4).

Related to the issue of regional differences in IQ is the entirely gratuitous assumption that the average intelligence difference found between Negroes and whites in the United States must have arisen in the 200 years or so since Negroes were brought to these shores as slaves. Bodmer and Cavalli-Sforza (1970, p. 25), for instance, make this assumption in order to argue that genetic selection due to differential birth rates of the more intelligent and the less intelligent segments of the Negro population could not have resulted in a mean Negro-white difference of 1 sigma (15 IQ points) in the 200 years (seven generations) since the importation of slaves from Africa. This argument assumes, of course, that the African populations from which slaves were recruited, and the slaves themselves, were equal in genetic potential for intelligence to the average of the white population. But this baseless assumption merely begs the question. There is no reason to assume that African and European populations have the same gene pools for intelligence, nor even to assume that the Africans who were recruited as slaves were a representative selection of Africans who remained in West Africa. We do know that studies of the intelligence of Negroes in Africa have found them to average at least one sigma below Europeans on a variety of tests[12] (Butcher, 1968, pp. 249-50; Evans, 1970, pp. 9-28). The meaning of this difference is, of course, quite unclear because of the problems posed by cross-cultural testing. But the evidence, such as it is, would give no reason to assume there is no difference between native Africans and Europeans or that there is a marked difference between Africans and American Negroes, although one might hypothesize a difference on the basis of the fact that the American Negro now has inherited some 20 to 25 percent of his genes from Caucasian ancestors[13] (Reed, 1969a).

Finally, one may raise the question of just how big a difference in average IQ one sigma really is. Is 1σ difference actually of any social, educational, or occupational consequence? There is of course no way of saying in absolute terms just how 'big' or how serious a difference of 1σ is. We can only note the various correlates and consequences of a 1σ difference in mean IQ in our society. The most disadvantageous consequences for any population group which is below the overall population mean have already been noted in connection with the properties of the normal curve, and the disproportionate representation of any two groups with bell-shaped distributions having different means when selective cut-offs are made at varying distances from the overall mean of the population. Selection for any characteristics correlated with intelligence will disfavor the subgroup with the lower mean in the percentage of its members who can meet the competition. No matter how much one may dislike the idea, the fact remains that much of the competition inherent in our society to some extent involves whatever the factors are that are assessed by intelligence tests, even when the individual's amount of formal education and the social status of his family background are held constant. The differences between persons in positions that are regarded as more or less desirable in our society involve differences in intelligence at least as much as in any other single factor, and the relationship is greater than many people would like to believe. For instance, persons in upper and middle management positions, while they are not thought of as being the intellectual elite, actually turn out, on the average, to be at the ninety-sixth percentile of the white population in intelligence, equivalent to an IQ of about 125 (Ghiselli, 1963). Many more whites than Negroes *per capita* fall above this point.

But perhaps the more serious consequences of the 1σ mean difference are at the lower extreme of the distribution. Persons who have been exposed to schooling for several years but who still have IQs below 70, especially on non-verbal and non-scholastic tests, are severely handicapped in the world of work, and can seldom succeed in *any* kind of skilled or semi-skilled work available in an industrial society. Most of them have difficulty finding employment in an urban economy and they are frequently dependent either upon relatives or public welfare for their support. Persons in our society today with IQs below 70 are generally regarded as mentally retarded and in school would be recognized as such even if there were no IQ tests. This degree of handicap cannot be passed off lightly as a 'cultural difference', because the behavioral correlates of an IQ below 70 are probably a handicap in *any* modern culture. Again, from the properties of the normal curve, any population subgroup whose mean is 1σ below IQ 100 can be expected to have approximately seven times as many persons with IQs under 70 as are found in a population whose mean IQ is 100. From a social standpoint, this is probably the gravest consequence of the average Negro-white IQ difference. If as many as one-sixth to one-fourth of the members of a community have IQs below 70, it is difficult to imagine that the quality of the environment would not be adversely affected. If the quality of the environment depends to some extent upon the intelligence of the persons who create the environment, we cannot argue, as some social scientists would do, that subpopulation intelligence differences can only be studied after complete environmental equality has been achieved, in which case presumably all differences would be eliminated and there would no longer be a problem calling for solution. Realistically, improving the environment in psychologically significant ways may depend even more upon improving the intelligence of its inhabitants than raising their intelligence depends upon improving the quality of their environment.

NOTES

1. 'Population' is a statistical concept. A population is defined by a set of operational criteria by which individuals are either included or excluded as members of the population. A population is thus defined also as all individuals who meet the criteria for inclusion. Mean values of various phenotypes in the population and their dispersion (variance or average difference among members of the population) are *estimated* on random samples drawn from the defined population. A sample is truly random when every member of the population has an equal chance of being included in the sample.

2. The term 'genetic value', (also called genic or genotype value), has a technical quantitative meaning. It does not imply any 'value judgment' about the trait in question. An individual's 'genetic value' is his hypothetical position on the trait's scale of measurement if he had developed in the 'average' environment of the population of which he is a member and in which h^2 has been estimated. Conversely, the individual's 'environmental value' is his hypothetical position on the trait scale if his genetic endowment were the average of the population. While 'genetic value' refers to *all* the genetic components that constitute the individual's genotype, the term 'breeding value' refers only to the additive genetic effects, or heritability in the narrow sense. An individual's breeding value is the hypothetical mean position on the scale of trait measurement of all of the individual's potential offsprings when his mate or mates are genetically at the population mean and when the offspring have developed in an average environment for the population.

3. It should be noted that a multiplicative model depends upon a scale with a true zero point and no zero or negative value; the multiplicative model cannot be applied to deviations from means, which is what practically all psychological test scores consist of. In any case, there is little difference in predictive precision between an additive and a multiplicative model unless the variations in G and E are very large in comparison to their means. There would be no practical difference between the models in estimating heritability when the coefficients of variation (i.e., the ratios σ_P/Mean G and σ_E/Mean E) are less than about 0·20.

4. A detailed treatment of the use of transformation of the scale of measurement in quantitative genetics can be found in Chapter 17 of Falconer's *Introduction to Quantitative Genetics* (1960).

5. *Epistasis* is the interactive (i.e., non-additive) effect among genes at different loci in the chromosomes. For example, the phenotypic effect of gene A plus gene B may be greater (or less) than the sum

of the separate effects of gene A and gene B. The epistatic effect, then, is the difference between $A+B$ and $A \times B$ (or any other non-additive combination of A and B). Epistasis generally has little effect on the heritability.

6. Assortative mating means a correlation between mates in the trait in question. A positive correlation between mates increases the phenotypic variance of the offspring in the population; a negative correlation decreases σ_P^2.

7. The covariance of G and E refers to the fact that genetic and environmental values may be correlated (positively or negatively) in the population. Numerically, the covariance of G and E (Cov GE) is equal to $2r_{GE}\sigma_G\sigma_E$.

8. *Dominance* in this case means that intelligence-enhancing genes exert more influence on the phenotype than non-enhancing genes. If **A** is a gene that enhances intelligence and **a** is a non-enhancing gene at the same locus, then we have three possible genotypes: **AA**, **Aa**, and **aa**. If **Aa** is exactly intermediate in effect between **AA** and **aa**, then there is no dominance; but if **Aa** is somewhat greater than the average of **AA** and **aa**, there is partial dominance; and if the effect of **Aa** is equal to that of **AA**, we have complete dominance. In the simplest case, that is, in a population in which the frequencies of **A** and **a** are equal, the *additive* effect of substituting gene **A** for gene **a** is merely half of the difference between the value **AA-aa**. The deviations from additive effects are called dominance deviations, and the total genetic variance is the sum of the variance due to additive effects and those due to dominance effects. Even with complete dominance a large proportion of the variance is additive unless the frequency of the dominant gene is greater than that of the non-dominant gene. Even in the latter case most of the variance can be additive if dominance is partial rather than complete. If dominance is complete, the proportion of genetic variance that is additive is $2q/(1+q)$, where q is the proportion of non-dominant (i.e., recessive) genes. (p is the proportion of dominant genes and $p+q = 1$.)

9. This was not presented by me as a 'contention' but as a 'reasonable hypothesis'. I wrote:

> It seems not unreasonable, in view of the fact that intelligence variation has a large genetic component, to hypothesize that genetic factors may play a part in this picture. But such an hypothesis is anathema to many social scientists. The idea that the lower average intelligence and scholastic performance of Negroes could involve, not only environmental, but also genetic, factors has indeed been strongly denounced. . . . But it has been

neither contradicted nor discredited by evidence. . . . The preponderance of the evidence is, in my opinion, less consistent with
a strictly environmental hypothesis than with a genetic hypothesis, which, of course, does not exclude the influence of
environment or its interaction with genetic factors. (Jensen,
1969a, p. 82)

10. What Jencks means, of course, is 'genetically superior *in IQ*'. It
is an interesting point that those who seem to oppose any hypothesis
of genetic differences also most frequently use the overly general
terms 'inferior' and 'superior' without the necessary qualification
of specifying the scale of the particular trait in question.

11. Most white-Negro mean differences reported in the literature probably underestimate the true population difference because of a
statistical artifact that enters into any comparison between two
groups which are not sampled from the total range of scores in the
population, as when samples are drawn from schools or the armed
forces which may exclude IQs below some rather low selection cut-
off. If on some metrical trait x two normally distributed populations
differ by some amount d, and if samples are drawn only between
the values a and b (i.e., the sample is restricted to the range of
values $a<x<b$), then the *lower* group is always favored, i.e., d is
always underestimated or, in other words, the sample means differ
less than the population means. The same thing is true if sampling
is restricted only by an upper or a lower selection cut-off.

12. The first attempt to estimate quantitatively the differences between
Africans' and Europeans' intelligence was made by Sir Francis
Galton (1870, p. 338). There were no intelligence tests at that time,
but Galton based his estimate on the relative proportions of men
in each race attaining certain levels of occupational skill and achievement and on his own first-hand impression while studying in Africa
– admittedly poor criteria by present-day standards. Galton estimated the Negro-white average intelligence difference as 'not less
than two grades, and it may be more'. 'Two grades' by Galton's
system of measurement is equivalent to 1·39 standard deviations
($1\cdot39\sigma$) or 20·85 points on an IQ scale with a σ of 15. It is interesting
to compare Galton's estimate with that of Kennedy *et al.* (1963)
for Southern Negroes as compared with whites, a difference of
21·1 IQ points (see Figure 8.2).

13. It is an interesting fact in its own right that while the number of
research studies and scholarly publications dealing with the mental
abilities of Negroes (African and American) numbers something
over a thousand, it is difficult to compile a bibliography of more than
a handful of references on the abilities of other racial groups. Euro-

pean colonialists in India, China, and Southeast Asia, for example, apparently were not stimulated to ask questions about the mental abilities of the peoples in these regions or to do research on the subject, while at the same time European psychologists and anthropologists were prolificly studying and writing about the mental capacities of Africans. (An extensive bibliography has been compiled by Andor, 1966.)

3   Intelligence and educability

Educability, which refers to the ability to learn school subjects under the ordinary conditions of classroom instruction, is quantitatively indexed by school grades and, more reliably, by scores on standardized tests of scholastic achievement. To what extent does educability depend upon intelligence? The question may seem rather circular, since intelligence tests were devised originally to predict scholastic performance, and scholastic criteria are still paramount in establishing the external validity of many standard intelligence tests. The correlation between IQ and measures of achievement is quite high, ranging from about 0·30 to 0·90 in various studies (the magnitude depending upon many conditions) with an average correlation of about 0·80 when corrected for attenuation (errors of measurement). In other words, something over 60 percent of the true variance in individual differences in scholastic achievement is accounted for by individual differences in intelligence. This evidence has been reviewed in detail by Bloom (1964, Ch. 4) and Tyler (1965, Ch. 5). A pupil's relative standing in achievement is quite stable over the school years, increasing in stability with each succeeding year, just as is the case for intelligence measures. Furthermore, the correlations between intelligence and achievement increase with years in school. Bloom (1964, p. 95) reports a correlation of 0·68 (or 0·85 when corrected for unreliability) between 9th year grades and college freshman grades. Another study (Bloom, 1964, p. 102) found a correlation between IQ at age 6 and school achievement at age 13 to be 0·60. And a correlation of 0·42 was found between Stanford-Binet IQ at age 4 and a scholastic achievement battery at age 13. So there can be no doubt that intelligence tests and achievement tests, even when they have no subject matter content in common, have considerable individual differences variance in common.

Furthermore, it is the general intelligence factor – the *g* which all tests of mental ability share in common – that correlates most highly with achievement. Differential abilities, such as those measured by Thurstone's Primary Mental Abilities (PMA) Tests (Verbal, Numerical, Reasoning, Spatial, etc.), do not show higher correlations with particular scholastic subjects than omnibus tests of general intelligence. The Verbal and Reasoning tests of the PMA battery, which have the largest *g* loadings, yield the highest correlations with achievement, and they correlate about equally with every scholastic subject (Tyler, 1965, p. 112). When a variety of achievement tests are factor analyzed along with a variety of intelligence tests and measures of personality, interests, etc., they are found to have their highest loadings on the *g* (general) factor, their next highest loadings on a verbal ability factor (labeled *V* : *ed*, i.e., verbal-educational, by British psychologists), and their next highest loadings on non-intellectual factors involving personality traits, interests, and family background characteristics. Other abilities having appreciable correlations with achievement, independently of *g* and *V* : *ed*, have not as yet been found. There *are* other ability factors, to be sure, but they have not been found to contribute to variance in scholastic achievement. It is possible that they might do so under quite different forms of instruction, but this has not yet been demonstrated for the learning of scholastic subjects. One of the major challenges to present-day educational researchers is to try and see if they can discover or invent learning environments or methods of teaching which can utilize abilities other than *g* and *V* : *ed* for the acquisition of scholastic skills and knowledge (see Cronbach & Snow, 1969; Bracht, 1970).

In view of the high correlation between IQ and achievement, how then can we distinguish between them? Traditionally, intelligence has been regarded as the *capacity* for acquiring knowledge and skills, while achievement *is* the knowledge and skills. And yet both intelligence and achievement can be measured only in terms of the person's actual performance, demonstrating knowledge and skills of certain types that we call cognitive, mental, or intellectual. The hypothetical *capacity* inferred to underlie acquisition is presumably the same for the knowledge and skills sampled by intelligence tests as for those sampled by scholastic achievement tests. In a sense, when we use intelligence tests to predict scholastic achievement, what we are doing is using achievement in one domain (non-scholastic) to predict achievement in another (scholastic).

The most obvious difference between tests of intelligence and of achievement is the breadth of the domains sampled by the tests. Achievement tests sample very narrowly from the most specifically taught skills in the traditional curriculum, emphasizing the 3 Rs. The test items are samples of the particular skills and items of information that children are specifically taught in school. Since this domain is quite explicitly defined and the criteria of its acquisition are fairly clear to teachers and parents, children can be taught and made to practise these skills so as to shape their performance up to the desired standard. Because of the circum-scribed nature of many of the basic scholastic skills, the pupil's specific weaknesses can be identified and remedied.

The kinds of skills and learning sampled by an intelligence test, on the other hand, represent achievements of a much broader nature. Much of what is tapped by IQ tests is acquired by *incidental* learning, that is to say, it has never been explicitly taught. Most of the words in a person's vocabulary were never explicitly taught or acquired by studying a dictionary. Intelligence test items typically are sampled from such a wide range of potential experi-ences that the idea of teaching intelligence, as compared with teaching, say, reading and arithmetic, is practically nonsensical. Even direct coaching and practice on a particular intelligence test raises an individual's scores on a parallel form of the test on the average by only five to ten points; and some tests, especially those referred to as 'culture fair', seem to be hardly amenable to the effects of coaching and practice. The average five-year-old child, for example, can copy a circle or a square without any trouble, but try to teach him to copy a diamond and see how far he gets! It is practically impossible. But wait until he is seven years old and he will have no trouble copying the diamond, without any need for instruction. Even vocabulary is very unsusceptible to enlargement by direct practice aimed specifically at increasing vocabulary.

This is mainly the reason that vocabulary tests are such good measures of general intelligence and always have a high *g* loading in a factor analysis of various types of intelligence tests, even those that are entirely non-verbal. The items in a vocabulary test are sampled from such an enormously large pool of potential items that the number that can be acquired by specific study and drill is only a small proportion of the total, so that few if any of the words one would acquire in this way are likely to appear in any given vocabulary test. Moreover, persons seem to retain only those words which fill some conceptual 'slot' or need in their own mental structures. A new word encountered for the first time which fills such a conceptual 'slot' is picked up and retained without conscious effort, and it will 'pop' into mind again when the conceptual need for it arises, even though in the meantime the word may not have been encountered for many months or even years. If there was no conceptual slot that needed to be filled, that is to say, no meaning for which the individual has a use and which the word serves to symbolize, it is exceedingly difficult to make the definition of the word stick in the individual's memory. Even after repeated drill, it will quickly fade beyond retrieval.

Since intelligence tests get at the learning that occurs in the total life experience of the individual, it is a more general and more valid measure of his learning potential than are scholastic achievement tests. But it should not be surprising that there is a substantial correlation between the two classes of tests, since both measure learning and achievement, one in a broad sphere, the other in a much narrower sphere. In recent years we have seen a trend in the construction of achievement tests which increases their correlation with intelligence tests, especially at higher grade levels. This results from devising achievement test questions that call for more than purely factual knowledge and require students to use their knowledge in novel ways, to reason from it, to see new relations, and to apply it to the solution of new problems. In short, achievement tests can be made to assess 'transfer of training' and this makes them correlate more highly with intelligence tests. An increased correlation could also result from an increased tendency to validate IQ tests against academic criteria. But generally, in a culturally homogeneous population, the broader based measures we call intelligence tests are more representative of the individual's learning capacities and are more stable over the years than the specific acquisitions of scholastic knowledge and skills.

One of the most impressive characteristics of intelligence tests is the great diversity of means by which essentially the same ability can be measured. Tests having very diverse forms, such as vocabulary, block designs, matrices, number series, 'odd man out', figure copying, verbal analogies, and other kinds of problems can all serve as intelligence tests yielding more or less equivalent results because of their high intercorrelations. All of these types of tests have high loadings on the *g* factor, which, as Wechsler (1958, p. 121) has said, '. . . involves broad mental organization; it is independent of the modality or contextual structure from which it is elicited; *g* cannot be exclusively identified with any single intellectual ability and for this reason cannot be described in concrete operational terms'. We can accurately define *g* only in terms of certain mathematical operations; in Wechsler's words, '*g* is a measure of a collective communality which necessarily emerges from the intercorrelation of any broad sample of mental abilities' (p. 123).

Assessment of scholastic achievement, on the other hand, depends upon tests of narrowly specific acquired skills – reading, spelling, arithmetic operations, and the like. The forms by means of which one can test any one of these scholastic skills are very limited indeed. This is not to say that there is not a general factor common to all tests of scholastic achievement, but this general factor common to all the tests seems to be quite indistinguishable from the *g* factor of intelligence tests. Achievement tests, however, usually do not have quite as high *g* loadings as intelligence tests but have higher loadings on group factors such as verbal and numerical ability factors, containing, as well, more content-specific variance.

It is always possible to make achievement tests correlate more highly with intelligence tests by requiring students to reason, to use data provided, and to apply their factual knowledge to the solution of new problems. More than just the mastery of factual information, intelligence is the ability to apply this information in new and different ways. With increasing grade level, achievement tests have more and more variance in common with tests of *g*. For example, once the basic skills in reading have been acquired, reading achievement tests must increasingly measure the student's comprehension of more and more complex selections rather than the simpler processes of word recognition, decoding, etc. And thus at higher grades, tests of reading comprehension, for those children who have already mastered the basic skills, become more or less indistinguishable in factorial composition from the so-called tests of verbal intelligence. Similarly, tests of mechanical arithmetic (arithmetic computation) have less correlation with *g* than tests of arithmetic thought problems, such as the Arithmetic Concepts and Arithmetic Applications subtests of the Stanford Achievement battery. Accordingly, most indices of scholastic performance increasingly reflect general intelligence as children progress in school. We found in one study, for example, that up to grade 6, verbal and non-verbal intelligence tests could be factorially separated, with the scholastic achievement tests lining up on the same factor with verbal intelligence (Jensen, 1971a). But beyond grade 6 both the verbal and non-verbal tests, along with all the scholastic achievement tests, amalgamated into a single large general factor which no form of factor rotation could separate into smaller components distinguishable as verbal intelligence *v.* non-verbal intelligence *v.* scholastic achievement. By grades 7 and 8 the Lorge-Thorndike Non-verbal IQ and Raven's Progressive Matrices are hardly distinguishable in their factor composition from the tests of scholastic achievement. At the same time it is important to recognize that the Lorge-Thorndike Non-verbal IQ and Raven's Matrices are not measuring scholastic attainment *per se*, as demonstrated by the fact that totally illiterate and unschooled persons can obtain high scores on these tests. Burt (1961a), for example, reported the case of separated identical twins with widely differing educational attainments (elementary school education *v.* a university degree), who differed by only one IQ point on the Progressive Matrices (127 *v.* 128).

Another important characteristic of the best intelligence test items is that they clearly fall along an age scale. Items are thus 'naturally' ordered in difficulty. The Figure Copying Test is a good example. The Figure Copying Test was developed at the Gesell Institute of Child Study at Yale University as a means for measuring developmental readiness for the traditional school learning tasks of the primary grades. The test consists of the ten geometric forms shown in Figure 3.1, arranged in order of difficulty, which the child must simply copy, each on a separate sheet of paper. The test involves no memory factor, since the figure to be copied is before the child at all times. It is administered without time limit, although most children finish in 10 to 15 minutes. The test is best regarded as a developmental scale of mental ability. It correlates substantially with other IQ tests, but it is considerably less culture-loaded than most usual IQ tests. It is primarily a measure of general cognitive development and not just of perceptual-motor ability. Children taking the test are urged

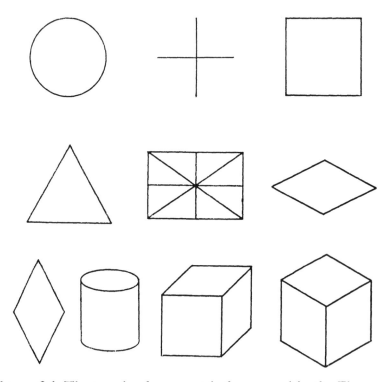

Figure 3.1 The ten simple geometric forms used in the Figure Copying Test. In the actual test booklet each figure is presented singly in the top half of a 5½″ × 8½″ sheet. The circle is 1¾″ in diameter.

to attempt to copy every figure. Ability to succeed on a more difficult item in the age scale is not functionally dependent upon success on previous items in the sense that the easier item is a prerequisite component of the more difficult item. By contrast, skill in short division is a component of skill in long division. The age differential for some tasks such as figure copying and the Piagetian conservation tests is so marked as to suggest that they depend upon the sequential maturation of hierarchical neural processes (Jensen, 1970b). Teaching of the skills before the necessary maturation has occurred is often practically impossible, but after the child has reached a certain age successful performance of the skill occurs without any specific training or practice. The items in scholastic achievement tests do not show this characteristic. For successful performance, the subject must have received explicit instruction in the specific subject matter of the test. The teachability of scholastic subjects is much more obvious than of the kinds of materials that constitute most intelligence tests and especially non-verbal tests.

Still another distinguishable characteristic between intelligence and achievement tests is the difference between the heritability values generally found for intelligence and achievement measures. But this topic is treated in Chapter 4.

GROWTH MODEL OF ACHIEVEMENT

Among the most interesting and theoretically important facts about scholastic achievement are the manner in which it increases or 'grows' over the years and the particular pattern of inter-correlations of individual differences in achievement from year to year over the course of schooling from first grade to high school graduation. In these aspects, the growth of scholastic knowledge closely resembles the growth of intelligence, and also, interestingly enough, it resembles the essential features of growth in physical stature. Total vocabulary size, one of the best indices of intelligence that can be measured on an absolute scale, also shows the same growth characteristics. The evidence relevant to the following discussion is derived from longitudinal studies in which the achievements of the same children are measured each year over the course of their schooling. Much of this evidence has been compiled by Benjamin Bloom (1964).

In the growth of scholastic knowledge and competence, just as in the growth of intelligence and of physical stature, individuals fluctuate in relative standing among their age peers throughout the course of development. The individual year-to-year fluctuations in relative standing are greater early in development and gradually diminish as individuals approach maturity. The year-to-year inter-correlations of scholastic achievement show a highly distinctive pattern. I have examined virtually all such longitudinal correlation

Table 3.1 Correlations (decimals omitted) among achievement test scores, and the first principal component (P.C.I), from grade 3 to high school (all columns, excepting P.C.I, from Vane, 1966).

				Grade				
Grade	3	4	5	6	7	8	HS	P.C.I
3		85	82	81	79	76	66	0·90
4	85		86	83	80	80	65	0·91
5	82	86		89	84	82	69	0·93
6	81	83	89		89	86	70	0·94
7	79	80	84	89		90	71	0·94
8	76	80	82	86	90		72	0·92
HS	66	65	69	70	71	72		0·80

Table 3.2 Correlations (decimals omitted) among achievement test scores, and the first principal component (P.C.I), from grade 2 to grade 9 (from Bracht & Hopkins, 1972).

					Grade				
Grade	2	3	4	5	6	7	8	9	P.C.I
2		73	74	72	68	68	66	60	0·80
3	73		86	79	78	76	74	61	0·86
4	74	86		87	86	84	81	70	0·92
5	72	79	87		93	91	87	77	0·95
6	68	78	86	93		93	90	81	0·96
7	68	76	84	91	93		94	85	0·96
8	66	74	81	87	90	94		86	0·94
9	60	61	70	77	81	85	86		0·86

matrices for achievement reported in the literature and have found no exception to this distinctive pattern.

Let us examine a couple of tables of actual correlations among year-to-year achievement measures. Table 3.1 shows the inter-correlations among standardized achievement scores of 272 white and Negro children attending integrated schools who had been tested at each grade level from 3rd grade to high school (from Vane, 1966, Table 1). Table 3.2 shows the year-to-year inter-correlations of achievement test scores of more than one thousand children from grades 1 to 9 (from Bracht & Hopkins, 1972, Table 2).

The first conspicuous feature of the correlations in Tables 3.1 and 3.2 is that they are quite high, ranging from about 0·60 to 0·90. This indicates a fairly high degree of stability of individuals' relative standing in scholastic achievement throughout the school years. Intelligence test scores show about the same degree of stability, although the correlations span a much wider range as we go down into the pre-school years. This can be seen in Table 3.3, which shows the intercorrelations among intelligence test scores of some 200 children from age 1·75 years of age to 18 years of age (from Honzik, MacFarlane, & Allen, 1948, Table III). Here the correlations range from close to zero (between ages 1·75 years and 18 years) up to about 0·90.

The most striking feature of all three correlation matrices, however, is the *pattern* of correlations, with the size of the correlations being largest near the principal diagonal and decreasing more or less regularly the further away they are from the diagonal. That is to say, the intercorrelations for temporally adjacent tests are high, and there is a regular decline in correlations as the interval between tests increases. All longitudinal test data on intelligence, vocabulary acquisition, physical stature, and scholastic achievement, it so happens, conform to this pattern when the measures are intercorrelated. Guttman (1954) has called this pattern of correlations a *simplex*. This point is worth knowing, because a simplex can be accounted for in terms of a very neat and simple model.

Before this model is described, a word is in order about the factor analysis or principal components analysis of a correlation matrix which is a simplex. A perfect simplex (i.e., one in which the correlations are not affected by sampling error or by differences

Table 3.3 Correlations (decimals omitted) among intelligence test scores* at different ages (from Honzik *et al.*, 1948), and the first and second principal components (P.C.I and P.C.II).

Age	1·75	2	3	3·5	4	5	6	7	8	9	10	14	18	P.C.I	P.C.II
1·75		71	52	48	38	39	27	29	27	22	20	14	07	0·43	0·72
2	71		69	60	46	32	47	46	43	37	37	28	31	0·59	0·62
3	52	69		71	58	57	57	55	49	43	46	36	35	0·69	0·51
3·5	48	60	71		76	71	64	60	50	54	60	47	42	0·77	0·38
4	38	46	58	76		72	62	59	61	60	64	49	42	0·77	0·21
5	39	32	57	71	72		71	73	70	69	71	61	56	0·83	0·03
6	27	47	57	64	62	71		82	77	74	74	69	61	0·86	−0·06
7	29	46	55	60	59	73	82		83	81	77	75	71	0·89	−0·13
8	27	43	49	50	61	70	77	83		92	88	83	70	0·90	−0·24
9	22	37	43	54	60	69	74	81	92		89	89	71	0·89	−0·31
10	20	37	46	60	64	71	74	77	88	89		86	73	0·90	−0·28
14	14	28	36	47	49	61	69	75	83	89	86		76	0·83	−0·41
18	07	31	35	42	42	56	61	71	70	71	73	76		0·75	−0·37

Age in Years

* Test at ages 1·75–5: California Preschool Schedule I or II.
Test at ages 6–14: Stanford-Binet Intelligence Scale.
Test at age 18: Wechsler-Bellevue Intelligence Scale.

in test reliability), when subjected to a principal components analysis that extracts as many components (i.e., hypothetical independent sources of variance) as there are tests, will yield (1) a large general factor (the first principal component), (2) a bipolar factor with positive loadings on early tests and negative loadings on late ones, (3) a factor that plots as a U with negative loadings in the middle of the series, (4) a factor with loadings that plot out a sine curve, and (5) a number of remaining nondescript, random factors (equal to the number of tests minus 4) which account for smaller and smaller proportions of the total variance among all the tests. In practice one applies some criterion for the number of components to be extracted (such as having Eigenvalues greater than 1), since each successive component accounts for less and less of the total test variance and beyond a certain point the components do not account for a significant percentage of the variance. In most of the correlation matrices of longitudinal intelligence and achievement data in the literature, only the first principal component has an Eigenvalue greater than 1 and it usually accounts for more than three-fourths of the total variance. The first principal component by definition is the one factor which accounts for most of the variance in all the tests, and in a simplex it is very large indeed, for as we shall see, there is really only one common factor plus as many random factors as there are tests in a simplex. The last column in Tables 3.1 and 3.2 shows the correlation of the achievement tests at each grade with the first principal component, which in both Table 3.1 and Table 3.2 accounts for 82 percent of the variance. In Table 3.3 the first two principal components had Eigenvalues greater than 1 and were therefore extracted; they account for 62 percent and 15 percent of the variance, respectively.

What kind of model will produce a simplex? Only two basic elements are required:[1] (1) a rate of *consolidation* factor, C, on which individuals maintain their relative positions in the population over the course of development, and (2) a random increment or gain, G, from time x to time $x+1$ (t_x to t_{x+1}). An individual's status, S, at any given time consists of the sum of $C \times G$ over all previous time plus the G of the immediate past. In effect, the consolidation factor C is a positive constant for a given individual; the gain factor G is a positive random variable in each time interval $t_x - t_{x+1}$. An individual's growth curve can then be represented as follows:

D

$t_1 : G_1$ (Gain since t_0)

$t_2 : CG_1 + G_2 = S_2$ (Consolidated gain from time 1 to time 2 plus unconsolidated gain at time 2 = status at time 2.)

$t_3 : CG_1 + CG_2 + G_3 = S_3$

$t_4 : CG_1 + CG_2 + CG_3 + G_4 = S_4$

$t_n : C(G_1 + G_2 + G_3 + G_4 + \ldots + G_{n-1}) + G_n = S_n$

For some measures, like height, one can never observe in the measurements themselves the gain G but only the consolidated gain CG, so that one always finds $S_1 < S_2 < S_3$, etc. This is not always the case for other characteristics such as the growth of body weight during development or the growth of intelligence or of scholastic achievement.

An actual simplex can be created simply by assigning some numerical values to C and G. Simulated individuals, for example, can each be assigned a C value selected from randomly distributed numbers from 0·10 to 1·00, and at each point in time G will be some value from 0 to 9 also taken from a table of normal random numbers. (To produce a growth curve which does not increase linearly but logarithmically, i.e., at a negatively accelerated rate characteristic of most growth curves, one can simply use the natural logarithm of S at each point in time. This will produce a quite typical looking growth curve, but the *form* of the growth function is not an essential aspect of the simplex. In the absence of an absolute scale, as is true of most psychological measurements, the form of the average growth curve, aside from being an increasing monotonic function of time, is quite arbitrary. The growth of vocabulary, a good index of intellectual development, can be measured on an absolute scale [number of words] and appears to be sigmoid. Over the period of schooling, from about age 5 to 18 years, however, the growth curve of vocabulary is logarithmic.) The S values at times t_1, t_2, t_3, etc. for 100 or more such simulated individuals when intercorrelated yield a correlation matrix with the simplex pattern. More complicated models can also produce a simplex; but this is the simplest model that will do it. The resulting simulated correlation matrix is virtually indistinguishable from those obtained from actual longitudinal intelligence and achievement test data.

Can we make a reasonable psychological interpretation of this model? The S values, of course, are no problem; they are simply the achievement measurements taken at different times. They are composed of consolidated gains, CG, plus unconsolidated gains, G, plus random errors of measurement, e.

The consolidation factor, C, is a variable which is more or less intrinsic to the individual; it is that aspect of individual differences in S values in the population at any cross-section of development which may be attributed to genetic and constitutional factors (which are not distinguishable in this model *per se*). The term consolidation as used here does not refer to the consolidation of short-term memory traces into long-term storage, but to the assimilation of experience (i.e., learning) into cognitive structures which organize what has been learned in ways that subsequently permit quick and adequate retrieval and broad transfer of the learning in new relevant situations. Stated in simplest terms, C is the process of *understanding* what one has learned. It is 'getting the idea', 'catching on', having the 'Aha!' experience that may accompany or follow experiencing or learning something, and the relating of new learning to past learning and vice versa. When learning takes place without C acting upon it, it is less retrievable and much less transferable for use in solving problems that are more or less remote from the original learning situation. C is what is generally meant by the term *intelligence*, but it can be manifested, observed, and measured only through its interaction with experience or learning. There can be learning without intelligence (i.e., without C) but intelligence cannot be manifested without learning. In our simple model we have represented the capacity for consolidation as a constant value for each individual; this is not an essential feature, although a more or less constant rank order of individuals' C values is essential. On the average, over the life span the C value probably increases up to maturity, levels off at maturity, and gradually declines in old age. Our concept of C comes very close to R. B. Cattell's concept of *fluid intelligence*. All intelligence tests measure S, but some tests reflect more of the C component (which Cattell would call tests of fluid intelligence) and some reflect more of the G component (which Cattell would call tests of crystalized intelligence) (see Cattell, 1971, Ch. 5).

The gain factor, G, consists of experience or learning and unconsolidated (or rote) memory of such learning. But is G properly represented as a random variable in our model? Consider the following quite well-established empirical findings. Learning abilities (which do not involve problem solving) have been found to show quite low, often negligible, correlations with intelligence. (For an excellent review, see Zeaman and House, 1967.) Moreover, a general factor of learning ability has not been found. There is a great deal of situation-specific or task-specific variance in learning, making for very low or even zero correlations among various kinds of learning. Therefore, learning *per se* in the vast variety of conditions under which it occurs in real life, cannot show much correlation, if any, with relatively stable individual difference variables such as intelligence.

Furthermore, consider the relative unpredictability or randomness of the individual's day-to-day experiences or opportunities for learning this or that, and the poorly correlated other variables, such as attention, motivation, and persistence, that can affect learning at any given moment. All these factors within a given interval of time add up in effect to a more or less random variable. It should be understood that random does not mean uncaused. A child may go down with measles and have to stay out of school for ten days and so miss out on a good many school learning experiences. Another child may miss out for a few weeks because his family moves to another city. Another child may learn a great deal for a period when the teacher is presenting something that especially interests him. And so on. The gains (or lack of gains) in any short period, though caused by a multitude of factors, appear in effect to be more or less random in the school population.

In his detailed and penetrating analysis of the mental test data of the Harvard Growth Study, Robert L. Thorndike (1966) noted that '*In considerable part, the factors that produce gains during a specified time span appear to be different from those that produced the level of competence exhibited at the beginning of the period.*' Thorndike reports the typical correlation between initial status and gain for a one-year interval to be $+0\cdot10$, which is about $+0\cdot22$ when corrected for attenuation. That is to say, initial status and gain after one year have less than 5 percent of their variance in common. (In Thorndike's analysis, status and gain were measured by experimentally independent measures, i.e., equivalent forms of the test, in order to avoid common errors of measurement lowering the correlation. One form of the test was used as the measure of initial status and an independent equivalent form was used as the base from which gains were computed.) This finding is consistent with the simplex model. Very little of the gain in a year's interval becomes consolidated as status. If it did, we should expect a much higher correlation between independent measures of status and of gain. Moreover, if a large random element did not enter into the short-term gains we should expect consistent individual differences in gains from one interval to the next and consequently substantial correlations between gains from one interval to the next. But this in fact is not the case. Thorndike gives the average correlation between two independent gain scores on intelligence tests for different intervals:

$$1\text{-year interval} = 0\cdot101$$
$$2\text{-year interval} = 0\cdot240$$
$$3\text{-year interval} = 0\cdot266$$
$$4\text{-year interval} = 0\cdot188$$
$$5\text{-year interval} = 0\cdot265$$

The longer the interval, of course, the larger is the proportion of the gain that has been consolidated and therefore the larger the correlations between gains over longer intervals. The same effect is reflected in the average correlations of initial status with gain based on experimentally independent tests:

$$1\text{-year interval} = 0\cdot045$$
$$2\text{-year interval} = 0\cdot006$$
$$3\text{-year interval} = 0\cdot031$$
$$4\text{-year interval} = 0\cdot139$$
$$5\text{-year interval} = 0\cdot329$$

These actual correlations are even smaller and somewhat less regular than would be predicted from the simplex model, probably because of measurement error, slightly changing factorial composition of the tests at different levels of difficulty (and thus at different ages), and unequal units of measurement over the full range of scores.

Another fact to be considered in this model is the heritability of the trait under consideration. This is quite high for intelligence and vocabulary, but lower for scholastic achievement, particularly in the elementary grades and for subjects such as spelling and mechanical arithmetic. Of all the growth characters on which there are good data, the highest heritability is for height. What high heritability means, among other things, is that a large part of the variance in status on the trait at maturity is, in principle, predictable at the moment of conception. That is to say, it is determined by genetic factors. If we take into consideration prenatally determined constitutional factors as well as the genetic factors, most of the variance in adult status for highly heritable characteristics like height, and to a slightly lesser degree intelligence, is theoretically predictable at birth. When something is highly predictable, it means nothing less than that it is predetermined. This is an unpopular but nevertheless accurate meaning of predictability. Predictability does not necessarily imply, however, that we have any control over the predetermining factors, nor does it necessarily imply the contrary. Although the correlation between Stanford-Binet IQ at age 2 and at age 18 is not higher than about $+0.3$, meaning that less than 10 percent of the variance in IQs at age 18 is predictable from a knowledge of IQs at age 2, heritability estimates indicate that some 70 to 80 percent of the variance in adult IQs is, in principle, predictable or predetermined at the time of conception. At each year from birth on, more and more of the predictable, predetermined aspect of the phenotype becomes manifest. This assumes, of course, that environmental influences throughout the course of children's development are no more variable than the actual environments in which the vast majority of children in our society are reared. It is the consolidation factor, C, in our simplex model which corresponds to the genetic and constitutional determining factors. Thus we should expect from this model that the heritability of IQ should increase from infancy to maturity as more and more experience is consolidated. This has been found in the increase of parent-child correlations from infancy to later childhood; such correlations strongly reflect heritability when the children have had no contact with their natural parents (because of adoption) with whom they show increasing correlations in intelligence as they mature, as was shown by Honzik (1957).

Also, from our model we would expect the squared loadings of the first principal component of the simplex matrix (P.C.I in Tables 3.1, 3.2, and 3.3) to approximate the amount of variance accounted for by individual differences in the C factor at any cross-section in the time scale of development. This can be clearly shown with simulated data in which the C values are of course known exactly. The estimates of variance accounted for by the *C* factor in the simplexes of actual data in Tables 3.1 to 3.3 should reflect the upper limits of the heritabilities in the broadest sense, i.e., the proportion of total variance attributable to all genetic factors and in part to the covariance of genetic and environmental factors (see Equation A.6 in the Appendix on Heritability). One would expect a quite large covariance component in scholastic achievement, and would expect it to increase over the course of schooling. The squared first principal components would yield inflated estimates of broad heritability to the extent that the *C* factor also includes non-genetic constitutional factors and any constant environmental effects over the course of development.

Intelligence thus can be thought of psychologically as that aspect of mental ability which *consolidates* learning and experience in an integrated, organized way, relating it to past learning and encoding it in ways that permit its retrieval in relevant new situations. The products of learning become an aspect of intelligence (or are correlates of intelligence) only when they are organized and retrievable, generalizable and transferable to new problem situations. This is why an adult with, say, only an eighth-grade education but with an IQ of 140 appears generally brighter and more capable at most things than a college graduate with an IQ of 110. It strikes many of those who have observed, taught, worked with, or employed both kinds of persons, that the advantage, in the long run, is usually with the person with the higher IQ rather than with the more education. Some of our social institutions unfortunately are set up so as to reward education more than intelligence. This will change, however, with increasing equality of educational opportunity. Then, not the amount of education, but the amount of consolidated achievement (i.e., intelligently usable and transferable knowledge and skills) will be the chief criteria for selection and promotion.

Material that is learned by rote association and repetition may appear as gains on an achievement test, but it does not necessarily become consolidated or integrated into the usable, transferable knowledge that we associate with intelligence. Unless it is constantly rehearsed, such knowledge acquired by rote quickly fades and is unretrievable. Anyone who has tried to improve his vocabulary by memorizing definitions of esoteric words appreciates this fact. Thus, no one has yet discovered any way of *teaching* intelligence to those who are not born with it. To teach intelligence might mean to point out more or less all the conceivable connections, generalizations, and possible transfer of every item of acquired information, and to elicit and reinforce the appropriate responses to these situations. This could involve teaching more than anyone could ever learn. Probably no one would live long enough ever to acquire even a mental age of six. The design of a computer that can 'learn' and 'think' both inductively and deductively is necessarily very different from that of the computer which merely records and stores items of information that can later be elicited by specific cues in a pushbutton fashion.

One of the ways in which scholastic achievement tests differ from intelligence tests is that at any given point in time, the usual achievement test scores reflect a relatively larger G or gain component, intended to assess what had been taught in the recent past in a particular grade in school. Since various subjects of the curriculum are newly introduced at different grades, the G component of achievement tests constitutes a larger proportion in relation to S than is the case for intelligence tests. The G component is largely a function of environmental influences, interests, motivation, and the like, acting at any given time. Bloom (1964, pp. 113-19) has reviewed convincing evidence that G is more related to environmental factors, while C is genetically and constitutionally determined. (Professor Bloom, however, may not concur in this interpretation.) Thus, accelerated achievement gains brought about by an enriched and intensified instructional program generally 'fade out' in a few months to a year. Without a strong consolidation factor, accelerated gains are not maintained without constant rehearsal of the acquired knowledge or skills. Because variance in achievement test scores reflects a larger gain component at any given time than do intelligence tests, which are designed to reflect the consolidation factor, one should expect populations that differ on the average on intelligence measures to differ significantly less on achievement measures at any cross-section in time, and this has been found to be the case (Coleman *et al.*, 1966; Jensen, 1971a). Consolidated achievement, however, provided it involves intellectual skills, should show about the same magnitude of population differences as are shown by intelligence tests.

An interesting difference between scholastic achievement scores and intelligence test scores (including vocabulary) is that the latter go on increasing steadily throughout the summer months while the children are not in school, while there is an actual loss in achievement test scores from the beginning to the end of the summer. Much of the most recently learned material prior to the summer vacation has not been sufficiently rehearsed to become consolidated. The loss is greatest for those school subjects that depend least upon general intelligence (i.e., the consolidation factor) and depend most upon sheer learning and memory, such as spelling, punctuation, grammar, and mechanical or computational arithmetic and number facts, as contrasted with reading comprehension and arithmetic concepts (Beggs & Hieronymus, 1968).

Gains in achievement (and intelligence test raw scores) are relatively greater early in learning than later, largely because it is easier to consolidate gains at the 'simple' end of the scale than at the more complex ('difficult') end of the scale of intellectual tasks. When students simultaneously begin a new course of study, the diligent but intellectually mediocre students can keep up or even excel for a time near the beginning of the course; but soon it becomes increasingly difficult to keep ahead as they progress further into the complexities of the subject matter. For the less intelligent students consolidation does not keep up with their gains to the same extent as for the brighter students. The growth of intelligence is not reflected mainly by an increase in the ability for simple learning through practice, but in the ability to consolidate and understand increasingly complex material. As Leona Tyler (1965, pp. 78-9) has put it: 'The child with an IQ of 80 is handicapped all through school not because he is slow or inept at learning things which are within the capacity of all the children at his age level, but because he is never *ready* to grasp new and more complex ideas at the time when they are ordinarily presented to children of his age.' *Readiness* in large part is the ability to *consolidate* the knowledge and skills gained through daily learning experiences.

According to our model, at any given point in time, a performance measure of achievement status (S) usually reflects more of the consolidated component (C) than of the gains component (G), and this is increasingly true over the course of development. Since C is largely genetic and stable and G is largely environmental and random, an inference from the model is that brighter siblings (and twins) should show higher correlations for achievement than duller siblings. (At any cross-section in time the recent [and random]

D*

gain component of the achievement test score would be a smaller proportion of total [consolidated] achievement for the brighter sibs and thus would not so attenuate the correlation between them. In other words, their phenotypic correlation would be closer to their genetic correlation.) This result is in fact what has been found. Burt (1943) divided sibling pairs into two groups: those above the median in IQ (i.e., 100 IQ) and those below the median. The correlation between siblings' scholastic achievement test scores was 0·61 for the above-average sibs and only 0·47 for the below-average sibs.

Another inference from our model is that sibling correlations (based on tests given at the same age for both sibs) in measures of intelligence should be substantial and should increase with age, while year-to-year measures of gain should show much lower or even negligible correlations. The status measures, which increasingly reflect C, therefore, would also increasingly reflect the genetic factors which the sibs have in common, while the gains, which reflect motivation and specific learning and largely fortuitous environmental factors, should show little, if any, sib correlation. This inference, too, has been substantiated in part in a longitudinal study conducted at the Fels Research Institute (McCall, 1970). The level (status) of intelligence at any given age was found to show much higher heritability than the pattern of *changes* (gains) in intelligence from one time to another (an average interval of 9 months). Although there is an increase in sib correlations with age, it is not statistically significant. The model also predicts that parent-child correlations should be higher when they are based on measures of the parent as an adult than measures of the parent taken at the same age as those on the child. McCall's (1970) study, which also included parent-child correlations of test scores obtained when both parent and child were between 3 and 12 years of age, showed significantly lower parent-child correlations than have been found in studies of parent-child correlations in which the parent was measured as an adult. (The one exception reported in the literature is Burt's [1966, Table 4] parent-child IQ correlation of 0·49 when the parents were adults and of 0·56 when the parents' childhood IQs were used.) McCall (1970, p. 647) concludes:

> ... although the general level of IQ appears to show heritability, the pattern of IQ change over age possesses far less heritability

(if any at all). . . . Siblings (and parent-child pairs) share some environmental elements (for example, general atmosphere of intellectual encouragement) as well as genes in common. However, whatever the factors that determine IQ change over age, apparently they are not simply the general family intellectual climate available to each sibling. Rather, one might speculate that the salient variables are relatively more specific events and intellectual circumstances which quite possibly interact with age, personality, social, and motivational factors.

The simplex growth model also predicts that individuals with higher genetic intelligence (i.e., higher C values in the model) should show greater intra-individual variability in measured IQ over the course of development. This was actually found to be the case in the data of Honzik *et al.* (see Table 3.3). A recent analysis of these data showed that children with the greatest year-to-year fluctuations in IQ manifested also a general upward trend in IQ and had the higher mean IQ over the course of development (Honzik and Gedye, personal communication).

ACHIEVEMENT AS A FUNCTION OF STUDY TIME

Carroll (1963) proposed a model of school learning in which the degree of learning, or amount learned, is a function of the ratio of time actually spent in learning to the time needed to learn. Time spent in learning is defined as the smallest value of either (*a*) time allowed for learning, (*b*) length of time the learner is willing to persevere, or (*c*) the amount of time needed to learn up to some criterion of mastery. The model can be expressed as follows:

$$\text{Amount of Learning} = f\left(\frac{\text{time spent}}{\text{time needed}}\right)$$

The time needed to learn a given amount of material or skill up to some criterion of proficiency is a function both of the type or quality of the instruction and of the learner's ability. The amount of time actually spent will be a function of the time allowed by the teacher or by other circumstances external to the learner (such as the number of hours in the school day and the amount of time the parents may require the child to spend at his homework or in being tutored) and also of the amount of time the learner can actually be attentive and engage in the kinds of activity that promote learning. This involves personality factors, interests, and motivation. Theoretically this model says that any learner, if allowed sufficient time and if able to persevere long enough, should be able to attain a mastery of any subject. This would be true only if it were assumed that all the learning got consolidated in ways that permitted retrieval and transfer to the learning of subsequent lessons.

This model makes it clear why we do not find a perfect correlation between ability and achievement: mental ability is only one element in the equation.

A study designed to test this model used programmed learning in order to achieve uniformity of the conditions of instruction (Sjogren, 1967). The subjects (all adults) studied three sets of programmed lessons concerning the solar system, set theory, and Chanukah. The learning conditions involved both self-pacing of the rate of presentation of the frames and presentation at a constant rate for all subjects. Following learning the subjects were given achievement tests on the topics studied. The part of the findings of interest here is that scores on the Wechsler Adult Intelligence Scale (WAIS) predicted the 'time needed' part of the equation, with correlations ranging from 0·50 to 0·66. In the constant study-time condition, therefore, the achievement was a function of intelligence. Independent estimates of the 'time needed' parameter added a slight but significant increment to the prediction of achievement scores when WAIS scores were included in a multiple regression equation, but only when the achievement test was administered *immediately* after the study period. The estimated 'time needed' parameter made no unique contribution over that of the WAIS (in which time is a factor in six of the eleven subtests) to the prediction of achievement when the achievement tests were administered *one week* after the programmed instruction.

This model highlights a major problem of school learning as it is traditionally managed: there is much less variability in 'time allowed' than in 'time needed' by various individuals, with the consequence that there are large differences in the amount learned. If the class is very heterogeneous, some students will have much more time than they need to learn the material presented and some will have much less time than they need. The misfortune of the former group is that they can waste time in class unless an enriched program is provided. The misfortune of the latter group is that some will never learn the material that was taught because the teacher moves on to new subjects. It has been found, for example, that some children do not learn the alphabet in twelve years of schooling, not because they were incapable of this simple learning throughout their twelve years in school but merely because they did not learn it when it was formally taught. And so it is with many school subjects, with more serious consequences when mastery is prerequisite for learning later subjects. The child who does not master multiplication will not learn division. To the extent that schools make some provision for differences in learning time for basic subjects they will tend to reduce achievement differences. Ideally, by the time children finish their schooling there should be a negligible correlation between proficiency in basic school subjects and intelligence. More intelligent students would simply have gone *further* educationally.

Schools approximate this condition to varying degrees, so that if we could measure both achievement and intelligence on an absolute scale (which we cannot do) we would expect to find greater variance in intelligence than in achievement. (Comparison of coefficients of variation of different measures is meaningless unless they are on an absolute scale.)

It is popularly supposed that disadvantaged Negro children differ from middle-class white children, on the average, more in scholastic achievement than in intelligence; but the largest studies of this issue have found just the opposite to be true. The Coleman Report, for example, found $0 \cdot 1\sigma$ to $0 \cdot 2\sigma$ less difference between Negro and white children on measures of scholastic achievement than on measures of intelligence. And Jensen (1971a) found in a California school district a Negro-white difference of $1 \cdot 08\sigma$ on a non-verbal intelligence test as compared with only $0 \cdot 66\sigma$ difference on the Stanford Achievement Tests. Negro pupils in these studies are closer to white pupils in scholastic achievement than in the non-scholastic, non-verbal abilities assessed by a variety of tests.

THE HIERARCHICAL NATURE OF MENTAL DEVELOPMENT

Although Carroll's model of school learning has been shown to fit the data derived from adults engaged in programmed learning, there is some question concerning its limitations for children's learning, where the amount learned may depend not only upon the time spent in learning but must also wait for the child's mental maturity to reach the level needed to learn (and consolidate) material of a certain degree of complexity. Some things are inordinately difficult or even impossible for a child to learn or consolidate, given any amount of time, if he has not attained an appropriate stage of mental maturity. There is now much evidence, exemplified in the work of Piaget (1960) and substantiated in numerous experiments by other child psychologists both here and abroad (for reviews see Flavell, 1963; Kohlberg, 1968; and Phillips, 1969), that the individual's cognitive development proceeds by distinct, qualitatively different stages in children's modes of thinking and problem solving at different ages. Piaget and others have demonstrated that children's thinking is not just a watered down or inferior approximation to adult thinking; it is radically and qualitatively different. The stages of mental development form an invariant sequence or succession of individual development. Each stage of cognitive development is a structured whole. Mental development thus does not consist of the mere accretion of specific stimulus-response associations. Cognitive stages are hierarchically integrated; higher stages reintegrate the cognitive structures found at lower stages. Also, as Kohlberg (1968, p. 1021) has pointed out, '. . . there is a hierarchical preference within the individual . . . to prefer a solution of a problem at the highest level available to him'. Sheldon White (1965) has amassed evidence for two broad stages of mental development, which he labels *associative* and *cognitive*. The transition from one to the other occurs for the vast majority of children between five and seven years of age. In the simplest terms, these stages correspond to *concrete-associative* thinking and *abstract-conceptual* thinking. The latter does not displace the former in the course of the child's mental development; in older children and adults the two modes co-exist as hierarchical layers. Mental development is known to take place at different rates among children, and the final level of ability attained can be viewed as a hierarchical composite of earlier developed abilities, each level of the hierarchy being necessary but not sufficient for development of the next higher level. At maturity persons differ with respect to the relative prepotence of different modes in the hierarchy of abilities and thus show differential capabilities for different kinds of learning and problem solving. The difficulty level of items in most standard intelligence tests (especially tests of the culture-fair variety, such as Raven's Progressive Matrices and Cattell's Culture-Fair Tests of *g*) reflects increasing dependence of the problem's solution upon higher mental processes.

Cumulative Deficit

The concept of 'cumulative deficit' is fundamental in the assessment of majority-minority differences in educational progress. Cumulative deficit is actually a hypothetical concept intended to explain an observable phenomenon which can be called the 'progressive achievement gap', or PAG for short. When two groups show an increasing divergence between their mean scores on tests, there is potential evidence of a PAG. The notion of cumulative deficit attributes the increasing difference between the groups' means to the cumulative effects of scholastic learning such that deficiencies at earlier stages make for greater deficiencies at later stages. If Johnny fails to master addition by the second grade, he will be worse off in multiplication in the third grade, and still worse off in division in the fourth grade, and so on. Thus the progressive achievement gap between Johnny and those children who adequately learn each prerequisite for the next educational step is seen as a cumulative deficit. There may be other reasons as well for the PAG, such as differential rates of mental maturation, the changing factorial composition of scholastic tasks such that somewhat different mental abilities are called for at different ages, disillusionment and waning motivation for school work, and so on. Therefore I prefer the term 'progressive achievement gap' because it refers to an observable effect and is neutral with respect to its causes.

When the achievement gap is measured in raw score units or in grade scale or age scale units, it is called *absolute*. For example, we read in the Coleman Report (1966, p. 273) that in the metropolitan areas of the Northwest region of the U.S. '. . . the lag of Negro scores [in Verbal Ability] in terms of years behind grade level is progressively greater. At grade 6, the average Negro is approximately $1\frac{1}{2}$ years behind the average white. At grade 9, he is approximately $2\frac{1}{4}$ years behind that of the average white. At grade 12, he is approximately $3\frac{1}{4}$ years behind the average white.'

When the achievement difference between groups is expressed in standard deviation units, it is called *relative*. That is to say, the difference is relative to the variation within the criterion group. The Coleman Report, referring to the findings quoted above, goes on to state: 'A similar result holds for Negroes in all regions, despite the constant difference in number of standard deviations.' Although the absolute white-Negro difference increases with grade in school, the relative difference does not. The Coleman Report states: 'Thus in one sense it is meaningful to say the Negroes in the metropolitan Northeast are the same distance below the whites at these three grades—that is, relative to the dispersion of the whites themselves.' The Report illustrates this in pointing out that at grade 6 about 15 percent of whites are one standard deviation, or $1\frac{1}{2}$ years, behind the white average; at grade 12, 15 percent of the whites are one standard deviation, or $3\frac{1}{4}$ years, behind the white average.

It is of course the absolute progressive achievement gap which is observed by teachers and parents, and it becomes increasingly obvious at each higher grade level. But statistically a more informative basis for comparing the achievement differences between various subgroups of the school population is in terms of the relative difference, that is, in standard deviation units, called sigma (σ) units for short.

Except in the Southern regions of the U.S., the Coleman study found a more or less constant difference of approximately 1σ (based on whites in the metropolitan Northeast) between whites and Negroes in Verbal Ability, Reading Comprehension, and Maths Achievement. In other words, there was no progressive achievement gap in regions outside the South. In the Southern regions, there is evidence for a PAG from grade 6 to 12 when the sigma unit is based on the metropolitan Northeast. For example, in the non-metropolitan South, the mean Negro-white differences (Verbal Ability) in sigma units are 1·5, 1·7, and 1·9 for grades 6, 9, and 12, respectively. The corresponding number of grade levels that the Southern Negroes lag behind at grades 6, 9, and 12 are 2·5, 3·9, and 5·2 (Coleman *et al.*, 1966, p. 274). The causes of this progressive achievement gap in the South are not definitely known. Contributing factors could be an actual cumulative deficit in educational skills, true subpopulation differences in the developmental growth rates of the mental abilities relevant to school learning, and selective migration of families of abler students out of the rural South, causing an increasing cumulation of poor students in the higher grades.

Selective migration, student turnover related to adult employment trends, and other factors contributing to changes in the characteristics of the school population, may produce a spurious PAG when this is measured by comparisons between grade levels at a single cross-section in time. The Coleman Report's grade comparisons are cross-sectional. But where there is no reason to suspect systematic regional population changes, cross-sectional data should yield approximately the same picture as longitudinal data, which are obtained by repeated testing of the same children at different grades. Longitudinal data provide the least questionable basis for measuring the PAG. Cross-sectional achievement data can be made less questionable if there are also socioeconomic ratings on the groups being compared. The lack of any grade-to-grade decrement on the socioeconomic index adds weight to the conclusion that the PAG is not an artifact of the population's characteristics differing across grade levels.

Another way of looking at the PAG is in terms of the percentage of variance in individual achievement scores accounted for by the mean achievement level of schools or districts. If there is an achievement decrement for, say, a minority group across grade levels, and if the decrement is a result of school influences, then we should expect an increasing correlation between individual students' achievement scores and the school averages. In the data of the Coleman Report, this correlation (expressed as the percentage of variance in individual scores accounted for by the school average) for 'verbal achievement' does not change appreciably from the beginning of the first school year up to the twelfth grade. The school average for verbal achievement is as highly correlated with individual verbal achievement at the beginning of grade 1 as at grade 12. If the schools themselves contributed to the deficit, one should expect an increasing percentage of the total individual variance to be accounted for by the school average with increasing grade level. But no evidence was found that this state of affairs exists. The percent of total variance in individual verbal achievement accounted for by the mean score of the school, at grades 12 and 1, is as follows (Coleman *et al.*, 1966, p. 296):

Group	Grade 12	Grade 1
Negro, South	22·54	23·21
Negro, North	10·92	10·63
White, South	10·11	18·64
White, North	7·84	11·07

Jensen (1971a) also failed to find any evidence of increasing sigma differences between whites, Negroes, and Mexicans in scholastic achievement over grades 1 to 8 in cross-sectional testing in a California school district.

Longitudinal studies outside the South show the same thing. Harris and Lovinger (1968) obtained a variety of intelligence and achievement test scores on the same disadvantaged Negro and Puerto Rican (in the ratio 9 to 1) children in grades 1, 3, 6, 7, 8, and 9. The school attended by these children had the lowest average achievement of any junior high school in the borough of Queens, New York. There was no evidence of declining IQs in this group. Eighth and ninth grade IQs were approximately equal to first grade IQs. Another longitudinal study by Rosenfeld and Hilton (1971) compared the academic growth of Negro and white students who attended the same high schools and were enrolled in the same curricula. Ability tests were obtained in grades 5, 7, 9, and 11. In absolute level of achievement the Negro students were one to two years behind the white students on most of the tests, and the absolute gap increased over time. But the *relative* gap, in sigma units, did not increase. The gap was no greater in the eleventh grade than would be predicted on the basis of the fifth grade differences in mean scores between the groups. When equated for initial differences in test scores, Negroes and whites gained academically at substantially the same rates between grades 9 and 11 on tests of Reading, Writing, Social Studies, and Listening. Whites, however, grew at a faster rate in Maths and Science achievement and in tests of verbal and quantitative reasoning. In analyzing the test results on students enrolled in academic and non-academic curricula, Rosenfeld and Hilton found no significant interaction between curriculum and race; that is, the overall academic growth of the Negro students relative to the white students did not depend on which curriculum they were enrolled in. The authors note:

> Generally, the Negro students in the academic programs have test scores similar to the white students in the nonacademic programs. And generally, the Negro students in the academic programs have SES (socioeconomic status) scores similar to the white students in the nonacademic programs. Overall, the white nonacademics are more like the Negro academics in SES than they are like the white academics.

The one longitudinal study conducted in the South (Georgia) showed no overall decline in mean IQ from grade 6 to 10 for either Negro or white students, who differed by a constant amount of approximately 20 IQ points (Osborne, 1960). The scholastic achievement scores show the usual divergence of white and Negro means from grade 6 to 12, but we cannot tell from Osborne's presentation of his results in terms of grade placement scores whether there is an increasing relative achievement gap in sigma units. Inspection of Osborne's graphs suggests that there is little, if any, increase in the relative achievement gap between Negroes and whites from grades 6 to 12.

The absence of a *relative* progressive achievement gap (PAG) as measured in sigma units between racial or socioeconomic groups means that the *absolute* PAG is *not* a matter of race or SES *per se* but a matter of differences in intellectual growth rates. It means that (*a*) the educational process is *not* treating children of the two races differently and (*b*) Negro and white children *per se* are *not* responding differently to the educational treatment. They are responding according to their individual intelligence levels, and not according to their racial membership. The absence of a relative PAG means, for example, that a Negro and a white child matched for IQ and other abilities will have the same growth curves for scholastic achievement. The Negro child, in other words, does not do worse in school than his white counterpart in IQ, and this is true when the matching on IQ is done at the very beginning of the child's schooling, before the schools can have had any cumulative effect on the child's IQ performance. In one study, large representative samples of Negro and Mexican-American children from kindergarten through the eighth grade in largely *de facto* segregated schools were compared with white children in the same California school district on a comprehensive battery of tests of mental abilities and of scholastic achievement, in addition to personality inventories and indices of socioeconomic and cultural disadvantage. It was found that when certain ability and background factors over which the schools have little or no influence are statistically controlled, there are no appreciable differences between the scholastic achievements (as measured by the Stanford Achievement Tests) of minority and majority pupils. And there is no evidence of a PAG between all majority and all minority pupils (who average about 1σ lower) when the differences are measured in sigma units (Jensen, 1971a).

NOTE

1. Actually, only one element is needed for a simplex, the random G element in the following model (as would be the case if $C = 1$ or was the same constant value for every member of the population). But this one-element model, consisting of cumulating random increments, as we shall see, would be too simple to reproduce all the essential characteristics of the growth curves and intercorrelations actually found in such characteristics as intelligence, stature, and achievement, e.g., the predictability or predetermination of the individual growth curves' asymptotic values implied by the substantial heritability of these characteristics.

4 The heritability of scholastic achievement

In an earlier review of evidence on the heritability of scholastic achievement, I stated: 'In general, individual differences in scholastic performance are determined less than half as much by heredity than are individual differences in intelligence. The largest source of individual differences in school achievement is the environmental differences *between* families. Variance in achievement due to differential environmental effects *within* families is extremely small' (Jensen, 1967, p. 153). I now believe this statement is too broad and too simple. No such *general* statement about the *magnitude* of the heritability of scholastic achievement seems warranted in view of the large number of factors that are now known to affect the magnitude of h^2 for achievement measures. This fact is reflected in the wide range of values of h^2 found in various studies. The values of h^2 estimated from correlations of MZ and DZ twins on six sets of achievement tests ranged from 0·05 to 0·82, with a mean of 0·40 (Jensen, 1967, p. 152). But the variations are not entirely haphazard and certain generalizations do seem warranted concerning the conditions affecting the magnitude of h^2 for achievement measures.

First, it is clear that at any given age or within any one sample of subjects on whom the heritability of intelligence and achievement have both been estimated from tests given at approximately the same time, h^2 for achievement is almost never higher than for intelligence and is usually much lower. Probably the best estimates of h^2 we can obtain for this comparison are the correlations between monozygotic (identical) twins reared together (MZT) and MZ twins reared apart (MZA). The two twin studies which obtained both intelligence and achievement scores on sufficiently large samples of MZT and MZA are those by Burt (1966) and by Newman, Freeman, and Holzinger (1937). Since intelligence tests are usually composed of a number of subtests of various types, it is best to compare them with the composite score on a scholastic achievement test made up of subtests of reading, spelling, arithmetic, etc. The correlations of MZT and MZA, along with dizygotic twins reared together (DZT) and unrelated children reared together (UT), on group and individual intelligence tests and on a composite achievement test are as follows:

| | Burt | | | | Newman *et al.* | | |
	MZT	MZA	DZT	UT	MZT	MZA	DZT
Number of Pairs	95	53	127	136	50	19	51
IQ							
Group Test	0·94	0·77	0·55	0·28	0·92	0·73	0·62
Individual Test	0·92	0·86	0·53	0·25	0·88	0·67	0·63
Scholastic							
Achievement	0·98	0·62	0·83	0·54	0·89	0·51	0·70

The pattern of these correlations is highly instructive. Note that in the case of MZ twins, being reared apart lowers the correlation between the twins much more for scholastic achievement than for IQ. And being reared together makes for a much higher correlation between unrelated children in achievement than in IQ. Dizygotic twins, with only half their genetic variance in common, when reared together are more alike in achievement than MZ twins reared apart, but this is not the case with IQ. This is strong evidence that the family environment exerts a greater influence on scholastic attainment than on IQ. Furthermore, the family environmental influences are greatest on the simpler school subjects such as spelling and arithmetic computation, which therefore have the lowest heritability. (When such subjects are tested outside the school context, however, they may reflect to a larger extent the consolidated aspects of the person's learning and would therefore have higher heritability.) The reason is quite easy to understand. Simple circumscribed skills can be more easily taught, drilled, and assessed; and the degree of their mastery by any individual will be largely a function of the amount of time he spends in being taught and in practising the skill. Thus children with quite different IQs can be shaped up to perform more or less equally in these elemental skills. If Johnny has trouble with his spelling or arithmetic, his parents may give him extra tutoring so that he can more nearly approximate the performance of his brighter brother. This is not so easily accomplished for more complex processes such as reading comprehension and arithmetic applications, which more nearly resemble IQ in degree of heritability.

Since school subjects increase in complexity with each grade level, and the consolidated portion of achievement correlates more and more with intelligence, we should expect that the heritability of scholastic achievement should also increase with age. There is evidence that this is the case. Husén (1963) found a decreasing environmental component in achievement variance from fourth to sixth grade. Increasing achievement differences among children as they advance in age then increasingly reflect their genetic intelligence differences. By the last year or two in high school, the heritability of comprehensive measures of scholastic achievement (rather than narrow tests which assess only the subject matter taught in the immediately preceding school year) is quite comparable to that of measures of general intelligence. This is shown in a study by Nichols (1965) who obtained the scores of large samples of MZ and DZ twins who, as high school juniors (eleventh grade), had taken the National Merit Scholarship Qualifying Test (NMSQT), which consists of subtests in English, mathematics, social studies, natural science, and word usage. Nichols notes that the intraclass correlations (on MZ and DZ twins) for the NMSQT composite score are very similar to correlations for measures of general intelligence obtained in other twin studies. These findings, at first glance, might seem to be in conflict with those of Newman *et al.* (1937), whose twins were adults but showed quite different correlations for IQ than for achievement. The reason is most likely that all the twins in Nichols' sample were very close to the same age and had the same number of years of schooling. The twins of Newman *et al.* had quite different amounts of schooling; for example, one twin went only through the third grade while her separated co-twin was a college graduate.

Newman *et al.* correlated the differences in educational backgrounds with differences of achievement for their pairs of MZ twins reared apart; the resulting r is 0·91! The same correlation for a group intelligence test (Otis IQ) is only 0·55, and for an individual intelligence test (Stanford-Binet IQ) it is 0·79. The achievement test has an h^2 of 0·51. For the Otis IQ h^2 was 0·73, and for Stanford-Binet IQ h^2 was 0·67. The total proportion of non-genetic variance, i.e., $1 - h^2$, not including error variance (estimated at 5 percent), is therefore 0·44 for achievement, 0·22 for Otis IQ, and 0·28 for Stanford-Binet IQ. The proportion of total variance accounted for by differences between twins in educational advantages, therefore, is given by the square of the correlation between difference in environments and difference in test scores, multiplied by the non-genetic variance $(1 - h^2)$, not including error variance. Thus, in the study by Newman *et al.*, twin differences in the index of educational environment account for the following proportions of total variance: in scholastic achievement = 0·36, in Otis IQ = 0·07, in Stanford-Binet IQ = 0·17.

Nichols (1965) also asked if the separate subtests (English, maths, etc.) of the NMSQT had any heritability after the general factor common to all the subtests was removed. He found that the 'residual' subtest scores had almost as high heritability as the composite score. Nichols comments, 'Thus, it appears that the specific abilities measured by the NMSQT subtests have about the same hereditary character as the more general ability which the subtests measure in common.' The general factor is probably identical with the *g* of intelligence tests. A factor analysis of several verbal and non-verbal intelligence tests and several achievement tests showed that all the tests had very similar loadings on the general factor (first principal component), and the proportion of total variance accounted for by the general factor increased from grades 4 to 8 (Jensen, 1971a, Table 5).

The heritability (h^2) of scholastic achievement depends also upon the degree of homogeneity or uniformity in the type and quality of the instructional program of the schools from which the individuals in the heritability analysis have been sampled. The school environment is more imposed upon the child than the extra-school environment, which generally allows the child much more freedom of choice of experiences according to his own proclivities.

School differences and teacher differences are more strongly reflected in those school subjects which are least apt to be taught or practised at home under parental supervision. Parents probably pay more attention to their children's reading and have more influence over it than any other subject, and therefore there should be relatively smaller sibling differences in reading skills. When parents pay little attention to children's scholastic progress, the environmental component of sibling differences is a function of teacher differences and, if siblings have different teachers or attend different schools with somewhat different curricula, there will be little or no sibling correlation between the specific environmental influences on their learning of school subjects.

Still another factor affecting the h^2 of achievement is the degree of correspondence between the school's curriculum and the subject content of the achievement tests. There is sometimes very poor correspondence between what is actually taught in class and what is assessed by the standardized achievement tests. Such discrepancies can either attenuate estimates of h^2 for scholastic achievement, or can leave the outcome ambiguous by causing the achievement test to become a measure of incidental learning in and out of school, rather than intentional learning in the classroom, thereby resembling more a general intelligence test. One of the characteristics of the more intelligent children is that they are better incidental learners; they somehow pick up and retain much more information than is directly taught to them or than they learn intentionally.

Thus, unlike the heritability of intelligence, the heritability of scholastic achievement as it is usually estimated is so conditional upon a large variety of other variables as to be a rather unstable datum.

FAMILY INFLUENCES ON SCHOLASTIC ACHIEVEMENT

One reflection of the relative environmental influences of the family and of the school on children's scholastic achievement is the magnitude of the intraclass correlation among full siblings. The total variance in test scores, σ_T^2, is analyzable into two main components: (*a*) variance *between* families,[1] σ_B^2, and (*b*) variance *within* families (σ_W^2). Thus, $\sigma_T^2 = \sigma_B^2 + \sigma_W^2$. The intraclass correlation, r_i, among siblings is[2]

$$r_i = \frac{\sigma_B^2}{\sigma_B^2 + \sigma_W^2} \qquad (4.1)$$

The value of r_i tells us how much alike siblings are as compared with children paired (or grouped) at random. If pairs of siblings are no more alike than pairs of children picked at random, $r_i = 0$. If all siblings in each family are identical, $r_i = 1\cdot00$. The theoretical *genetic* correlation, σ_G, between siblings (when there is no genetic correlation between their parents) is $0\cdot50$. If the parents have some degree of genetic resemblance, the correlation between siblings will be slightly greater than $0\cdot50$.[3]

If reliably different sibling correlations are found between two tests in the same population or between two subpopulations on the same test, what can it mean? To answer this, we need an explicit model of the components that make up a sibling correlation (or any set of paired individuals). An individual's score, X, on a scholastic test can be represented as follows:

$$X = G + E_F + E_S + e \qquad (4.2)$$

where X = test score in deviation units
$\quad\ G$ = genetic value (in deviation units)
$\quad\ E_F$ = family environmental influence (in deviation units)
$\quad\ E_S$ = school environmental influence (in deviation units)
$\quad\ e$ = measurement error.

The heritability, h^2, of the test scores is:

$$h^2 = \frac{\sigma_G^2}{\sigma_G^2 + \sigma_{E_F}^2 + \sigma_{E_S}^2 + \sigma_e^2} \qquad (4.3)$$

and the 'environmentability', E^2, is: $1 - h^2$.[4]

The correlation, r_{AB}, between the test scores of paired individuals, A and B, can then be represented as follows, assuming that the family and school environments are uncorrelated:

$$r_{AB} = \rho_G h^2 + \rho_{E_F} E_F^2 + \rho_{E_S} E_S^2 \qquad (4.4)$$

where r_{AB} = obtained correlation between paired persons A and B
$\quad\ \rho_G$ = genetic correlation between persons
$\quad\ h^2$ = heritability of the test scores in the population sampled
$\quad\ \rho_{E_F}$ = correlation between family environmental influences on persons A and B

ρ_{E_S} = correlation between school environmental influences on persons A and B

E_F^2 = family 'environmentability' (i.e., proportion of test score variance attributable to environmental differences among families)

E_S^2 = school 'environmentability' (i.e., proportion of test score variance attributable to variability in schooling).

If the paired individuals are genetically unrelated, and were not reared in the same family, and have not attended the same classes in school (or the same or similar schools), then ρ_G, ρ_{E_F}, and ρ_{E_S} will all be zero and r_{AB} will be zero. Values of r_{AB} greater than zero can be due to any combination of the values of the several components given in the above formula.

If now we have obtained sibling correlations (r_S) in two subpopulations, 1 and 2, and if we assume that (*a*) the genetic correlation of siblings is the same in both subpopulations, (*b*) the heritability (h^2) is the same in both groups, and (*c*) the school influences are the same for both subpopulations, then the difference between the sibling correlations in the two subpopulations should be an estimate of their difference in proportion of test variance attributable to the (between) *family* environmental effects, i.e.,

$$r_{S_1} - r_{S_2} = \sigma_{E_{F_1}} E_{F_1}^2 - \rho_{E_{F_2}} E_{F_2}^2 \qquad (4.5)$$

The value $\rho_{E_F} E_F$, of course, tells us nothing about the quality or direction (poor *v.* good) of the family environmental influences. It merely estimates the proportion of sib correlation attributable to this source. And $r_{S_1} - r_{S_2}$ estimates how much two subpopulations differ in $\rho_{E_F} E_F^2$, i.e., family environmental influences on scholastic achievement.

I have obtained sibling correlations (intraclass r_i, using all the school-age siblings in each family) on large samples of white and Negro children in a California school district. The sample sizes on which the sibling correlations are based represent virtually all the siblings in the elementary school district (fourteen schools) who had taken either the same tests or sufficiently similar tests to permit intercorrelation.

All of the tests were administered by a staff of specially trained testers in order to maximize uniformity of testing procedures. The raw test scores (as well as measures of height and weight) were converted to normalized standard scores within each 6-month age interval for all the children in the elementary grades (K-6), totalling over 8000 children. This was done separately within each racial group. Table 4.1 shows the intraclass correlations of siblings in the white and Negro samples, the sample sizes for each test, and the value for determining the statistical significance of the difference between the r_i's of the two racial groups. We see that even though all but two of the tests show statistically significant differences between the sibling correlations for whites and Negroes, the actual magnitudes of the differences are generally quite small. The differences for the Lorge-Thorndike intelligence tests are of about the same magnitude as for height and weight. Sibling correlations for height provide a good reference point, since the heritability of height is very high and the genetic correlation between siblings for this trait is at least 0·50 or slightly more. If one racial group or the other had in it a larger proportion of half-siblings misidentified as full siblings, it would show up in the correlation; the group with more half-siblings would have the lower correlation, since half-sibs have a genetic correlation of only 0·25. Half-sibs who were identified as such were, of course, not included in this analysis. There were many more half-sibs excluded in the Negro sample. The fact that the Negro sibling correlation for height is even slightly higher than for whites suggests that the other Negro sib correlations are not likely to be attenuated by the presence of misidentified half-sibs in the sample. The same thing holds true for weight, although to a slightly lesser degree, since the heritability of weight is not quite as high as for height. In other studies, the heritability of weight has been found to be very close to that for intelligence, and our sibling correlations are consistent with this. The intelligence test sibling correlations average just about the same as those for weight. The overall impression to be gained from Table 4.1, then, is that there is no marked difference between the white and Negro samples in the degree of family environmental influence on most tests.[5] The largest differences are found for a memory test which involves repeated trials, i.e., each digit series is repeated three times, instead of only once, prior to recall by the subject. Figure copying (the child copies 10 geometric forms of increasing complexity) shows a considerably higher sib correlation for Negroes (0·36 *v.* 0·26 for whites). Of the scholastic achievement tests, spelling and arithmetic computation show the largest sib correlation differences between whites

Table 4.1 Intraclass correlations among siblings in white and Negro elementary school samples and white-Negro mean difference (in white sigma units)

| Measure* | Correlation | | | Sample Size** | | $\frac{W\text{-}N}{\sigma_W}$ |
	White	Negro	z†	White	Negro	
Motor-Motivational Tests						
1. Making Xs, 1st Try	0·10	0·14	−11·39	619	342	−0·12
2. Making Xs, 2nd Try	0·10	0·13	−7·90	618	343	−0·36
Memory Tests						
3. Immediate Recall	0·26	0·22	7·48	429	260	0·66
4. Repeated Trials	0·27	0·15	20·40	428	259	0·55
5. Delayed Recall	0·27	0·23	6·15	424	253	0·68
Intelligence Tests						
6. Figure Copying	0·26	0·36	−19·13	435	277	0·85
7. Lorge-Thorndike, Primary	0·44	0·43	1·71	277	162	1·26
8. Lorge-Thorndike, Verbal	0·38	0·36	5·64	707	346	1·41
9. Lorge-Thorndike, Non-verbal	0·39	0·34	14·84	709	359	1·44
Achievement Tests						
10. Word Meaning	0·33	0·35	−2·44	206	278	1·65
11. Paragraph Meaning	0·37	0·30	10·26	213	270	1·58
12. Spelling	0·37	0·21	6·47	84	64	1·10
13. Language (Grammar)	0·29	0·23	2·67	94	69	1·66
14. Arithmetic Computation	0·31	0·45	−6·44	88	76	1·04
15. Arithmetic Concepts	0·24	0·22	1·03	89	71	1·53
16. Arithmetic Applications	0·34	0·35	−2·92	85	69	1·54
Physical Measures						
Height	0·42	0·45	−9·33	744	414	
Weight	0·38	0·37	2·12	743	414	

* These measures are described in the Appendix at the end of Chapter 4.
† z is the standardized deviation from the mean of the normal distribution, used here for testing the statistical significance of the difference between the sibling correlations for whites and Negroes. The various significance levels of z are: $z_{(0.05)} = 1·96$; $z_{(0.02)} = 2·33$; $z_{(0.01)} = 2·58$; $z_{(.001)} = 3·09$.
** Number of families.

and Negroes, with whites showing the higher correlation for spelling and Negroes for arithmetic computation. The Lorge-Thorndike IQ tests show very small race differences in sib correlations and they also yield the highest sib correlations except for height.

Since the correlation between paired individuals is $r_{AB} = \rho_G h^2 + \rho_E E^2$, and since the genetic correlation (ρ_G) between siblings is approximately 0·5 (or slightly more assuming assortative mating), it is evident that as the value of h^2 approaches 1·00, the sibling correlation, r_s, must converge on 0·5. Sibling correlations departing in either direction from 0·50 must involve lower heritability. While it is possible to obtain sibling correlations of close to 0·50 when the value of h^2 is low, it is impossible to obtain sibling correlations that depart significantly from 0·50 when h^2 is very high. Therefore, the absolute deviation of the sibling correlation from 0·50 provides a rough index of the degree of non-genetic variance in the measurements. (It is a 'rough' index because the theoretical genetic correlation between sibs is 0·50 only under assortative mating and when there is no dominance variance; each of these effects may differ for different tests, but it is most unlikely that the effect of either alone would be more than±0·05. Since assortative mating and dominance deviation have *opposite* effects on the genetic correlation between siblings, their effects tend to cancel out, so that 0·50 is probably the best overall estimate of the genetic correlation between sibs. Test reliability, of course, also effects the E' index.) This index, which we will call E', is the absolute difference between the sibling correlation, r_s, and 0·50, which is theoretically the sibling correlation if $h^2 = 1·00$. That is, $E' = |r_s - 0·50|$. (Note that E' can range only from 0 to 0·5.) Because values of r_s close to 0·5 can arise even when h^2 is low or even zero, low values of E' are more ambiguous and the higher values of E' are more valid indicators of non-genetic variance in test scores. If E' is an index of non-genetic effects, $1 - E'/\rho_G = H'$, which can be called an index of genetic effects, on the same scale as h^2, going from 0 to 1·00. Reference to Table 4.1 shows that values of H', based on the sibling correlations in the white samples, range from about 0·20 for the Making Xs up to 0·76, 0·78, and 0·88 for the three forms of the Lorge-Thorndike IQ Test. (In the Negro sample, H' for the three forms of the Lorge-Thorndike are 0·68, 0·72, and 0·86.) H' for height is 0·84, and for weight is

0·76. (In the Negro sample the corresponding values are 0·89 and 0·74). The seven Stanford Achievement Tests have H' values in the white sample ranging from 0·48 to 0·74 with a median of 0·66. (In the Negro samples, H' ranges from 0·42 to 0·90 with a median of 0·60.) All these values of H' are very similar to values of h^2 (or other heritability indices) for intelligence tests, physical traits, and scholastic achievement when h^2 is estimated by more elaborate and more accurate means than is possible by estimation from sibling correlations alone. The fact that the values we obtain for H' are very consistent with those obtained by better means (e.g., twins reared apart, comparison of monozygotic and dizygotic twins, and the correlation between genetically unrelated children who have been reared together) is presumptive evidence that our H' index, and consequently also E', are reasonably valid indicators of genetic and environmental effects on test scores. They are admittedly a poor substitute for h^2 estimates based on a variety of kinship correlations used together in more complex heritability formulas such as I have described elsewhere (Jensen, 1967). Yet, in the present data, as was pointed out, our inferences from the sibling correlations, via E', are quite in keeping with more dependable estimates of heritability.

Just as we could use h^2 in testing certain hypotheses about the degree of genetic and non-genetic determination of test variance in different subpopulations, so we can use our environmental index E' in the same way, albeit with greater reservations.

If we hypothesize that the mean white-Negro difference in ability test scores is entirely attributable to environmental factors (and, conversely, that no genetic factors enter into the difference), then we should predict that the mean white-Negro difference in test scores is directly related to the non-genetic index, E'. The more that a particular test reflects environmental influences in either the white or Negro populations, the greater should be E' for that test and the greater should be the mean difference in test scores between whites and Negroes if the hypothesis is true that the mean difference is entirely environmental. One possible way of testing this hypothesis would be to obtain the correlation between the mean white-Negro difference ($\bar{W}$-$\bar{N}$) and E' on a variety of ability tests which differ in their values of $\bar{W}$-$\bar{N}$ and E'. The environmental hypothesis would predict a *positive* correlation between these two variables. A genetic hypothesis would predict a *negative* correlation. Often genetic and environmental hypotheses of subpopulation differences lead to the same predictions so that one cannot decide between them on the basis of empirical outcomes. But here we have a situation in which environmental and genetic hypotheses predict diametrically *opposite* outcomes.

Using the data of Table 4.1 (omitting height and weight), we can determine the correlation between E' and $\bar{W}-\bar{N}/\sigma_W$. The mean white-Negro difference must be divided by the standard deviation in the white sample (σ_W) in order to express all the differences on the same scale for the various tests. The differences are thus expressed in white sigma units.[6] Figure 4.1 shows the scatter diagram relating $\bar{W}-\bar{N}/\sigma_W$ (the Y axis) and $E' = |r_s - 0.50|$ (the X axis). The white samples are plotted as white triangles and the Negro samples as black triangles. The two bivariate means are indicated by white and black circles. The regression lines for the regression of Y on X are shown for both the white and Negro groups. The regression line for whites has a somewhat steeper slope than for Negroes. But in both cases the slope is *negative*, which is opposite to the prediction from the environmental hypothesis. The Pearson r between $\bar{W}-\bar{N}/\sigma_W$ and $E' = |r_s - 0.50|$ is -0.80 for whites and -0.61 for Negroes. The correlation between the Negro and white values of E' is 0.71. This r of 0.71 means that the various tests are quite similar for whites and Negroes in the degree to which they reflect non-genetic factors. (Since the reliabilities of all these tests are quite uniformly high and about the same for Negroes and whites, corrections for attenuation would have a negligible effect on the results.)

Since extreme values on either the X or Y axis can inflate the Pearson r, it is desirable to obtain a measure of correlation which is free of the effects of scale and cannot be spuriously inflated by extreme values. Spearman's rank order correlation (rho) provides this measure. For whites rho is -0.56 and for Negroes rho is -0.47. The rho between white and Negro E' values is 0.64.

The most extreme values on both X and Y variables are those of tests #1 and #2, the Making Xs Test, which is not a cognitive test but a motor skills test and was intended largely to reflect test-taking motivation and effort. It is known to be sensitive to instructions and situational factors and so it is not surprising that it should show the highest E' index. We should also determine the correlations when these two tests are eliminated, to make sure that all of the correlation is not caused by these two parts of a single test which does not measure mental ability to any appreciable degree. When tests #1 and #2 are eliminated, the Pearson r's for whites and Negroes are -0.44 and -0.34, respectively. The r between Negro and white E' values is 0.54. The rank order

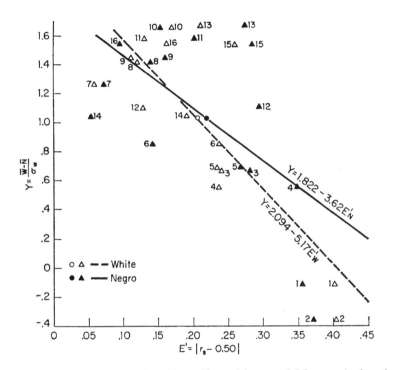

Figure 4.1 The regression lines (for whites and Negroes) showing the mean white-Negro difference in white sigma units (Y) on 16 ability tests (numbered 1 to 16) as a function of the absolute difference from 0·50 of the sibling correlation for each test (E'). Circles indicate the bivariate means; triangles indicate the various tests, which are numbered as follows: 1. Making Xs (neutral instructions); 2. Making Xs (motivating instructions); 3. Memory – immediate recall; 4. Memory – after repetition; 5. Memory – delayed recall; 6. Figure Copying; 7. Lorge-Thorndike IQ, Levels I and II (pictorial); 8. Lorge-Thorndike, Verbal IQ; 9. Lorge-Thorndike, Non-verbal IQ; 10. Stanford Achievement: Word Meaning; 11. Stanford Achievement: Paragraph Meaning; 12. Stanford Achievement: Spelling; 13. Stanford Achievement: Language (grammar); 14. Stanford Achievement: Arithmetic Computation. 15. Stanford Achievement: Arithmetic Concepts; 16. Stanford Achievement: Arithmetic Applications.

E

correlations (rho) after tests #1 and #2 are eliminated are -0.34 for whites and -0.20 for Negroes. The rho between white and Negro E' values is 0.46. Thus, when the two non-cognitive tests are left out and rank order correlation is used, the correlations are unimpressive. The most impressive aspect is that they are negative, while the environmental hypothesis predicts positive correlations. This analysis, based as it is upon E' with its ambiguity at the low end of the scale, does not warrant strong statistical inference, but it seems safe to say at most that the results do nothing to support the environmental hypothesis and, if anything, tend in the opposite direction. It is best regarded as a prototype for more elaborate studies in which the most precisely obtainable estimates of h^2 are correlated with the magnitude of the racial differences on a wide variety of tests. Ideally, a much larger number of tests would be used, so that moderate correlations (as obtained in the present study) could be statistically significant at a high level of confidence. Also, tests would have to be specially sought or devised to have a wider range of h^2 values in both racial groups. The present tests were not selected with this purpose in mind. Thus, the essential methodology is made clear by the present study and it may be followed by more definitive studies in this vein.

One such independent replication of these findings has already been made by Nichols (1972) in the Dight Institute of Human Genetics at the University of Minnesota. Nichols used an entirely different set of tests from those used in the study by Jensen. He used 13 tests: the Information, Comprehension, Vocabulary, Digit Span, Picture Arrangement, Block Design, and Coding Subscales of the Wechsler Intelligence Scale for Children; the Bender-Gestalt Visual Motor Test (ability to copy figures of varying complexity); the Illinois Test of Psycholinguistic Abilities; the Goodenough-Harris Draw-A-Man IQ Test; and the Spelling, Reading, and Arithmetic tests of the Wide Range Achievement Test. The subjects were 543 full sibling pairs, each tested at 7 years of age, with about equal numbers of whites and Negroes drawn from seven large cities in various parts of the United States. (The subject pool was obtained from the nation-wide Collaborative Study of the National Institutes of Health.) From the sibling correlations Nichols estimated the heritability of each of the 13 tests. This estimate assumes an environmental correlation of 0.15 between the sibs. (Nichols' method of estimating h^2 from sib correlations can be shown algebraically to be perfectly correlated [negatively] with the E' index used in the previous study.) Nichols then obtained the correlation of the heritabilities of each of the 13 tests with the magnitudes of the average difference (in standardized units) between whites and Negroes on each of the tests. This correlation was $+0.67$. That is, the higher the heritability of the test, the greater is the white-Negro difference, which is what was found in the Jensen study employing essentially the same methodology. Nichols also pooled the white and Negro samples and obtained the correlation between test scores and an index of socioeconomic status (SES). Some tests reflected SES differences more than others. The correlation between h^2 for each test and the test's correlation with SES was $+0.86$; when race is partialed out of this correlation (giving, in effect, the average correlation between h^2 and the tests' correlation with SES *within* each racial group), the correlation becomes $+0.74$. This high positive correlation between tests' heritability and the tests' correlations with SES (within racial groups) is what one should expect if there is a genetic component in social class differences in mental ability (see Chapter 6).

SIBLING REGRESSION

The correlation among siblings of close to 0.40 on the Lorge-Thorndike Intelligence Tests in both the white and the Negro samples has an interesting consequence which may seem puzzling from the standpoint of a strictly environmental theory. It is entirely expected if one assumes a genetic model of intragroup and intergroup differences. This is the phenomenon of sibling regression toward the population mean. If one picks children who are tall for their age, it is found that their siblings are about halfway between the tall children and the mean of the population from which they were sampled. Conversely, if one picks short children, their siblings will be taller – about halfway between the short children and the population mean. The same is true for numbers of fingerprint ridges and all other polygenically inherited characteristics. It is also true of IQ. Genetic theory predicts the precise amount of regression.

We have clearly established in our research (and it has been corroborated in many other studies [see Stanley, 1971; Sattler,

1972]) that if we match Negro and white children for IQ, their performance on scholastic achievement tests is so equivalent as not to differ statistically even with very large sample sizes. In other words, the IQ test gives the same prediction of scholastic performance for Negro children as for white children.

But if we match a number of Negro and white children for IQ[7] and then look at the IQs of their full siblings with whom they were reared, we find something quite different: the Negro siblings average some 7 to 10 points lower than the white siblings. Also, the higher we go on the IQ scale for selecting the Negro and white children to be matched, the greater is the absolute amount of regression shown by the IQs of the siblings.[8] For example, if we match Negro and white children with IQs of 120, the Negro siblings will average close to 100, the white siblings close to 110. The siblings of both groups have regressed approximately halfway to their respective population means and not to the mean of the combined populations. The same thing is found, of course, if we match children from the lower end of the IQ scale. Negro and white children matched for, say, IQ 70 will have siblings whose average IQs are about 78 for the Negroes and 85 for the whites. In each case the amount of regression is consistent with the genetic prediction. The regression line, we find, shows no significant departure from linearity throughout the range from IQ 50 to 150. This very regular phenomenon seems difficult to reconcile with any strictly environmental theory of the causation of individual differences in IQ that has yet been proposed. If Negro and white children are matched for IQs of, say, 120, it must be presumed that both sets of children had environments that were good enough to stimulate or permit IQs this high to develop. Since there is no reason to believe that the environments of these children's siblings differ on the average markedly from their own, why should one group of siblings come out much lower in IQ than the other? Genetically identical twins who have been reared from infancy in *different* families do not differ in IQ by nearly so much as siblings reared together in the same family. It can be claimed that though the white and Negro children are matched for IQ 120, they actually have different environments, with the Negro child, on the average, having the less intellectually stimulating environment. Therefore, it could be argued he actually has a higher genetic potential for intelligence than the environmentally more favored white child with the same IQ. But if this were the case, why should not the Negro child's siblings also have somewhat superior genetic potential? They have the same parents, and their degree of genetic resemblance, indicated by the theoretical genetic correlation among siblings, is presumably the same for Negroes and whites.[9]

Similar regression would be expected between parents and children but there are no adequate cross-racial studies of this for IQ. A rigorous study would require that the Negro and white parents be matched not only for education, occupational status, and income, but also for IQ. A genetic hypothesis would predict rather precisely the amount that the offspring of Negro and white parents matched for these variables would differ in IQ. The only existing evidence relevant to this hypothesis is the finding, in a number of studies which attempted to match Negroes and whites for socioeconomic status, that the *upper*-status Negro children average 2 to 4 IQ points *below* the *low*-status white children (Shuey, 1966, p. 520; Scarr-Salapatek, 1971a; Wilson, 1967), even though it is most likely that the upper-status Negro parents were of higher IQ than the low-status white parents. The regression-to-the-mean phenomenon could account for the crossover of the average IQs of the children from the two racial groups.

NOTES

1. A 'family' in this analysis is a group of two or more full siblings who have been reared together.

2. In this formula for r_i the σ_B^2 and σ_W^2 are population values. When estimates of these population values are made from samples of the population, s_B^2 and s_W^2, the formula for the intraclass correlation is

$$r_i = \frac{s_B^2 - s_W^2}{s_B^2 + (\bar{n}-1)\, s_W^2}$$

where $\bar{n}$ is the arithmetic mean of the number of cases in each class (i.e., siblings in each family). Whenever the number of cases differs considerably from one class to another, a method other than the simple arithmetic mean is needed for obtaining the value of $\bar{n}$. For a more detailed discussion of intraclass correlation see Blalock (1960, pp. 266-9).

3. A good rough estimate (which, if anything, errs on the conservative side, i.e., slightly too low) of the sibling genetic correlation, ρ_{G_s}, given the parental genetic correlation, ρ_{G_P}, is

$$\rho_{G_s} = \frac{\rho_{G_P}+1}{\rho_{G_P}+2}$$

4. Both h^2 and E^2 can be corrected for attenuation due to unreliability of measurements by subtracting the error variance, σ_e^2, from the denominator in the formula for h^2. The corrected heritability and environmentability are abbreviated as h_C^2 and E_C^2.
5. Nichols (1972), however, found a lower sib correlation for Negroes than for whites on the 4-year Stanford-Binet IQ.
6. Another possible way of expressing the racial difference on a common scale for all tests would be by the point-biserial correlation (r_{pbs}) between test scores and the racial dichotomy (quantized as 0 and 1). But r_{pbs} bears a non-linear relationship to $(\bar{W}-\bar{N})/\sigma_W$ and when used as an index to be correlated with another variable could result in a non-linear but monotomic relationship to the other variable which would underestimate the degree of relationship if the Pearson r were used. In such a case, either the correlation ratio (eta) or Spearman's rank order correlation (rho) should be used as the measure of degree of relationship instead of the product-moment correlation (Pearson's r).
7. Technically speaking, the Negro and white children are matched on 'regressed true scores' (regressed to the common mean), that is, the IQ scores they would be expected to obtain if errors of measurement were eliminated. This is a standard statistical procedure generally called for in studies based on the matching of individuals from two or more groups.
8. We have tested the linearity of sibling regression in IQ in large white and Negro samples of school-age children and have found it does not depart significantly from linearity throughout the IQ range from about 50 to about 150. Such linearity of regression is consistent with a simple genetic model; it is not predictable from any environmental hypotheses that have been put forth as explanation of the average Negro-white IQ difference.
9. Actually, the genetic sibling correlation would be slightly higher in whichever group had the highest degree of assortative mating (i.e., correlation between spouses) for IQ. At present there is no good evidence concerning the degree of assortative mating for IQ in the Negro population, although one study found no Negro-white difference in degree of assortative mating for amount of formal education. (Warren, 1966)

Appendix A: Description of Tests in Table 4.1

Speed and Persistence Test (Making Xs)

The Making Xs Test is intended as an assessment of test-taking motivation. It gives an indication of the subject's willingness to comply with instructions in a group testing situation and to mobilize effort in following those instructions for a brief period of time. The test involves no intellectual component, although for young children it probably involves some perceptual-motor skills component, as reflected by increasing mean scores as a function of age between grades 1 to 5. The wide range of individual differences among children at any one grade level would seem to reflect mainly general motivation and test-taking attitudes in a group situation. The test also serves partly as an index of classroom morale, and it can be entered as a moderator variable into correlational analyses with other ability and achievement tests. Children who do very poorly on this test, it can be suspected, are likely not to put out their maximum effort on ability tests given in a group situation and therefore their scores are not likely to reflect their 'true' level of ability.

The Making Xs Test consists of two parts. In Part I (1st try) the subject is asked simply to make Xs in a series of squares for a period of 90 seconds. In this part the instructions say nothing about speed. They merely instruct the child to make Xs. The maximum possible score on Part I is 150, since there are 150 squares provided in which the child can make Xs. After a two-minute rest period the child turns the page of the test booklet to Part II (2nd try). Here the child is instructed to show how much better he can perform than he did on Part I and to work as rapidly as possible. The child is again given 90 seconds to make as many Xs as he can in the 150 boxes provided. The gain in score from Part I to Part II reflects both a practice effect and an increase in motivation or effort as a result of the motivating instructions, i.e., instructions to work as rapidly as possible.

MEMORY TESTS

Memory for Numbers Test

The Memory for Numbers Test is a measure of digit span, or more generally, short-term memory. It consists of three parts. Each part consists of six series of digits going from four digits in a series up to nine digits in a series. The digit series are presented on a tape recording on which the digits are spoken clearly by a male voice at the rate of precisely one digit per second. The subjects write down as many digits as they can recall at the conclusion of each series, which is signaled by a 'bong'. Each part of the test is preceded by a short practice test of three digit series in order to permit the tester to determine whether the child has understood the instructions, etc. The practice test also serves to familiarize the subject with the procedure of each of the subtests. The first subtest is labeled *Immediate Recall* (I). Here the subject is instructed to recall the series *immediately* after the last digit has been spoken on the tape recorder. The second subtest consists of *Delayed Recall* (D). Here the subject is instructed not to write down his response until ten seconds have elapsed after the last digit has been spoken. The ten-second interval is marked by audible clicks of a metronome and is terminated by a bong sound which signals the child to write his response. The Delayed Recall condition invariably results in some retention decrement. The third subtest is the *Repeated Series* test, in which the digit series is repeated three times prior to recall; the subject then recalls the series immediately after the last digit in the series has been presented. Again, recall is signaled by a bong. Each repetition of the series is separated by a tone with a duration of one second. The repeated series almost invariably results in greater recall than the single series. This test is very culture-fair for children in second grade and beyond who know their numerals and are capable of listening and paying attention, as indicated by the Listening-Attention Test. The maximum score on any one of the subtests is 39, that is the sum of the digit series from four through nine.

INTELLIGENCE TESTS

Figure Copying Test

This test was given only in grades K-4. The test is shown in Figure 3.1 and is also described there (pp. 77-8).

Lorge-Thorndike Intelligence Tests

These are nationally standardized group-administered tests of general intelligence. In the normative sample, which was intended to be representative of the nation's school population, the test has a mean IQ of 100 and a standard deviation of 16. It is generally acknowledged to be one of the best paper-and-pencil tests of general intelligence.

The Manual of the Lorge-Thorndike Test states that the test was designed to measure reasoning ability. It does not test proficiency in specific skills taught in school, although the verbal tests, from grade 4 and above, depend upon reading ability. The reading level required, however, is intentionally kept considerably below the level of reasoning required for correctly answering the test questions. Thus the test is essentially a test of reasoning and not of reading ability, which is to say that it should have more of its variance in common with non-verbal tests of reasoning ability than with tests of reading *per se*.

The tests for grades K-3 do not depend at all upon reading ability but make use exclusively of pictorial items. The tests for grades 4-8 consist of two parts, *Verbal* (V) and *Non-verbal* (NV). They are scored separately and the raw score on each is converted to an IQ, with a normative mean of 100 and *SD* of 16. The chief advantage of keeping the two scores separate is that the Non-verbal IQ does not overestimate or underestimate the child's general level of intellectual ability because of specific skills or disabilities in reading. The Non-verbal IQ, however, correlates almost as highly with a test of reading comprehension as does the Verbal IQ, because all three tests depend primarily upon reasoning

E*

ability and not upon reading *per se*. For example, in the fourth grade sample, the correlation between the Lorge-Thorndike Verbal and Non-verbal IQs is 0·70. The correlation between Verbal IQ and the Paragraph Meaning Subtest of the Standard Achievement Test is 0·52. The correlation between the Non-verbal IQ and Paragraph Meaning is 0·47. Now we can ask: What is the correlation of Verbal IQ and Paragraph Meaning when the effects of Non-verbal IQ are partialled out, that is, are held constant? The partial correlation between Verbal IQ and Paragraph Meaning (holding Non-verbal IQ constant) is only 0·29.

The following forms of the Lorge-Thorndike Intelligence Tests were used:

Level 1, Form B	Grades K-1
Level 2, Form B	Grades 2-3
Level 3, Form B. Verbal and Non-verbal	Grades 4-6

ACHIEVEMENT TESTS

Stanford Achievement Tests

Scholastic achievement was assessed by means of the so-called 'partial battery' of the Stanford Achievement Tests, consisting of the following subtests: Word Meaning, Paragraph Meaning, Spelling, Word Study Skills, Language (grammar), Arithmetic Computation, Arithmetic Concepts, and Arithmetic Applications. The Stanford Achievement battery was administered in grades 1 through 6.

5   *Between-groups heritability*

The heritability of *individual differences* in intelligence *within* the white population (European and North American Caucasians) is so well established by a number of independent studies – to the effect that genetic factors are about twice as important as environmental factors as a cause of individual differences in IQ – that this conclusion is now generally accepted by scientists who are familiar with the evidence. The situation regarding *mean* differences in intelligence *between* subpopulation groups is quite another matter. Not only does there prevail a marked *a priori* preference for environmental explanations of group differences – particularly if different racial groups are involved – but in most discussions even the possibility of genetic differences is never raised. The investigator's task is assumed to be solely that of hypothesizing or identifying the environmental factors responsible for the mean intelligence difference between the two groups in question. Usually any and all environmental differences found to exist between the groups, in whatever degree, are deemed adequate to explain the IQ difference, whatever its magnitude. In many instances this results in attributing quite large differences to very weak causes as judged from the correlation between the hypothesized environmental effect and IQ variance *within* either of the population groups being compared. But, logically, unless a direct causal relationship (rather than just a correlation) between an environmental factor and IQ is established, there is no more basis for preferring an explanation in terms of some *visible* environmental difference than in terms of some invisible genetic difference. And in the case of race differences in IQ, there are even *visible* genetic differences (e.g., skin color, hair texture, etc.) between the groups, the purely logical status of which, in relation to IQ, is not different from the visible environmental differences between the groups. In both cases, the visible differences may or may not make a causal difference in IQ. The visible environmental differences and the visible physical genetic differences between two racial groups may have no causal connection with IQ; both may be merely correlated with some other factors which directly influence IQ. Since we know from studies of the heritability of individual differences in IQ that genetic factors have comparatively powerful effects and environmental factors have comparatively weak effects, is there probabilistically more reason to hypothesize environmental factors as of greater importance than genetic factors in explaining group differences in IQ? The *a priori* preference for strictly or preponderantly environmental explanations seems to stem more from ideological than from any logical or scientific considerations. Thus, Jencks (1969, p. 29) writes, 'While a significant number of black children may well suffer serious prenatal damage, Jensen's evidence suggests that we should probably look elsewhere to explain racial differences in IQ scores. But it hardly follows that we must look to genes. We might do equally well to look at patterns of child rearing.' This clearly expresses a preference which could determine one's research strategy, but the preference would seem to run counter to the probabilities suggested by already established evidence. Genes have already been established as having powerful effects on IQ; individual genetic differences correlate about 0·85 to 0·90 (the square root of the heritability) with IQ. Correlations between child-rearing practices and IQ *within* racial groups are minute by comparison, and the extent of their causal connection with IQ differences *between* racial groups has not been determined. (If the broad heritability, including *GE* covariance, of IQ is 0·75, for example, the maximum correlation between IQ and *all* environmental effects combined would be only $\sqrt{1-0\cdot75} = 0\cdot50$ within the population in question.) Pointing to some environmental difference whose causal relationship to IQ is not established is logically no more plausible as an environmental explanation of a mean IQ difference than is pointing to some clearly genetic difference, such as skin color, as a genetic explanation of the difference.

The preference for environmental explanations of group differences reaches its zenith in a few studies. Gross (1967), for example, compared two Brooklyn Jewish groups on a variety of cognitive tests. The 90 Jewish boys, averaging about 6 years of age, came from either Sephardic families (immigrants from Arabic or Oriental countries) or Ashkenazic families (immigrants from Europe). All their mothers were native-born and English was the household language. All were middle class and lived in the same community. Yet the Ashkenazic boys scored higher than the Sephardic boys on the several cognitive tests and differed by as much as 17 IQ points on the Peabody Picture Vocabulary Tests. The investigators studied the family environments intensively for clues that could explain the significant IQ difference between these two groups. No significant differences could be found between the groups in a host of family training and background experiences – except for one item in the questionnaire of parental attitudes. Twice as many Ashkenazic mothers said that earnings were 'unimportant' in their desires for their children, and three times as many Sephardic mothers said they wanted their sons to be 'wealthy'. This single, subtle attitudinal factor, then, supposedly explains the 17 points IQ difference. There is no suggestion of the possibility that Sephardic and Ashkenazic groups may have different gene pools for many characteristics, including intelligence. The study is cited by other writers (e.g., Havighurst, 1970, p. 321) as an example of how subtle environmental differences can influence cognitive development. It is interesting that no one has produced IQ differences nearly as large as 17 points in non-disadvantaged groups even by the most intensive training. Direct coaching on a particular IQ test results in only about 9 or 10 points gain. Another zenith of environmentalism: as an example of the effects of environmental differences on IQ, Klineberg (1956) points to an IQ difference of 47 points (58 *v.* 105)[1] between a group of rural Negro children in Tennessee and a group of urban Negro children in Los Angeles. Since the largest difference ever reported between a pair of identical twins reared apart is 24 IQ points (Newman, Freeman & Holzinger, 1937), it seems most improbable that a mean difference of 47 IQ points would be attributable entirely to environmental differences. It is, of course, not *impossible*, but it is highly *improbable*. Preferences obviously do not always correspond to probabilities.

Since researchers with a penchant for exclusively environmental explanations of subpopulation IQ differences seldom attempt to rule out any plausible hypothesized environmental effects or to determine the relative importance of various environmental factors as causes of group differences, we must ask if there are any feasible means for assessing the relative plausibility of different environmental explanations. The prevailing preference for the null hypothesis when any other than environmental causes of group differences are considered has actually hindered exercise of the kinds of experimental and psychometric ingenuity that could possibly lead to rejection of the null hypothesis. There are prejudices in this area which have retarded even the zeroing-in on truly causal environmental factors. One prominent prejudice is the notion that any *possible* environmental explanation is an *adequate* explanation. Rarely is an attempt made to determine how much of the variance is actually accounted for by the hypothesized environmental variable or set of variables. Just because some factor *could* be causal does not mean that in fact it *is*. Another prejudice is the opinion that studies designed to test a genetic hypothesis should not be considered unless the single study can yield a 100 percent definitive answer, leaving no residual of unanswered questions concerning the whole issue of genetic racial differences. This intransigent perfectionism regarding the testing of genetic hypotheses is not only in marked contrast to the research philosophy that prevails with respect to environmental hypotheses, but it is incompatible with what we know of how scientific progress has been achieved in dealing with other problems.

Answers to complex questions are usually attained gradually, by working on very limited aspects of the problem, one at a time. The first study of a phenomenon is rarely the definitive study, and most often there is no single definitive experiment. The theory of evolution, for example, does not rest upon a single definitive study but upon a preponderance of evidence, each piece of which reduces the uncertainty about some small relevant aspect of the total complex consequences of evolution. The heredity-environment uncertainty with respect to particular subpopulation differences, similarly, will in all likelihood not be resolved by any one study but will come about through a large number of studies which attempt to reduce uncertainty about many limited aspects of the question. Any single study should be judged by its degree of success in answering the limited question to which it is addressed and not in terms of whether it provides a definitive answer to the general question.

How often have studies which could have led to the rejection of certain specific environmentalist hypotheses been swept aside as if they were worthless, simply because they did not provide a definitive proof of a genetic hypothesis? Many easily disproved environmental hypotheses are allowed to prevail because a genetic counter-hypothesis remains unproven. However, it is possible to disprove many specific environmental hypotheses without having to propose any counter-hypothesis. But we have seen exceedingly little of such research. When a researcher is wedded to environmentalism, apparently it does not much matter to him which particular environmental hypotheses have some truth to them and which do not. If one environmental explanation is knocked down by contrary evidence, another can always be readily posited in its place. It is pure environmentalism rather than any particular environmental hypothesis that must stand at all costs. Some hypothesized environmental factors, without any supporting evidence, do not even have the advantage of plausibility, whereas high plausibility of an alternative genetic hypothesis makes it highly suspect and open to vociferous attack from some circles.

The very *ad hoc* nature of environmentalist explanations seems to me antithetical to the ways of science. Scientific progress is won through an unrelenting battle against *ad hoc* explanations of natural phenomena. Therefore, in studying subpopulation differences in mental abilities, does it not seem a more scientific approach to consider *all* factors which are known to cause individual differences within groups? And is it not reasonable, if for practical reasons of research strategy we must assign some priority to the hypothesized causes we wish to consider, that the evidence derived from studies *within* groups should serve as a guide to the kinds of hypotheses most worth entertaining about the causes of differences *between* groups? And does not this lead us directly to the hypothesis of genetic factors as being among the undoubtedly multiple causes of racial subpopulation differences in mental abilities? Furthermore, it is practically axiomatic in biology that any characteristics showing individual variation *within* subgroups of a species will also show variation *between* subgroups of the species.

DEFINITIONS OF RACE

Biologically speaking, races are subdivisions of a species. In the human species, races are subpopulations characterized by a higher degree of *intra*breeding than *inter*breeding. The greater the geographic or racial isolation of the subpopulations, the higher is their degree of intrabreeding and the lower is the degree of interbreeding. The more time that various subpopulations are isolated from each other, the more they will differ in the relative frequencies of genes for various characteristics, so that in many centuries of isolation sufficient differences in various gene frequencies accumulate as to make for pervasive and obvious differences in physical appearance. Social classes within a society are also breeding populations, although the degree of isolation and hence the ratio of intrabreeding to interbreeding is much less than is the case for the major racial groups. The major racial groups are characterized as the largest subdivisions of mankind between which gene flow has been the most restricted for the longest periods, usually because of geographical isolation. They therefore show the largest differences in gene frequencies for the largest number of characteristics.[2]

The five major continental divisions are the Caucasians, Negroes, Mongoloids, American Indians, and Oceanic peoples. Each of these groups can be further subdivided into breeding populations with lesser degrees of isolation and less restricted gene flow. How far one wishes to carry on the subdivision into smaller and smaller subpopulations is quite arbitrary and depends upon one's purposes. The ratio of intrabreeding to interbreeding for subpopulation groups, as well as the extent of differences in gene frequencies, are clearly continuous variables, and whether two subpopulation groups are regarded as genetically different, that is, qualify as different racial groups, depends upon where the line is drawn. In a very coarse-grained classification Europeans and Hindus would be found in the same racial group; in a much more fine-grained classificatory system even different castes of Hindus would be regarded as 'racially' different groups, i.e., breeding populations differing in the frequency of one or more genes. Almost without exception in nature, any genetically conditioned characteristic that varies among individuals within a population also varies between populations. Among the genetically conditioned traits most well established as varying between major racial groups are body size and proportions; cranial size and cephalic index; pigmentation of the hair, skin, and eyes; hair form and distribution on the body; numbers of vertebrae; fingerprints; bone density; basic metabolic rate; number of sweat glands; fissural patterns on the chewing surfaces of the teeth; blood groups; various chronic diseases; frequency of dizygotic (but not monozygotic) twinning; male/female birth ratio; ability to taste phenylthiocarbamide (PTC); length of gestation period; and degree of physical maturity at birth (as indicated by degree of ossification of cartilage). No such strong claim can yet be made for behavioral characteristics, especially those involving cognitive abilities, but probably all geneticists would concur in the statement by Spuhler and Lindzey (1967, p. 413) '. . . it seems to us surprising that one would accept present findings in regard to the existence of genetic, anatomical, physiological, and epidemiological differences between the races . . . and still expect to find *no* meaningful differences in behavior between races'.

Most subpopulation differences, physical or behavioral, cannot be ranked on any absolute scale of desirability; they are relative to particular environmental and cultural requirements. A trait which is highly adaptive under one set of environmental conditions may be neutral or maladaptive under another set of conditions. As Penrose (1951, p. 397) has remarked:

> Everyone is accustomed, quite erroneously, to regard the group from which he has originated as being the normal. Judged by world standards, his group is likely to be abnormal and he may have to fall back on the assumption that, though unusual, it may represent a specially desirable set of gene frequencies. He is perhaps justified only in inferring that his group has a genetical structure well suited in the past to its environment, else it would not have maintained itself.

While racial groups differ in gene frequencies for various characteristics, the differences are usually continuous and rarely discrete. There are no clear-cut boundaries between racial groups, since varying degrees of hybridization are found among all major races. Social criteria of racial group membership, however, usually do not recognize genetic gradations but classify persons discretely into this racial group or that. The social criteria of race are simple;

they are the ethnic labels people use to describe themselves and the more obvious physical characteristics such as skin color, hair form, facial features, etc., by which persons roughly judge one another's 'race'. Ordinary social criteria make for unreliability in the classification of 'borderline' or ambiguous cases. Nevertheless, for the major racial groups there is undoubtedly a high degree of correspondence between social and biological criteria. If one were to sort school children, for example, into three racial groups – Negro, Oriental, and Caucasian – by the ordinary social criteria, one would find a very high concordance of classification if one used strict biological criteria based on the frequencies of blood groups, anthropometric measures, and other genetic polymorphisms. What the latter measures would reveal are degrees of racial admixture, and a consequent continuity of genetic differences from one group to another, with only *modal* genetic differences between the groups. Studies of behavioral differences in relation to ethnic classification would be much improved by using biological in addition to social criteria of racial membership, so that correlations between continuous variables could be obtained as well as mean (or median) differences between groups. But most studies of race differences in mental characteristics have compared groups selected solely by social criteria. If the observed behavioral differences are due only to social factors, then the social definition of race should be quite adequate, and, in fact, it should be the most appropriate definition. But if the groups are, in fact, genetically overlapping because each one's gene pool contains some admixture of the other, use of the social criterion alone can only result in a blurring and underestimation of the racial genetic aspect of the measured behavioral difference. Because of varying degrees of racial admixture in different groups and localities, one should expect to find variable differences between socially defined racial groups. A common error is to think of socially defined racial groups as genetically homogeneous. They surely are not.

Another block to clear thinking is to regard a race as a kind of Platonic ideal, without reference to any actual population group. Observable samples of subpopulations, however they are defined, cannot be regarded as representative of some Platonic racial group. Such Platonic racial groups do not, in fact, exist, except in some people's imaginations. Samples of a subpopulation (racial, socio-economic, or whatever) are merely representative (if properly selected) of the clearly specified population group from which they were selected.

Population subgroups which have migrated are not necessarily representative of their native parent populations. Studies of racial or national groups in the United States, therefore, cannot automatically be generalized abroad, and the reverse is also true. This does not mean, however, that meaningful comparative studies of various subpopulations within the United States (or elsewhere) are not feasible.

INFERENCE FROM WITHIN-GROUPS TO BETWEEN-GROUPS HERITABILITY

The first explicit recognition of this problem which I have come across in the psychological literature is attributable to E. L. Thorndike (1940, pp. 320-1). It is quite interesting to note how close his estimate of heritability, based on the rather meagre evidence of his day, comes to the estimates based on our present more sophisticated methodology and more extensive data. He ascribed the following percentages to the components of variance in individual differences in intelligence:

Genes	80%
Training	17%
'Accident'	3%

After discussing the predominantly genetic basis of *individual* differences in intelligence, Thorndike goes on to say the following about *group* differences:

Most of what has been said here about individual mental differences is applicable to the mental differences of families and races. Such exist as a consequence of differences between the genes or training or both, of one family from another, one race from another. A sample of man isolated from the rest in breeding will only by rare accident have genes identical with the rest of man. Whatever selective forces operate in the begetting of that sample's children will only rarely be just the same as operate in the rest of man. But it is easy to overestimate these family and racial differences, and in the interest of one or another theory or prejudice this has often been done. The popular notion that all the persons of each race are closely alike mentally and very different from all the persons of any other race is sheer nonsense. There is usually great variation within the race and great overlapping between races. The case about which most is known is intelligence in American Negroes, including Negro-white hybrids, and whites mostly of English and North European descent. (p. 321)

And Thorndike goes on to estimate the overlap[3] here for persons who have had equal numbers of years of schooling; his estimate is that 10 percent of Negroes exceed the white median, which, assuming normality of the two distributions, corresponds to a mean difference of approximately 1·3 sigmas or $1·3 \times 15 = 19·5$ IQ points. (This is a slightly larger difference than the 12 percent median overlap estimated by Shuey on the basis of all existing evidence up to 1965.)

Most modern geneticists would agree that Thorndike's main point is essentially correct. Any breeding groups are virtually certain to have different gene pools and the only real questions that remain concern the magnitude of the genetic difference (i.e., the heritability of the phenotypic group difference), its direction (i.e., which group is higher on the characteristic in question), and its significance in terms of the demands made by the environment. Some differences, though real and statistically significant, do not make any practical difference under existing conditions. The large racial differences in ability to taste phenylthiocarbamide, for example, are of no personal or social consequence. Differences in mental abilities, on the other hand, can have important practical consequences, depending upon their magnitude, both for individuals and for society. What Thorndike recognized was the high probability of genetic group differences, but he made no attempt to estimate their magnitude, which is the more important question in a practical sense. We are hardly any further ahead today.

The simple fact is that one cannot, in any strict, formal sense, infer between-groups heritability from a knowledge of within-groups heritability. This is true even if the heritability of the trait is perfect (i.e., $h^2 = 1·00$) within each group and there is absolutely no overlap of the phenotypic distributions of the two groups. As a clear example we can point to various kinds of grasses. Grown in complete darkness, their colors will vary from white to pale yellow, without the slightest trace of green. The heritability of the color differences is perfect. The same grasses grown in sunlight vary in color from light green to dark green, and here the heritability is perfect. The large color difference between the white-yellow and the green grass is entirely attributable to a difference in a single environmental factor, in this case an obvious one – the presence or absence of visible light, without which the photosynthesis of chlorophyll, the green element in plants, cannot occur. By the same token, environmental differences can completely obscure genetic differences, even to the extent that the phenotypic and genotypic differences are in reverse directions. A genetically light green strain of grass, for example, will be darker green when grown in direct sunlight than a genetically darker green strain grown in the shade. Then there is the third possibility of two genotypically different strains looking phenotypically exactly alike when grown in the same environment. Under some other environmental conditions, although they are exactly the same for both strains, the two strains will reveal quite large phenotypic differences. For example, one type of golden rod when grown in the shade is dwarfed, while another type is tall; but both are of medium height when grown in direct sunlight (Thoday, 1969). Thus even phenotypic and environmental similarity are not sufficient for inferring genetic similarity. In principle, there can be the same lack of correlation between phenotypes and genotypes for different subpopulations of the human species, even granted a very high correlation between phenotypes and genotypes within the subpopulation groups. But we must inquire under what actual conditions this is likely to be true.

If there is no *formal* relationship between within-group heritability and between-group heritability, is there any kind of relationship at all? Is the estimation of heritability within groups in any way relevant to the discussion of racial differences or any other kinds of subpopulation differences? It is – in a probabilistic or likelihood sense.

Let us look at a clear-cut example of human differences. Two particular subpopulations on the African continent – the Pygmies and the Watusi – differ in mean stature by 5 to 6 standard deviations (in terms of the variability in height of Europeans), which is about 11 to 13 inches (Martin & Saller, 1959).[4] As far as I can determine no one has ever proven that this is entirely a genetic difference or even that genetic factors are in any way implicated. A completely environmental explanation of the difference in stature has not been ruled out by evidence. Certainly the environments of the two groups differ enormously: Pygmies inhabit the rain forests while the Watusi live on the plains; their living habits and diets differ markedly, as do the kinds of illnesses and misfortunes to which they are liable. Yet, despite these facts, it would be difficult to find anyone who would seriously proffer a nongenetic or environmentalist explanation of this difference in stature between Watusi and Pygmies. Why?

The first reason is that apparently no one emotionally *needs* to believe that differences in height are not inborn. Differences in height have relatively minor social correlates; few people attach any great importance to height and, if anything, the average is generally regarded as more desirable than either of the extremes. Furthermore, no subpopulation has ever been socially or economically handicapped, as far as we know, because of its average difference in height from that of other groups. If for some religious, political, or ideological reasons it were thought repugnant to regard differences in stature, at least between population groups, as innate, it is likely that the prevailing explanation of the Watusi-Pygmy difference would be in terms of their environmental differences, and some persons might make strenuous efforts to maintain this belief and try to make everyone else subscribe to it.

But the rational grounds for attributing the stature difference to genetic factors is not because it has been proven in any formal sense, but merely because it seems highly plausible. It is instructive to examine the reasons for this plausibility. It rests on four main factors:

(*a*) The mean difference *between* the groups is large, being more than $\frac{5}{6}$ of the total range *within* either group.

(*b*) The heritability of height within populations is known to be very high, usually over 0·90. Thus, the total range of environmental variations within populations only accounts for about 10 percent of the phenotypic variance. The distribution of environmental effects will have a standard deviation which is equal to the square root of the environmental variance. Taking the total phenotypic within-group variance of height as 5 inches, the environmental variance would be 0·10 × 5 inches = 0·5 inches, and the standard deviation (*SD*) of the environmental effects would be $\sqrt{0.5} = 0.71$ inches. This means, in effect, that two genetically identical individuals (e.g., monozygotic twins) who differ by 0·71 inches can be said to differ by 1 *SD* in the effects of all environmental factors influencing stature. We can then express the mean difference of, say, 10 inches between Watusi and Pygmies in terms of the number of *SD*s by which they must differ in the environmental factors affecting height *within* a population, if we are to explain all of the differences in terms of these environmental factors. This amounts to 10 inches/0·71 inches = 14·8 *SD*s difference between the two groups in the effects of environment. Two normal distributions whose means differ by as much as 14·8 *SD*s are so extremely far apart that there would be absolutely no overlap between the two groups in the environmental factors affecting height. In other words, the probability is practically infinitesimal that even the very largest environmental differences affecting height *within* either population could begin to explain the 10 inches difference *between* the two populations. No naturally occurring environmental effects within either population would alter height more than about 6 *SD*s (which includes 99·8 percent of the total range of a normal distribution) or 6×0.71 inches = 4·3 inches. Thus, the mean difference *between* groups is something more than twice as large as the largest differences within groups that could be attributable to naturally occurring environmental effects *within* the groups. This is therefore so highly improbable, that in order to go on entertaining a strictly environmental hypothesis of the cause of the mean difference in statures one would have to hypothesize that the environments of Watusi and Pygmies differ in some very potent unknown factor (or factors), 'X', which is present in one population and not in the other and which affects *all* individuals in the one population and *none* in the other. Furthermore, if factor 'X' does not have an equal or constant effect on all members of the population in which it is present, and if the two populations are genetically identical for stature in accord with the environmental hypothesis, then we should expect to find a lower heritability for stature in the population affected by factor 'X', since it is a variable environmental effect which acts in the one population and not in the other. If genetically identical, both populations should be expected to respond similarly to the environmental factors common to both. If the heritabilities of stature do not differ significantly in the two populations, there would be two ways of getting around this fact while still maintaining an environmental hypothesis. We can posit that factor 'X' has a *constant* effect on every member of the population in which it occurs. Or we can posit *two* unknown factors, 'X' and 'Y', which (*i*) have *opposite* effects on stature, (*ii*) exist exclusively in one population or the other, and (*iii*) have equally variable effects on stature, thus increasing the non-genetic variance by equal amounts. If these conditions seem untenable to us, we are apt to call factors 'X' and 'Y' genetic and reject the environmental hypothesis. But this is admittedly a subjective judgment and neither a scientific, statistical proof of a genetic hypothesis nor a disproof of the environmental hypotheses. But we do know that genes *can* have such large effects on stature (as can be proven by selective breeding of plants and animals) and thus the genetic hypothesis seems more reasonable than the hypothesis of unknown factors 'X' or 'Y'.

(*c*) The third reason that we intuitively accept a genetic hypothesis in this case is that height is not the only physical difference we see between Pygmies and Watusi. Suppose there are differences in hair texture and distribution, in proportional differences in body build, in facial features, and so on. In short, there would be a whole consistent *pattern* of differences, not just differences along a single dimension. Because of this consistent pattern of physical differences, short Watusi still would not much resemble tall Pygmies. The correlations among various body measurements, after the general factor of stature is partialled out, would be different for Pygmies and Watusi. This finding would accord with our observation that Pygmies and Watusi look different even if one ignores the overall difference in stature. All these differences could, of course, be environmental, but it would be up to the environmentalist to explain what kinds of environmental effects could produce such consistently marked and different patterns of characteristics in the two populations. The genetic hypothesis would be more plausible because most of the elements entering into the pattern differences are known to be highly heritable within each population.

(*d*) The fourth reason that an environmental hypothesis strikes us as implausible is that the extreme environmental conditions which have the most extreme effects on stature within either population also have *other* effects on the individual. These would make him differ from his fellows in more than just stature. Severe malnutrition might make a Watusi abnormally small – perhaps as small as the larger Pygmies. But malnutrition also makes Watusi physically weak, while normal Pygmies, though small in stature, are physically very strong. A Pygmy with pituitary gigantism might be as tall as some normal Watusi, but he would be much weaker physically. In other words, the extreme differences produced by non-genetic factors *within* the populations involve a constellation of other differences which do not resemble the differences *between* the typical individuals of each population.

These four 'arguments' for the *plausibility* of genetic group differences in stature, however, cannot *prove* a genetic hypothesis, or, conversely, cannot disprove an environmental hypothesis, because we can always posit factor 'X' as the unknown but crucial environmental difference responsible for the difference between the groups in stature. If there are specific hypotheses about causal environmental differences, these hypotheses can be tested and rejected without proving the genetic hypothesis. But at least we could determine which environmental factors do *not* cause the group difference in stature. If every known environmental difference, singly or in combination, fails to account for the difference, then the environmentalist must fall back on some unknown factor 'X'. Unless he can formulate testable hypotheses concerning the nature of 'X', we are left with an explanation which has little utility in terms of prediction or control of the variable we wish to explain. Even if a genetic hypothesis were wrong, the fact of high within-group heritability leaves no doubt that the mean difference between the populations could be decreased by genetic selection. On the other hand, hypothesizing factor 'X' as the cause of the difference provides no basis for control. But if such approaches can never prove or disprove genetic or environmental hypotheses, how can such hypotheses be put to scientifically definitive tests – as definitive, that is, as anything can be in an empirical science?

Discontinuous Traits

As Thoday (1969) has pointed out, there is usually little or no problem in establishing genetic differences between populations in discontinuous traits. Such traits are all-or-none and are due to the presence or absence of a single gene. The genetic basis of the trait can be established from family pedigrees and concordance rates for various degrees of kinship. If samples of the two populations being compared are sufficiently large in relation to the base rate frequency of the gene (or the alternate allelic forms of the gene) in the two populations, then the relative frequency of the gene in each population can be determined. This has been done with blood groups and many other physical characteristics which show discrete rather than continuous variation. So far as we know, there are very few genes that are exclusive to any one population; only a few of the 70-odd identified blood types fall into this category. As Thoday (1969, p. 4) notes, 'Populations of a species do not differ absolutely, but in the relative frequency of different genotypes.'

Continuous Traits

The characteristics we are most interested in, however, are continuous variables, like height and IQ. Their wide variability over a continuous range of values is said to be polygenic, that is, a result of the combined effects of many genes, each one independently either adding, not adding, or subtracting a small increment of the trait. Each person's genotype for a particular trait is comprised of a random assortment of the parental genes; thus individuals inherit genes, not genotypes. Parents can only pass on their genes to their progeny, not their genotypes. Since many different assortments and combinations of the parental genes are possible, we see considerable variations both among parents and their children and among the children of the same parents. For polygenic traits, like height and IQ, how can we prove genetic differences between populations?

Coming back to our Watusi and Pygmy example, we can perform what plant geneticists call a 'transplant' and animal geneticists call 'cross-fostering'. That is, we rear members of one population in the habitat of the other and vice versa. Shortly after birth, Pygmy infants would be given to Watusi for rearing and Watusi infants would be given to Pygmies. Will their adult height come closer to the mean of the population of their origin or of their adoptive population? If the sample sizes are large enough, this method could establish with considerable accuracy the relative contributions of 'nature' and 'nurture' to the mean height difference between Pygmies and Watusi. The uncontrolled factor in this case, of course, is prenatal environmental effects. The experiment could be slightly improved by cross-fostering the mothers themselves, so that at least two generations of samples from each group would be exposed to the same environmental conditions of the other groups. This would still not clinch the question of prenatal effects, however, because there could be genetic differences in the intra-uterine environments provided by Pygmies and Watusi which could affect the infants' later growth potential, so that prenatal environmental differences affecting growth could be mistaken for genetic differences in stature. No heritability study could reveal this prenatal effect if its variance *within* groups were very small relative to other sources of environmental variance. Someone might argue that it does not matter whether the phenotypic difference is due to a genetic difference in the characteristic itself or is the indirect result of a genetic difference in qualities of the intra-uterine environment. This, however, is a scientifically unacceptable answer. It leads neither to further understanding nor to the possibility of control. The aim of a scientific approach is to localize causal factors as precisely as possible.

Therefore, if cross-fostering, with all the controls appropriate to this method, does not wipe out the stature difference between our groups, we have only proved that differences in the postnatal, external environment are not the cause of the mean group difference. To determine the contribution of prenatal effects, we would have to resort to another method – a cross-breeding experiment. The environmental hypothesis would predict that Pygmy women artificially inseminated by Watusi should have children whose adult stature is much closer to the Pygmy mean than to the Watusi mean, and vice versa. A genetic hypothesis based on the simplest additive model (i.e., no dominance, epistasis, or genotype × environment interaction) would predict that the offsprings' height would fall halfway between the height of the parents. If the heritability of height within these populations had already been worked out in detail so that a more elaborate model could be applied, taking account of more than just the additive genetic effects, a more precise prediction would be possible. If there is some degree of dominance for tallness, for example, we should expect the offspring mean to be somewhat displaced above the midparent value.

If for some reason we could not perform a breeding experiment, or if we could not wait for a generation to determine the results of such an experiment, we might look for a breeding experiment that had occurred in nature. Say we found a pair of neighboring Watusi and Pygmy villages in which a limited amount of inter-marriage between the groups had occurred for several generations. The distributions of heights of the two groups would then be much less bimodal; there would be continuous variation from the shortest Pygmy to the tallest Watusi. If all families in these villages kept complete and accurate genealogies extending back to the time before any intermarriages took place, our method would be simple. We would determine each individual's percentage of Watusi ancestors and correlate this with individuals' heights, or plot a graph showing the form of the relationship between these two variables. We could then say how much of the variability in stature was accounted for by degree of Watusi ancestry. If there were a significant positive correlation, it would not necessarily clinch a genetic hypothesis, though it would surely be consistent with it. But there would remain the possibility that in any inter-marriage, the offspring who lived in the Pygmy village occasionally ate Watusi foods and those who lived in the Watusi village occasionally ate Pygmy food. One might argue that certain Watusi foods stimulated skeletal growth and Pygmy foods stunted growth. Then the progeny of intermarriages would tend toward inter-mediate heights, and perhaps the more remote the original ancestor of the other group, the less inclined would the descendants be to eat the food of the ancestor's village. Thus stature could be a continuous, increasing function of percentage of Watusi ancestry due to purely environmental (i.e., dietary) causes. To rule out this explanation, we would need to do one of two things: either demonstrate a lack of correlation between percentage of Watusi ancestry and dietary habits, or between stature and dietary habits, or study half-siblings differing in Watusi ancestry but reared together in the same family, where the same dietary conditions would exist for both children. Under these conditions, a genetic hypothesis would predict that the half-sib with the more Watusi ancestry would be the taller, on the average. The only remaining source of contamination would be a dietary difference resulting indirectly from genetic differences in appearance (say, facial features) having nothing to do with stature, which might cause the parents or others to treat the more Watusi-looking child more like a Watusi, so that occasionally he would get Watusi food while his less Watusi-looking half-sib would not. But there is a way to control for this, too. Since there could be considerably less than perfect correlation between facial features and percent of Watusi ancestry, we will be able to find some half-sibling pairs in which the least Watusi-looking child actually has the most Watusi ancestry. If in these cases the amount of Watusi ancestry is positively correlated with height, the environmental hypothesis can be rejected.

What if family genealogies are not known? Are we then at a total loss? No, not if there are certain genetic characters, such as blood groups, which have markedly different frequencies in the Watusi and Pygmy population, since the genes for these characters (and the socially invisible characters, like blood groups) are the best for our purposes to determine probabilistically the relative amounts of Watusi and Pygmy genetic admixture of our subjects. Optimal weights for the presence or absence of each characteristic can be summed in a multiple regression equation (or a discriminant function analysis) for rank ordering individuals in terms of percentage of Watusi admixture. As a simple example, say we use four hypothetical blood groups – U and V, both of which are found exclusively in all pure Watusi, and Y and Z, both of which are found exclusively in all pure Pygmies. Given this information, we can assign children in our villages in which some intermarriage has taken place to one of three categories: (*i*) full Watusi (UV), (*ii*) mixed (UY, UZ, VY, VZ), and (*iii*) full Pygmies (YZ). The more different distinguishing blood groups that are used, the more categories of the 'mixed' group are possible.[5] We could then compare the mean stature in the various categories, and if they are found to differ significantly, an exclusively environmental hypothesis would be rejected.

Thus one can see how difficult it would be to prove in any definitive scientific sense something that is so easy to accept in terms of its high commonsense plausibility – that the greater stature of Watusi than of Pygmies is not entirely due to an environmental difference. Proving genetic intelligence differences between subpopulations is even more difficult – first, because the differences are much smaller (the average Negro-white difference, for example, amounts to less than one-fifth of the total range [i.e., $\pm 3\sigma$] of intelligence within the white population); second, because a much greater variety of environmental factors can be hypothesized to affect behavioral traits than physical traits and therefore more controls are necessary; and third, because the measurement of intelligence is a much less obviously simple and unambiguous procedure than the measurement of height.

Thoday (1969, p. 13) has suggested a much simpler technique which can establish a genetic difference between two populations but cannot prove the *direction* of the genetic difference, since environmental factors could completely obscure or even reverse the difference in the phenotypes of the two populations. If two populations differ genetically for a given trait, the genetic variance of the progeny of hybrids will be greater than the mean genetic variances within the parent populations.[6] We could estimate genetic variance by comparing the within twin-pair variance of identical twins with that of fraternal twins, i.e., $V_F - V_I$. If the value $V_F - V_I$ is greater in the hybrids than the average of the corresponding values in the two parent populations, this is evidence that the populations are genetically different in the trait in question.[7] The same analysis could be performed using full sibs (*FS*) and half-sibs (*HS*) to obtain $V_{HS} - V_{FS}$ in the hybrid and parent populations, although larger numbers of *FS* and *HS* pairs than of twin pairs would be needed to achieve the same degree of statistical precision, since the difference between *FS* and *HS* in genetic variance is only about half the difference between identical and fraternal twins. Using both kinds of data (twins and siblings) would, of course, make for a stronger test of the genetic hypothesis than either set of data alone.

The main point to be emphasized from all this is that determination of within-group heritability cannot formally establish a genetic difference between groups. But the higher the within-group heritability, the greater is the *plausibility*, or the *a priori* probability, that genetic differences exist between the groups. Plausibility is a subjective judgment of *likelihood*. If we examined a large number of traits for heritability within two groups and could establish with certainty whether there were or were not genetic group differences for each of these traits, we would find that the higher the within-groups heritability, the higher would be the probability of a genetic between-groups difference. But this is a probabilistic, not a necessary, relationship. A between-group genetic difference produced by selection in opposite directions in the two groups *could* be accompanied by lowered within-group heritabilities. But the opposite relationship is more likely. It is much like the probabilistic but not necessary relationship between the number of years since a person's birth and whether or not he is living or dead. If, in a city's birth register, we look up a particular person, John Doe, and know only his birthdate, we can consult a life insurance company's actuarial tables and determine the probability of living to the age of John Doe. The probability of living to John Doe's age will be some value *between* 0 and 1. But no actuarial probability tables can help us in establishing that John Doe is in fact living or dead. The more years that have elapsed since his date of birth, the greater is the likelihood that we will be right if we assume (i.e., hypothesize) that John Doe is dead. We could always be wrong, but the likelihood of this decreases the greater the time elapsed since the birth of John Doe. And so it is with the likelihood of there being a genetic difference *between* subpopulations; the greater the heritability of a trait within groups, the greater is the likelihood that between-group differences in the trait involve genetic factors. But *proof* of the genetic hypothesis for any particular trait depends upon other evidence, just as proof that a particular John Doe is alive cannot be *proved* by the actuarial tables. But if John Doe was born in 1870, how many of us would want to place our bet on the hypothesis that he is alive today? Of essentially the same nature is our acceptance of the Watusi-Pygmy difference as genetic without formal proof.

The same thing holds true, though to a lesser degree of likelihood, in the case of intelligence differences between social classes and racial groups. This valid limitation of generalizing heritability studies within populations to differences between populations is vigorously and correctly insisted upon by some writers (who, however, usually fail to point out the increasing likelihood relationship) while at the same time they show no hesitancy whatever about generalizing environmental sources of variance from one population to another. Hirsch (1970), for example, cites a study[8] of mid-Eastern Jewish children in Israel brought up in a kibbutz who had IQs 30 points higher than similar children brought up in individual homes. Hirsch concludes: 'There is no basis for expecting different overall results for any population in our species' (Hirsch, 1970, p. 101). How does this differ from generalizing the heritability of intelligence from, say, Cyril Burt's

English samples to any other population in our species? If a statement about genetic variance (h^2) cannot be generalized across racial groups, how can Hirsch justify generalizing a statement about the effects on IQ of environmental variance, which is the complement of heritability, i.e., $1 - h^2$? If we cannot answer the question of the magnitude of the genetic component of social class or race difference in mean IQ, equally we cannot answer the question of the magnitude of the environmental component in these differences, for the two questions are in fact the same.

Theoretically it is quite erroneous to say there is no relationship whatsoever between heritability *within* groups and heritability *between* group means. Jay Lush, a pioneer in quantitative genetics, has shown the formal relationship between these two heritabilities (Lush, 1968, p. 312), and it has been recently introduced into the discussion of racial differences by another geneticist, John C. DeFries (in press). This formulation of the relationship between heritability *between* group means (h_B^2) and heritability *within* groups (h_W^2) is as follows:

$$h_B^2 \simeq h_W^2 \frac{(1-r)\rho}{(1-\rho)r}$$

where

h_B^2 is the heritability *between* group means;

h_W^2 is the average heritability *within* groups;

r is the intraclass correlation among *phenotypes* within groups (or the square of the point biserial correlation between the quantized racial dichotomy and the trait measurement);

ρ is the intraclass correlation among *genotypes* within groups, i.e., the within-group genetic correlation for the trait in question.

Since we do not know ρ, the formula is not presently of practical use in determining the heritability of mean group differences. But it does show that if for a given trait the genetic correlation among persons within groups is greater than zero, the between-group heritability is a monotomically increasing function of within-groups heritability. This is illustrated in Figure 5.1, which shows between-groups heritability as a function of within-groups heritability for various values of the within-group genetic correlation when the mean phenotypic difference between the two groups involved is one standard deviation.

Environmental variables hypothesized to account for some of the between-groups difference are most unamenable to empirical evaluation if they have little or no variance *within* at least one of the groups and preferably both. When there is no within-group variance in some factor, it is impossible to demonstrate a correlation between that factor and IQ. If, for example, we hypothesize that all Negroes experience a feeling of 'alienation' which depresses

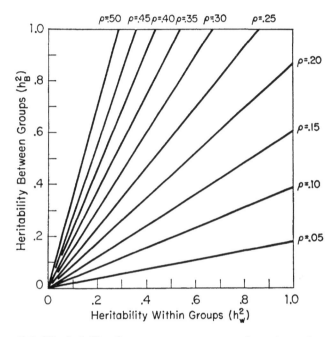

Figure 5.1 Heritability between groups as a function of average heritability within groups for different values of within-group genetic correlation (ρ) for two populations which differ pheno-typically by one standard deviation.

the IQ, we must show that 'alienation' is, in fact, correlated with IQ. Unless variance in 'alienation' can be measured in some way, there is no way of showing its correlation with IQ. If there is variance, a correlation coefficient significantly greater than zero will establish a relationship, but not necessarily a causal one. Clearly the most potentially fruitful environmental hypotheses we can investigate are those involving environmental factors which have the highest correlations with IQ (or other measures of mental abilities) *within* population groups. If a *causal* connection between the environmental factor and IQ can be established, so much the

F

better. We already know with a high degree of certainty that genetic factors have a causal relationship to IQ and that in the white populations in which the heritability of IQ has been studied the correlation between IQ and genotypes is of the order of 0·80 to 0·90 (i.e., the square root of the heritability). No combination of environmental factors in these populations, consequently, correlates with IQ much more than about $\sqrt{1-h^2} \simeq 0·50$. If it is agreed that a rational research strategy in terms of what we already know is to investigate the largest sources of variance first, then a genetic hypothesis of subpopulation differences would seem to have the most obvious priority.

NOTES

1. According to the author (Willis Clark) of the Los Angeles study cited by Klineberg, this mean of 105 is in error – it is actually 95.
2. For an excellent detailed discussion of the concept of race from the standpoint of population genetics, see Laughlin (1966).
3. The term 'overlap' as it is used in comparing the score distributions of two groups is frequently misunderstood. It is best referred to as *median overlap*. It is a useful index of the difference between two groups and it has the advantage of being unaffected by the shape of the distribution or the scale properties of the measurements so long as they are at least an ordinal scale. It tells us the percentage of individuals in the lower group whose scores exceed the median score of the higher group. If the medians of the groups do not differ, the overlap is 50 percent.

   There is another satisfactory measure of overlap originally proposed by Tilton and explicated by Elster and Dunnette (1971). This overlap measure (O) is defined as the percentage of persons in the lower group whose scores may be matched by persons in the higher group or vice versa (assuming equal numbers in both groups). The values of O for mean differences (in standard deviation units) between groups have been tabled by Elster and Dunnette (1971, p. 687). In terms of this O statistic, the Negro-white percentage of overlap in the Stanford-Binet IQ distribution of Kennedy, Van De Reit, and White (1963) is 47 percent (see Figure 8.2, p. 212).
4. I am using this Pygmy-Watusi comparison only analogically as an intuitively understandable example and do not intend the analogy to hold at every point that is non-essential to this use of it. Nor is it

intended necessarily to give a completely accurate account of Pygmy-Watusi differences. An expert in genetical anthropology comments:

> The Pygmies are known to be genetically similar to the peoples in the area in which they live. That is, in skin pigmentation, hair structure, blood types, and other non-stature traits they are very much the same as their taller neighbors. The secondary morphological features (jaw type, etc.) seem to follow from the general aberration of growth pattern. The Pygmy example provides a partially acceptable analogy. However, we don't know of 'cultural' factors relating to height and we surely do for IQ; Pygmies seem to produce Pygmies wherever they are; and we don't know of any environmental factors which would depress height to such an extent. On the whole it seems reasonable to adopt a genetic hypothesis for the Pygmies. You must agree that it is 'more likely' than the comparable genetic hypothesis for white-Negro IQ differences. The reasoning is the same but the likelihood is different.

5. In practice this method unfortunately is not as simple as it may appear. The method is weak to the degree that one does not have separate lines or groups each having its own average percentages of genes from one parental population and which differ considerably from group to group. For example, if one took a population produced by crossing F_1 individuals *inter se*, the percentage of Watusi genes would have only very little correlation with the blood group genes U, V, Y, and Z in our hypothetical example. The more generations the mixed group is from the F_1, the lower would be the correlation between percentage of Watusi genes and the Watusi blood groups; most of this attenuated correlation between genes would be due to linkage.

6. 'Parent population' in this case means simply the populations from which the parents of the hybrids originated; it does not imply that the variances must be determined for the actual parents of the hybrids. The variance estimates in the 'parent populations' are best obtained on samples most resembling the hybrid sample in age and other background characteristics. Hybrids, in this usage, are for the most part later than the F_1 generation.

7. This test is more sensitive (i.e., there would be a larger difference between $\bar{V}_F$ and $\bar{V}_I$ in the hybrids) if the observed difference between the races were due to only a few genes. If the same observed difference were in fact due to many genes each with a small effect, the increase in variance (i.e., the greater $\bar{V}_F$-$\bar{V}_I$ in the hybrids) would be relatively small and hence the test would be statistically less sensitive.

8. This Israeli kibbutz study is frequently referred to in conferences and writings by persons who wish to cite evidence of the powerful effects of social environmental effects on IQ. The reference given by Hirsch and others is to a letter to the editor of the *Harvard Educational Review* by Benjamin Bloom (1969). My attempt to evaluate the study mentioned by Bloom, however, led to naught. A letter from Bloom referred me to Dr Moshe Smilansky of Israel, the author of the original study. A letter from Dr Smilansky informs me that the study had not been completed, the data were not analyzed, and there was as yet no written report of the study that I could obtain. Consequently, it cannot be evaluated by me or anyone else at this time. Such anecdotal reports, though they may be true to the facts, are hardly admissible as scientific evidence, and unless explicitly designated as merely anecdotal are obviously unwarranted in articles or letters published in scholarly journals.

6 Social class differences in intelligence

Intelligence differences between social classes (*within* racial groups) are the one type of subpopulation difference in which a substantial genetic component is really no longer in dispute among geneticists, psychologists, and sociologists who have studied the research evidence on this topic.[1]

Social class or socioeconomic status (SES) today is largely a matter of educational and occupational status. The substantial correlation, averaging between 0·40 and 0·60 in various studies, between indices of SES and phenotypic intelligence is one of the most consistent and firmly established findings in psychological research, and it holds true in every modern industrial society in which it has been studied. When a population is stratified into four or more SES levels, mean IQ differences of more than one standard deviation, at times as large as two *SD*s, are generally found between the extreme groups. Intelligence variation *within* social class categories is great, especially when a few broad categories are considered. The within-class variation among the offspring of the parents on whom the SES classification is based is, of course, still greater. Practically the entire range of abilities is found within each stratum, although the median overlap between the lowest and highest may be exceedingly small. The incidences of mental retardation and of intellectual giftedness will differ by a factor greater than six in groups whose means are separated by one *SD* or more.

In any society which provides more or less equal educational opportunities and a high degree of social mobility, and in which social stratification is based largely on education, occupation, and income, the abler members of the society will tend to move upwards and the less able gravitate downwards in the SES hierarchy. In so doing, they of course take their genes for intelligence with them. The high degree of assortative mating for intelligence (correlations between spouses ranging from 0·40 to 0·60 in most studies) increases the segregation of genes for mental ability and helps to maintain the substantial correlation between SES and intelligence. Thus, social classes are breeding populations differing in gene frequencies, especially for genetic factors related to ability and very likely for the genetic component of those personality traits which favor the development, educability, and practical mobilization of the individual's intellectual potential. But there is considerable mobility between social classes which works against their becoming castes. In fact, if social classes rigidified into castes at some period in history, genetic intelligence differences between them would most likely be reduced, since all of the IQ variability arising within classes in each generation would remain as within-class variance. A high degree of social mobility correlated with ability, on the other hand, in each generation 'converts' a substantial proportion of the within-class variance to *between*-class variance. Thus, classes separated by more than two or three steps in the SES hierarchy can in time undergo wide separation in the distributions of genetic factors related to ability. This trend increases the closer we approach equality of educational and occupational opportunity and the more that SES mobility reflects ability factors rather than inequalities in opportunity.

Burt (1959; see also 1943 and 1961b) has shown the distributions in England of sons according to their own and their father's social class, when SES is grouped into three broad categories, as follows:

Father's Status	Son's Adult Status			
	I	II	III	Total
I (High)	51·7	34·5	13·8	100·0
II (Middle)	23·3	46·9	29·8	100·0
III (Low)	13·7	36·9	49·4	100·0

These figures show, for example, that of sons who had fathers in class I, 51·7 percent remained in the class in which they were born, while the rest moved to a lower class. A study by Young and Gibson (1965) showed that when siblings in the same family changed their social status as adults, it was the more intelligent who moved up and the less intelligent who moved down the SES scale. Since we know that the largest part of the IQ difference between siblings is due to genetic factors, it follows that social mobility must lead to some segregation of the gene pool for abilities. This has been shown most strikingly in a recent study by Waller (1971b), who found that the greater the difference in IQ test score between father and son (both tested at high school age), the greater is the probability that the son will be socially mobile, for both upward and downward social mobility. The correlation between father-son IQ difference and father-son difference on a composite index of SES is +0·29±0·08. When the two most extreme classes (I and V) of fathers were excluded, the correlation based on classes II, III, and IV is +0·37±0·07. The correlation between high school IQ and adult SES is +0·69 for the fathers and +0·57 for the sons. It has been noted in several studies that this correlation increases gradually with age, as persons approach their own highest levels of occupational attainment.

Using fruit flies (*Drosophila melanogaster*), Thoday and Gibson (1970) have demonstrated experimentally how genetic differences can arise between classes or groups even in a phenotypic characteristic largely controlled by environmental factors and with relatively low but significant heritability in the total population ($h^2 = 0·25$). The continuous phenotypic character chosen for study was the number of sternopleural bristles on the fly; more bristles develop on flies raised at lower temperatures. Flies were divided into two environments differing in temperature – 20°C *v.* 25°C. In each generation the virgin flies from both environments are pooled; those with the larger number of bristles are put into the 20°C environment. Another generation of flies is produced and the same procedure is repeated. In the early generations the temperature (an environmental effect) is by far the chief determinant of bristle number, and the selection was such that overall genetic and environmental effects were operating in the same direction. Thus, flies with more bristles, for whatever combination or interaction of genetic and environmental effects, were segregated in each generation from those flies with fewer bristles. The amount of mobility from 20°C to 25°C in each generation was 20 to 30 percent of the total fly population. After nine generations, all progeny were grown under uniform environmental conditions, permitting an experimental determination of the heritability of the characteristic. It was found that after nine generations the *within*-groups heritability had become 0·13 and the *between*-groups heritability had become 0·42. The overall heritability for the total population (i.e., between-groups + within-groups) of the ninth generation was not significantly different from that of the first generation ($h_1^2 = 0·25$ v. $h_9^2 = 0·30$). But in the ninth generation genetic factors accounted for more of the difference *between* groups than for individual differences *within* groups. The authors concluded:

> Inter-group mobility dependent upon a variable does lead to genetic differences between groups even under conditions where there are strong environmental differences between groups. In fact, in the particular conditions of this experiment the genetic and environmental differences between groups are not of very different importance. On the other hand, despite the environmental difference, much of the genetic variation has sorted out *between* groups at the expense of within-group variance.

The human situation is much more complex than that in our experiment. For example, there is intra- as well as interclass social heredity in the human situation, whereas in our experiment the parent-offspring environmental correlation is entirely between groups; the correlation between human social mobility and any particular variable is incomplete, whereas we have tried to make it complete in our experiment; and the environmental difference between human classes is complex and doubtless very heterogeneous, whereas in our experiment we have made the controlled environmental difference between groups simple and have made it correlated completely with groups. Further, we stress that no importance should be attached to the actual heritabilities or components of variance obtained in our experiment, for they would have differed had we used a smaller or greater temperature difference, a base stock with different initial heritability, or one showing genotype-environment interaction with respect to temperature. It is therefore obvious that extrapolation from our experiment, or indeed from any other animal experiment, must be made only with extreme caution.

Nevertheless, we do feel that our experiment is relevant to the human situation inasmuch as it strengthens the expectation that social mobility related to a heritable variable will give rise to some genetic difference between class means despite strong parent-offspring environmental correlation. We therefore believe that our experimental results support those who hold the view that neither cultural nor genetic approaches alone are likely to lead to adequate explanations of social class phenomena. (Thoday & Gibson, 1970, p. 992)

If the environmentalist hypothesis that there is no genetic component to social class intelligence differences were true, it would mean that all the factors involved in social mobility, educational attainments, and the selection of persons into various occupations have managed scrupulously to screen out all variance associated with genetic factors among individuals in various occupational and social strata. The probability that the selection processes have led to there being only environmental variance in intelligence among various socioeconomic groups and occupations – a result that could probably not be accomplished even by making an explicit effort toward this goal – is so unlikely that the argument amounts to a *reductio ad absurdum*. If individual differences in intelligence are due largely to genetic factors, then it is virtually impossible that the average intelligence differences between social classes (defined by educational and occupational criteria) do not include a genetic component.

The statistical argument goes as follows: The correlation between phenotypes (the measurable characteristic) and genotypes (the genetic basis of the phenotype) is the square root of the heritability, or h. An average estimate of h for intelligence in European and North American Caucasian populations is 0·90. An estimate of the average correlation between occupational status and IQ is 0·50. A purely environmentalist position says that the correlation between IQ and occupation (or SES) is due entirely to the environmental component of IQ variance. In other words, this hypothesis requires that the correlation between genotypes and SES be zero. So we have correlations between three sets of variables: (*a*) between phenotype and genotype, $r_{pg} = 0·90$; (*b*) between phenotype and

F*

status, $r_{ps} = 0.50$; and (c) the hypothesized correlation between genotype and status, $r_{gs} = 0$. The first two correlations (r_{pg} and r_{ps}) are determined empirically and are here represented by the average values reported in the literature. The third correlation (r_{gs}) is hypothesized to be zero by those who believe genetic factors may play a part in *individual* differences but not in SES *group* differences. The question then becomes: is this set of correlations possible? The first two correlations we know are possible because they are empirically obtained values. The only correlation seriously in question is the hypothesized $r_{gs} = 0$. Now we know that mathematically the true correlations among a set of three variables, 1, 2, 3, must meet the following requirement:[2]

$$r_{12}^2 + r_{13}^2 + r_{23}^2 - 2r_{12}r_{13}r_{23} < 1$$

The fact is that when the values of $r_{pg} = 0.90$, $r_{ps} = 0.50$ and $r_{gs} = 0$ are inserted into the above formula, it yields a value greater than 1.00. This means that r_{gs} must in fact be greater than zero.

Another, more intuitive way of stating this problem is as follows: if only the environmental component (i.e., $1-h^2$) determined IQ differences between status groups, then the h^2 component of IQs would be regarded as random variation with respect to SES. Thus, in correlating IQ with SES, the IQ test in effect would be like a test with a reliability of $1-0.80 = 0.20$. Therefore, the theoretical maximum correlation of IQ with SES would be close to $\sqrt{0.20} = 0.45$. This value is slightly below but still very close to the average value of obtained correlations between IQ and SES. So if we admit no genetic component in SES IQ differences, we are logically forced to conclude that persons have been fitted to their SES (meaning largely educational and occupational attainments) almost *perfectly* according to their environmental advantages and dis-advantages. In other words, it would have to be concluded that persons' innate abilities, talents, and proclivities play no part in educational and occupational selection and placement. This seems a most untenable conclusion. The only way we can logically reject the alternative conclusion – that there are average genetic intelligence differences among SES groups – is to reject the evidence on the heritability of individual differences in intelligence. But this evidence is among the most consistent and firmly established research findings in the fields of psychology and genetics.

NOTES

1. For more comprehensive reviews of SES and intelligence the reader is referred to Tyler (1965, Ch. 12), Eckland (1967), and Gottesman (1968).
2. This requirement, known as the 'consistency relation' among correlations, is explicated by Walker and Lev (1953, pp. 344-5).

7 *Race differences in intelligence*

If we are able to draw strong conclusions concerning genetic factors involved in social class intelligence differences, why are we any less able to do so in comparing racial groups? In terms of genetic criteria, social classes and racial groups differ only in degree – both are breeding populations which differ in gene frequencies for various characteristics. The essential difference that concerns us is in the factors that influence social mobility. The main factor in upward mobility *within* racial groups is ability of one kind or another, including intelligence. Thus mobility and assortative mating based to some extent on ability make for SES stratification within racial groups and a corresponding, though imperfect, segregation of those genetic factors associated with mobility in the SES hierarchy. This movement is vertical *within* racial groups, but does not necessarily cut across racial boundaries. Thus, a certain SES status within the framework of one racial group cannot necessarily be directly equated with the corresponding status within a different racial group. As Eckland (1967, p. 191) has put it:

Both social classes and races *can* be treated as Mendelian populations. On the other hand, when describing . . . the selecting and sorting mechanisms that increase the between-group variance in intelligence, whites and Negroes cannot be thought of as being joined in this selection process. For all practical purposes, the fact persists that the American Negro, owing to discriminatory practices, is part of an adjacent but clearly separate structure which makes any comparisons of

phenotypic traits between Negroes and whites especially tenuous, except for skin color. (This is not true of social classes
within either structure.)

Differences in gene frequencies among SES groups, furthermore,
are more or less directly attributable to the selecting and sorting
mechanisms involved in social mobility. The much larger variety
of genetic differences among racial groups, on the other hand, has
much more obscure origins tracing back through the history of the
race for hundreds or thousands of generations and has involved a
host of selective factors other than those involved in social mobility
since the industrial revolution. Genetically selective factors, such
as differences in climatic and social adaptation, may or may not
involve genes which are relevant to present-day social mobility.
Yet it seems more likely than not that some of the cultural adapta-
tions in the past history of a racial group would have genetically
selective effects which could make for racial differences, on the
average, in educability and types of occupational performance.
Spuhler and Lindzey (1967, p. 412) have noted

> . . . the enormous discrepancies between races in the efficiency
> with which culture is transmitted (for example, the difference
> between literate and nonliterate societies). Some of these
> differences are closely associated with race differences, have
> existed for many thousands of years, and presumably have been
> accompanied by very different selection pressures in regard to
> characters potentially relevant to culture transmission, such as
> 'intelligence'.

The gene pools of racial groups are relatively much more isolated
than is the case for social classes. And assortative mating is based
on skin color and other physical racial characteristics. To the
extent that these characteristics enter into occupational and social
mobility, genetic differences in ability factors, which have very
imperfect correlations with the physically distinguishing characteristics, will have a lesser tendency to become selectively stratified
along SES lines. Thus, relatively unadulterated ability and other
behavioral traits will be the preponderant determinants of mobility
within the white population. But in the history of the Negro
population in America, those ability and personality factors
normally making for upward SES mobility have been markedly

attenuated by intrinsically irrelevant racial characteristics such as skin color. These irrelevant characteristics may operate negatively or positively (i.e., as hindrances or advantages in upward socio-economic mobility) to weaken the correlation between ability and SES. If there were no racial discrimination of any kind, SES differences would be determined equally by ability in all racial groups. SES differences among races would then be merely an incidental correlate of ability differences among racial groups. Since this has surely not been the case, we can place much less confidence in SES as an index of genetic ability differences *between* racial groups than *within* groups. And we can also place less confidence in the meaning of SES differences *within* those racial groups for whom variations in irrelevant physical characteristics such as skin color may also play a part in social mobility. As all forms of racial discrimination diminish, we can expect SES increasingly to reflect the same ability and personality traits *between* as well as *within* racial groups. It has been pointed out by Duncan (1969) that in 1964,

> . . . the earnings of Negro men aged 25 to 34 were about 55 percent as great as those of white men of the same age. The dollar gap amounted to some $3,000. Eighteen percent of this gap could be attributed to the disadvantageous social origins of Negro men, indexed by the educational and occupational levels of the heads of families in which they grew up. An additional 3 percent was due to the racial differential in size of families of orientation. Some 22 percent of the gap not already accounted for arose from differences in the realized mental abilities of white and Negro children, as revealed in standard tests. Apart from differences in family size and socioeconomic level, and apart from differences in mental test scores, length of schooling accounted for 2 percent of the income differential. Another 12 percent turned on the differences between white and Negro men in the occupations followed, excluding factors of education, mental ability, number of siblings, and social origins. Altogether, the calculation accounts for some four-sevenths of the income gap. The remaining three-sevenths (43 percent) is due to the fact that Negro men in the same kinds of occupations, with the same amount of schooling, with equal mental ability, having come from families of the same size and socioeconomic position,

had annual earnings only three-quarters as high as those of white men with the stated average characteristics of the Negro men.

TWIN DIFFERENCES AND RACE DIFFERENCES

Social scientists who are most critical and disapproving of any suggestion of the possibility that genetic factors are implicated in racial differences in intelligence apparently believe there is an important argument in their favor to be gleaned from comparisons of identical twin differences and race differences in IQ. For example, in a widely published statement by the Council of the Society for the Psychological Study of Social Issues (1969)[1] we read: 'In an examination of Jensen's [1969a] data, we find that observed racial differences in intelligence can be attributed to environmental factors. Thus, identical twins reared in different environments can show differences in intelligence test scores which are fully comparable to the differences found between racial groups.' This argument has been emphasized and elaborated upon by a number of psychologists (e.g., Gottesman, 1968, p. 28; Deutsch, 1969, p. 549; Kagan, 1969, p. 275; Burgess & Jahoda, 1970). Because twin differences in IQ have thus been held up as one of the major arguments against the hypothesis of genetic differences between racial groups, we must carry this analysis through to its logical conclusion.

Two major criticisms may be made of the argument as it has been presented by its proponents (viz., all of those cited above). First, they pick and choose among the twin differences that they wish to consider. In not one of the comparisons has the total available evidence been examined. Instead, selected cases of the most extreme twin differences on record are compared with the average Negro-white difference in IQ. Second, it is never noted that measurement error constitutes part of the average twin difference but does not enter into the mean difference between population groups. Therefore comparisons are always made between twin differences *including measurement error* and group differences *free* of measurement error.[2] Let us remedy these two faults and see what conclusions can validly follow from a comparison of twin differences with race differences.

Only monozygotic (MZ) twins are of interest to us here, since they have identical genotypes and any difference between them must be due entirely to non-genetic factors. Moreover, since our interest here is in the effects of environmental differences on the IQs of genetically identical persons, we shall look only at MZ twins who have been separated early in life and have been reared apart. MZ twins reared apart show larger IQ differences than MZ twins reared together. Most of the MZ twins reared apart who have been reported in the world literature on twins and on whom IQs are available are contained in four studies, by Burt (1966), Juel-Nielsen (1965), Newman, Freeman and Holzinger (1937), and Shields (1962). There are 122 twin pairs in all. I have re-analyzed the original data from all these published studies of the IQs of MZ twins reared apart (Jensen, 1970a). The essential statistics are summarized in Table 7.1. The analysis shows that the mean

Table 7.1 Statistics on IQs of MZ twins reared apart (from Jensen, 1970a)

Study	N (Pairs)	Mean IQ	SD	$|\bar{d}|$	$SD_{|d|}$	r_i	r_d
Burt	53	97·7	14·8	5·96	4·44	0·88	0·88
Shields	38	93·0	13·4	6·72	5·80	0·78	0·84
Newman *et al.*	19	95·7	13·0	8·21	6·65	0·67	0·76
Juel-Nielsen	12	106·8	9·0	6·46	3·22	0·68	0·86
Combined	122	96·8	14·2	6·60	5·20	0·82	0·85

Tests: Burt – 'final assessments', a composite score of two or more verbal and non-verbal group and individual intelligence tests scaled to a population mean = 100, $SD = 15$; Shields – composite of the Mill Hill Vocabulary Test and the Domino D-48 (non-verbal reasoning) Test; Newman *et al.* – Stanford-Binet (1916); Juel-Nielsen – Danish adaptation of the Wechsler-Bellevue (Form I).

$|\bar{d}|$ = mean absolute difference between co-twins
r_i = intraclass correlation
r_d = correlation based on the twin differences, i.e.,

$$r_d = 1 - \left(\frac{|\bar{d}|}{|\bar{d}_p|}\right)^2$$

where $|\bar{d}_p|$ = mean absolute difference between all possible paired comparisons in the general population

$$|\bar{d}_p| = \frac{2\sigma}{\sqrt{\pi}} = 1·13\sigma \text{ (Population } \sigma \text{ for IQ is 15)}$$

absolute difference in IQ between twins for the data of all studies combined is 6·60, $SD = 5·20$. The mean differences range from 5·96 to 8·21 in the various studies – differences which are not statistically significant, so that 6·60 is the best available estimate of the mean IQ difference between MZ twins reared apart. But we cannot compare this value directly with any mean difference between racial groups, because the mean absolute difference between twins includes the test's measurement error, while the difference between the means of two groups does *not* include measurement error. Therefore, to make the mean absolute difference between twins comparable to the mean difference between, say, Negroes and whites, we must either remove the measurement error from the twin differences or include it in the racial mean difference. It is more logical to do the former. If the reliability of the IQ tests is assumed to be 0·95 (the upper bound of reliability of the Stanford-Binet) and we correct the mean difference of 6·60 for attenuation by removing measurement error, the 'true-score' absolute difference between the MZ twins is 5·36 IQ points.[3] This, then, is the twin difference which should be compared with the mean Negro-white difference of 15 IQ points. But we should go further and look at the entire distribution of the true-score differences between the members of each MZ twin pair. A so-called 'regressed true score' is the statistically best estimate of an individual's 'true' score on a test, i.e., the estimated score he would have obtained if the test scores were free of measurement error.[4] Figure 7.1 shows the distribution of true-score differences for the 122 MZ twin pairs.[5] It should be noted that of the total of 122 pairs of MZ twins reared apart, only six pairs (5 percent) show true-score differences greater than the mean Negro-white difference of 15 IQ points and only three pairs (2·5 percent) show true-score differences greater than 16 points (18, 20, and 22).

The distribution of twin differences in IQ, it turns out, does not differ significantly from the theoretical χ (chi) distribution. This is convenient, since the χ distribution is, in a sense, one-half of a normal distribution. If we were to graph a frequency distribution of the absolute differences between a very large number of randomly paired values each selected at random from a normal (Gaussian) distribution, the result would approximate a χ distribution. Now, since the only difference between the MZ twin pairs is due to non-genetic or environmental factors, and since the twin differences in IQ closely approximate a χ distribution, we can conclude that the effects of environment on IQ have a normal distribution in this twin sample. Moreover, it is possible to determine the standard deviation (SD) of the distribution of the effects of environmental differences on IQ. The SD is 4·74 IQ points.[6]

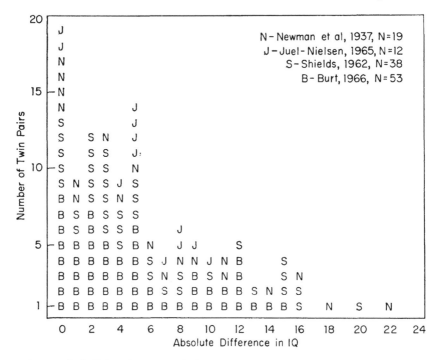

Figure 7.1 Distribution of absolute differences ($|d|$) in regressed true-score IQ between co-twins reared apart. This distribution closely approximates the chi distribution.

Since in a normal distribution six sigmas encompass virtually 100 percent of the population (actually all but 0·27 percent), and since the SD of environmental effects on IQ in the total twin sample is 4·74, it can be said that the total range of environmental effects in a population typified by this twin sample is $6 \times 4\cdot74 = 28\cdot4$ IQ points. This value is referred to by geneticists as the *reaction range* of IQ under natural conditions. This determination of the reaction range is slightly greater than the values conjectured by Gottesman (1968, p. 34) of 24 points, by Bloom (1964, p. 71) of 20 points, and by Cronbach (1969, p. 343) of 'more than 25 points'.

Thus, we now have a *scale* of the effects of environment (in populations similar to the twin samples), with one SD on the scale being equivalent to $4 \cdot 74 \pm 0 \cdot 3$ IQ points. That is to say, two genetically identical individuals who differ by $4 \cdot 74$ IQ points (true-score values) can be said to differ by one SD on the scale of the effects of environment on IQ.[7]

If, then, we hypothesize that the mean difference of 15 IQ points between Negroes and whites is due entirely to non-genetic causes, we must conclude that the two populations differ by $15/4 \cdot 74 = 3 \cdot 2$ SDs on our environmental scale. With a difference this large, only $0 \cdot 07$ percent of the lower group exceeds the median of the higher group.

But here we are considering the *total* non-genetic or environmental effects in the twin samples. The total environmental variance can be analyzed into two parts: (*a*) variance due to environmental effects (i.e., differences) *between* families, and (*b*) variance due to environmental effects *within* families, including unequal prenatal effects on each member of a twin pair. (These environmental differences operating *within* families and making for environmental differences among children reared together are sometimes referred to as *micro-environmental* effects.) The proportions of variance attributable to the *between* and *within* components are estimated from the difference between MZ twins reared together in the same family (MZT) and MZ twins reared apart in different families (MZA). The differences between the mean absolute difference among MZA and MZT give an estimate of the within-families and between-families effects. The difference between MZ twins reared apart is attributable to both the *within*-families and *between*-families environmental effects; the difference between MZ twins reared together is attributable only to the *within*-family effects. Subtracting the difference for MZT from the difference for MZA, therefore, gives us the difference attributable to between-family effects. When this is done on MZT and MZA data where both types of twins are from comparable populations, the *within*-families environmental effect actually turns out to be slightly larger than the *between*-families effect on IQ (Jensen, 1970a, p. 145). But to keep the argument simple, let us assume that the between and within variances are approximately equal. This would mean that half the within-MZA twin variance is due to environmental differences between families. Since the variance of *total* (i.e., between and within) environmental effects on IQ is $(4 \cdot 72)^2$

or 22·5, the *SD* of the *between*-families environmental effects $\sqrt{22\cdot5/2} = 3\cdot35$ IQ points. That is to say, a difference of one *SD* in the effects on IQ of differences among families' environments is equivalent to 3·35 IQ points difference between genetically identical twins.

Environmental theories of Negro-white IQ differences usually assume that the causal environmental factors are predominantly those we normally classify as between-family differences, such as parental occupations, education, income, maternal and child nutrition and health care, cultural advantages in the home, and the like. Social reformers do not seriously propose to eliminate *within*-family sources of variance. When racial differences or social class differences in IQ are attributed to environmental causes, what is usually meant are the kinds of effects that are responsible for *between*-families environmental variance.

So, if one *SD* of between-families environmental difference corresponds to 3·35 IQ points in our twin population, the mean difference of 15 IQ points between Negroes and whites is equivalent to $15/3\cdot35 = 4\cdot48$ *SD*s on the *between*-families environmental scale. Two normal distributions with means more than 4 sigmas apart are almost totally non-overlapping. A strictly environmental hypothesis of the racial IQ differences based on existing twin data, therefore, leads to the conclusion that the distributions of total environmental effects on IQ are only slightly overlapping in the Negro and white populations and the *between*-families environmental effects are practically non-overlapping. These distributions are shown in Figure 7.2. The burden of demonstrating that an average environmental difference of either magnitude exists between the average Negro and the average white of course must rest upon those who insist upon a purely environmental explanation of the racial IQ difference and at the same time claim that twin studies support their thesis. It must be noted that the twin studies used in our analysis are *all* studies of MZ twins reared apart on whom there are IQ data; these separated twins cover a wide range of environmental variation, including all levels of socioeconomic status in the European and North American populations from which the twins were drawn. These data, therefore, strongly suggest that if the Negro-white IQ difference is attributable entirely to non-genetic factors, these must exist in some as yet unmeasured aspect of the environment, for no one has yet identified or measured any set of environmental conditions on which the Negro and white populations differ, on the average, by even half as much as 3 sigmas.[8] A multiple point-biserial correlation (R) between a host of environmental measures and the Negro-white dichotomy (treated as a quantized variable) would have to be

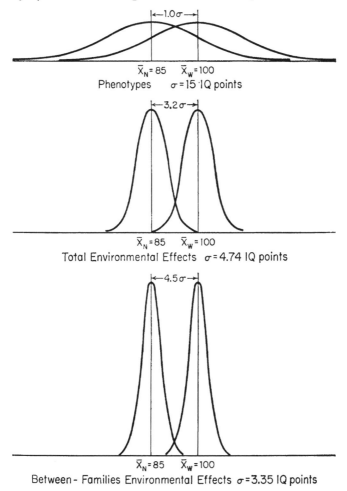

Figure 7.2 The top curves represent two IQ distributions each with $\sigma = 15$ IQ points and the means differing by 15 points or 1σ. The middle set of curves shows the effect of removing all genetic variance, leaving only the total environmental variance; the means then differ by $3 \cdot 2\sigma$ of total environmental effects. The lower curves show the effect of removing both the genetic and the within-families environmental variance, leaving only between-families environmental variance; the means then differ by $4 \cdot 5\sigma$ of between-families environmental effects. The area under all curves is the same.

approximately 0·8 for the sigma difference between the group means on the environmental scale to be as great as 3 sigmas and R would have to be 0·9 for the mean environmental difference to be as great as 4·5 sigmas. Is there any known set of environmental variables which when optimally combined in a multiple regression equation will yield an R with race (i.e., Negro *v.* white) of 0·8 or 0·9? The

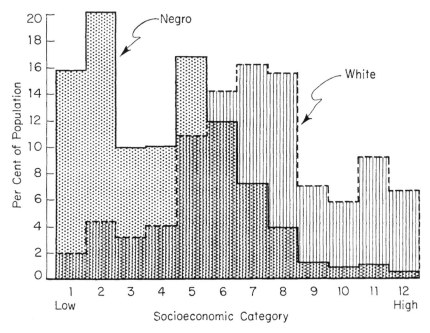

Figure 7.3 Percentages of total U.S. Negro and white populations falling into 12 socioeconomic status (SES) categories. The point-biserial correlation between race (Negro = 0, white = 1) and SES is 0·53. For the Negro distribution the mean = 4·05, SD = 2·40; for the white distribution the mean = 7·23, SD = 2·72. (From U.S. Census of Population, 1960, *Subject Reports: Socioeconomic Status.* Final Report PC (2) −56, p. 50. U.S. Government Printing Office, Washington, D.C.)

production of such an R stands as a challenge to the environmentalists.

In this connection we might look at the distributions of the Negro and white populations of the United States on the 12-category socioeconomic scale used in the 1960 Census, as shown in Figure 7.3. The median overlap between the distributions is about 10 percent, and the point-biserial correlation between the quantized racial dichotomy (Negro $= 0$ $v.$ white $= 1$) and SES (if the Negro and white groups are of equal size) is $+0.53$. (The median SES of the Negroes and whites differs by about one SD.) The usual argument is that SES does not measure the most important environmental variables, which, if included in the SES index, would greatly increase the correlation between the quantized racial variable and the improved SES index. It is most likely, however, that a 12-point SES index pulls along with it many other more subtle environmental factors which are not explicitly measured by the index. Thus many other environmental indices combined along with SES in a multiple regression equation will raise the multiple correlation (R) between 'environment' and race (or between 'environment' and IQ) only slightly.

There are a few environmentally relevant variables on which we can express the (United States) Negro-white difference in terms of standard deviation units, assuming an approximately normal distribution of the variable in both populations. These estimates have been made by Shockley (1969, p. 1432). Based on statistics for all family annual incomes in the U.S. population from $3,000 to $15,000 from 1947 to 1966, the mean family income of Negroes was -0.80 ± 0.15 SDs below that of whites. The SD units by which the Negro mean falls below the white on other variables is: -0.33 for unemployment rate, -0.52 for completing high school, -0.87 for children living with both parents, -1.0 for rate below 'poverty line'. None of these SD differences comes near the 3.2 SDs (for total environmental effects) or 4.48 SDs (for between-families environmental effects) derived from the twin studies as being the environmental difference required to produce a 1 SD mean IQ difference between two genetically identical populations.

Does a variable seemingly as non-psychological as family income pull along with it enough other factors reflecting the qualities of the environment that would affect children's mental development such that taking family income into account as an environmental index would improve the prediction of children's IQs (from the parental IQs) over the prediction that would be derived from a genetic model alone?

Data which may help to answer this question are found in Terman's (1926) monumental study of gifted children. In 1922, over 1,500 children with Stanford-Binet IQs of 140 or above were selected from California schools; their educational and occupational careers were followed into adulthood (Terman & Oden, 1959). The Stanford-Binet IQs of more than 1,500 of the children of the gifted group were obtained. These data, therefore, permit an interesting genetic prediction.

The simplest additive genetic model used by agricultural geneticists for predicting the mean value of some attribute in the offspring of a specially selected parent population is given by Crow (1970, p. 157), as follows:

$$\bar{O} = \bar{M} + h_N^2 \, (\bar{P} - \bar{M}) \qquad (7.1)$$

where

$\bar{O}$ = predicted mean of the offspring
$\bar{M}$ = general population mean
h_N^2 = narrow heritability[9]
$\bar{P}$ = parental mean

The population mean, $\bar{M}$, is 100. The mean IQ of the gifted group (as children) was 152. Terman estimated their spouses' mean Stanford-Binet IQ from his Concept Mastery Test as 125. Thus the parental mean, $\bar{P}$, would be $(152 + 125)/2 = 138\cdot5$. The best available estimate of narrow heritability (h_N^2) for intelligence is given by Jinks and Fulker (1970, pp. 342, 346) as $0\cdot71 \pm 0\cdot01$. Substituting these values in the formula given by Crow, we have

$$\bar{O} = 100 + 0\cdot71 \, (138\cdot5 - 100) = 127\cdot33$$

as the predicted mean IQ of the offspring. We can compare this genetic prediction with the mean Stanford-Binet IQ actually obtained by Terman and Oden (1959, Table 61) on 1,525 offspring of the gifted group. The IQ distribution of the offspring is shown in Figure 7.4, with a mean of 132·7 and *SD* of 16·5.[10] The obtained mean is 5·4 IQ points higher than our predicted value. But the prediction was based on the assumption of no difference between the average environment provided by the gifted parents and average environment in the general population. Therefore, the discrepancy of 5·4 IQ points over the predicted IQ may be viewed as due to the environmental advantages of the offspring of the gifted. This would be a 'between-families' environmental effect, one *SD* of which, according to our MZ twin analysis, is equivalent to 3·35 IQ points. So the offspring of the Terman gifted group could be regarded as having enjoyed environmental advantages $5\cdot4/3\cdot35 = 1\cdot6$ *SD*s above the average environment in the general population. It is interesting, therefore, that the average family income of the gifted is 1·45 SDs above the national average. Using only income as an index of environmental advantage, we would estimate the IQ of the offspring of the gifted as the genetic prediction (IQ = 127·3) plus the environmental advantage (1·45 × 3·35 = 4·9 IQ points) as 132·2, which does not differ significantly

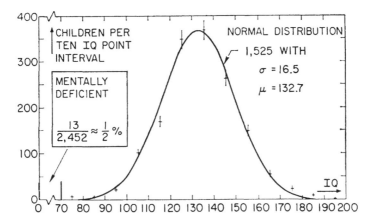

Figure 7.4 Distribution of Stanford-Binet IQs of the offspring of Terman's gifted subjects. A normal curve is superimposed on the actual data indicated by crosses. (Terman and Oden's [1959, Table 61] data were plotted in this figure by W. Shockley, who notes that 'The offspring [of the Terman gifted group] have an accurately normal distribution in the same IQ range in which the parents do not fit the tail of a normal distribution' (personal communication). This point is interesting in that this result is predictable from a polygenic model with a large [e.g. > 20] number of loci and a considerable amount of heterozygosity in the parents. Under these conditions, theoretically the offspring should show a nearly normal distribution despite marked skewness of the distribution of the parental values, and this in fact is what is found in these data.)

from the obtained mean IQ of 132·7. Thus, our model fits the Terman gifted data very well.

By reckoning from the same model, the average Negro income gap of − 0·80 ± 0·15 would account for about 0·80 × 3·35 = 2·7 IQ points (or 18 percent) of the 15 IQ points difference between the racial IQ means. It must be concluded that income differences can account for only a small fraction (less than one-fifth) of the 15 points mean IQ gap between Negroes and whites.

A frequent criticism of basing estimates of environmental variance on the pooled data from studies of MZ twins reared apart is that the distribution of environmental differences in these samples is probably somewhat less than the total range of differences found in the general population. But since we have used the actual *SD* of twin samples in our analysis, we have taken the reduced variability into account, and this criticism therefore is not valid. The valid conclusion is that if one is talking about the kinds and amounts of environmental effects that produce IQ differences between genetically identical twins reared apart, it is highly improbable that the mean Negro-white difference can be explained by such environmental effects. The Negro and white populations of the United States would have to be assumed to differ by 3 to 5 sigmas on the scale of environmental effects which are responsible for the twin differences. As yet, no one has identified any environmental variable or optimally weighted combination of variables which are causally related to IQ and on which Negro and white populations differ by anything like 3 sigmas.

It seems more sensible, however, to base our environmental scale on broader estimates of heritability than just those derived from MZ twins reared apart. Such an estimate can be obtained by using all the kinship correlations reported in the literature, including all twin data. When this was done, an overall h^2 of 0·77 (or 0·81 when corrected for attenuation) was obtained (Jensen, 1969a, p. 51). If we use $h^2 = 0.80$, the distribution of environmental effects on true-score IQs (assuming test reliability = 0·95) will have a standard deviation of $\sqrt{1-0.80 \{(0.95) (15)^2\}} = 6.5$ IQ points, and the total reaction range of environmental effects (from the 'worst' environment in a thousand to the 'best' in a thousand) would be $6 \times 6.5 = 39$ IQ points. Using the environmental $SD = 6.5$, a mean difference of 15 points between Negroes and whites, explained environmentally, would therefore require a difference of 2·3 *SD*s on this environmental scale. The *SD* of *between-families* environmental effects would be about 4·6 IQ points, and on this scale the Negro and white populations would have to differ by 3·3 *SD*s if we wish to entertain the hypothesis that all of the 15 IQ points difference is due to differences between family environments. Thus, even using a larger environmental component than that estimated from MZ twins reared apart, the differences between Negro and white means required by the environmental hypothesis are still much larger than any actual environmental differences reported between Negro and white populations.[11]

GENOTYPE × ENVIRONMENT INTERACTION

The genotype × environment $(G \times E)$ interaction often figures prominently in discussions of the genetics of race differences in intelligence (e.g., Gottesman, 1968, pp. 30-2; Bodmer & Cavalli-Sforza, 1970, p. 29). The $G \times E$ interaction means either one, or both, of two things: (*a*) that what constitutes a good environment for one genotype may constitute a bad environment for some other genotype in terms of the development of the phenotype; and (*b*) that environmental advantages (or disadvantages), though acting in the same phenotypic direction for all genotypes, may have unequal phenotypic effects on different genotypes. For example, a good environment may result in great phenotypic similarity for genotypes A and B, while a poor environment may lower A's phenotype only slightly but may drastically push down B's phenotype. The possibility of $G \times E$ interaction for a given trait thus holds out the hope that if only the optimal environment were found, or genotypes were optimally matched to different environmental conditions, the phenotypes could be equalized on the trait in question despite genotypic differences. All of the examples ever cited of such $G \times E$ interaction are taken from plant and animal breeding experiments and involve a relatively narrow characteristic. The favorite example is the experiment by Cooper and Zubek (1958), who, through selective breeding, established 'dull' and 'bright' strains of rats in maze learning ability and found that when both strains were raised under conditions of sensory deprivation they performed almost equally poorly in maze learning, and when both strains were raised in a sensorily 'enriched' environment they performed almost equally well; only when the groups were raised under normal laboratory conditions (the same as the selectively bred parental generations) did they show large differences in maze learning. In short, the magnitude of the phenotypic differences between the strains varied markedly under different environmental conditions – a perfect example of $G \times E$ interaction.

Such interaction with respect to human intelligence, and

particularly genetic racial differences in intelligence, cannot be ruled out on the basis of present evidence. But it is seldom noted by those who emphasize $G \times E$ interaction that no evidence for it has been turned up in any of the studies of the heritability of human intelligence. It should show up in lower correlations between monozygotic (MZ) twins and between dizygotic (DZ) twins than those predicted from a simple additive model with assortative mating, and possibly with some dominance (which can be distinguished from $G \times E$ interaction by examining the parent-offspring correlations). The correlations obtained between DZ twins (also parent-child and sibling correlations) do not depart sufficiently from a genetic model without $G \times E$ interaction as to give much indication that any such interaction exists for human intelligence, at least in the Caucasian populations that have been sampled.

One of the conceptually neatest methods for detecting one kind of $G \times E$ interaction, first proposed by Jinks and Fulker (1970, pp. 314-15), is applicable to our data on MZ twins reared apart. We can ask: Are different genotypes for intelligence equally affected by environmental advantages (or disadvantages)? In the case of genetically identical twins, any phenotypic difference between them reflects some environmental difference. One twin can be said to be environmentally advantaged and the other disadvantaged, relative to one another. While the phenotypic *difference* between the twins, $| t_1 - t_2 |$, reflects only environmental effects, the average of their phenotypes, $(t_1 + t_2)/2$, reflects their genotypic value (plus the average of their environmental deviations). If this correlation is significantly greater than zero, we can claim a $G \times E$ interaction. A positive correlation would mean that genotypes for high intelligence are more susceptible to the influence of good or poor environments; a negative correlation would mean that genotypes for lower intelligence are more sensitive to the effects of environment. The correlation of IQ differences with IQ averages of the 122 MZ twin pairs is -0.15, which is not significantly different from zero. When measurement error is removed by using regressed true scores instead of the obtained IQs, the correlation falls to -0.04. Thus the twin data reveal no $G \times E$ interaction. This finding is consistent with Jinks and Fulker's (1970) failure to find any evidence for a $G \times E$ interaction in their analysis of a number of studies of the heritability of intelligence.

A THRESHOLD HYPOTHESIS OF ENVIRONMENTAL EFFECTS

Several years ago I proposed the hypothesis that the environment, with respect to mental development, displays 'threshold' effects (Jensen, 1968a, pp. 10-14). What this means is that environmental variations in one part of the total scale of environmental advantages have quantitatively or qualitatively different effects on the development of the phenotype than variations in another part of the scale. Such threshold effects for many characteristics are well known to geneticists (e.g., Falconer, 1960, Ch. 18) and there seemed reason to believe that intelligence might show similar threshold effects. In reviewing the literature reporting large shifts in IQ resulting from environmental changes, it was clear that all instances of large gains in IQ were found in children whose environments had been changed from very poor to average or superior, while no IQ gains of comparable magnitude have been reported for children whose environments have changed from average to superior. This suggests a non-linear (or non-additive) effect of environment on mental development. Going from a typical slum environment to an average middle-class environment would presumably have a larger effect on IQ than going from a middle-class to an upper-class environment. We know that nutrition behaves more or less in this fashion with respect to stature. When the diet is deficient in certain vitamins, minerals and proteins, physical growth is stunted, but when adequate amounts of these foods are provided, growth is normal and further supplements to the diet will produce little effect. If we determined the heritability of stature in a population that included a sizeable percentage of persons whose nutrition had been inadequate for the full realization of their genetic potential for stature, we should find a much lower heritability than in a population in which everyone had adequate nutrition. In other words, the presence of threshold effects, or of a non-linear relationship between environment and phenotype, should result in lower heritability for populations located largely in the below-average part of the environmental scale as compared with populations located largely in the above-average part of the scale. This is illustrated in Figure 7.5. The phenotype/genotype ratio can be thought of as the degree to which the potential for development (genotype) is realized in actual development or performance (phenotype). It is assumed that phenotypic performance cannot exceed genotypic potential. The curves showing the hypothesized relationship between environment and the phenotype/genotype ratio are made to asymptote at some unspecified point below 1·00, since I do not wish to engage in a futile debate over whether persons ever realize their full intellectual potential.[12] It should be understood that the asymptotic values of these curves for indi-

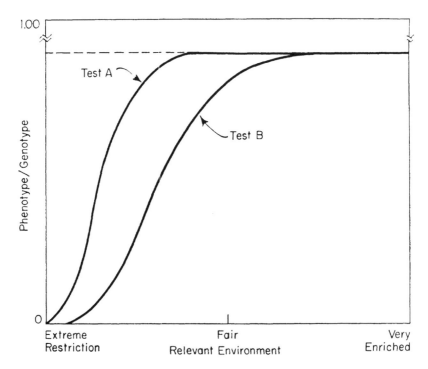

Figure 7.5 Hypothetical curves showing the relationship between the degree to which genetic potential is realized in the phenotype (i.e. actual performance) and the quality of the environment. Test A represents a relatively culture-free test, Test B a more culturally loaded test.

viduals are assumed to be approximately normally distributed in the population. Test A in Figure 7.5 represents a relatively culture-free or culture-fair test; Test B is a more culturally loaded test.

Figure 7.6 depicts an environmental hypothesis of Negro-white IQ difference. The hypothetical frequency distributions of the Negro and white populations are plotted on the same environmental scale as that shown in Figure 7.5. The bulk of the Negro population is shown to be in the range of environment below the threshold of adequacy for full realization of genetic potential, while the bulk of the white population is above the environmental threshold for the full development of genetic potential. The consequence of this hypothetical state of affairs is that the reaction range of IQ should be much higher in the Negro than in the white population, and the heritability of IQ should be lower in the Negro

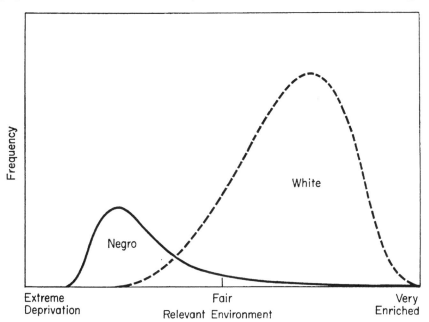

Figure 7.6 Hypothetical frequency distributions of Negro and white populations of the United States with respect to environmental variables relevant to intellectual development. When compared with Figure 7.5, which has the same abscissa, it illustrates the hypothesis that many Negroes may be reared in environmental conditions that do not permit the development of genetic intellectual potential to the same extent as in the white population.

than in the white population. In other words, this hypothesis shows the bulk of the Negro population to be located in that part of the environmental scale that makes the most difference in mental development.

This seems to be a plausible hypothesis. But it has been legitimately criticized. Bereiter (1970, p. 294), for example, points out that there is no strong evidence for the threshold hypothesis and that, at the time it was presented (Jensen, 1968a, 1969a), the only evidence for it was the large IQ gains, amounting to an average of some 30 points, shown by severely deprived orphanage children, at about 18 months of age, when they were put into a more stimulating environment and were eventually reared in good adoptive homes (Skeels & Dye, 1939; Skeels, 1966). Bereiter argues that this magnitude of IQ gains is within the reaction range of IQ, assuming a heritability of 0·80 and equal additivity of environmental effects across the whole range of environments. But a 30-point mean difference in *group means* suggests some individual changes outside the normal reaction range for IQ. In fact, four of the thirteen subjects in Skeels' study showed IQ gains greater than 30 points (Skeels, 1966, Table 1). So perhaps the threshold hypothesis may be needed after all in order to account for these data.

Probably the best evidence for the threshold hypothesis would be the finding of significantly higher heritability in groups that are above average in SES and environmental advantages than in groups of low SES.[13] No one has ever done this systematically. The gifted children in Terman's study came mostly from the higher SES levels and unquestionably had considerably better than average environmental advantages for intellectual development. The mean IQ of their siblings was 123 and the correlation between the IQs of the gifted and their siblings, estimated from the sibling regression, is 0·44, which, when corrected for attenuation, is close to the genetically predicted sibling correlations of 0·5 (with random mating) or 0·6 (with an assortative mating coefficient of 0·5), and does not differ much from sibling correlations reported in the general literature. The gifted group as adults were, on the average, of higher SES than their own parents. Thus the offspring of the gifted probably enjoyed even greater environmental advantages. The narrow heritability of IQ in this group, estimated from the midparent-midchild regression, is 0·85. This is significantly higher than the best estimate of narrow heritability (0·71) given by Jinks and Fulker (1970, p. 342) on the basis of Burt's data, which includes a wide range of SES in the English population. It is also higher than the midparent-midchild correlation (0·69 ± 0·03) found in a largely rural population sample in Vermont in 1920, with environmental advantages presumably much below those provided by the Terman gifted and their spouses (Jones, 1928, p. 69). These heritability findings, then, are consistent with the threshold hypothesis. But the total evidence for the hypothesis must still be regarded as quite ambiguous. A clear finding of an appreciable difference between h^2 in the Negro and white populations, however, would be consistent with the hypothesis depicted in Figures 7·5 and 7·6. It could mean, in effect, that the scale of environmental effects differs for the bulk of the two populations and not simply that the two populations are distributed about different means on the same additive (i.e., equal interval) scale of environments. So now we must examine what meager evidence exists on the estimation of h^2 in Negro populations.

Estimations of h^2 in Negro Populations

Recognizing that the threshold formulation implies a lower heritability of IQ in the Negro population if in fact a substantial proportion of them have been subjected to environmental conditions in that part of the scale with the largest effects on cognitive development, Vandenberg (1970) sought evidence to test this hypothesis, viz., that there is a greater proportion of environmental variance in IQs in a Negro (or any environmentally deprived) population. Vandenberg estimated heritability by comparing MZ and DZ twins. Let us look at the genetic model and its assumptions, which form the basis for this method of estimating heritability.

The total phenotypic variance,[14] V_p, can be partitioned into two main components: variance attributable to differences (both genetic and environmental) *between* families (V_B) and differences (both genetic and environmental) *within* families (V_w). The between-families variance (V_B) can be partitioned into genetic and environmental components: V_{BG} and V_{BE}, respectively.

The model assumes that the total variance is the same for MZ and DZ twins, i.e., $V_{MZ} = V_{DZ}$. The total variance for DZ twins[15] is composed of $V_{DZ} = \frac{1}{2}V_{BG} + \frac{1}{2}V_{WG} + V_{BE} + V_{WE}$. The total variance for MZ twins is composed of: $V_{MZ} = V_{BG} + V_{BE} + V_{WE}$. From the data we can obtain the *between* and *within* variances for DZ and MZ twins. If we subtract the *between*-families DZ variance from the *between*-families MZ variance, we obtain one-half of the *between*-families genetic variance:

$$V_{BMZ} = V_{BG} + V_{BE}$$
$$\underline{V_{BDZ} = \frac{1}{2}V_{BG} + V_{BE}}$$
$$\text{Difference} = \frac{1}{2}V_{BG}$$

G

Doubling $\frac{1}{2}V_{BG}$ gives the total genetic variance V_G, and this value divided by the total phenotypic variance $(V_{MZ} = V_{DZ} = V_P)$ gives the heritability, $h^2 = V_G/V_P$.

If we subtract the *within*-families MZ variance from the *within*-families DZ variance, we again obtain one-half the genetic variance:

$$
\begin{aligned}
V_{WDZ} &= \tfrac{1}{2}V_{WG} + V_{WE} \\
V_{WMZ} &= \phantom{\tfrac{1}{2}V_{WG} + {}} V_{WE} \\
\hline
\text{Difference} &= \tfrac{1}{2}V_{WG}
\end{aligned}
$$

And again, doubling $\frac{1}{2}V_{WG}$ gives the total genetic variance.

Obviously, if there is any *within*-family genetic variance in the trait, V_{WDZ} must be greater than V_{WMZ}. This fact permits a preliminary statistical test to determine if any further analysis is even warranted. If the so-called variance ratio,[16] $F = V_{WDZ}/V_{WMZ}$, is not significantly greater than 1, the data can be said to show no evidence of heritability. (The smaller the number of cases in the sample, the larger must F be in order to attain statistical significance.)

Vandenberg (1970) used this method on 31 MZ and 14 DZ Negro twin pairs and 130 MZ and 70 DZ white twin pairs. All twins were given a battery of twenty cognitive tests covering verbal, reasoning, numerical, spatial, and perceptual abilities. Vandenberg did not carry his analysis beyond computing the variance ratios, V_{WDZ}/V_{WMZ}, and reporting the significance levels of the resulting Fs for each test. The F, of course, only tells us whether there is any statistically significant genetic component in the test; F does not tell us the magnitude of the heritability.[17] Among the twenty tests, only 6 showed F ratios significant beyond the 10 percent level in the Negro group as compared with 13 significant Fs in the white group. But this comparison is misleading because the significance of the F depends upon the sample size, and the white sample is much larger than the Negro. For some tests, the white F, though significant, is smaller than the Negro F. The mean F for all tests is 1·33 (non-significant) for Negroes and 1·68 $(p < 0·01)$ for whites. The corresponding values of Holzinger's H coefficient are 0·25 (Negro) and 0·41 (white). These values do not differ significantly. But it is not very logical in this case to compare the overall F for Negroes with the overall F for whites, combining all tests together. What is actually needed is a statistical test of the significance of the difference between the Negro and white Fs for each test.[18] If they do not differ significantly, there is little support in these data for the hypothesis that the heritability for a given test differs between the Negro and white populations. The largest Negro-white difference in F on any of twenty tests in Vandenberg's study is on the spelling test (Negro $F = 1.58$, n.s., white $F = 2.94$, $p < 0.001$). But the difference between even these most extreme Fs is not significant at the 10 percent level, so of course none of the other differences is significant. Vandenberg's data, therefore, hardly provide statistically reliable support for his conclusion that 'there is good evidence for the thesis that the ratio between hereditary potential and realized ability was generally lower for Negroes than for whites . . .' (Vandenberg, 1970, p. 283). Clearly, the trouble with this study is the small number ($N = 14$) of DZ twin pairs in the Negro group. With so few cases, the sampling error of the variance estimate is simply too large to permit any statistically reliable inference.

There are only three other published heritability studies which have included Negroes. One of these combines the Negro and white MZ and DZ twin samples in arriving at heritability estimates for a variety of tests of spatial ability (Osborne & Gregor, 1966). The results, therefore, do not allow any comparison of Negro and white heritabilities for these traits. The data, furthermore, could not be analyzed separately for the two racial groups, since for both groups combined there are only 33 pairs of MZ and 12 pairs of DZ twins. These samples are much too small to detect significant differences in heritabilities within the range we might expect. The standard error of h^2 with these size samples would be approximately 0.10, so group differences in h^2 smaller than about 0.20 could not be detected as statistically significant.[19]

Another paper based on the same twin samples as those of the previous study estimated heritability for seven tests of simple arithmetic (Osborne, Gregor, & Miele, 1967). The value of h^2 for the composite score of all seven tests is 0.80 ± 0.10; the intraclass correlations for MZ and DZ twins are 0.84 and 0.44, respectively. But again, since there was no separation of Negro and white twin samples, the study tells us nothing about racial differences in h^2. Moreover, the practice of estimating h^2 in mixed samples from two distinctive populations seems indefensible, since the only population to which the result can be generalized is one comprised of the same proportions of the two racial groups. Also, heritability estimates can be biased in one direction or the other depending upon the relative proportions of the two racial groups in the MZ and DZ samples. The *between*-families (or twin pairs) variance will generally be increased relative to *within*-families (pairs) variance when racial groups with widely differing means are combined in heritability analyses.

In a third study, the twin samples were separated by race, and heritabilities were computed separately for Negroes and whites (Osborne & Gregor, 1968). The white sample was composed of 140 MZ and 101 DZ twin pairs; the Negro sample of 32 MZ and 11 DZ pairs. Nine tests of spatial ability were used. Heritabilities for the white sample are in the range generally found for cognitive tests, going from $h^2 = 0.38$ to 0.82, with a mean h^2 of 0.54. In the Negro sample the values of h^2 range from 0.02 to 1.76, with a mean of 0.94. Four of the nine estimates of h^2 are larger than 1.00! This makes the estimates highly suspect, and no doubt the trouble is in the large sampling error of the Negro estimates, based as they are on Ns of 32 MZ and 11 DZ twin pairs. Despite an average h^2 value of 0.94, only two of the nine tests show heritability values significantly greater than zero at the 5 percent level of significance. (All the white h^2 values, however, differ significantly from zero at the 1 percent level.) There is no significant difference between the white and Negro heritabilities, but this study could not have statistically detected quite substantial group differences in heritability even if such differences actually existed. The fact that a statistically significant genetic component of variance shows up on only two of nine tests for Negroes and on all of the tests for whites certainly provides no support for the authors' conclusion that 'environment does not play a more significant role in the development of spatial ability of Negro children than of white children' (p. 736). But neither does this study provide any support for the opposite conclusion. Because of the very few cases in the Negro sample, the study throws no light whatever on Negro-white differences in the heritability of mental abilities.

Even the largest study of IQ heritability in a Negro population is statistically unsatisfactory in terms of sample size (Scarr-Salapatek, 1971a). Since Scarr-Salapatek obtained all her data from public school files, she was not able to determine the twins' zygosity (i.e., whether they are monozygotic or dizygotic). She had to estimate the proportions of MZ and DZ twins in her white and Negro samples from the percentages of like-sex and unlike-sex twin pairs. The MZ and DZ twin correlations, in turn, are based on these estimates (along with the correlations for like and unlike sex pairs) and are not the directly obtained correlations between test scores for MZ and DZ twins. This estimation procedure used by Scarr-Salapatek greatly enlarges the standard errors of the estimated twin correlations and, of course, of the heritability estimates derived therefrom. This serious statistical inadequacy of the study is not emphasized in Scarr-Salapatek's report, which contains no statistical tests of significance of any of her h^2 values, few, if any, of which would have proven sufficiently reliable statistically to permit rejection of the null hypothesis or of one or another of the alternative hypotheses under consideration. For this reason, the present account of Scarr-Salapatek's findings refers only to her particular sample and procedure. The study permits no strong inferences concerning the heritability of IQ in white and Negro *populations*. Unless such studies in the future are done with sufficiently fastidious methodology and large enough samples to permit strong statistical inference with respect to clearly formulated models, the mounting data will serve merely as a kind of Rorschach inkblot into which researchers project their particular biases and discern any interpretation that suits their fancy. Hunches may be gleaned, but hypotheses remain untested.

Scarr-Salapatek searched through the records of a total of 250,258 children from kindergarten to twelfth grade in the Philadelphia schools and found 1,521 twin pairs (493 of opposite sex and 1,028 of same sex). The racial distribution of the twin sample was 36 percent white and 64 percent Negro. Group-administered IQ and scholastic achievement test scores were available. Scarr-Salapatek's heritabilities in the white sample, both for IQ and scholastic achievement, are lower than the median values typically found in other studies of white populations in England and the United States. The heritability for both IQ and achievement is slightly lower in Scarr-Salapatek's Negro sample than in the white, but the white and Negro heritabilities are about the same within social classes. In the Negro and in the white samples heritability increased as a function of social class, but the trend toward lower heritabilities for low SES holds only for the intelligence measures, while the achievement tends to go in the opposite direction. In short, subgroups of whites and Negroes roughly equated for social class had about the same heritabilities, and lower-class subpopulations of both racial groups had significantly lower heritabilities for the aptitude tests. The lower heritability in this group seems to be due principally to greater *within*-pair variance for same-sex twins, which, of course, includes all MZ twins. Scarr-Salapatek's interpretation of this finding is in terms of the threshold hypothesis, viz., that environmental deprivations in the lowest SES group have increased differences between co-twins and decreased variance among unrelated individuals, with a consequent reduction of genetic variance, relative to environmental variance, in test scores. When the lowest SES groups were not included in the analysis, Scarr-Salapatek found similar heritabilities in the Negro and white samples. But despite higher heritabilities of both verbal and non-verbal aptitude in middle-class Negroes than in middle-class whites, Scarr-Salapatek's data show that the Negro scores are distributed around means that are nearly a standard deviation below whites of comparable and lower SES. This is difficult to reconcile with the hypothesis that Scarr-Salapatek seems to favor as an explanation of the mean white-Negro ability difference. Scarr-Salapatek's hypothesis should predict that the heritability of the mental tests would be in general lower in the Negro sample than in the white. Such a finding (which in fact was not found) could be interpreted as consistent with an explanation of the mean Negro-white IQ differences in terms of environmental factors such as cultural deprivation. Scarr-Salapatek writes: 'The lower mean scores of disadvantaged children of both races can be explained in large part by the lower genetic variance in their scores' (p. 1293). She adds: 'If most black children have limited experience with environmental features relevant to the development of scholastic skills, then genetic variation will not be as prominent a source of individual phenotypic variation; nor will other between-family differences such as SES [socioeconomic] level be as important as they are in a white population' (p. 1294).

The data shown in Scarr-Salapatek's Table 3 (p. 1288), however, make this interpretation highly questionable. These data allow comparison of the mean scores on the combined aptitude tests for Negro children whose parents' level of education and income are both *above* the median (of the Negro and white samples combined) with the mean scores of white children whose parents' education and income are both *below* the common median. The lower-status white children still score *higher* than the upper-status Negro children on both the verbal and the non-verbal tests. Although non-verbal tests are generally considered to be less culture-biased than verbal tests, it is the non-verbal tests which in fact show the greater discrepancy in this comparison, with the *lower*-status whites scoring higher than the *upper*-status Negroes. But in this comparison it is the upper-status Negro group that has the *higher* heritability (i.e., greater genetic variance) on both the verbal and non-verbal tests. Thus, the lower heritability which Scarr-Salapatek hypothesizes as being consistent with Negroes' generally poorer performance because of environmental deprivation applies in this particular comparison to the lower-status white group. Yet the lower-status white group out-performs the upper-status Negro group, which has the highest heritability of any of the subgroups in this study (see Table 9, p. 1292).

This finding is more difficult to reconcile with a strictly environmental explanation of the mean racial difference in test scores than with a genetic interpretation which invokes the well-established phenomenon of regression toward the population mean. In another article Scarr-Salapatek (1971b) clearly explicated this relevant genetic prediction, as follows:

> Regression effects can be predicted to differ for blacks and whites if the two races indeed have genetically different population means. If the population mean for blacks is 15 IQ points lower than that of whites, then the offspring of high-IQ black parents should show greater regression (toward a lower population mean) than the off spring of whites of equally high IQ. Similarly, the offspring of low-IQ black parents should show less regression than those of white parents of equally low IQ. (Scarr-Salapatek, 1971b, p. 1226)

In other words, on the average, an offspring genetically is closer to its population mean than are its parents, and by a fairly precise amount. Accordingly, it would be predicted that upper-status Negro children should, on the average, regress *downward* toward the Negro population mean IQ of about 85, while lower-status white children would regress *upward* toward the white population mean of about 100. In the downward and upward regression, the two groups' means could cross each other, the lower-status whites thereby being slightly above the upper-status Negroes. Scarr-Salapatek's data (Table 3) are quite consistent with this prediction. Her finding is not a fluke; the same phenomenon has been found in other large-scale studies (see Chapter 4, pp. 117-19).

Scarr-Salapatek's exceedingly low (and often even zero or negative) heritability values in the lower SES groups (both Negro and white) raises the question of the adequacy of the particular tests and testing procedures and their comparability with those in other major studies of the heritability of intelligence. It is a reasonable conjecture that these group-administered tests, designed for particular grade levels rather than for the full range of ability, were too difficult to allow much spread of scores for many of the low SES children and are therefore less reliable for the low SES than for the higher SES groups. Consistent with this conjecture is the fact that the intercorrelations among the several tests are lower for subjects below the SES median than for those above the SES median (see Table 4, p. 1289). And what is the effect of truncating the range by excluding 99 twin pairs who were in retarded classes, four-fifths of whom were Negro (footnote 26)? Could this differentially attenuate correlations for Negro and white twins?

The most reasonable, albeit statistically weak, conclusions we can draw from Scarr-Salapatek's study (1971a) are: (*a*) The heritability of IQ and scholastic achievement is lower in the lowest social class group than in middle and higher SES groups. This is consistent with the threshold hypothesis and suggests that the threshold aspect of the environment exists only in that segment of the population, regardless of race, which is most likely to suffer from poor prenatal and postnatal maternal health and nutrition and other disadvantages of poverty. (*b*) The Negro and white groups do not differ appreciably in heritability for the abilities measured in this study, although these groups differ, on the average, by almost one standard deviation (equivalent to about 15 IQ points) in these abilities. Therefore, it would appear that even if the threshold hypothesis is correct, the threshold is far down the environmental scale and the hypothesis is not adequate to account for the average Negro-white difference that occurs in groups that are not environmentally deprived, as indexed by SES. An environmental theory of the racial group difference must therefore posit some hypothetical factor or factors (e.g., racial discrimination) having no within-group variance to account for the between-groups difference. Other hypothetical environmental factors responsible for the between-groups difference have been suggested. Crow (1969, p. 308), a geneticist, writes, 'It can be argued that being white or being black in our society changes one or more aspects of the environment so importantly as to account for the difference in mean IQ. For example, the argument that American Indians score higher than Negroes in IQ tests – despite being lower on certain socioeconomic scales – can and will be dismissed on the same grounds: some environmental variable associated with being black is not included in the environmental rating.' Another geneticist, Lederberg (1969, p. 612), posits 'racial alienation' as the primary cause of the educational achievement gap between the races.[20]

Within-family variance, V_{WF}, is in some ways a more interesting scientific datum than between-families variance, V_{BF}, or total variance, V_T. V_{WF} seems to be more stable; it shows less sampling fluctuation than V_{BF}. The employment opportunities in a particular locality, for example, can considerably influence the characteristics of the population of that locality, making it more or less homogeneous in genetic and environmental factors. A community that encompasses a wide range of educational, occupational, and socioeconomic levels will have much greater genetic and environmental diversity than a community with a narrow range on these factors, and these community differences will be reflected in the *between-families* IQ variance, while the within-families variance remains relatively uniform. In other words, the between-families variance in any given sample is much more likely to be a function of demographic factors than is the within-families variance. Within-families variance (based on all full siblings within each family) is analyzable into two main components, genetic and environmental. (In the environmental component we include any variance due to genotype × environment interaction.) Thus,

$$V_{WF} = V_{GWF} + V_{EWF}$$

An important determinant of the genetic component, V_{GWF}, when regarded as a proportion of the total genetic variance, is the degree of assortative mating, i.e., the genotypic resemblance between parents in the characteristic in question.[21] The higher the parental correlation, the smaller is the proportion of total variance

G*

contributed by V_{GWF}. If we assume that two populations have identical gene pools for a given trait such as intelligence, and also have the same degree of assortative mating, then any difference between the V_{WF} of the two populations should reflect differences in the environmental component of variance, V_{EWF}, since the populations are presumed to be equal in V_{GWF}. We have compared V_{WF} for Lorge-Thorndike IQ scores on all Negro and white families having two or more full siblings enrolled in the elementary grades (K-6) of a California school district. The value of V_{WF} does not differ significantly in the white and Negro samples ($F = 1.01$, $df = 1210/649$, $p > 0.05$). If we assume that the two groups have essentially the same gene pools for intelligence, the fact that V_{WF} does not differ in the two groups can mean either that (*a*) the racial groups do not differ either in assortative mating or in within-families environmental variance, or (*b*) they differ in environmental variance but the group with the greater environmental variance also has a higher degree of assortative mating, so that the effects balance each other, leaving V_{WF} the same in both groups. Since according to the threshold hypothesis the Negro group should have the larger V_{EWF}, we would have to assume a higher degree of assortative mating in the Negro than in the white group for V_{WF} to be equal for both. Since it is improbable that in this particular community, in which the Negro population is educationally and socioeconomically much less stratified than the white population, there would be a higher degree of assortative mating among Negroes than among whites (if anything, the reverse is more likely), the finding of Negro V_{WF} = white V_{WF} must be regarded as not supporting the threshold hypothesis, at least in this Negro population, which, on the whole, is probably much less environmentally disadvantaged than the Negro population used in Scarr-Salapatek's twin study. It comes close to resembling Scarr-Salapatek's population after her lowest SES group was excluded, and in which also no white-Negro difference in environmental variance was found. Yet in our California samples, as in Scarr-Salapatek's Philadelphia sample, the Negro-white IQ difference is of the order of one standard deviation. Again, if the difference in group means is due to some environmental factors depressing Negro performance, these factors apparently do not increase within-family environmental variance in IQ or decrease its heritability.

Proponents of an entirely environmental theory of the between-groups difference who acknowledge large and equal within-groups heritability of IQ recognize the problem of accounting for the between-groups difference in terms of the same kinds of distributed, variance-producing environmental factors that account for within-groups IQ variance. Thus, Sitgreaves (1971), a statistician, criticizing a genetic hypothesis of racial differences and proposing a purely environmental hypothesis instead, presented the following argument:

> The hypothesis proposed for study by Professor Jensen states that the observed differences in the means and variances of the IQ scores reflect differences in the distribution of the genetic component in the two groups. The alternative hypothesis proposed here considers that this distribution is the same in both the white and Negro populations with the result that
>
> $$\bar{G}_2 = \bar{G}_2 = 100,$$
>
> and
>
> $$V_{G_1} = V_{G_2} = 160.[22]$$
>
> Now, if we assume that for Negroes in the South,[23] the totality of the environmental effects, represented by the component, E, is to *depress each IQ score by a fixed amount* [emphasis added], and we assume that this amount is 15 points, we have
>
> $$\bar{E}_2 = -15, \ V_{E_2} = 0,$$
>
> so that
>
> $$\bar{P}_2 = \bar{G}_2 + \bar{E}_2 = 100 - 15 = 85$$
>
> and
>
> $$V_{P_2} = V_{G_2} + V_{E_2} = 160 + 0 = 160$$
>
> Thus, we obtain from the model exactly the values that have been observed.

Note that a central feature of this environmental model (which accepts the constraint of equal heritability within both groups) is that the environmental difference between the populations has no within-group variance but operates to depress the IQs of all members of the Negro population by a fixed amount. No environmental variables are yet known which produce quantitatively uniform psychological effects on all persons. If such a factor does exist, why should it depress the IQs of Negro subpopulations in various localities (but all presumably having the same gene pool) by different amounts? If the well-established regional differences in IQ among Negroes are due to environmental factors, then these factors must contribute to the variance in the Negro population. Sitgreaves' model, therefore, appears highly implausible.

The key question raised by Sitgreaves' unconvincing effort is: Can an environmental model of the racial IQ difference be devised which accepts the constraints of realistic values for within-group heritability and still appear plausible?

Social Allocation Models

Just such an attempt was made by Light and Smith (1969) in a form they refer to as a 'social allocation model'. They state:

> By social allocation we mean a process whereby members of different racial groups are assigned to environments non-randomly. This model differs from the classic environmentalist position because it grants that individual differences in IQ (although not racial differences) are largely genetic. With respect to the racial differences, the 25 percent non-genetic component accounts for all the observed difference. We differ from the interactionists in believing that the majority of the variation in intelligence can be separated into additive genetic and environmental components. (p. 487)

In brief, this model accepts the findings on the heritability of individual differences in intelligence; it assumes approximately the same heritability in white and Negro populations; and within these constraints it attempts to account for the 15-points mean IQ difference between the racial groups in entirely environmental terms, positing equality in the racial distribution of genotypes for intelligence.

Light and Smith proceed by constructing two grids, one for whites and one for Negroes, each with 10 columns and 12 rows, making 120 cells in all. The 10 columns are the genetic categories, each containing one-tenth of the population. Since the total variance of IQ is $15^2 = 225$ and h^2 is 0.75, the genetic variance will be $0.75 \times 225 = 168.75$. The mean IQ values of the 10 columns (genetic values) are then simply the mean value of each tenth of a normal distribution with an overall mean of 100 and a variance of 168·75. The Negroes and whites have the same distributions of genotypes (column means) in this model. The 12 rows represent environmental categories, which have different distributions for whites and Negroes, based on the 12 socioeconomic categories of the 1960 U.S. Census (see Figure 7.3). Since the non-genetic variance is $1 - h^2 = 0·25$, the environmental component of IQ variance will be $0·25 \times 225 = 56·25$, with an overall mean of 100. The mean IQs of the 12 rows are obtained by assuming a normal distribution of environmental effects on IQ (an assumption which is supported by twin studies) and dividing this normal distribution (with mean $= 100$, variance $= 56·25$) into 12 unequal parts with frequencies corresponding to the Census data. Thus, from the 10×12 grid's row means and column means, assuming additive effects of genetic and environmental factors, one can obtain the mean IQ within each of the 120 cells. The resultant overall mean IQs for whites and Negroes are 100 and 91·26, respectively. Since this difference falls short of the 15-points difference that needs to be accounted for, Light and Smith introduce the assumption of 1 percent 'interaction' variance into the model.[24] This means that low genotypic IQs are more depressed by poor environment than higher genotypic IQs. Light and Smith had a computer find the optimal 'malicious' allocation (as they call it) of Negro genotypes to environmental categories in producing this 1 percent interaction effect so as to maximize the overall Negro-white IQ difference. This brings the white and Negro means to 100 and 86·81, respectively, which is very realistic in terms of the empirical values of white and Negro mean IQs. Light and Smith went further and assumed a 10 percent interaction due to 'malicious' allocation of poor genotypes in poor environments; the optimal allocation of 10 percent interaction effects by the computer to maximize the white-Negro difference resulted in mean IQs of 100 and 82·59. Light and Smith state: 'We may therefore conclude that with an interaction component of variance somewhere between 0·01 and 0·10, the black mean IQ may be expected to be approximately 85, even though blacks are distributed identically with whites over the genetic categories' (1969, p. 498). Thus, the claim is made that this environmental allocation model can accept the available heritability estimates for IQ and, by assuming a small interaction component of between

1 and 10 percent of the variance, can account for the mean Negro-white difference of about 15 IQ points *without* assuming any genetic intelligence difference between the two racial populations. The Light and Smith environmental allocation model is, so far, undoubtedly the most complex and ingenious attempt to explain the racial IQ difference in purely environmental terms while accepting the evidence on the heritability of intelligence *within* populations.

But the Light and Smith model has a number of serious – indeed, fatal – faults, which have been proved mathematically in a detailed analysis of the model by Shockley (1971a).[25] Without going into the detailed mathematical analysis that Shockley provides, the major deficiencies which it turns up in the model are as follows:

1. Probably the gravest deficiency of the model is the fact that the magnitude of the Negro-white difference it can account for under the given constraints is completely a numerical artifact of the number of rows and columns used. The selection of a 10×12 array is essential for the particular results obtained by Light and Smith. If more than 15 IQ points difference between the racial groups had to be accounted for, one need only use more rows and columns to produce the desired result. The finer one slices up the environmental and genetic distributions, the larger the group difference that can be 'explained' environmentally. Shockley points out that a 1000×1200 array would account for about a 50-points mean IQ difference. Pick any size difference you please – the Light-Smith model can explain it by using whatever size of array is necessary. The number of categories into which one divides up the genetic and environmental distributions is, of course, entirely arbitrary, or at best is limited by the size of the smallest units of the measuring scales for IQ and SES. A model that allows arbitrary parameters and can thereby be made to fit any set of facts is scientifically untestable. Even if there were actually a genetic difference between two groups, as long as there was any environmental difference (where favorableness of the environment is positively correlated with IQ) between the groups, the Light-Smith model could show that *all* the between-groups differences, no matter how large, were explainable environmentally.

2. The 'malicious' allocation aspect of the model assumes inter-

action that works only in one direction, such as to lower the Negro IQ. If the sign of the interaction were reversed (such that good environments raised low genotypic IQs more than high genotypic IQs) the 'malicious' allocation would become a 'beneficent' allocation and the Negro mean IQ could be 7 points *higher* than the white mean under the 10 percent interaction condition. Thus, the assumption of the particular *direction* of the interaction (for which there is no empirical evidence) is necessary to produce the outcome desired by Light and Smith. As Shockley notes:

> That such a procedure *per se* is logically unsatisfying can be appreciated by noting that it could explain away a real genetic difference. . . . Light and Smith's methodology could be used, even if a genetic offset (difference) did exist, to argue the case for subtle, immeasurable, but significant environmental causes not detectable at the crude level of the Census Bureau's SES Categories. . . . Thus, unless some operationally defined means of assessing the subtle differences that might exist for interaction within cells of the 10×12 array can be devised, methodology based purely on analysis of variance puts the question of genetic differences . . . in the class that Bridgman defines as a 'meaningless question'. (Shockley, 1971a, p. 243)

3. The IQ distribution for whites resulting from the Light-Smith calculations corresponds perfectly to the empirically obtained normal, bell-shaped curve, with mean $= 100$, $SD = 15$. But the Negro IQ distribution generated by their model, except for the mean, is in violent disagreement with actual data, both as to the variance and the form of the distribution. The variance of the Negro distribution generated by the model is 340 for the 0·01 interaction condition and 617 for the 0·10 interaction condition! (The actual variance of Negro IQs obtained in one of the largest normative studies of the Stanford-Binet is 154 [Kennedy, Van De Reit, & White, 1963], and in nearly all other studies the Negro IQ variance is less than the white variance of about 225 to 260.) Also, the form of the Negro IQ distribution generated by the model shows an exaggerated skewness to the left, whereas in fact empirically obtained distributions of Negro IQ display a slight degree of skewness to the right. Another peculiarity is that there is a *decrease* in the hypothetical Negro IQs from the eighth to the tenth SES category (tenth is the higher SES).

4. In the examples of the model produced by Light and Smith, it can be deduced that the within-family genetic variance is extremely small in the hypothetical Negro population, implying a much higher heritability of IQ for Negroes than for whites. (The evidence presented by Scarr-Salapatek, 1971a suggests that, if anything, within-family variance is slightly larger for Negroes.) The Negro sibling correlation should be about the same as for identical twins reared together, according to the results generated by the model. Furthermore, the 'malicious' allocation of Negro genotypes to SES categories produces a much higher correlation between SES and IQ than any correlations found empirically, and most of the SES IQ differences would be genetic. The IQ differences between SES groups are actually not nearly as great as those generated by Light and Smith. Phenotypic IQ differences of nearly 50 points between the same genotypes are produced by SES differences *within* the Negro group!

5. Since in the particular allocations of genotypes to environments almost 90 percent of the Negroes in the two lowest genetic categories also fall into the two lowest environmental categories, Shockley notes that a logical consequence of this feature of the Light-Smith model is dysgenics: even if there is no Negro genetic deficit in a given generation, the model predicts that there will be one in the *next* generation, since it is well-established that birth rates are higher for Negroes in lower SES as compared with higher SES categories. Much smaller dysgenic effects would be expected for whites, according to this model, because birth rates are much less negatively correlated with SES status than is the case in the Negro population.

From his analysis of the Light-Smith model, Shockley, noting its serious short-comings amounting practically to absurdities, concludes, 'Thus their attempt to construct an environmental explanation constitutes in fact a *reductio ad absurdum* basis for rejecting their premises' (1971a, p. 233).[26] Thus far neither Light and Smith nor anyone else has produced a model which can simultaneously take account of (*a*) the evidence on within-groups heritability, (*b*) the correlation between SES and IQ within groups, and (*c*) the between-groups difference, strictly in environmental terms, without the models also generating other features which grossly fail to accord with empirical findings.

NOTES

1. A critique of the SPSSI Council's statement was published by Jensen (1969c).
2. *Obtained* scores can be conceived of as analyzable into two components: *true*-scores plus an *error* component. The reliability (r_{tt}) of a test is defined as the ratio of true score variance to obtained score variance and the proportion of variance due to measurement error, therefore, is $1 - r_{tt}$. Errors of measurement, being random, cancel each other when scores are averaged to obtain a group mean. Adding a random number (half of which are + and half −) to each score in a distribution, where the number of scores is large, will increase the variance of the distribution but will not significantly alter the mean. On the other hand, when the *absolute* difference (i.e., a difference regardless of its sign, + or −) between a pair of scores is obtained, it includes the measurement error. For example, imagine a set of many pairs of 'true' scores (i.e., scores without any error) in which the scores of both members of each pair are identical (although the mean of each pair may differ from the mean of every other pair). The mean of the absolute differences within pairs, therefore, will be zero. Now imagine adding random numbers (i.e., error) to every individual score. Then the mean of the absolute differences within pairs will be some value greater than zero. This value constitutes measurement error.
3. The correlation between twins can be determined from the mean absolute difference $|\bar{d}_k|$ between twin pairs from the following formula

$$ r = 1 - \left(\frac{|\bar{d}_k|}{|\bar{d}_p|}\right)^2 $$

where

$|\bar{d}_k|$ = mean absolute difference between kinship members,
$|\bar{d}_p|$ = mean absolute difference between all possible paired comparisons in the general population, and

$$ |\bar{d}_p| = \frac{2\sigma}{\sqrt{\pi}} = 1 \cdot 13\sigma $$

Since the population σ for IQ is 15, and the twin difference is 6·60, the above formula yields a value for $r = 0\cdot85$. Thus, if the genetic variance for IQ $= 0\cdot85 \times 15^2 = 191\cdot25$, and the error variance is $(1 - r_{tt})\sigma^2$ [where r_{tt} is test reliability] $= (-1\cdot95)15^2 = 11\cdot25$, and the total variance is $15^2 = 225$, then the environmental variance (i.e., the remainder) must equal 22·50, which has a standard deviation of $\sqrt{22\cdot50} = 4\cdot74$. Assuming a normal distribution of environmental effects, the mean absolute difference in IQ due to environmental differences is $1\cdot13 \times 4\cdot74 = 5\cdot36$.

4. An individual's estimated true score $\tilde{X}t$, is:

$$\tilde{X}_t = r_{tt}\,(X - \bar{X}) + \bar{X}$$

where
   r_{tt} is the reliability of the test
   X is the individual's obtained score
   $\bar{X}$ is the mean of the population from which the
      individual was sampled

5. This distribution of true-score differences may be compared with that of the obtained-score differences for the same 122 twin pairs (Figure 4 in Jensen, 1970a).
6. The details of this statistical analysis are given by Jensen (1970a).
7. In a classic study, Burks (1928) estimated the effects of environment on IQ from an analysis of correlations between detailed ratings of the home environment and the IQs of adopted children. A multiple correlation (corrected for attenuation) between the actual environmental ratings and IQ was 0·42. (The correlation between IQ and the theoretical environmental scale derived in our twin study is 0·32.) Burks concluded from her analyses of the IQs and environments of adopted children that

> 1. The total effect of environmental factors one standard deviation up or down the scale is only about 6 points, or, allowing for a maximal oscillation of the corrected multiple correlation (0·42) of as much as 0·20, the maximal effect almost certainly lies between 3 and 9 points. 2. Assuming the best possible environment to be three standard deviations above the mean of the population (which, if 'environments' are distributed approximately according to the normal law, would only occur about once in a thousand cases), the excess in such a situation of a child's IQ over his inherited level would lie between 9 and 27 points – or less if the relation of culture to IQ is curvilinear on the upper levels, as it may well be. (Burks, 1928, p. 307)

The geneticist Sewell Wright (1931) later performed a genetical analysis, using his method of 'path coefficients', on Burks' data. He showed that Burks' correlation between environment and adopted child's IQ could be broken down into two components: the *direct* effect of home environment on IQ and the *indirect* effects of the foster parents' IQ on the child's environment. The *direct* correlation of home environment and child's IQ was 0·29; that is, about 9 percent of the IQ variance was attributable to variance in home environments, independently of the intelligence of the foster parents. The *SD* of these environmental effects thus would be equivalent to 4·39 IQ points and the total reaction range of home environments on IQ would be approximately this value multiplied by the number of *SD*s in a normal distribution, or $4·39 \times 6 = 26·34$ IQ points. (If the indirect effects of foster parents' IQ is included with the direct effects of home environment, the total reaction range is 36 IQ points.) The occupational status of the foster parents in Burks' study spanned a wide range, from professional to unskilled labor, although a majority were in occupations that would be classified as middle- and upper-middle SES. The reaction range of 26 means, in effect, that improvement of a child's home environment (without changing his parents' IQs) would raise the IQ 26 points for those children who shortly after birth are moved from the most unfavorable environment in a thousand to the most favorable environment in a thousand. A gain of 36 points would occur if, *in addition*, the child exchanged the 'worst' parents in a thousand for the 'best' parents in a thousand.

8. A comparison of large representative samples of Negro and white school children in a California school district showed them to differ by 0·61 sigmas on the Home Index (Gough, 1949), a 25-item inventory of the child's home environment and SES (Jensen, 1971b). On a non-verbal intelligence test (Raven's Progressive Matrices) these same Negro and white samples differ by 1·07 sigmas.

9. In predicting offspring values from parental values, the narrow heritability (h_N^2) is used, since its value is the proportion of total phenotypic variance which is 'additive', that is, which breeds true and accounts for resemblance between parents and children. Theoretically, h_N^2 is defined as the correlation between midparent and midoffspring. In estimating total non-genetic or environmental variance, on the other hand, we use heritability in the broad sense (h_B^2), since this is the proportion of variance attributable to *all* genetic factors (additive + dominance + epistasis). Thus $1 - h_B^2 = e^2$, the proportion of variance due to non-genetic factors. Theoretically, h_B^2 is defined as the correlation between MZ twins reared apart in random (i.e., uncorrelated) environments.

10. These data were plotted in Figure 7.4 by Professor W. Shockley (personal communication, 5 October 1969). It is also interesting to compare the IQs of the offspring of the gifted parents with the IQs of children adopted by gifted parents. Shockley (personal communication) has made the only statistical analyses of this point in

Terman's data, as follows. There were about 100 adopted children but only 18 were given IQ tests, and Terman has not reported their mean. However, it is stated that 6 of the 18 had IQs above 135 and none had IQs above 146. If the distribution of IQs of the adopted children were the same as of the natural offspring, we should expect, among 18 cases, to find 8·1 above IQ 135 and 4·1 above IQ 146. The corresponding obtained frequencies for the adopted children (6 and 0, respectively) fall significantly below the expected frequencies ($\chi^2 = 4·65$, $p < 0·05$).

11. A sociologist, acknowledging this logic by making a similar analysis, writes:

> To explain the variation between Negro and white IQ on this environmental basis, we need to find determinants of IQ on which there is a difference of two and one-half standard deviations between Negroes and whites, assuming a linear relationship between the variables. This is a difference such that, for a normally distributed variable, about one percent of Negroes would be above the average of the whites. It does not seem to me outrageous that a well-measured variable of oppressiveness of conditions of life and cultural deprivation might show such a difference. (Stinchcombe, 1969, p. 517)

Presumably, if there were, in fact, any evidence for a two-and-a-half standard deviations environmental difference between Negroes and whites in the U.S., Stinchcombe would have reported it rather than merely surmising that such a possibility does not seem 'outrageous.'

12. This is a futile topic for discussion because no operational means are ever specified which would permit one to know when the individual's genetic potential has been realized. 'Genetic potential' is a hypothetical construct and is meaningless without reference to a specified environment. The high heritability of intelligence indicates that most persons come about equally close to realizing their genetic potential, although we cannot say just how far below the upper limit of this potential everyone is. The theoretical upper limit cannot be specified, since we can never know all possible environmental influences on mental development. In the range of natural environments in which the middle 99 percent of the population actually live today, however, the 'reaction range' of environment on intelligence is most probably something between 30 and 40 IQ points.

13. It is assumed that in making comparisons of heritability in different subpopulation groups that estimates of h^2 should take into account

possible subpopulation differences in assortative mating, test reliability, and 'range-of-talent' (i.e., differences in variance).

14. We shall assume only true-score variance in this model. In practice, variance due to measurement error (test unreliability) can be determined and removed at any one of several stages in the analysis. It is simplest to remove it from the total variance at the outset.

15. In this example we assume random mating for the sake of simplicity. In practice, we take assortative mating into account. Under random mating, one-half of the additive genetic variance is *within* families for DZ twins (and ordinary siblings) and one-half is *between* families. The effect of assortative mating (correlation between parents) is to proportionally decrease variance *within* families and increase variance *between* families. When the correlation between parents is 0·50, the proportions of *between*- and *within*-families genetic variance are about 0·60 and 0·40, respectively.

16. The variance ratio, labeled F after Sir Ronald Fisher, the English geneticist and statistician who invented the method known as 'the analysis of variance', is explicated in virtually all modern statistical textbooks, e.g. Walker and Lev (1953).

17. It is possible, however, to obtain Holzinger's (1929) H coefficient – a kind of index of heritability – from the F ratio. $H = (F-1)/F$. H has been frequently called heritability, but it is actually not the same as h^2, which is V_G/V_P, i.e., the proportion of genetic variance. $H = (V_{WDZ} - V_{WMZ})/V_{WDZ}$. [Or, from twin correlations, $H = (r_{MZ} - r_{DZ})/(1 - r_{DZ})$.] In terms of variance components, H consists of:

$$H = \frac{\frac{1}{2}V_{BG}}{\frac{1}{2}V_{BG} + V_{WE}}$$

This coefficient can be seen to differ considerably from true heritability:

$$h^2 = \frac{V_{WG} + V_{BG}}{V_{WG} + V_{BG} + V_{WE} + V_{BE}} = \frac{V_G}{V_P}$$

18. The significance of the difference between two Fs is tested by transforming the Fs to a unit normal variate and referring the difference to the normal distribution to determine its p value. The appropriate transformation is given by Paulson (1942).

19. A simple approximation to the standard error of h^2 as determined by the twin method is given by Newman Freeman & Holzinger (1937, p. 116):

$$SE_h^2 = \frac{1-r_{MZ}}{1-r_{DZ}}\sqrt{\frac{(1+r_{MZ})^2+(1+r_{DZ})^2}{N}}$$

where r_{MZ} and r_{DZ} are the MZ and DZ twin correlations and N is the total number of twin pairs (MZ+DZ pairs).

20. It is not entirely clear if Lederberg extends this alienation hypothesis also to IQ and other ability differences. He writes:

'intelligence' undoubtedly does have a very large and relatively simple genetic component. In fact, the genes are all too visible: they control the color of the skin. In our present milieu, these genes may lead a student with the highest intellectual potential to turn his back on the hard work of learning physics, chemistry, and mathematics (which will measure out as intelligence by middle-class standards) in favor of black studies that he hopes may meet his more urgent needs in other spheres. (Lederberg, 1969, p. 612)

21. The degree of assortative mating in any single generation affects the total genetic variance in the population; positive assortative mating increases the total genetic variance. The degree of assortative mating, however, does not influence the within-family variance (i.e., the difference among full siblings) in any one generation, so that the *proportion* of within-family genetic variance is decreased by positive assortative mating and the *correlation* among siblings is increased. The additive genetic variance within families is strictly a function of the heterozygosity (i.e., number of pairs of dissimilar alleles) of each of the parents and not of their genotypic similarity or dissimilarity. However, within-family genetic variance for polygenic traits may be decreased after continued assortative mating for several generations. (For a good discussion of the quantitative genetics of assortative mating, see Crow and Felsenstein, 1968.)

22. Sitgreaves assumes $h^2 = 0.80$ in both populations, and assumes a true-score phenotypic variance for IQ of 200, so that $(0.80)(200) = 160$ as the genetic variance (V_G) in each group.

23. It is not clear why Sitgreaves refers specifically to Negroes in the South – perhaps to emphasize environmental disadvantages – but the fact is that 15 IQ points is an underestimate of this group's deviation from the white national mean of 100. The best estimate of Stanford-Binet IQ in Negro school children in the South gives a mean of 80·7, $SD = 12.4$ (Kennedy, Van De Reit, & White, 1963).

24. Light and Smith obtain this 1 percent interaction by noting that the median correlation between identical twins reared apart is 0·75,

and the median correlation between unrelated children reared together is 0·24. Thus, $G+E+I_{GE} = 0·75+0·24+0·01 = 1·00$, where I_{GE} is the variance due to genotype $\times$ environment interaction. One cannot take this seriously, since the values of 0·75 and 0·24 are just estimates of population values with large standard errors; the fact that they should add up to more or less than 1·00 is therefore not at all surprising. $G \times E$ interaction is never estimated in this way in population genetics. The 1 percent interaction used by Light and Smith must be regarded as an assumption of their model, not as an empirical fact which they have incorporated. At present there is no statistically significant evidence for a $G \times E$ interaction with respect to human intelligence, nor is there any good evidence that would disprove an interaction as small as 1 percent. However, interactions as large as 10 percent, if they actually existed, would surely be detectable with present evidence. The fact that an interaction has not been detected means it is either very small or non-existent.

25. Although the Light and Smith paper appeared in the *Harvard Educational Review*, its Board of Editors refused to consider the publication of Shockley's critique, which has subsequently appeared in the *Review of Educational Research*, a publication of the American Educational Research Association. This decision by the *HER*'s Editorial Board was preceded by their refusing to publish an article solicited by them on the 'Jensen controversy' by Professor Scriven (1970). A similarly solicited article from Professor Ellis B. Page, who wrote more critically of Jensen's critics than of Jensen, was also refused publication.

26. A reply by Light and Smith (1971) and a rejoinder by Shockley (1971c) add nothing essentially new to the discussion nor do they alter the conclusions drawn here.

8   Multiple and partial correlation methods

The literature on social class and racial differences in intelligence is replete with reports of correlations between innumerable environmental, attitudinal, and personal variables and IQ. Correlations have been reported between IQ and variables such as family size, absence of father, prematurity, child-rearing practices, birth weight, family income, parental education, protein intake, books in the home, mother's age, position in family – the list is almost endless. Each variable may yield some non-zero correlation with IQ, however small, and since some racial groups differ on many of these variables in the same direction as they differ in IQ and in the same direction that the variables are correlated with IQ, it creates the impression that the racial IQ difference must be easily explainable in terms of the racial differences on all of these environmental factors. The fallacy in this, of course, is that the IQ variance (either within or between racial groups) accounted for by all these environmental factors is not equal to the *sum* of all the various environmental influences. In accounting for IQ variance, environmental measures, not being independent sources of variance, must be added up in the fashion of a multiple regression equation. That is to say, the contribution to IQ variance of each environmental factor must be added up *after removing* whatever IQ variance it has in common with all the previous factors added in. The greater the correlation between the environmental factors, the smaller is the contribution to IQ variance of each successive factor which is added to the composite of environmental variables.

Because of the lack of independence among environmental

variables, we need more studies of the multiple correlation (R) between environment and IQ. Environmental measures such as family income, father's occupation, or some composite index of SES are commonly regarded as excessively 'crude' measures of the environment, with the implication that these measures fail to include important influences on IQ caused by more subtle and refined environmental variables. The important question, however, is how much *more* of the IQ variance is accounted for[1] by the 'subtle' environmental factors over and above the IQ variance already accounted for by a 'crude' environmental index, such as SES? Could one find more than five or six environmental measures which *independently* add significant increments to the multiple correlation with IQ? In a study of the correlation between adopted children's IQs and environmental factors, Burks (1928) found a correlation of 0·33 between the children's IQs and their family's income. When two quite elaborate and detailed ratings of the home environment (Whittier Home Index and Culture Index) were included, along with family income, in a multiple correlation, the resultant R was 0·34, just 0·01 greater than for income alone. Similarly, mothers' vocabulary correlated with the adopted children's IQs 0·249; the multiple R between mother's vocabulary +mother's mental age+mother's education and children's IQs was 0·254. The multiple R between children's IQs and a number of environmental factors, which taken singly had correlations with children's IQs between 0·15 and 0·30, was only 0·35 (0·42 corrected for attenuation). Significantly higher correlations between environment and the parents' own children are obtained, because parental intelligence is correlated with the environment and the children. The multiple R between the several environmental variables and children's IQs was 0·61. But since the correlations between midparent intelligence and child's IQ is 0·60 and between parental intelligence and environmental rating is 0·77, most of the correlation between child's IQ and environment is attributable to the parents' intelligence and the genetic correlation between parents and children. The multiple correlation of the environmental indices with children's IQs when the parental contribution is removed is only 0·183. Even in the case of the adopted children, the single most important environmental factor contributing to variance in children's IQs was the foster mother's intelligence. The single best index of the quality of the environment is probably midparent intelligence, since in Burks' study it correlates 0·77 with a very elaborate composite index of the quality of home environment.

Thus, environmental indices such as SES, parental education, occupation, and income are 'crude' not in the sense that they do not account for a major proportion of the environmental variance in IQ, but only in the sense that they are not analytical – they do not pinpoint the most potent specific sources of environmental variance encompassed within these broad or 'crude' measures.

The theoretical upper limit of environmental variance that can be accounted for by environmental factors, of course, is $1 - h^2$, and the highest possible multiple R between environmental variables and IQ is $\sqrt{1 - h^2}$. Thus, when h^2 is 0·75, the highest possible R is 0·50. Burks' (1928) multiple R between environment and IQ of adopted children is 0·42. When correlations between IQ and environment much above 0·50 are found, it most likely means that there is a correlation between the environmental measures and genetic factors. But this should not be unusual, since probably the most important environmental factor is the parents' intelligence.

The method which is suggested by all this and has not been sufficiently exploited in the study of environmental factors in intelligence is to obtain multiple Rs between a host of environmental factors hypothesized to be important and (*a*) measures of mental ability and (*b*) the quantized racial groups, and between the mental measures and the quantized racial groups.[2] Since multiple R^2 like zero-order r^2 accounts only for variance in one variable due to its linear regression on another variable or set of variables, the form of the relationship between continuous variables should be tested for statistically significant departures from linearity, which can only lower the correlations. To remedy non-linear relationships so that linear correlation methods can have their maximum efficiency one can seek transformations of the scale which will help to create linear relationships between variables. When correlations have not been tested for departures from linearity, it is best assumed that if they err, they err on the side of underestimation of the true degree of correlation between the variables in question.

Thus, we can obtain three correlations:

(1) The multiple correlation, R_{EI}, between a number of environmental measures (E) and intelligence (I)

(2) The multiple correlation, R_{ER} between the environmental measures and the racial dichotomy treated as a quantized variable

(3) The point-biserial correlation, r_{RI}, between the racial dichotomy and intelligence.

From these three correlations we can then obtain partial correlations, that is, correlations between each pair of variables with the effects of the third statistically held constant. Unfortunately, there are no data in the literature which permit the optimal use of this method, which consists of having multiple correlations of a large number of environmental variables with IQ and race. But we can illustrate the method using a single composite measure of the environment. A study by Tenopyr (1967) is interesting because it involves control of SES both by selection of subjects and by statistically partialling out SES from the correlations between race and abilities. The subjects were 167 Negro and white machine-shop trainees recruited from the low socioeconomic areas of the community (Los Angeles). They had an average of 11·9 years of education and their mother's average education was 11·1 years. The whites were slightly but not significantly lower than the Negroes on a composite SES index based on the education of the subject, his mother's education, and the status level of his father's job. In addition to the SES index, three ability tests were given to all subjects: Verbal Comprehension (V), Numerical Ability (N), and Spatial Visualization (S). The correlations among all the variables are as follows:

	N	S	Race	SES
Verbal (V)	0·30	0·11	0·27	0·21
Numerical (N)		0·21	0·18	0·14
Spatial (S)			0·21	0·04
Race*				−0·09

* Negro = 0, White = 1

From these above correlations, we can obtain the following *partial* correlations:[3]

$$r_{V,\ \text{Race.SES}} = 0\cdot30\ p<0\cdot01$$
$$r_{V,\ \text{SES.Race}} = 0\cdot24\ p<0\cdot01$$

$$r_{N,\ \text{Race.SES}} = 0\cdot19\ p<0\cdot01$$
$$r_{N,\ \text{SES.Race}} = 0\cdot16\ p<0\cdot05$$

$$r_{S,\ \text{SES.Race}} = 0\cdot21\ p<0\cdot01$$
$$r_{S,\ \text{SES.Race}} = 0\cdot06\ \text{n.s.}$$
$$r_{S,\ \text{Race.SES, V}} = 0\cdot19\ p<0\cdot01$$

All correlations are rather low due to restriction of the range on all variables caused by the method of subject selection. But the partial correlations remain interesting. Note that every test has a higher partial correlation with race than with SES and that the difference is largest for the spatial ability test, which is the least culturally and educationally loaded of the three. Also note that partialling out *both* SES and Verbal Ability (the most culturally loaded test) still leaves a significant partial r of $0\cdot19$ between race and spatial ability. In other words, the racial difference on all of these tests cannot be accounted for by whatever environmental influences are summarized in the SES index. Moreover, it should be remembered that since SES most probably has some correlation with the genetic component of ability, when we partial out SES from the correlation of race with ability we are partialling out too much; that is, we remove something more than just the environmental component of the correlation between SES and ability.

Much higher correlations than Tenopyr's between race, SES, and IQ are available from large unselected samples of Negro ($N = 655$) and white ($N = 628$) school children in Georgia (Osborne, 1970): IQ was measured by a group test (California Test of Mental Maturity) and SES was measured on a rather elaborate 25 item questionnaire. Race is quantized as Negro $= 0$, white $= 1$. The correlations are:

$$r_{\text{Race, IQ}} = 0\cdot691$$
$$r_{\text{SES, IQ}} = 0\cdot615$$
$$r_{\text{Race, SES}} = 0\cdot638$$

The partial correlations are:

$$r_{\text{Raec, IQ.SES}} = 0\cdot493$$
$$r_{\text{SES, IQ.Race}} = 0\cdot312$$

The point-biserial correlation of 0·493 between race and IQ with SES partialled out corresponds to a mean IQ difference between the races of about 1σ. (Figure 8.1 shows the relationship between the point-biserial correlation, r_{pbs}, and mean group difference, d, in sigma units, when the two groups have equal Ns and equal σs.) The correlation of SES and IQ with race partialled out is signific-

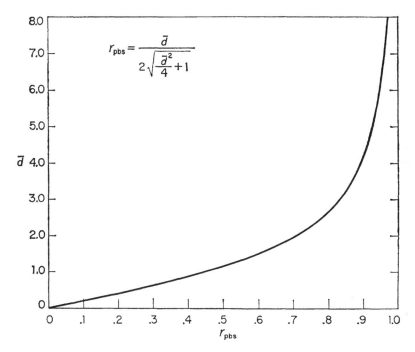

Figure 8.1 The relationship between the point-biserial correlation (r_{pbs}) and the mean difference (d) between groups in sigma units on the continuous variable, assuming equal sigmas and equal Ns in the two groups.

antly smaller than the correlation between race and IQ with SES partialled out. All this can mean is that the environmental factors summarized in the SES index at most account for $(0·691)^2 - (0·493)^2 = 0·23$ of the total IQ variance which is associated with SES differences between races.

This value of environmental variance *between* the races is close to twice the estimates of between-families environmental variance *within* races. In other words, the environmental index (SES) accounts for only about as much of the mean racial differences as would be accounted for if we assumed that the between-groups heritability is about the same as the within-groups heritability, i.e., both the between-groups and within-groups differences are comprised of about 20 to 25 percent environmental variance. Notice that the correlation between SES and IQ (with race partialled out) is 0·312, so that SES accounts for about 0·10 (i.e., r^2) of the variance in IQ *within* racial groups – a value slightly greater than estimates of between-families environmental variance (e.g. Jensen, 1967). And this is about what should be expected, since the SES index reflects the between-families part of the environmental variance. The environmental difference between the racial groups is treated as a part of the between-families variance when the data of both groups are analyzed together, as we have done here. These results from Osborne's study, then, are consistent with the hypothesis that the between-racial-groups heritability is about the same as within-groups heritability. The mean IQ difference clearly cannot be accounted for entirely in terms of the SES differences. Now, if in addition to the composite SES index used in this study we had been able to include in a multiple R a host of other environmental factors which have been hypothesized as causes of the Negro-white IQ difference, the test of the hypothesis would be markedly strengthened. As noted previously, however, it is doubtful that adding more environmental variables to a composite SES index in a multiple regression equation will result in a multiple R with IQ which is much larger than the zero-order r between the SES index and IQ.

If we knew the heritability, h^2, of test scores in the combined racial populations on two or more tests which differ significantly in h^2, it should be possible to determine the point-biserial correlation between the racial dichotomy and genotypic intelligence.[4] Say we have two tests which differ in amount of cultural loading and therefore reflect environmental influences to different degrees. Such tests should therefore differ in h^2. We also must have evidence that the two tests are measures of the same factor (say, g) and are not measuring two different abilities. (For example, the vocabulary and the block design tests are both highly loaded on g, although a vocabulary test can be made much more culturally loaded than a block design test. It is also possible mathematically to regress out the minor irrelevant ability factors on which the two tests may differ.) Suppose test 1 has an h_1^2 of 0·50 and test 2 has an h_2^2 of 0·80 in the total population. To keep the illustration of the method simple, we will assume no correlation between genotypes and environments, although a solution could be obtained by this method if there were an independent estimate of the $G \times E$ covariance. With this simplifying assumption of zero $G \times E$ correlation, we can only *underestimate* the true proportion of genetic variance or heritability, so, if anything, we err in favor of environment.[5] The total variance of tests 1 and 2 can be represented as follows:

$$\text{Test 1: } \sigma_1^2 = \sigma_G^2 + \sigma_E^2$$

and, since $h_1^2 = 0.5$,

$$\sigma_1^2 = 0.5\sigma_1^2 + 0.5\sigma_1^2$$
$$\sigma_{G_1}^2 = 0.5\sigma_1^2$$
$$\sigma_{E_1}^2 = 0.5\sigma_1^2$$

$$\text{Test 2: } \sigma_2^2 = 0.8\sigma_2^2 + 0.2\sigma_2^2 \text{ (since } h^2 = 0.8)$$
$$\sigma_{G_2}^2 = 0.8\sigma_2^2$$
$$\sigma_{E_2}^2 = 0.2\sigma_2^2$$

Now, the point-biserial correlation between race (R) and Test 1, r_{R_1}, and between race and Test 2, r_{R2}, can be represented as follows (assuming all correlations have been corrected for attenuation):

$$r_{R1} = 0.7r_{RG_1} + 0.7r_{RE_1}$$
$$r_{R2} = 0.9r_{RG_2} + 0.45r_{RE_2}$$

The coefficients in these equations are the square roots of the variance components, σ_G^2 and σ_E^2.

Given the empirically ascertained values of h_1^2, h_2^2, r_{R1}, r_{R2}, we can solve the simultaneous equations for r_{RG}, that is, the correlation between the racial dichotomy and the genetic component of the test variance. For example, assume that Test 1 is more culturally loaded than Test 2 and that their respective correlations with race are $r_{R1} = 0.5$ and $r_{R2} = 0.4$. (Approximately such correlations would be obtained if the mean racial difference on Tests 1 and 2 were 1σ and 0.75σ, respectively.) So we solve the simultaneous equations:

$$0.5 = 0.7r_{RG} + 0.7r_{RE}$$
$$0.4 = 0.9r_{RG} + 0.45r_{RE}$$
$$r_{RG} = 0.18$$
$$r_{RE} = 0.53$$

We see that in this case most of the racial difference is accounted for by the correlation of race with environment, $r_{RE} = 0.53$, while the correlation between race and the genetic component, r_{RG} = 0·18, is small – and it could be zero or even a negative correlation, given somewhat more extreme values of r_{R1} and r_{R2}.

Taking the example further, suppose that these correlations were reversed, that is, the mean racial difference is greater for the test with the higher heritability. Then

$$0\cdot4 = 0\cdot7r_{RG}+0\cdot7r_{RE}$$
$$0\cdot5 = 0\cdot9r_{RG}+0\cdot45r_{RE}$$
$$r_{RG} = 0\cdot55$$
$$r_{RE} = 0\cdot02$$

And here we see that the racial difference is largely accounted for by the correlation of race with the genetic component of test variance. It would be desirable to obtain the relevant data on more than two tests differing from one another in heritability and in their correlations with race, so that the system of equations would be overdetermined, thereby permitting a test of the adequacy of this model in accounting for the empirically obtained correlations.

At present we have no ideal data for this kind of analysis. However, it can be noted that such data as do exist seem to be less in accord with the first example above than with the second. Tests that appear to be more culture-loaded, contrary to popular belief, usually show *smaller* racial mean differences than tests which are designed to be more culture-fair. For example, Negroes do less well, relative to whites, on Raven's Progressive Matrices Test than on the much more obviously culture-loaded Peabody Picture Vocabulary Test. (Although the reverse is true for another socioeconomically disadvantaged group, the Mexican-Americans.) Also, contrary to popular belief, scholastic achievement tests, which have generally been found to have h^2 values around 0·4 to 0·6 (as compared to 0·7 to 0·8 for intelligence tests), generally show a smaller mean Negro-white difference than is found with intelligence tests. Comparison of large representative samples of Negro and white children in grades 1 through 8 in a California school district, for example, showed an average race difference of $0\cdot66\sigma$ on a battery of scholastic achievement tests and a difference of $1\cdot08\sigma$ on a set of non-verbal intelligence tests (Jensen, 1971). The cultural contents of the two sets of tests differ strikingly, yet both sets of tests have their largest factor loadings on the g factor (or first principal component). Although these findings are hardly persuasive in terms of the type of analysis suggested above, since all the relevant parameters have not been precisely estimated in the very same populations, the direction of all of the relationships is such that it would be surprising indeed if a rigorous application of this method would show $r_{RG} < r_{RE}$, that is, a smaller correlation of race with the genetic than with the environmental component of test variance.

PROBLEMS OF UNEQUAL VARIANCES

Quantitative genetics and heritability estimation are based on the analysis of variance, and sooner or later in comparing heritability estimation in different population groups one is confronted with the problem of unequal variances on the trait being compared across populations. As regards the treatment of IQs or other ability measures in comparing white and Negro populations the problem is essentially unsolved. In fact, it is seldom faced. Researchers in this field should remain aware of the problems created by unequal variances.

Shuey (1966, pp. 200-1), in her comprehensive review of studies of Negro IQ, found 200 studies which permitted comparison of the variances of Negro and white groups on the same mental measurements. In 67 percent of the comparisons, the white group had significantly larger variance; the Negro groups showed larger variance in 26 percent of the studies. The largest normative study of Stanford-Binet IQ in a Negro population shows the Negro IQ variance to be only 57 percent as great as the variance of the normative white population (Kennedy, Van De Reit, & White, 1963). Also, the distribution of IQs in the Negro population does not as closely approximate the normal curve as in the white population; the Negro distribution is slightly skewed to the right, as shown in Figure 8.2. A similar skew is seen in the Negro distribution of scores on the Armed Forces Qualification Test for all the nation's youths tested in 1968, and on which the Negro variance is only 72 percent as great as the white variance (Office of Surgeon General, 1969, p. 53). Thus it seems well established that Negroes show less variance than do whites on mental tests. Does this mean there is less genetic variance in the Negro population, or less environmental variance, or less of both? It is hard to

H

say. If one assumes a strictly additive model of genetic and environmental effects (that is, no genotypes × environments interaction), and if it is hypothesized that there are no differences, either in means or variances, in the *genotypic* distributions of Negroes and whites for mental ability, then it follows that the environmental variance must be less in the Negro population. If this is true, the broad heritability of IQ should be higher in the Negro than in the white population, unless we assume that the

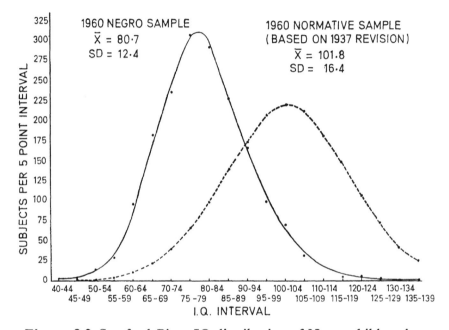

Figure 8.2 Stanford-Binet IQ distribution of Negro children in five Southeastern states (solid line) and of white children in the 1960 normative sample. (From Kennedy, Van De Reit & White, 1963.)

groups differ in the size or direction of the gene-environment correlation which may or may not comprise part of the broad heritability (see Equation A.6 in Appendix on Heritability). But there is no suggestion of this in what little evidence we have.

In the study by Kennedy *et al.* (1963), the Negro and white IQ variances are $(12·4)^2 = 153·76$ and $(16·4)^2 = 268·96$, respectively. If we estimate the heritability of IQs in the white population as $0·80$, the white genetic variance is $0·80 × 268·96 = 215·17$. But this is greater than the *total* Negro IQ variance. In fact, the heritability of IQ in the white group would have to be assumed to be 0·57 for the white *genetic* variance to equal the *total* IQ variance of the Negro group, and surely some of the Negro variance is non-genetic. Furthermore, no reported study of the heritability of Stanford-Binet IQs is as low as 0·57 in the white population. Thus, the hypothesis of identical distributions of genotypes for IQ in the Negro and white samples of the Kennedy *et al.* study is untenable – if we accept the additive model of genetic and environmental effects. If we could support a multiplicative model, on the other hand, there would be no problem. A multiplicative model would hold that since the phenotype, P, equals $G \times E$ (rather than $G + E$), a poor environment would reduce the variance of P, even if the variances of G and E were the same in the Negro and white populations. If G and E actually combine multiplicatively rather than additively, then a logarithmic transformation of the phenotypic measures should be appropriate for the additive model, since if $P = G \times E$, the $\log P = \log G + \log E$. Interestingly enough, when the IQs in the Kennedy *et al.* study are transformed to natural logarithms,[6] the skewness is eliminated, the Negro distribution becomes more nearly normal, and the variances of the Negro and white distributions become equal, although the means are slightly further apart. Thus, the smaller IQ variance of Negroes than of whites could be merely an artifact of our scale for measuring intelligence.

Perhaps the proper scale for IQ should be the suggested logarithmic transformation. How are we to decide which scale is preferable? The writer has not yet found sufficient data for a solid basis for such a decision, but some of the criteria for a choice of scale usually employed in quantitative genetics can be mentioned. In general, the preferable scale is one which (*a*) minimizes the correlation between the means and variances of subgroups within the population, (*b*) closely approximates a normal (Gaussian) distribution in the population, (*c*) the effects of both genetic and environmental factors are as additive as possible, thereby minimizing $G \times E$ interaction. Often not all of these conditions are satisfied by any one scale, and then a decision must be made in terms of which of the conditions it is most desirable to preserve. Criterion (*a*) is probably least important. Height as measured on an interval scale, for example, satisfies all the conditions quite well except (*a*). When children are grouped by age, there will be a correlation between the means and variances of the various age groups – ten-year-olds, for example, are both taller and more variable in height than three-year-olds. Similarly, both the mean and the variance of Stanford-Binet mental age are greater in ten-year-olds than in three-year-olds, and, as in the case of height, we accept this intuitively as a correct reflection of the 'state of nature'. Are we correct, then, to expect that two subpopulations matched for chronological age but differing in mean mental age should also show a difference in variance? (On the other hand, combining all age groups into a single distribution can contradict the above criterion (*b*), and possibly (*c*).)

A statistical test could be applied to determine if the lesser variance of the Negro IQ distribution is an artifact of the scale or a 'fact of nature'. One would determine, for both Negro and white population samples, separately and together, whether there is any significant correlation (both linear and non-linear relationships should be sought) between family means (based on fraternal twins or siblings[7]) and within-family variances. Since the total variance (V_T) of a subpopulation is comprised of the between-families variance (V_B) plus within-families variance (V_W), we should determine if two subpopulations which differ in V_T differ in V_B or V_W or in both. If they differ only in V_B, this suggests a 'fact of nature' rather than an artifact of scale, and this interpretation is strengthened if it is found that there is no significant correlation between family means and within-family variances. A correlation between within-family variances and family means suggests a scale artifact which might be eliminated by a transformation of the scale. These tests, however, would not be worthwhile unless performed on quite large and representative samples of the sub-populations in question. If it is found that the most adequate scale from all these standpoints shows marked differences in IQ variance for Negroes and whites, and if the heritabilities of IQ were either closely comparable in both populations, or smaller in the Negro population, the genetic uniformity hypothesis would be very untenable. It would indicate less genetic variance in the Negro population. (The results could, of course, go in the opposite direction, but the evidence based on the existing scales of mental ability indicates less variance in the Negro samples.) Smaller variance, with the consequence of a lesser proportion of the subpopulation having higher values on the intellectual ability scale, even if the mean were the same as in the general population, would have important social consequences for the subpopulation with the lower variance in terms of the proportion of its members who are able to compete successfully in those endeavors in which proficiency is most highly correlated with intellectual ability. J. B. S. Haldane (1965, pp. xcii-xciii) noted that 'For cultural achievements high variability may be more important than a high average. . . . When we say the ancient Greeks were great mathematicians we are in fact thinking of about 20 men. We know nothing about the average Greeks in this respect.'

Why should two populations have different genetic variances? Differences in gene frequencies and in the degree of assortative mating are the chief causes.[8] A difference in gene frequencies for a given characteristic will cause different means and variances, although if the number of gene loci is large, the difference in variances will be relatively less than the difference in means. If the genetic means in both populations are equal, the most likely explanation of unequal genetic variances is differences in degree of assortative mating. That is, the tendency for like to mate with like with respect to a particular trait. It is known that there is a high degree of assortative mating for intelligence in the white population. (There are no published studies of assortative mating for intelligence in non-white populations.) Assortative mating increases the total genetic variance in the population; it also increases the between-families variance relative to within-families variance. Some 15 to 20 percent of the total variance in the white population is attributable to assortative mating for intelligence. Assortative mating *per se* has no effect on the mean, so if both the genetic means *and* variances differ between two populations, we can suspect differences in gene frequencies as well as differences in assortative mating. One can see this most clearly in a simple illustration involving only a single pair of genes, one allele[9] of which adds to the trait (**A**) and the other of which has no effect on intelligence (**a**). The genetic mean of a population is determined by the proportion of $\mathbf{A}/(\mathbf{A} + \mathbf{a})$ alleles in its gene pool. Such a simple genetic system, used here only for simplicity of illustration, will produce a distribution of the trait having only three values. With many pairs of genes involved, as in the case of a polygenic trait such as intelligence, the distribution of the trait will cover a range of many values. Assume that in population X the frequencies of **a** and **A** alleles are equal, i.e., the proportions are $0.5\mathbf{a} + 0.5\mathbf{A}$. Since every individual receives two alleles (one from each parent), the proportions of all possible combinations[10] of the alleles in the population (assuming random mating – a simplifying but not a necessary assumption) is given by the binomial expansion of $(\cdot 5\mathbf{a} + \cdot 5\mathbf{A})^2$, which is

$$0.25\mathbf{aa} + 0.50\mathbf{aA} + 0.25\mathbf{AA}.$$

The frequency distribution, with three categories (or 'scores'), will thus have one-fourth of the population in the low category, one-half in the 'average' or intermediate category, and one-fourth in the high category. Now consider a hypothetical population Y, in which the proportions of **a** and **A** alleles are 0.6 and 0.4, respectively. In this case, the expansion of $(0.6\mathbf{a} + 0.4\mathbf{A})^2$ is

$$0.36\mathbf{aa} + 0.48\mathbf{aA} + 0.16\mathbf{AA}$$

and 36 percent are in the low category, 48 percent in the intermediate category, and 16 percent in the high category.

If we assign the value of 1 to **A** and 0 to **a**, the mean of population X will be 1.00 and the mean of Y will be 0.80. The variance is 0.50 in population X and 0.48 in population Y. Also, the distribution in population X is symmetrical, while the distribution of Y is skewed to the right. If, in producing the next generation of population X, we assume perfect assortative mating and no loss of genes through selection, the mean would remain 1.00, but the variance would increase to 0.75. (The proportions would be $0.375\mathbf{aa} + 0.250\mathbf{aA} + 0.375\mathbf{AA}$.) We can see that assortative mating increases variance in the population by increasing the proportions of homozygotes (individuals with the same alleles on both chromosomes, i.e., **AA** and **aa**) and decreasing the proportion of heterozygotes (i.e., **Aa**).[11]

NOTES

1. Note that 'accounted for' does not mean 'caused by'. Correlations (zero, order, multiple, or partial) do not and cannot demonstrate causality, although they are a useful basis for hypothesizing causal factors which then must be proved to be causal by other than correlational methods.

2. Groups are quantized by assigning a single numerical value to each member of a group, e.g., male $= 0$, female $= 1$; Negro $= 0$, white $= 1$, etc. In this way it is possible to obtain a product-moment correlation coefficient (called a point-biserial correlation, r_{pbs}) between the quantized variable and a continuous variable such as IQ and SES indexes. Quantized variables are also sometimes called 'dummy' variables.

3. A partial correlation between variables 1 and 2, with variable 3 held constant, is symbolized as $r_{12 \cdot 3}$. The formula for partial correlation is:

$$r_{12 \cdot 3} = \frac{r_{12} - r_{13} r_{23}}{\sqrt{(1 - r_{13}^2)(1 - r_{23}^2)}}$$

Higher order partials, controlling more than one variable, are possible (see Walker & Lev, 1953, pp. 340-4).

4. As far as I can determine, this method was first suggested by Dr Carl Bereiter (personal communication, 3 February 1970).

5. It can be shown that genotype-environment correlation has no effect on h^2 when it is estimated by the most common method of comparing the intraclass correlations for MZ and same-sex DZ twins and the assumption is made that the intrapair environmental effects are the same for MZ and DZ twins. Under an assumption of greater intrapair environmental differences for DZ than for MZ twins, however, increasing values of the genotype-environment correlation result in increasing the genetic variance and consequently the value of h^2. (See Appendix on Heritability, especially Equation A.6.)

6. The transformation is $100(1 + ln \text{ IQ}/100)$, which leaves the mean IQ at 100. (*ln* is the natural logarithm.)

7. Twins would be preferable, especially MZ twins, but they are too scarce to be generally feasible for making a strong statistical test of an hypothesis. In using ordinary siblings, on the other hand, one must take account of age differences. Within-family variance in IQs may be related to within-family variance in chronological age (CA), in which case the within-family CA variance should be partialled out of the correlation between within-family IQ variance and family means.

8. Covariances between genetic and environmental factors can also increase the total phenotypic variance. This source of variance is classifiable, strictly speaking, neither as genetic nor environmental. If environmental differences were reduced, there would be not only less environmental variance but also less covariance due to the correlation of genetic and environmental factors. The total phenotypic variance would therefore be decreased, but the genetic

variance would remain unchanged. Consequently there would be an increase in $V_G/V_P = h^2$.

9. An *allele* is one of two (or more) alternative forms of a gene, occupying the same locus in paired chromosomes.

10. Assuming two kinds of alleles in the population, **A** and **a**, only one of which increases the trait, the distribution of all possible combinations resulting under random mating is given by the binomial expansion of $(p\mathbf{A}+q\mathbf{a})^{2n}$, where p and q are the proportions of **A** and **a** alleles in the population and $p+q = 1$, and n is the number of gene loci (i.e., gene pairs having the same locus on homologous chromosomes). The larger the number of gene loci (n) involved in the trait, the greater must be the disparity from $p = q = 0.5$ to produce a given deviation of the distribution from normality and to produce skewness of the distribution. The number of gene loci involved in intelligence is not known, but various hypotheses have put it in the range from 10 to 100. Jinks and Fulker (1970, p. 343) estimate that at least 22 and perhaps as many as 100 or more genes are involved in determining individual differences in IQ.

11. A detailed account of the quantitative genetics of assortative mating is provided by Crow and Felsenstein (1968).

9 Intelligence of racial hybrids

Those social scientists who insist that there are no racial genetic differences in ability are often the most critical of studies which have used a social criterion of race rather than more precise genetic criteria. The Council of the Society for the Psychological Study of Social Issues (SPSSI), for example, published a statement saying, 'Many of the studies [on white-Negro IQ differences] cited by Jensen [1969a] have employed a social definition of race, rather than the more rigorous genetic definition. Conclusions about the genetic basis for racial differences are obviously dependent on the accuracy of the definition of race employed' (Council of SPSSI, 1969). The SPSSI Council seems not to have considered the idea that if the observed IQ differences between racial groups are due only to social-environmental factors, then the social definition of race should be quite adequate, and, in fact, should be the only appropriate definition. If it is argued that two socially defined racial groups which differ in mean IQ are not racially 'pure' and that one or both groups have some genetic admixture of the other, it can mean only that the biological racial aspect of the IQ differences, if such exists, has been *under*estimated by comparing socially, rather than genetically, defined racial groups.

For this reason, a few investigators have attempted to study the relationship between intelligence and more refined biological criteria of race than is afforded by the crude social classification of persons as 'Negro' or 'white'. The results of these attempts to date are highly ambiguous and contribute little, if anything, to reducing the uncertainty concerning the possible genetic basis of

H*

racial differences in the distribution of intelligence. The research possibilities implicit in this approach, however, are considerable, but they depend upon genetically quite sophisticated methodologies which have been recently suggested but have not yet been applied to the problem. Earlier studies based on highly visible physical characteristics as criteria for degree of racial hybridization were virtually doomed to inconclusiveness.

American Negroes are racial hybrids. In 1926 Herskovits found that 70 percent of a U.S. Negro sample reported having one or more white ancestors (Herskovits, 1926), and in 1969, T. E. Reed, a leading student of this subject, asserted that there are probably no Negroes of pure African descent being born in the United States today, unless they are born to African exchange students (Reed, 1969a). Reed states that the American Negro usually has 'between 2 and 50 percent of his genes from Caucasian ancestors, and these genes were very probably received after 1700' (Reed, 1969a, p. 165). All but a negligible proportion of the slaves brought to the United States arrived between 1700 and 1800 and totalled somewhat less than 400,000. Most of the introduction of Caucasian genes into the American Negro gene pool occurred during the period of slavery. Today the average percentage of Caucasian genes in American Negroes is estimated, on the basis of blood groups, at something between 20 and 30 percent. (These estimates are based largely on population samples from northern urban areas.) The evidence has been summarized by Reed (1969a). The most representative estimate is probably that of Negroes in Oakland, California, with 22 percent Caucasian genes. Due mainly to selective migration, the percentages differ in various parts of the country, being generally lowest in the 'Deep South' and highest in the North and the West. The average in two counties in Georgia is 11 percent. Representative samples in other localities are New York (19 percent), Detroit (26 percent), Baltimore (22-31 percent), Chicago (13 percent), Washington and Baltimore (20-24 percent), Charleston, South Carolina (4-8 percent). Within each of these Negro subpopulations there is considerable variability among individuals in their percentage of Caucasian genes. The Oakland, California Negro population, with its mean of 22 percent Caucasian genes, has an estimated standard deviation of 14 percent (Shockley, 1970b), which means that the variability of the degree of Caucasian admixture among the California Negroes is at least as great as the average differences in Caucasian admixture between Negroes in the South and those in the North and West. The frequency of genes of African origin in the white population, on the other hand, is estimated at less than 1 percent (Reed, 1969b).

The method of estimation of degree of racial admixture is based on analysis of blood groups. There are a number of blood proteins, or antigens, which have markedly different frequencies in African and European populations. When the average frequencies of these blood groups are known for the ancestral populations (in this case West Africans and West Europeans) which gave rise to the hybrid population, it is possible to determine the relative degree of admixture of the two ancestral populations in the hybrid group by analysis of the frequencies of the blood groups in the hybrid sample. The accuracy of the estimate depends upon several factors: (*a*) the size and representativeness of the sample, (*b*) the number of blood groups used, (*c*) the exactness of the estimates of the frequencies of the blood groups in the ancestral populations, and (*d*) the lack of selection, mutation, or genetic drift for the indexed genes. Given these conditions, or a reasonable approximation thereto, the proportion of Caucasian genes (*M*), can be estimated by the formula originated by Glass and Li (1953), two geneticists who first applied this method to determine the Caucasian admixture of Negroes in Baltimore (estimated at 30 percent and later revised to less than 25 percent on the basis of a better estimate of the frequency of Rh in Africa).

$$M = \left| \frac{N_h - N_A}{C - N_A} \right| \tag{9.1}$$

where

M is the proportion of Caucasian genes in the Negro hybrid population

N_h is the proportion of the Negro hybrid population showing the particular blood group

N_A is the proportion of the Negro African ancestral population showing the blood group

C is the proportion of the Caucasian population showing the blood group

The larger the number of blood groups used and the higher the agreement in *M* used, the more confidence we can place in the average estimate. At least a dozen different blood groups can now be used in this determination. Those blood groups which show the largest differences in frequency between West Africans and Caucasians are, of course, the more useful, and the best blood groups for this purpose are those which are totally absent in one or the other ancestral population. The Duffy blood group gene *Fyᵃ* is frequently used because it is virtually absent in the West Africans from whom the original slave populations were derived and it occurs in over 40 percent of Caucasians. For this reason *Fyᵃ* has been called the 'Caucasian gene'. In this case $M = N_h/C$.

SKIN COLOR AND IQ

Skin color is inherited and Negro-Caucasian differences in skin color are attributable most probably to only 3 to 4 pairs of genes (Stern, 1970).[1] Various genetic models for skin color postulate anywhere from 2 to 8 loci to explain the distribution of skin colors found in hybrid groups. Although skin color is definitely related to degree of African-Caucasian admixture for the average of *groups* having different degrees of admixture, skin color is not a highly reliable index of Caucasian admixture in individuals (Harrison *et al.*, 1967; Stern, 1970). When so few genes are involved in a characteristic, the individual variability of the characteristic among persons having exactly the same ancestry is great. The offspring of true mulattoes (who are the offspring of Caucasian and African parents), for example, show a wide range of skin color even within the same family. Estimates of the correlation of skin color in Negroes with amount of Caucasian ancestry are about 0·30 to 0·40. Thus, in terms of measurement theory, where the reliability of a measurement is the square of the correlation between true score and the observed score, the reliability of skin color ('observed score') as an index of Caucasian ancestry ('true score') would be at most about $0·40^2$ or 0·16. If now we hypothesize that there is a correlation between Negroes' IQs and the amount of their Caucasian ancestry and that this correlation is slightly higher than for skin color (since more genes are involved in intelligence), say about 0·50 as an upper limit of the correlation, the reliability of IQ as an index of Caucasian ancestry would be about $0·50^2$ or 0·25. The highest correlation that can be obtained between two measures is the square root of the product of their reliabilities. So the highest correlation we could expect to find between IQ and skin color would be about $\sqrt{(0\cdot16)\,(0\cdot25)} = 0\cdot20$. Any higher correlation than this would most probably be attributable to factors other than racial admixture *per se*. The fact that the correlations between skin color and IQ should be about $0\cdot20$ at most, if in fact there is a genetic racial difference in intelligence, and the fact that a correlation this high or higher between color and IQ could arise for quite other reasons make it a weak and inconclusive type of evidence with respect to the central hypothesis.

Shuey (1966) has reviewed all the studies which attempted to relate IQ to skin color in racial hybrids. In 12 of the 18 studies, the hybrids lighter in color score higher than the darker; in 4 other studies the lighter scored higher in the majority of tests given, i.e., in 3 out of 4 or 3 out of 5; and in two of the comparisons there was no evidence of a relationship between the visible indexes of white ancestry and test score. These studies leave little doubt of a true relationship between skin color (and other visible features ranged along a Negroid-Caucasoid continuum) and scores on intelligence tests. The actual correlation between lightness of skin and test scores was determined in several studies, all reviewed by Shuey (1966, pp. 456-63). Correlations range from $0\cdot12$ (Klineberg, 1928), to $0\cdot17$ (Herskovits, 1926) and $0\cdot18$ and $0\cdot30$ (Peterson & Lanier, 1929). But, as Herskovits (1926) pointed out, the question that such studies do not answer is the extent to which these correlations are a result of racial admixture. They could be just the result of assortative mating patterns which bring about a genetic correlation between skin color (and other visible characteristics) and intelligence. If lightness of skin is a socially valued characteristic, it would be a factor in assortative mating, along with other factors such as intelligence and its correlates of educational and socioeconomic status. Thus, genes for skin color and for intelligence would become segregated together, resulting in a phenotypic correlation between these two characteristics which would have nothing to do with *racial* intelligence differences. In fact, in such a situation the preponderance of genes for intelligence theoretically could have come from the hybrids' African ancestors. Furthermore, some part of the correlation between skin color and IQ could be a direct consequence of attitudes in the social environment which favor lighter colored Negro children and adults. Freeman *et al.* (1966) found a significant positive relationship between lightness of skin and income, socioeconomic status, and educational attainment in Negroes. There was also a correlation between spouses in skin color, showing that this characteristic is a factor in assortative mating in the Negro population. Obviously, to establish any direct correlation between intelligence and degree of Caucasian admixture in Negroes would require the use of non-visible genetic characteristics, which are therefore not a basis for assortative mating or social discrimination, as an index of Caucasian admixture.

GENETIC BIOCHEMICAL POLYMORPHISMS AND IQ

The use of genetic polymorphisms in the blood for researching this problem was suggested independently by Shockley (1966), a physicist noted for the invention of the transistor, and by Heston, a psychiatric geneticist noted for his research on the genetics of schizophrenia (e.g., Heston, 1966). Essentially, Heston has proposed obtaining correlations between skin color (measured with a reflectance spectrophotometer on the underside of the upper arm) and mental test scores, on the one hand, and between percentage of Caucasian admixture (based on a dozen or more blood groups) and intelligence scores, on the other, and then testing the hypothesis that the non-visible index of Caucasian admixture (blood groups) correlates more highly with intelligence than the visible index of skin color. If the blood groups measure of M (proportion of Caucasian genes) correlates more highly with, say, IQ than does skin color, the hypothesis of a racial genetic difference in intelligence would be supported. Blood groups are a more reliable basis than skin color for estimating Caucasian admixture because more genes are involved and because blood groups, being non-visible, do not enter into mate selection.

Heston, with quantitative geneticist Oscar Kempthorne and statistician James Hickman, worked out a method for statistically estimating the proportion of Caucasian genes in *individual* Negroes, which is a more complex problem than the estimation of M, the proportion of Caucasian genes in a particular hybrid Negro *population*. The method for estimating the Caucasian admixture of individual Negroes is as follows:

We have two ancestral racial groups, Caucasian (C) and African (A). Also, we have some measurable genetic polymorphism, G, which has 1, 2, 3 ... k forms. (A polymorphism is 2 or more genetically different forms at the same locus on the chromosome [and therefore mutually exclusive], for example, Rh-positive and Rh-negative blood types.) In addition, we know the probability, P (i.e., the gene frequency), of each of these blood polymorphisms in each of the ancestral populations. (The frequencies of many blood polymorphisms in European and African populations are given in Race & Sanger, 1968.) We can represent this information as follows:

Genetic Polymorphism	Ancestral Population	
	C	A
$G1$	P_{CG1}	P_{AG1}
$G2$	P_{CG2}	P_{AG2}
$G3$	P_{CG3}	P_{AG3}

Now, say we have a sample from a hybrid population representing a genetic mix of the C and A populations. We can determine the probability, b, that an observed polymorphism, say, $G1$, originated in C. (The probability that it originated in A is, then, of course, $1-b$.) It is $b = |H-A/C-A|$, where H is the proportion of the hybrid population showing $G1$, and C and A are the proportions of the two ancestral populations showing $G1$ (i.e., the values P_{CG1} and P_{AG1} in the above table). So, for the hybrid Negro population (N), we have the following probability matrix for each of the 3 forms of the polymorphism G.

Genetic Polymorphism	Population Sample	
	C	N
$G'1$	$(b-1)P_{CG1}$	bP_{AC1}
$G'2$	$(b-1)P_{CG2}$	bP_{AG2}
$G'3$	$(b-1)P_{CG3}$	bP_{AG3}

Now, say we draw an individual from the hybrid Negro sample, N, and we find this individual possesses the $G1$ form of the blood group; since these alternate forms occupy the same locus and are therefore mutually exclusive, he will not possess G2 or G3. So, for this individual, $G'1 = 1$ and $G'2 = G'3 = 0$. This individual, then, is represented in the top right-hand cell ($b\,P_{AG1}$) of the above matrix. The estimated probability $E(b')$ that this individual's $G'1$ blood type originated from Caucasian ancestors is thus:

$$E(b') = \frac{\bar{M}P_{AG1}}{\bar{M}P_{AG1} + (1 - \bar{M})P_{CG1}} \tag{9.2}$$

where P is the value shown in the first table above and $\bar{M}$ is the proportion of Caucasian genes in the hybrid group, being the *average* of a number of determinations using blood groups for which the estimated ancestral frequencies are most reliable, such as the Duffy Fy^a gene. For each individual $E(b')$ is determined similarly from a number of polymorphisms, mostly various blood antigens, and an average of the b's, $\bar{b}'$, will be the estimate of the proportion of Caucasian genes in an individual. Since there is non-random mating in natural populations, there should be a correlation between individual estimates of b' for various genes; that is, because of assortative mating, genes of Caucasian origin would have tended to stay together to some greater than chance degree in the Negro hybrids. The extent of this deviation from random assortment can be computed. If it can be shown that the value of b' for one assessed phenotypic character (e.g., a particular blood group) can reliably predict the average b' for all the other assessed phenotypes, then it can be presumed that it also predicts the genetic mix in the unassessed phenotypes. If the estimates of b' for individuals meet these criteria with a high level of statistical significance, the b's for individuals can be correlated with measures of skin color and of mental ability. If the correlation of b' with intelligence is significantly larger than with skin color (or if the partial correlation of b' and IQ, with the effect of skin color removed, is significantly greater than zero) we would reject the hypothesis of no genetic racial difference in ability.

Since variation in skin pigmentation, because of its social-environmental consequences, is controlled in this research design, any direct biochemical connection between degree of skin pigmentation and intelligence must be either ruled out or, if such a relationship is established, its consequences for the present design must be assessed. The possibility of a biochemical connection between skin pigmentation and intelligence is not totally unlikely in view of the biochemical relation between melanins, which are responsible for pigmentation, and some of the neural transmitter substances in the brain. The skin and the cerebral cortex both arise from the ectoderm in the development of the embryo and share some of the same biochemical processes.

If there is some correlation between amount of Caucasian ancestry of a Negro child and the cultural-environmental influences acting upon him, it could be argued that this approach does not sufficiently control or 'read through' environmental determinants of intelligence to allow any definitive conclusion. However, if the correlation between proportion of Caucasian genes and intelligence showed up substantially even in environmentally quite homogeneous samples, such evidence would surely strengthen a genetic hypothesis of racial intelligence differences. A further control, but one that would require the screening of very large samples for the optimal blood groups, would involve maternal half-siblings. Pairs of half-sibs would be selected to differ in their proportions of Caucasian genes, as estimated by the methods just described, and would also be measured for skin color and IQ. In other words, we would have matched controls for both prenatal and postnatal environmental effects. It is hard to imagine any reason why, on the average, the environments should favor the child with the more Caucasian genes when the independent effects of skin color and other visible characteristics are statistically controlled. It might be possible to find environments which favor the more Negroid characteristics, so that finding a positive correlation between Caucasian genes and IQ in such circumstances would be even more compelling.

Since studies of this kind have not yet been done, there is no good basis for speculating about their probable outcome when and if they are carried out.[2] Shockley (1971b)[3] has noted that California Negroes have twice as high a percentage of their genes from Caucasian ancestors as do Georgia Negroes and that the IQ difference between Negroes in California and in Georgia (estimated from army pre-induction test results) is about 10 points. But this observation can carry little conviction, since differences in the cultural and educational conditions of Negroes in Georgia and in California are completely confounded with differences in Caucasian gene frequencies as possible causes of the IQ difference.[4]

OFFSPRINGS OF NEGRO-WHITE MATINGS

Theoretically, if most of the variation in intelligence is due to additive genetic effects, the average intelligence of the offspring of parents from each of two racial groups with different genetic means should be approximately intermediate between the means of the two groups. And if genetic factors were all-important, the offsprings' average should be the same regardless of whether the mother or the father had the higher IQ or came from the group with the higher mean. If the test scores of the offspring were *not* independent of the mother's race, this would constitute evidence for non-genetic factors in racial IQ variation – provided a crucial condition is met, viz., that the average parental IQ is the same for either maternal or paternal racial combination. Failure to meet this requirement makes the only published study of this type wholly inconclusive. Willerman, Naylor, and Myrian-thopoulos (1970) compared the IQs of four-year-old children resulting from all four of the possible combinations of matings of Negro and white men and women. They found that the interracial offspring of white mothers were significantly higher than of inter-lacial Negro mothers. Nearly all of this effect was due to the very low IQs of the male children of unmarried Negro mothers. Maternal race was a significant factor in the results only among the children of the unmarried Negro mothers, whose children, particularly the males, had the lowest IQs. This finding accords with others show-ing the greater vulnerability of males to unfavorable prenatal, perinatal, and postnatal conditions (Jensen, 1971b). But the study sheds little, if any, light on racial genetic differences, since there was no measurement of the parental IQs in the two interracial combinations.[5] Persons involved in interracial marriages or matings cannot be regarded as representative of the general population of whites or Negroes. For example, a study (reported in Goldhammer, 1971) of racial intermarriages between 1914 and 1938 in Boston showed that Negro grooms were occupationally well above the average employed Negro male, whereas white grooms were occupationally far below employed white males in general. Both white and Negro brides in interracial marriages were occupation-ally below the average of women in their respective racial groups. In interracial marriages, the average IQ of Negro grooms is probably higher than of white grooms. Thus the higher IQs of interracial children born to white mothers could be due to the genetic effect of the superior Negro father rather than to any prenatal or postnatal environmental advantage afforded by having a white mother.

NOTES

1. Skin pigmentation is usually measured by one of two methods. The oldest method is by means of a 'color top', a disc having adjustable sectors of different colors (e.g., black, white, red, yellow) which are blended by spinning the disc; the sizes of the colored sectors are adjusted so that when they are blended, they match the individual's skin color. The calibrated sizes of the colored sectors thus provide a reasonably reliable, objective index of skin color. A more recent method is based on the measurement of skin reflectance with a photoreflectometer; reflectances are usually measured in three key color ranges of the visible spectrum, using blue, green, and amber tri-stimulus filters. The readings with each filter are usually made on the underside of the upper arm, on the forehead, and on the back of the neck, and the readings for the various sites are averaged. The range of values found between African Negroes and English whites follows a straight line; the genes for pigmentation appear to be additive in effect. Technical details can be found in Harrison (1957) and Harrison and Owen (1956, 1964).

2. The feasibility of this kind of study at the present time is not universally unquestioned among geneticists. In a personal communication, geneticist Peter L. Workman writes:

> Since American Negroes do not comprise an equilibrium population, morphological characters constituting an African appearance segregate together with African genes. Holding constant external appearance (skin color, lip breadth, etc.) might also partial out most of the relevant information. Further, Heston's method doesn't account for the non-equilibrium structure. Thus, although the experimental idea is a good one, and MacLean and I will present the appropriate methods in print shortly, I am very skeptical that it could be done at this time. We need more African data [on blood group frequencies].

3. Shockley (1970b) has also suggested dividing a large Negro group, such as the total enrolment in an all-Negro school or college, into two halves on the basis of some assessment of intellectual ability

(e.g., above or below the median in IQ, college entrance tests, grade-point average, etc.) and then determining the proportion of the lower and higher groups showing the Duffy Fy^a 'Caucasian gene'. This test must assume no correlation between Fy^a and socially visible features which could affect IQ and no correlation between Fy^a and IQ in the white population. The feasibility of this proposal has been questioned because the American Negro population probably has not yet reached genetic (Hardy-Weinberg) equilibrium, so there would probably be a great deal of genetic linkage of visible African morphological features and blood polymorphisms. Controlling or partialling out the visible racial characteristics would therefore also partial out some of the IQ variance associated with the blood groups used as an index of the degree of African-Caucasian admixture. If it could be argued that the socially visible African features did not themselves constitute an 'environmental' disadvantage that might adversely affect mental development or performance on intelligence tests, the proposal would have merit despite genetic disequilibrium in American Negro racial hybrids.

4. If a 10 percent admixture of Caucasian genes raises the IQ of Negro-white hybrids by 10 points, one would have to assume a great deal of genetic interaction or some kind of hybrid vigor to explain why a 100 percent admixture of Caucasian genes would raise the IQ only about 15 points. If an admixture of Caucasian genes had the large effect suggested by Shockley, one should expect there to be much greater genetic variance among Negroes, and there is no evidence of this. If anything, the evidence is for less genetic variance in the Negro population. The 10-points IQ difference between Georgia and California Negroes would therefore most reasonably be attributed mainly to selective migration and environmental differences.

5. For further comments see the four critiques of the study by Willerman *et al.* in the Letters to *Science*, 1971, **172**, 8-12, with a reply by Willerman *et al.*

10 *Environmental rationalization versus environmental research*

In the chapters that follow, it is necessary to distinguish 'environmentalism' from research on the environment. *Environmentalism* is the scientifically anomalous attitude that ignores, shuns, or denigrates any hypothesis of genetic causation in specific classes of human individual or group differences. Environmentalists differ among themselves in the kinds of differences from which they exclude the possibility of genetic influences. Thus we see environmentalists who accept the findings on the heritability of individual differences in intelligence but who vehemently argue against the suggestion that genetic factors may be involved in any subpopulation differences, social-class or racial. Still others acknowledge the evidence on genetic intelligence differences among social classes *within* racial groups, but categorically reject without evidence the hypothesis that specific racial groups differ genetically in mental abilities. Some will admit genetic explanations, or at least grant their plausibility, regarding racial differences in physical and sensory capacities, while not allowing the possibility of genetic differences in more complex mental capabilities. The idea that certain small and isolated racial groups, such as the Australian Bushmen, might differ genetically from major racial groups in mental capacities is viewed only with a mild skepticism by some environmentalists, who vociferously denounce those who would question wholly environmental theories of intelligence differences between major racial groups.

The aim of the environmentalist, almost as a matter of principle, is to 'explain' a given human difference as due wholly to environmental causes. As already noted, environmentalists often differ in the particular kinds of traits and groups to which they extend their insistence upon a wholly environmental explanation of human differences. This tendency results in the uncritical acceptance of almost any environmental factor that anyone suggests as an explanation, regardless of its often purely *ad hoc* status, its inconsistency with other data, and often the failure even to show any *correlation*, much less causation, between the suggested environmental causes and the behavioral traits in question. Since an environmental explanation is decreed as necessary and sufficient, almost any environmental factor will do, without the need to demonstrate its causal connection, or even correlation, with intelligence or scholastic achievement. Some environmental factors are formulated clearly enough to be put to the test of evidence; as each of the hypothesized factors is rejected on the basis of evidence, other increasingly subtle environmental deficits are postulated to explain the differences. Baratz and Baratz (1970, p. 35) have noted this tendency in various attempts to account for the failure of intervention programs such as Head Start to appreciably raise IQ and scholastic performance:

> Postulation of one deficit which is unsuccessfully dealt with by intervention programs then leads to the discovery of more basic and fundamental deficits. Remediation or enrichment gradually broadens its scope of concern from the fostering of language competence to a broad-based restructuring of the entire cultural system. The end result of this line of argument occurs when investigators such as Deutsch and Deutsch (1968) postulate that 'some environments are better than others'.

Inconsistencies abound in environmentalist arguments. Unrelated children adopted at birth and reared together are much less alike in IQ than true siblings, it is said, because of subtle factors within the family environment which makes them dissimilar in intelligence. In the next breath it is argued that identical twins reared apart in different families are highly similar in IQ because of subtle influences common to both families (though they may be at opposite ends of the SES spectrum and have no knowledge of one another) which make for a high correlation between the twins' IQs. How often do we see environmentalists propose any experiment, statistical study, type of evidence, or any combination thereof, which could cause them to question the null hypothesis regarding genetic differences, or even to reject a particular environmental factor which has been postulated as a cause of IQ differences? Various environmental factors are constantly repeated in the environmentalist literature as a cause of IQ differences, even when studies specifically designed to test these hypotheses have yielded largely negative results. There seems to be no way for the environmentalist to give up any hypothesized environmental factor; regardless of the outcomes of empirical tests, each newly hypothesized factor is added to the growing list of purported environmental causes of IQ differences.

The principal environmentalist fallacy consists of looking for any environmental differences that exist between two subpopulation groups which differ in mean IQ and merely *assuming* that the environmental differences are the cause of the IQ difference; usually it is not even regarded as necessary to demonstrate that a non-zero correlation between the hypothesized environmental factor and IQ exists *within* the groups. At least three critical questions need to be answered about every hypothesized environmental factor before one can even begin to consider whether it is a causal factor: (1) Does it correlate with the trait in question *within* the two groups being compared? (2) How much do the groups differ on the environmental factors? (3) Does the factor make any significant contribution to within-groups or between-groups variance in the trait independently of other hypothesized factors? As pointed out in a previous section, one cannot properly assess the importance of a large number of intercorrelated environmental factors from the single (zero order) correlations of each one with IQ. It is each variable's independent contribution to the multiple correlation that counts. When major environmental factors fail to account for IQ differences sufficiently to sustain the environmental hypothesis, other subtler environmental factors are then postulated, and they may be tested in a new study and be found to show some correlation with the IQ difference. But rarely are they combined with the variables of the first study to see if they in fact add any significant increment to the coefficient of multiple determination (R^2). Even if they do, the direction of the causality often remains an open question which can be answered only by evidence other than correlational data. The pattern of multiple correlations at best narrows the range of possibilities in seeking the most probably fruitful environmental variables for experimental manipulation.

It is this approach which distinguishes research on environmental factors, which is a legitimate scientific enterprise, from dogmatic environmentalism. Behavior geneticists recognize the influence of non-genetic factors in all forms of behavior and in all individual and group differences, and they are interested in understanding these non-genetic factors precisely and in learning what proportions of the variance they contribute, singly and in combination, and how much is due to additive, interactive, and covariance effects in the population. Developmental behavior genetics seeks to understand how the individual phenotype develops through the genotype's interaction with and utilization of the environment. Variance in genotypes for any trait, within or between groups, is not ruled out or restricted on any *a priori* basis. Environmentalism, on the other hand, simply decrees the null hypotheses *a priori* with respect to certain classes of genetic variance, and in order to fill the void must posit a number of environmental influences or measurement biases which often are accepted merely on the grounds of plausibility. It is possible, however, to bring research evidence to bear on many specific environmental factors and test biases which environmentalists assume are the main causes of subpopulation differences in intelligence and related performance. Under such examination of the relevant evidence, some of the main pillars of the environmentalist argument regarding Negro-white intelligence differences simply collapse, still others are seen to be resting on extremely flimsy foundations in fact, while the remainder are so vaguely formulated as to be insusceptible to empirical proof or disproof.

11 Equating for socioeconomic variables

In comparative studies of the mental abilities of racial groups, environmentalists are most insistent that the racial samples being compared on intelligence be matched, or otherwise equated, on indices of socioeconomic status (SES), which usually includes father's occupation, education of parents, income, quality of housing, and place of residence. When groups are thus 'equated' and a substantial mean IQ difference still shows up, it is claimed that not enough environmental factors were controlled. As one sociologist put it: '. . . the kinds of socioeconomic measures that have been used so far in attempting to control on environmental effects appear to omit a wealth of cultural and psychological factors'. This is a testable hypothesis; it should be determined how much the cultural and psychological factors (assuming they can be specified and measured) add to the multiple R^2 with IQ over and above the R^2 yielded by good indices of SES.

But the whole notion of equating for SES, in the first place, involves what has been called the 'sociologist's fallacy'. This fallacy is seen in full bloom in one sociologist's criticism of studies of Negro-white IQ differences which equated the groups for SES or other environmental factors: 'Actually in most of the studies he [Jensen, 1969a] reports on, the most important environmental variable, the IQ of the parent, has not been equated at all' (Stinchcombe, 1969, p. 516). Apart from the strictly *environmental* effect of parental IQ,[1] it is obvious that, since IQ variance contains a large genetic component, equating groups for parental IQ means equating them for genetic factors more than for environmental factors. The same is true, though to a lesser degree, when we equate for SES. When typical Negro children are equated with white children on some index of SES, one is comparing a *majority* of the Negro population with some lower fraction of the white population.[2] The white comparison group, therefore, is not genetically representative of the entire white population but is genotypically (as well as environmentally) lower by some substantial degree. Thus, if one supposes one is equating only for environmental influences, equating on SES equates *too much*. The method would be a proper control of environmental factors if *all* children had been placed in their SES categories completely at random, in the nature of a true experiment. But as it is, SES classification is more a result than a cause of IQ variance.

Consider the fact that there is a much *lower* correlation between IQ and the SES in which one is reared than between IQ and persons' SES as adults. If SES *per se* were an important environmental determinant of IQ, we should expect children's IQs to correlate at least as much with the SES of their parents as with the SES the children attain as adults, but this is far from being the case. Burt (1961b) found in England that approximately 30 percent of the population changes SES (half going up and half going down) in each generation (based on father's occupation divided into six classes, from 'higher professional' to 'unskilled labor'). There is probably similar intergenerational mobility in the United States, at least in the white population. In Minnesota, for example, Waller (1971b) found a correlation of 0·724 between men's IQs (measured when they were in high school) and their adult occupations but a correlation of only 0·32 between their IQs and their own fathers' adult occupations. (The corresponding correlations in an English population were 0·77 and 0·36 [Burt, 1961b].) The *SD* of parental IQs *within* occupational classes is generally much less (about one-half) than that of children's IQs within occupational classes, which is usually only one or two points less than the *SD* of the total population (see Gottesman, 1968). This very great variance of children's IQs within each class is embarrassing to environmental theories. It is predictable from the polygenic theory of intelligence.

Although matching for SES in comparing racial groups most likely works *against* a genetic hypothesis of the racial difference, because it matches to some degree for genetic as well as environmental factors, it is nevertheless instructive to note the results of studies which have attempted to control for SES by actual matching or by statistical equating of groups. In reviewing all the studies of this type up to 1965, Shuey (1966, p. 518) summarizes the results as follows:

> With two exceptions, the colored averaged below the white groups in mental test performance in all of the 42 investigations. [The two exceptions were studies which showed ambiguous results or presented insufficient statistical analysis to permit an evaluation.] Average IQs were reported in 33 of the studies including a total of about 7,900 colored and 9,300 white *S*s, and from these a mean difference of 11 points favoring the whites was obtained [in contrast to a mean difference of 15-16 IQ points when random samples are compared]. . . . Twenty-five of the 41 studies were located in the North, and in at least fourteen of the researches the colored and white children were not only attending the same school, but were living in the same district or neighborhood. The combined mean difference in IQ between the 2,760 colored subjects tested in the North and the whites of comparable socioeconomic status or occupation was 7·6. Nearly all of these *S*s in the eighteen studies were of school age, the whites and Negroes attending the same school and living in the same areas, many with large Negro populations.

A more recent study by Tulkin (1968) controlled not only SES but a number of subtle family environmental factors. Controlling SES alone did not overcome the racial difference in mean IQ. After the familial behavioral differences were equated, however, Tulkin concluded, 'When family differences were also statistically controlled, there were no significant racial differences on test scores in the upper socioeconomic group, although differences remained significant in the lower socioeconomic group.' Two critical points should be made about this particular study, however. First, the upper SES Negro group was small ($N = 52$), and though it did not show a statistically significant difference from the white upper SES group, the difference was in the same direction as in most other studies.[3] Second, Tulkin's analysis, which controlled (by covariance analysis) for various family factors within SES groups, was based on a composite score of verbal and non-verbal IQ plus five scholastic achievement tests. The composite score is thus more heavily weighted with scholastic achievement than with intelligence. As was noted previously, achievement scores (*a*) have lower heritability than IQ, (*b*) are more susceptible to family environmental influences, and (*c*) generally show smaller racial differences than does IQ, as is also true in Tulkin's study when the social and family variables are not controlled. Controlling these variables, therefore, should make a greater impression on achievement than on IQ tests. Even among the several achievement tests the magnitude of the difference between the upper SES white and upper SES Negro groups is greater for the *less* culturally loaded subject matter. The upper SES white sample exceeds the Negro upper SES sample, for example, by only 0·18 *SD* on the language achievement test but by 0·51 *SD* on the arithmetic test, a highly significant difference. When we compare the upper and lower SES white samples on these two achievement tests, on the other hand, the reverse occurs: the SES difference is greater for language than for arithmetic. These results, then, are consistent with the general finding, which is reviewed in a subsequent section, that the largest differences between Negroes and whites appear on tests that are the least culturally loaded. Tulkin's study also shows the composite achievement score to be more highly correlated with verbal IQ than with non-verbal IQ, and the overall Negro-white difference is greater on non-verbal IQ. Tulkin's investigation might have been more interesting if he had also applied the covariance control of family variables to non-verbal IQ alone rather than only to a composite score heavily weighed with achievement tests.

But as was pointed out, the method of matching racial groups for SES or other environmental variables and then comparing their mean IQs cannot tell us anything of importance, except that the SES matched groups are usually more alike in IQ than unmatched groups, for some indeterminate combination of genetic and environmental causes. We can go a step further, however, and seek a set of circumstances in which environmentalist and genetic theories should predict opposite results. The environmentalists' emphasis on equating for SES, and even for parental intelligence, is based on the idea that the SES variable has a predominantly causal connection with IQ, and therefore racial IQ differences will be eliminated to the extent that we are successful in equating SES and other environmental factors. The logic at least is clear, even if the premises are questionable. But the logic suggests an interesting comparison. What if we compared (*a*) Negro children reared in upper-middle-class homes by Negro parents whose educational and occupational status and income were well above the average of the white population with (*b*) white children reared in the lowest SES category, whose parents are well below the average in intelligence, have less than an average education, and are either in unskilled work or on welfare?

Even if parental IQs were not measured, there would be little doubt in such a case that the high SES Negro parents would have higher IQs in general than the low SES white parents. If these SES factors are more important determinants of IQ than genetic factors, there can be no doubt that the predicted result should be a much higher mean IQ for the upper SES Negro children than for the lower SES white children. An ideal study along these lines has not yet been done; it would involve obtaining IQs of both parents of every child and making a prediction of the child's IQ based on a genetic model. Since there is some regression toward the population mean from parent's IQ to child's IQ, a genetic theory of the racial intelligence difference would predict that Negro and white children should regress toward different population means. In the two SES groups we are considering here, the regression would be in opposite directions: the children of the high SES Negro parents would on the average regress to some degree downward toward the Negro population mean, and the low SES white children would regress upward toward the white population mean. Because the Negro population mean is about one standard deviation below the white population mean, the mean IQs of our two hypothetical groups of children would be much closer together than if we compared the mean IQs of low and high SES white children, and this should be so, according to our genetic hypothesis, even if the high SES Negro and white parents were perfectly matched on IQ. The conformity of actual data to the predictions from this genetic model will, of course, be attenuated to the degree that the parents' and offsprings' environments have been dissimilar with respect to factors influencing mental development.

Facts relevant to this hypothesis have been summarized by Shuey (1966, pp. 519-20): 'Where Negro pupils have been compared with whites of the same occupational or socioeconomic class and where children from two or more classes have served as subjects, a greater difference has been found between the racial samples at the upper than at the lower level.' The eight relevant studies were all in agreement in this finding. Shuey (p. 519) continues: 'The combined mean difference in IQ between the 617 colored *S*s of higher status and their white counterparts is 20·3, in contrast with a combined mean difference of 12·2 between the 3,374 colored and 2,293 white children of low status.' Overall, the mean IQ of the high status Negro children is 2·6 points *below* the mean IQ of the low status white.[4] Since the publication of Shuey's review in 1966, this finding has been repeated in three major studies based on very large samples (Coleman *et al.*, 1966; Wilson, 1967; Scarr-Salapatek, 1971a). In each study, when Negro and white children are classified by the same criteria into from 3 to 5 categories according to parental SES, the *mean mental test scores of the lowest SES white group exceeds the mean IQ of the highest SES Negro group*. It is significant that no major study has found contradictory results. Also, data from the Coleman Report indicate that, with the exception of Puerto Ricans, other minority groups (American Indians, Mexican-Americans and Orientals), which are socioeconomically less advantaged than the white majority population, do not show this phenomenon – that is, their upper SES group in every case exceeds the white lower (and usually also middle) SES group in test scores.

NOTES

1. The environmental contribution of parental IQ can best be assessed by means of adopted or foster children, since there is little or no genetic correlation between foster children and their foster parents. In a study of this kind by Burks (1928), it was found that the *total* environmental contribution to the IQs of the foster children was only 17 percent (which is close to $1 - h^2$ when h^2 is based on twin studies). The independent *environmental* contribution of parents' intelligence (mother and father combined) was about 3 percent. Burks (1928, p. 301) states: 'We should not expect this *environmental* contribution of parental intelligence to be over four or five percent, however, because the correlations (even when corrected for attenuation) between child's IQ and foster parents' M.A. (mental age) are so very low.' The correlation was 0·09 for foster father and 0·23 for

foster mother. A study by Honzik (1957) showed approximately the same correlation between foster children and their biological parents, with whom they have had no contact since birth, as found for children reared by their own parents. The adopted children did not correlate significantly with their adopting parents. In the frequently cited study by Skodak and Skeels (1949), children of rather low IQ mothers (mean = 85·75) were adopted into superior foster homes. They showed a correlation of 0·38 with their true mothers with whom they had no contact beyond infancy. The adopted children's average IQ, however, was approximately 11 points higher than the mean IQ that would be predicted from a genetic model assuming that the children represented a random selection of the offspring of mothers with a mean IQ of 85 and were placed in randomly selected environments in the population. Actually, of course, these children were selected by the adoption agency as suitable for adoption and the adoptive homes were selected for their favorable environmental attributes. The 11 points, however, is very likely an overestimate of any environmental effect on these children's IQs, since the children put out for adoption, most of them illegitimate, were not a random selection of such children, and it has been indicated by Leahy (1935) that illegitimate children who become adopted have a higher average IQ than illegitimate children in general or than legitimate children placed for adoption. Readers interested in a detailed and trenchant critique of the Skodak and Skeels studies should read Terman (1940, pp. 462-7) and McNemar (1940).

2. The Negro and white populations of the U.S. today differ about 1 *SD* in SES in terms of the *SD* of SES in the white population. Thus the average SES difference between the races is approximately the same as the average absolute difference among persons within the white population.

3. The mean IQs of the white upper and lower SES groups in Tulkin's study are at the 81st and 34th percentiles of the white population norms; the corresponding percentiles of the upper and lower SES Negro samples, based on Negro population parameters ($\bar{X} = 85$, $\sigma = 14$) are 95th percentile and 66th percentile, respectively.

4. Shuey (1966, p. 520, footnote 55) gives the following means (of children's scores) for the combined studies:

Socioeconomic Status

Children	Upper	Lower	Difference
White	111·88	94·22	17·66
Negro	91·63	82·04	9·59
Difference	20·25	12·18	

Assuming a single parent-offspring regression of 0·50 and no assortative mating, which is the simplest possible genetic model, and assuming a white population mean of 100 and a Negro population mean of 85, the mean IQs of the most extreme parent (probably the father or the one who chiefly determines the family's SES) are estimated as follows:

Socioeconomic Status

Parent	Upper	Lower	Difference
White	124	88	36
Negro	99	79	20
Difference	25	9	

It can be seen that the race × SES crossover in children's IQs (shown by the diagonal in the top table) must result because the upper SES white and Negro parents differ quite markedly in IQ, assuming a genetic interpretation of Shuey's data is correct. If the Negro parent mean IQs were perfectly matched to the white IQs, this simple genetic model, given the assumptions previously stated, would predict mean IQs of 104·5 and 86·5 for the upper and lower SES Negro children.

It also appears that, in terms of IQ, the high SES white samples in those studies summarized by Shuey may represent a slightly more select upper segment of the white population while the high SES Negro samples may represent a somewhat less select upper segment of the Negro population. The white children's mean IQ of 111·88 is at approximately the 73rd percentile in the white population while the Negro children's mean of 91·63 is only at about the 70th percentile in the Negro population, assuming equal σ in both populations. If the Negro σ is smaller than the white σ, as is true in the majority of studies, then the high SES Negro samples in Shuey's summary could be a more select segment of the Negro population than is true of the high SES white sample.

12 *Accentuated environmental inequalities*

Negro-white IQ comparisons usually mean comparison of an environmentally less favored group with a more favored group. When the IQ difference is in the same direction as the environmental difference, the interpretation is problematic. Gottesman (1968, p. 34) has expressed the commonly held view: 'It is only when two individuals or two groups come from equally favorable environments that a difference in measured IQ can be interpreted to indicate a difference in genetic potential.' But what about environmental inequalities that are *opposite* in direction to the IQ difference? Kuttner (1968, p. 147) first noted the methodological possibilities suggested by this set of conditions:

> If two populations can be studied which have experienced long-standing differential treatment, and yet both achieve at the same level, then grounds exist for presuming superior potential in one group. Or if one of the two groups responds to ameliorative conditions with a more markedly improved performance, then the same conclusion can be entertained. This procedure avoids artificially equating a disadvantaged group with a favored majority who may enjoy psychological and cultural benefits that are secondary products of status and hence beyond tabulation. At the same time, comparing deprived groups may isolate the significant variables that contribute most heavily to overall performance.

Kuttner then proceeds with a detailed comparative analysis of

I

Negro and American Indian environmental conditions and their mental and scholastic test performance.

On all the socioeconomic, educational, and health factors which sociologists have generally pointed to as causes of the Negro-white differences in IQ and scholastic achievement, the American Indian population has been about as far below Negro standards as the Negro ranks below whites. In 1960 Indian median income was 59 percent of Negro, which was 55 percent of white. Life expectancy, reflecting nutrition and health care, is much lower for Indians than for Negroes. In educational disadvantages, unemployment, poor housing, and infant mortality Indians are considerably worse off than Negroes. The Coleman Report (1966) used a scale composed of 12 categories of environmental variables[1] deemed important by social scientists as having a causal relationship to children's intellectual development. In this nationwide survey, which included more than 645,000 children in 4,000 public schools, Indians were lower than Negroes in all 12 environmental categories, and, overall, Indians averaged further below Negroes than Negroes averaged below whites. The relevance of these environmental indices is shown by the fact that *within* each ethnic group they correlate in the expected direction with tests of intelligence and scholastic achievement. Since health, parental education, employment and family income, in addition to the 12 more subtle environmental factors rated in the Coleman study, are all deemed important for children's scholastic success, the stark deprivation of the Indian minority even by Negro standards ought to be reflected in a comparison of the intelligence and achievement test performance of Indians and Negroes. The interesting fact is, however, that on all tests, from first to twelfth grade, Indians scored *higher* than Negroes. Since many Indian children are bilingual, they can be most fairly compared with white and Negro children on non-verbal tests of intelligence, especially in the early school years. Coleman *et al.* (1966, p. 20) found that on a non-verbal intelligence test the mean score of Indian children in the first grade (approximately 6 years of age) exceeded the mean score of Negro children by 0·96 *SD*s, which is equivalent to about 14 IQ points. The first-grade intelligence test scores (with an overall national mean of 50 and an *SD* of 10) of all the ethnic groups in the Coleman study (Table 9, p. 20) are shown below:

Group	Non-verbal	Verbal
White	54·1	53·2
Negro	43·4	45·4
Indian	53·0	47·8
Puerto Rican	45·8	44·9
Mexican-American	50·1	46·5
Orientals	56·6	51·6

Thus, the Indian-Negro difference in a host of environmental factors is in just the *opposite* direction to the differences in mean performance on tests of non-verbal and verbal intelligence, reading comprehension, and maths achievement.

Attempts to explain away these striking findings of the Coleman Report have invoked the ideas of unrepresentative sampling of the Indian population, effects of the racial composition of the school, and differences in motivation, self-concept, and educational aspiration between Negroes and Indians. For example, Bodmer and Cavalli-Sforza (1970, p. 27) write: 'According to the Coleman report, however, American Indians typically go to schools where whites are in the majority, which is not the case for most of the schools attended by black children.' Several comments about this statement are in order. It was pointed out earlier that Negro children in this study are about 1 *SD* below Indian children on the non-verbal test in the first grade. Since racial composition of the school *per se* has not been shown by the Coleman study or any other study to be related to achievement, it is most unlikely that the effect of racial composition of the school will have had sufficient effect by first grade to account for 1 *SD* IQ difference.[2] Moreover, Coleman *et al.* (1966, p. 40) report that 48 percent of the Indians in the first-grade sample were in schools in which the *majority* of pupils were Indians. If this argument of Bodmer and Cavalli-Sforza carried any conviction, we should predict that in the case where Negroes attend schools which have a majority of white pupils, they should do as well as Indians in similar circumstances. The Coleman Report provides the conditions for examining this hypothesis (pp. 40 and 243). At the twelfth grade, 92 percent of non-metropolitan North and West Negroes attend schools in which Negroes are in a minority; 91 percent of all twelfth-grade Indians attend schools in which they are in a minority. Yet on the non-verbal intelligence test, non-metropolitan North and West Negroes score approximately 0.8 SD (equivalent to 11-12 IQ points) below the national average, while the Indians score about 0.1 SD (2-3 IQ points) below the national average. Even on the verbal ability test the largely bilingual Indians exceed this Negro group by 0.4 SD (about 6 IQ points). Thus these data lend no support to Bodmer's and Cavalli-Sforza's conjecture. But they go on to argue that Coleman's Indian sample *may* not adequately represent the 70 to 80 percent of American Indians who live on reservations. This is mere surmise, but in any case it is irrelevant to the point being made by these data: they are the very same Indians who were tested in the Coleman study who also rated much lower than Negroes on all the environmental indices. Despite this environmental disadvantage, these same Indians scored higher than Negroes on the ability and achievement tests.

But what about motivation, self-esteem, and educational aspirations? These factors are commonly mentioned as explanatory variables in discussions of Negroes' mental test and scholastic performance. Gordon (1970, p. 254), for example, states: 'Moreover, socially disadvantaged children have been determined by several investigators to be less highly motivated and to have lower aspiration for academic and vocational achievement than do their middle and upper class school peers.' Further on in the same passage, Gordon (p. 255) writes: 'As important as these attitudes toward school and learning may be, it is in the area of attitude toward self and others that the crucial determinants of achievement and upward mobility may lie. . . .' Coleman *et al.* attempted to take account of these motivational and attitudinal factors.

If poor environmental conditions, discrimination, and minority status depress academic motivation, aspiration, and self-esteem as a student, we should expect the Indian students to show lower ratings on these variables than Negroes. If it is argued that Negroes suffer greater prejudice, discrimination, and the psychological handicaps they may engender, than do Indians, we should expect this to show up in Coleman's motivational and attitudinal assessments. But on a questionnaire of 16 items intended to assess school-related attitudes, motivation, self-concept, and educational aspirations, Negroes showed higher (more favorable) scores than Indians; in the twelfth grade, Negroes were higher on 14 of the 16 items. Overall, the several ethnic groups ranked as follows on these 16 motivational indices, from highest to lowest: whites, Orientals, Negroes, American Indians, Mexican-Americans, and Puerto Ricans. The three ethnic groups showing a lower standing than Negroes on the motivational measures all score higher on all tests of ability and scholastic achievement given in the first grade as well as in the twelfth grade, with only one exception – first-grade Puerto Ricans scored 0·05 *SD* (less than 1 IQ point) below Negroes on the verbal ability test.

Although these motivational indices correlate significantly in the expected direction with test performance *within* each of the ethnic groups (Coleman *et al.*, 1966, p. 299, Table 3·221·1), showing that they are indeed relevant to academic attainment, the ordering of the several ethnic groups' mean test scores clearly do not correspond to their ordering on the motivational factors. At twelfth grade, the rank-order correlation between mean test scores (the average of five ability and achievement tests) of the six ethnic groups and the rank order of their motivation indexes is 0·66. If the Negro group is omitted from the ranking, the rank-order correlation becomes 1·0, i.e., perfect. The large rank-order discrepancies on both sets of variables between the Negro and Indian groups can hardly be attributable to differential school drop-out rates; even at ages 16 and 17 Negroes have only a 3·1 percent higher enrolment rate than Indians (Coleman *et al.*, 1966, p. 450). Even if all of the 3·1 excess of Indian drop-outs consisted of the 3·1 percent with the lowest IQs in the Indian distribution, their not being included would raise the Indian mean test score by only 0·07 *SD*s (about 1 IQ point).[3] But the overall Indian-Negro test difference is 0·4 *SD*s (6 IQ points) at twelfth grade, so at the very most only one-sixth of this difference could be attributed to differential drop-out rates.

Coleman (p. 219) notes that Negro-white differences are more uniform across various tests than are the differences between the other ethnic groups in the study:

The disadvantage for the various groups differs for different areas of achievement. For those from different linguistic cultures, Oriental Americans, Mexican-Americans, Indians, and Puerto Ricans, the disadvantage shows most clearly for reading comprehension and verbal ability. For Negroes, the disadvantage appears to be about the same for all areas tested. . . . The Negroes' averages tend to be about one standard deviation below those of the whites, which means that about 85 percent of Negro scores are below the white average.

Comparisons of white, Negro, and Mexican children in a California school district yield similar conclusions (Jensen, 1971a). Table 12.1 shows the results of this study in terms of the sigma units (i.e., standard deviation of the test scores in the white sample) by which the minority group falls below the white group. The Stanford Achievement battery consists of Word Meaning, Paragraph Meaning (reading comprehension), Spelling, Language (grammar), Arithmetic Computation (mechanical arithmetic), Arithmetic Concepts, and Arithmetic Applications (thought problems). The non-verbal intelligence tests were a composite of the Lorge-Thorndike Non-Verbal IQ, Raven's Progressive Matrices, and Gesell's Figure Copying Test (see Figure 3.1). The Home Index (Gough, 1949, 1971) is a 25-item inventory of socioeconomic status based on educational and occupational level of parents, material possessions in the home, parental participation in the middle-class and upper-middle-class social and civic activities, and cultural advantages in the home, e.g., music lessons and art.

It can be seen in Table 12.1 that at every grade level from 1 to 8 the Negro group is further below the white group than is the Mexican group, and the difference is greater for the non-verbal tests than for the scholastic achievement tests. Yet on the Home Index, the Mexicans are further below the Negroes than the Negroes are below the whites. The relevance of the Home Index is shown by its positive correlations with test performance within groups, and in a multiple-regression equation for predicting scholastic achievement the Home Index makes a unique contribution to the overall prediction of achievement. Also a questionnaire similar to that used in the Coleman study to reflect attitudes of self-confidence, self-esteem, and educational aspirations showed only small Negro-white differences, while scores were generally much lower for the Mexican group. None of these indices reflects the added disadvantage of the Mexicans' bilingualism. In the present sample, the percentage of Mexican children whose parents speak only English at home is 19·7 percent as compared with 96·5 percent for whites and 98·2 percent for Negroes. In 14·2 percent of

Table 12.1 Number of white sigma units by which minority group means fall below the white mean

Grade	Sample Size (N)			Stanford Achievement Tests		Non-verbal Intelligence		Home Index (SES)		Adjusted Achievement Means	
	White	Negro	Mexican	Negro	Mexican	Negro	Mexican	Negro	Mexican	Negro	Mexican
1	285	218	258	0·25	0·34	1·07	0·53	—	—	−0·09	0·15
2	229	162	250	0·57	0·37	1·03	0·70	—	—	0·15	0·06
3	281	207	241	0·83	0·68	0·98	0·53	0·58	1·13	0·11	0·05
4	237	189	239	0·69	0·59	0·95	0·48	0·38	1·18	0·17	0·15
5	242	198	211	0·75	0·54	0·05	0·62	0·70	1·18	0·21	0·10
6	219	169	218	0·84	0·69	1·23	0·67	0·47	1·36	0·09	0·02
7	388	262	305	0·71	0·57	1·13	0·72	0·71	1·36	0·07	0·08
8	356	289	303	0·64	0·62	1·18	0·79	0·77	1·34	0·06	0·08
Mean				0·66	0·55	1·08	0·63	0·60	1·26	0·10	0·09

the Mexican homes Spanish or another foreign language is spoken exclusively, as compared with 1·1 percent for whites and 0·5 percent for Negroes. Many of the parents of the Mexican children grew up in Mexico where they had little or no education. Most of them came to the central valley of California (in which the present study was conducted) as agricultural workers living in overcrowded, unsanitary migratory camps that follow the fruit and vegetable crops. Because of the nomadic life of the parents, many of these

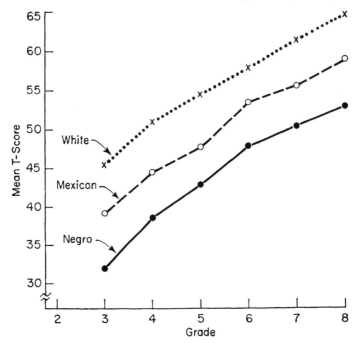

Figure 12.1 Mean T scores ($\bar{x} = 50$, $SD = 10$) on Raven's Progressive Matrices.

children have poor records of school attendance. The adjusted achievement means (the last two columns of Table 12.1) refer to the achievement test means after they have been adjusted by analysis of covariance using intelligence and SES as the control variables. In effect, these two columns represent the sigma units by which the minority groups fall below the white in achievement when all groups are statistically equated for intelligence and SES. The achievement differences that remain are practically negligible and can be even further reduced by including additional control variables, such as motivational and personality tests, in the covariance analysis.

On Raven's Progressive Matrices, a non-verbal, culture-fair test of the *g* factor of intelligence, the Mexicans were intermediate between whites and Negroes, as shown in Figure 12.1, despite the lower SES and poorer motivation of the Mexican pupils.

Finally, a factor analysis was performed on the intercorrelations among all the variables in all three ethnic groups combined. Four major factors emerged: (I) scholastic achievement and verbal intelligence, (II) non-verbal intelligence, (III) rote memory ability,

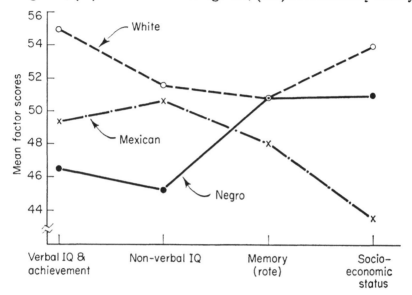

Figure 12.2 Factor scores (mean = 50, SD = 10 within each grade level) for four variables, comparing white, Mexican-American and Negro samples in grades 4, 5 and 6. The factor scores are independent of one another; that is, the scores on any one factor reveal differences between subjects who are statistically equated on the three other factors. (From Jensen, 1971a, Table 6.)

(IV) socioeconomic status. Minor factors were (1) speed, motivation, and persistence, (2) neuroticism, (3) extraversion, (4) age in months. These variables are, in effect, partialled out of the major factors. Since the four major factors are orthogonal (i.e., uncorrelated with one another) by virtue of the type of factor analysis used (varimax rotation of the principal components), each one can be viewed as a 'pure' measure of a particular factor in the sense that the influences of all the other factors are held constant. Factor scores were obtained for every pupil on each of the four main factors. (The factor scores have an overall mean of 50 and a standard deviation of 10.) The mean factor scores of the three

I*

ethnic groups are shown for grades 4, 5, and 6 (total $N = 1,179$) in Figure 12.2. On factor I (verbal IQ and achievement) all three ethnic groups differ significantly from one another. On Factor II (non-verbal IQ) the Negro-white and Negro-Mexican differences are significant, but the Mexican-white difference is not. On Factor III (rote memory) the only significant difference is between Mexicans and Negroes at grades 4 and 5. On Factor IV (SES) the Mexicans fall significantly below whites and Negroes, whose SES factor scores differ only slightly in this school population.

The test results for various minorities reported in the Coleman study in many ways are paralleled by the percentages of the various groups employed in professions that depend upon educational attainments. Weyl (1969) has made these comparisons, based on the 1960 U.S. Census, in terms of an index consisting of the ratio of the total proportion of the ethnic minority in the profession to the statistical expectation, which is the proportion of the total population constituted by the ethnic minority times the proportion of the population constituted by the members of the profession. An index value of 100 means the ethnic group is represented in a given profession according to statistical expectation; one of 50 means that it contributes half the expected number of professionals, and one of 200 means it supplies twice the statistical expectation. The index figures are shown in Table 12.2. It is interesting to

Table 12.2 Index figures of the contribution of five ethnic groups to American professions in 1960*

Profession	White	Negro	Indian	Japanese	Chinese
Accountants	112	7	38	166	174
Architects	110	5	0	232	506
Artists and Writers	110	16	133	209	136
College Professors	107	32	0	143	537
School Teachers	103	76	86	120	318
Engineers	111	5	57	124	303
Natural Scientists	109	20	0	205	438
Lawyers and Judges	111	11	19	54	53
Clergymen	104	66	124	89	23
Physicians	108	21	10	182	302
Nurses	106	54	124	116	76
Technicians	107	36	86	201	197

* From Weyl (1969, p. 114).

note that Orientals, who in Coleman's study scored higher than any other groups in non-verbal and mathematical abilities, have the highest index figures in accounting, architecture, engineering, and natural sciences. Negroes, who were lowest in non-verbal abilities and relatively higher in verbal, show the lowest indices for professions involving spatial and quantitative abilities, such as architecture and engineering, and are most heavily represented in such verbal professions as school teaching and the clergy.

If prejudice and discrimination are more important than abilities in determining a group's representation among the professional classes, then it should be puzzling that two minorities – the Japanese and Chinese – who have also been subject to discrimination and other social disadvantages in the United States should have considerably higher indices than the white majority. The group labeled white in Table 12.2 includes Jews, whose separate overall average is an index of 282, which is by far the highest, and nearly triple the index for non-Jewish whites, although Jews have experienced prejudice and social discrimination. The figures of Table 12.2 lend support to the popular characterization of Jews and Orientals as America's intellectual elite. The reasons, undoubtedly complex, probably involve selective migration, selective and assortative mating patterns, differential job opportunities and other associated genetic and cultural factors.

NOTES

1. The environmental variables were: (1) reading material in home, (2) items in home (cultural amenities), (3) structural integrity of home, (4) foreign language in home, (5) preschool attendance, (6) encyclopedia in home, (7) parents' education, (8) time spent on homework, (9) parents' educational desires for child, (10) parents' interest in school work, (11) child's self-concept (self-esteem), (12) child's interest in school and reading.
2. The largest and methodologically most thorough study of this question showed that racial composition of the classroom of itself had no effect on IQ (Wilson, 1967).
3. If from a normal distribution, with mean = 0, $\sigma = 1$, a segment of the distribution lying between two points on the abscissa, z_1 and z_2, is eliminated, the resulting mean $(\bar{X}_s)$ of the eliminated segment is:

$$\bar{X}_s = \frac{Y_1 - Y_2}{\text{area between } z_1 \text{ and } z_2}$$

where Y_1 and Y_2 are the values of the ordinate at z_1 and z_2. The mean of one tail of a distribution then is simply

$$\bar{X}_t = \frac{Y_1}{\text{area beyond } z_1}$$

13 *Inequality of schooling*

Some writers have pointed to supposed educational inequalities as a cause of poor Negro performance in IQ and achievement tests. Thus, Bodmer and Cavalli-Sforza (1970, p. 27) write: 'Black schools are well known to be generally less adequate than white schools, so that equal number of years of schooling certainly do not mean equal educational attainment.' This statement clearly implies that the Negro-white scholastic achievement gap (generally equivalent to two to four grade levels at high school graduation) is attributable, at least in large part, to the superior school facilities enjoyed by white children. But there is now massive evidence which clearly contradicts this claim.

The well-known Coleman Report (Coleman *et al.*, 1966) was funded by the U.S. government specifically to determine the degree to which inequalities in educational performance are attributable to inequalities in school facilities. This enormous survey of the nation's schools found that very little (overall, less than 10 percent) of the variance among schools in scholastic achievement was due to differences in school facilities, including variables such as physical facilities, class size, curricula, teacher salaries, experience and qualifications, special services, etc. The report concluded: 'Differences in school facilities and curriculum which are the major variables by which attempts are made to improve schools, are so little related to differences in achievement levels of students that, with few exceptions, their effects fail to appear even in a survey of this magnitude' (p. 316). More specifically, the major findings of the Coleman study are summarized as follows (p. 325):

Taking all these results together, one implication stands out above all: That schools bring little influence to bear on a child's achievement that is independent of his background and general social context; and that this very lack of an independent effect means that the inequalities imposed on children by their home, neighborhood, and peer environment are carried along to become the inequalities with which they confront adult life at the end of school. For equality of educational opportunity through the schools must imply a strong effect of schools that is independent of the child's immediate social environment, and that strong independent effect is not present in American schools.

In an analysis of relationships between (a) minority enrolment, (b) IQ, and (c) reading scores, on the one hand, and (d) pupil expenditure, (e) teacher salary, (f) pupil/teacher ratios, and (g) number of school administrators, on the other hand, in 191 school systems in California, it was found that the school-related variables have negligible correlations with IQ and reading scores, while percentage of minority enrolment has very high negative correlations with the school's mean IQ and reading level. At the same time, there is a slight, but non-significant, positive correlation between minority enrolment and the indices of school quality (Jensen, 1971a).

The fact is that the achievement level in a school is predictable from a number of demographic characteristics over which the school itself has no control whatsoever. Thorndike (1951), for example, correlated average IQ and an average scholastic achievement index (based on half a million children) with twenty-four census variables for a wide range of communities, large and small, urban and rural. Eleven of the correlations were significant at the 1 percent level. Census variables showing the highest correlation with IQ and achievement were educational level of the adult population (0·43), home ownership (0·39), quality and cost of housing (0·33), proportion of native-born whites (0·28), rate of female employment (0·26), and proportion of professional workers (0·28). In a multiple correlation these census variables predict IQ and achievement between 0·55 and 0·60.

Statistics based on all schools (over 900) in New York City show a strong *negative* correlation between pupil expenditures and scholastic achievement, since the school's financial resources are positively correlated with the proportion of Negro and Puerto Rican enrolment (Gittell, 1971). The 30 elementary schools in New York with a per pupil expenditure of more than $1,100 per year (mean of $1,330) showed reading and arithmetic scores five to seven months *below* the scores of pupils in the 101 schools with an expenditure below $600 (mean of $551). Pupil-teacher ratios in the high-scoring schools were more than twice as high as in the low-scoring schools. In other words, by most objective indices of advantages provided by the majority of schools in New York, the minority children are more favored than majority children. The report states:

> The evidence we have accumulated is somewhat surprising. We have recorded traditional variables that supposedly affect the quality of learning: class size, school expenditure, pupil/teacher ratio, condition of building, teacher experience, and the like. Yet, there seems to be no direct relationship between these school measurements and performance. Schools that have exceptionally small class registers, staffed with experienced teachers, spend more money per pupil, and possess modern facilities do not reflect exceptional academic competence. (Gittell, 1971, p. 2)

Jensen (1971a) compared large representative samples of Negro and Mexican-American pupils with white pupils from kindergarten through eighth grade in largely *de facto* segregated schools in the same California school district, using a comprehensive battery of tests of mental abilities and of scholastic achievement, in addition to personality inventories and indices of socioeconomic and cultural disadvantage. It was found that when certain ability and background factors over which the schools have little or no influence are statistically controlled, there are no appreciable differences between the scholastic achievements of minority and majority pupils. The study lends no support to the hypothesis that the schools are discriminating unfavorably against Negro pupils, whose average scholastic achievement was 0·66 *SD* below the white mean. (On non-verbal tests of intelligence, the average difference was 1·08 *SD*.) Furthermore, it was found that Negro children are as far below the white IQ mean, in sigma units, at kindergarten or first grade as at twelfth grade. If the schools contributed to the Negro-white IQ difference, one should expect to find an *increase* in the difference from kindergarten to twelfth grade. When race is entered as a variable into a multiple regression equation, along with a number of measures of mental ability and social background, to predict scholastic achievement, race *per se* makes no significant independent contribution to the prediction. This means, in effect, that a Negro pupil and a white pupil who are matched for IQ and home background will perform equally well in school. The average Negro-white achievement difference is thus related to race only incidentally, through association with intelligence. There is no evidence that the schools have contributed to this difference, and, in fact, there is evidence to the contrary – schools tend to have a leveling influence, so that Negroes and whites actually differ less in scholastic performance than in intelligence as measured by non-verbal tests at an age before the school could have had any appreciable impact.

The fact that Negro children have been shown to lag less far behind white children on scholastic achievement tests than on non-verbal intelligence tests which tap skills that are not taught in school (but which predict scholastic performance) belies the theory which blames the Negroes' lower achievement on poor teaching by the schools. Kenneth Clark (1968), for example, rejects the cultural deprivation theories of Negro scholastic performance:

> The picture of deprivation given by these theories is one of total stark, bleak deprivation. The degree of poverty in urban working-class Negro homes is so stark that the child has absolutely no sensory stimulation whatsoever . . . many of these studies talk about lower class culture as if it were totally isolated from all communication with the rest of our society. Not one of these reports, to my knowledge or memory, ever talks about the reality: there is no sub-culture in our large society that is so deprived as to be unable to have some communication with the larger culture through our mass media, television, etc. . . . The sophisticated version of the cultural deprivation explanation of academic retardation for Negro children has seemed to have built up a mythology of cultural isolation that does not seem to be supported by reality. (pp. 181-2)

Clark then goes on to blame the schools for the academic lag of Negro children:

To what extent are they not being taught because those who are in charge of teaching them do not believe that they can learn, do not expect that they can learn, and do not relate to them in ways that are conducive to their learning? (p. 183)

This is a currently popular hypothesis, but I can find no objective evidence that supports it. It is not sufficient merely to note that there are some teachers and schools which have undesirable attitudes toward minority children and provide an inferior educational environment for such children. We must examine those schools which have taken pains to give Negro children every advantage that is provided for the white children, and in which the teachers, both white and Negro, have been specially selected for their dedication and favorable attitudes toward minority pupils. Where these conditions exist, has there been found an appreciably smaller achievement gap between the races? I believe there has been some reduction in the achievement gap in the California schools in which I have collected data and where there has been a concerted effort to give every advantage to Negro children. It is under these conditions that the scholastic achievement difference is about 30 percent less than the average difference in intelligence, when intelligence is measured by very non-scholastic, non-verbal tests. There is no reason to believe that good teaching and good educational facilities will not improve Negro scholastic performance.[1] But there is equally no evidence to support the belief that the Negro-white difference that still persists under these conditions is a result of some subtle, invisible discrimination by teachers whose attitudes and expectations depress Negro performance.

NOTE

1. One critic of this interpretation has argued that unless the relative achievement gap can be shown to decrease during the school years, more parsimonious explanations would involve differentiated selection (e.g., drop-out rates) of students or, more likely, the presence of non-IQ variance in scholastic achievement.

14 Teacher expectancy

Credence in the notion that lower Negro performance on IQ tests results from teachers' expectations was widely promulgated by one of the most highly publicized studies in the recent history of educational research – the famous *Pygmalion in the Classroom* study by Rosenthal and Jacobson (1968). The main thesis of these authors is that a teacher's expectation of what pupils are able to do creates a 'self-fulfilling prophecy' which actually raises or lowers the children's IQs and level of scholastic achievements. Thus, initial differences in test scores, if known to the teachers, should become magnified in subsequent testings as a result of teacher expectations. And similarly, on the basis of previous experience, preconceptions, etc. concerning the relative abilities of Negro and white children, teachers' expectations should, according to this hypothesis, create or magnify performance differences between Negro and white pupils.

Rosenthal and Jacobson (1968) attempted to test this hypothesis by having teachers administer a group paper-and-pencil intelligence test to all pupils from kindergarten through sixth grade in a South San Francisco elementary school. Teachers were told that the test was intended '. . . to predict which youngsters are most likely to show an academic spurt'. In September, each teacher was given a list of those children (actually selected by a table of random numbers) who were supposedly predicted by the test to be most likely to show an academic spurt during the school year. The children were tested again by the teachers in January and May. The authors' conclusion, which has been repeated and accepted so widely in educational circles, is that the teachers' expectancies influenced the mental development (or test performance) of the children.

But the evidence presented in the study does not in the least support this conclusion, as is emphatically pointed out in the major critical reviews of the study (Thorndike, 1968; Snow, 1969; Elashoff & Snow, 1971). In the first place, the data themselves present so many bizarre features as to make them totally suspect. For example, in one grade the control group (i.e., non-expectancy of a spurt) had a mean IQ of 31! This is just barely at the imbecile level; such defective children actually are never enrolled in regular classes. Even if we accept the authors' conclusions without questioning the quality of the data or their analyses, the 'prophecy' effects shows up in only nineteen pupils in two grades (one of which has the control group with a mean IQ of 31). As Thorndike comments in his review: 'If these present data show anything, they show that the testing was utterly worthless and meaningless' (p. 710). Thorndike concludes that the study

. . . is so defective technically that one can only regret that it ever got beyond the eyes of the original investigators! Though the volume may be an effective addition to educational propagandizing, it does nothing to raise the standards of educational research. . . . In conclusion, then, the indications are that the basic data upon which this structure has been raised are so untrustworthy that any conclusions based upon them must be suspect. The conclusions may be correct, but if so it must be considered a fortunate coincidence.

But *are* the conclusions of Rosenthal and Jacobson in fact correct? Fortunately, the expectancy hypothesis has since been subjected to rigorous tests with the proper controls and appropriate methodology. Since Rosenthal and Jacobson reported finding the strongest expectancy effect in the first-grade pupils, Claiborn (1969) attempted to demonstrate the effect, using procedures similar to those of Rosenthal and Jacobson, in twelve first-grade classes. He found no evidence of the expectancy effect.

The largest study, by Fleming and Anttonen (1971), involved 1,087 second-grade pupils in 39 classrooms in 22 schools representing two socioeconomic levels – low SES and middle SES. The design of this study was more complex than that employed by

Rosenthal and Jacobson, so that the influences of a number of factors could be assessed – the effect of the teachers' attitudes toward intelligence tests, the effect of giving the teacher the results of the tests *v.* withholding test scores, the effect of giving the teacher grossly inaccurate IQs (inflated by 16 points) on some children, and the differential effect of all these variables on children's retest performance as a function of SES. Two intelligence tests were used (Kuhlman-Anderson and Primary Mental Abilities). Pre- and post-testing occurred at the beginning and end of the school year. All post-testing was conducted by graduate assistants who were unaware of the nature or purpose of the study. The results of the post-test analysis revealed no significant differences among the four treatment groups (viz., *a.* teachers given IQ scores; *b.* withholding of IQ information; *c.* teachers given Primary Mental Abilities percentiles; *d.* teachers given IQs inflated by 16 points). There was a significant effect of teachers' opinions of IQ tests as assessed by a questionnaire, but the effect appeared only for the middle SES children. When teachers were categorized into three groups (High, Middle, and Low) on their opinion of the validity of IQ tests, the low opinion teachers' pupils, in the middle SES classes, received significantly lower IQs than were obtained by pupils whose teachers had a high opinion of IQ tests. The effect was in the same direction for low SES children, but was so small as to be non-significant even with the large sample sizes employed. When teachers were asked to assess the accuracy of the IQ scores given to them, based on knowledge they gained of the child throughout the school year, they significantly judged the IQs inflated by 16 points as less accurate than the regular IQs.[1] Fleming and Anttonen (1971, p. 250) conclude:

> It appears that, in the real world of the teacher using IQ test information, the self-fulfilling prophecy does not operate as Rosenthal hypothesizes. We can only conclude that teachers are more sensitive to the functioning level of students than previously believed, since teachers, in fact, identified the inflated group as less accurate. Recognition of the deception by the teachers suggests that day to day living with the academic performance and behavior of children, at least for this group of teachers, provides more input than the results of an intelligence test administered on one given day.[2]

To date there have been nine attempts all together to replicate the Rosenthal and Jacobson (RJ) *Pygmalion* effect. Elashoff and Snow (1971, pp. 158-9) in their review of these studies concluded

> ... it can be seen that of nine studies (other than RJ) attempting to demonstrate teacher expectancy effects on IQ, none has succeeded. Of twelve expectancy studies including pupil achievement measures as criteria, six have succeeded. Of seven studies including measures of observable pupil behavior, three have succeeded. And of seventeen studies including measures of observable teacher behavior, fourteen have succeeded. Thus it seems that teacher expectancy effects are most likely to influence proximal variables (those 'closest' in a psychological sense to the source of effect, e.g., teacher behavior) and progressively less likely to influence distal variables (or variables psychologically remote from the source of expectations). IQ, the most remote of pupil variables, is unlikely to be affected. These results are consistent with a Brunswikian view of teacher-learner interaction. . . . They suggest that teacher expectancies may be important and are certainly deserving of study, but they fail utterly to support *Pygmalion's* celebrated effect on IQ.

NOTES

1. Unfortunately, this study did not include IQs that were *deflated*. Teachers' judgments of the degree of accuracy of their pupils' IQs may not be symmetrical for *inflated* and *deflated* values; that is to say, teachers may be more (or less) sensitive to an overestimate of their pupils' intelligence than to an underestimate.

    Teachers are capable of making fairly accurate judgments of their pupils' intelligence based on their classroom performance. The writer recently asked teachers in eight elementary school classes (grades 4, 5, 6) to rate their own impression, near the end of the school year, of each pupil's intelligence. Each pupil was rated on a 5-point scale. None had been given any psychometric tests prior to the teachers' assessments. The teacher ratings had the following correlations: Lorge-Thorndike Verbal IQ, 0·66; Lorge-Thorndike Non-verbal IQ, 0·58; Raven's Standard Progressive Matrices, 0·49; Rote Memory Test, 0·44. The teacher's rating had a loading of 0·79 on the first principal component in a principal components analysis of the intercorrelations among these tests and other measures.

2. There is one peculiarity to be noted in this study and about which the authors make no comment. The mean IQs of all groups are unusually high (overall mean = 112·15). While the IQ difference between low and middle SES groups was by far the largest effect in the experiment, the SES IQ difference was still smaller than is generally found. The mean post-test IQs of low and middle SES groups were 106·86 and 117·18, respectively. Nothing is said about the racial composition of the samples, but a mean IQ of 106·86 is certainly well above that generally found for either white or Negro samples classed as 'low SES'. This atypical peculiarity of the data in an otherwise impeccable study may limit its generalizability to more typical populations.

15 *Motivational factors*

A number of motivational factors have been investigated in attempts to explain at least some of the Negro-white difference in intelligence test performance in terms of differences in motivation. The evidence to date does not support the differential motivation hypothesis. This should not be too surprising, since experimental studies of the effects of motivational factors on intelligence testing have generally shown either very small or non-significant effects, and when differences have been found they tend to show that conditions most typical of those in which intelligence tests are normally given yield the best scores. Burt and Williams (1962), for example, found that children obtained slightly higher scores when taking tests for school promotion rather than for experimental purposes. Intelligence tests are quite insensitive to external motivational manipulations. Tiber and Kennedy (1964) tested middle- and lower-class white children and lower-class Negro children with and without several different incentives, such as praise after each test item, verbal reproof, and candy reward. These various testing conditions had no significant effects on Stanford-Binet IQs and showed no interaction with social class or race. Tiber and Kennedy concluded that the IQ differences usually found between such social class and racial groups cannot be attributed to motivational differences. This conclusion is too sweeping, of course, since other motivational factors not under the experimenter's control could affect test performance. But the fact remains that scores on IQ tests have proved highly resistant to experimental manipulations of incentives and motivational sets.

SELF-CONCEPT

The testee's self-concept or self-esteem has been claimed to be an important determinant of test performance, and Negro-white IQ differences have been attributed to the purported lower self-confidence and self-esteem of Negro children, at least in test situations. The dozen or so studies of this topic are about evenly divided in supporting or failing to support some hypotheses related to this issue (Zirkel and Moses, 1971). But the present evidence is so ambiguous that no really strong conclusion in either direction seems to have emerged. What has *not* been at all consistently shown, however, is that assessments of self-concept (or self-esteem, etc.) jointly (*a*) differ for Negroes and whites, (*b*) are correlated with IQ or scholastic achievement, and (*c*) are not merely a reflection of the pupil's more or less objective appraisal of his own scholastic standing and aptitudes. Inventories intended to assess the pupil's self-concept of his abilities typically contain items such as, 'I feel that I just cannot learn', 'How do you compare in ability with your friends (or classmates)?', 'Do you have the ability to complete high school (or college)?' etc. (e.g., Anderson & Johnson, 1971, p. 295). If pupils' answers to such questions in any way reflect an awareness of their standing among their age mates in scholastic ability, it should not be surprising that their self-concept scores are correlated with objective measures of intelligence and scholastic performance. Children are quite perceptive about the relative standing of themselves and their schoolmates in 'brightness'.

Coleman *et al.* (1966, p. 323), in the largest study employing a pupil attitude and self-concept inventory, found one attitude questionnaire item which, far more than any others, differentiated minority and white children and also correlated with scores on intelligence tests. It was the item 'good luck is more important than hard work for success', which is referred to as a 'control of environment' attitude. The largest differences, which were found in the ninth grade, indicate that those minority pupils (Negro, Mexican-American, Indian, and Puerto Rican) who *disagree* that 'good luck is more important than hard work' obtain significantly higher verbal test scores, on the average, than white pupils who *agree* with the statement. Thus it is clear that the factor tapped by this particular question is correlated with verbal intelligence (to about the same degree in all ethnic groups) and also shows significant ethnic group differences. (The correlation of this item with non-verbal intelligence is considerably lower, but is still significant.) But the *causal* connection between response to this questionnaire item and intelligence scores is not established. Does the attitude directly affect test performance, or are less intelligent pupils merely more likely to attribute success to 'good luck' rather than to 'hard work'? The latter explanation seems more probable. Gough (1953) was able to produce a non-cognitive 'intelligence test', made up of 'personality'-type questions, which correlated remarkably with scores on standard intelligence tests. Not a single item of the Gough questionnaire calls for mental ability *per se*. All the items are questions such as 'I have often been frightened in the middle of the night' (keyed *False*), and 'I gossip a little at times' (keyed *True*). Few would argue that being frightened at night will lower one's intelligence, or that by gossiping one can raise one's IQ. Belief in 'luck' probably falls into this same category of attitude items that comprise Gough's non-intellectual intelligence test.

The study which has used what is probably the most elaborate and most reliable index of self-esteem, the 42-item Coopersmith Self-Esteem Inventory, administered to groups of white, Negro, and Puerto Rican fifth and sixth graders matched for SES and IQ, came to this conclusion:

> Support was thus given for the growing number of studies which indicate that the self-concept of Negro children does not differ significantly from and may even be higher than that of white children. It also appears that the self-concept of Puerto Rican children is significantly lower not only than the self-concept of white children, as shown in the minimal amount of previous research, but also than that of Negro children. (Zirkel & Moses, 1971, p. 260)

The fact that the ethnic groups were selected so as to be highly similar in SES and IQ unfortunately makes the results rather tenuous. If it is claimed that lower IQs are partly a result of poor self-concept, then matching ethnic groups for IQ and SES could well minimize differences in the self-concept scores.

268 *Educability and Group Differences*

COMPETITION AND FAILURE THREAT

Still another motivational theory of low Negro IQ and scholastic attainment, originally suggested by the experimental research of Irwin Katz (1964, 1968), holds that Negro test performance is depressed by a constellation of factors comprised of (*a*) *failure threat* – the Negro's expectancy of a low probability of success in competition with whites or white norms on an intelligence test, and (*b*) *social threat* –emotional responses of fear, anger, and humiliation that are presumably detrimental to performance and may be elicited by a white examiner, especially if the examiner is perceived as unsympathetic, supercilious, and authoritarian. Katz has tested these hypotheses experimentally by administering test-like tasks to Negro college students with and without instructions that it was or was not an intelligence test, that the testees were or were not competing with whites or white norms, with white or Negro examiners, threatening or friendly examiners, and with or without external threats such as strong electric shock. This research, although interesting and important in its own right, has unfortunately been misrepresented as indicating that these situational factors manipulated in Katz's experiments affect Negro perform- ance on standard intelligence tests and in situations that are typical of those in which intelligence tests are ordinarily admini- stered (e.g., Watson, 1970). It has not been demonstrated that the effects hypothesized by Katz account for any of the Negro-white difference in IQ as measured by any of the standard individual or group administered tests of intelligence. Whether or not it is possible significantly to influence subjects' performance on certain experimental tasks, specially selected for their sensitivity to distraction and emotional arousal, under conditions that are very atypical of ordinary intelligence testing (such as threatening instructors, examiners acting hostile and authoritarian, and threat of electric shock while performing the task) is not at issue.

The several experiments of Katz and his co-workers (recently reviewed by Sattler, 1970)[1] did not use intelligence tests, but timed experimental tasks depending mainly on *speed* of performance, rather than mental power. Such speed tasks are known to be more sensitive to distractions, emotional states, and the like. One of the tests, for example, was simple arithmetic – but the subjects were college students. This makes sense in terms of the effect Katz was trying to detect in his experiment. The aim was to use a test which was so easy that not intelligence but mainly a speed factor, highly sensitive to distraction, would be the greatest source of variance in the experiment. The experimental tasks that come closest to resembling anything found in standard intelligence tests are the digit-letter substitution and digit-symbol tests, which resemble the digit-symbol subtest of the Wechsler Intelligence Scale. But of the eleven subtests comprising the Wechsler, digit symbol has by far the lowest loading on *g* (correlated for attenuation) and the lowest correlation of any subtest with the total IQ. Thus the tests used by Katz could hardly have been a better selection if the aim was to reveal the effects of situational variables on performance. But they were not intelligence tests and the conditions of administration that produced lower scores were not typical of normal testing. Moreover, Katz used Negro college students, and since college students are selected mainly for intelligence, this would have the effect of narrowing the range of variance that intelligence might contribute to performance on the tests, permitting personality and emotional factors to contribute a relatively larger proportion of the variance. Then, too, it should be noted that the Katz experiments are not concerned with comparing Negro and white performance on tests but with showing variation in Negro performance under different testing conditions. So we do not know how much Negro-white difference on any test would be accounted for by the Katz hypotheses. The magnitude of the score decrements found by Katz, even under the most extremely unfavorable conditions, are small in relation to the standard deviation in the population and do not invariably show up in the predicted direction from one experiment to another. When results are in the opposite direction to the hypothesis, it seems not to cast doubt on the hypothesis but to give rise to *ad hoc* rationalizations, such as, 'In the last study the results when the tester was Negro were in the opposite direction, regardless of the kind of feedback used. There may be a simple regional explanation for these contradictory findings, since the earlier experiment was done in Florida, and the latter one in Tennessee. Perhaps the Negro student in the Deep South is more fearful of competition with white peers than is the Negro student in the Upper South' (Katz, 1968, p. 281).

RACE OF EXAMINER

Despite the many conjectures (see Sattler, 1970, pp. 143-4) that the race of the examiner affects Negro-white differences on actual intelligence tests, the evidence does not support this belief. The most adequate published study intended to examine the testee and tester racial interaction used three Negro and three white female testers giving the Stanford-Binet Intelligence Test and the Peabody Picture Vocabulary Test to Negro and white children enrolled in a Head Start program in Tennessee. Race of the examiners was found to have no significant effect on the test scores of either the Negro or the white children (Miller & Phillips, 1966). Shuey (1966) compared the nineteen studies of Negro IQ in elementary school children in the South where the testing was done by a Negro with the results obtained on all Southern Negro school children. Shuey concludes:

> The 2,360 elementary school children tested by Negroes earned a mean IQ of 80·9 as compared with a combined mean of 80·6 earned by more than 30,000 Southern Negro school children, an undetermined but probably a large number of whom were tested by white investigators. The present writer also calculated the combined mean IQ achieved by 1,796 Southern colored high school pupils who were tested by Negro adults. This was 82·9 as compared with a mean of 82·1 secured by nearly 9,000 Southern colored high school students, many of whom were examined by white researchers. From these comparisons it would seem that the intelligence score of a Negro school child or high school pupil has not been adversely affected by the presence of a white tester. (p. 507)

The most recent and comprehensive review of this topic concludes: 'The experimenters' race affects subjects' picture and doll preferences, but may not influence their scores on intelligence tests and personality measures' (Sattler, 1970, p. 137).

DIFFERENTIAL TEST PERFORMANCE

If generalized attitudes that depress Negro but not white performance accounted for the Negro-white IQ difference, it would be hard to explain why some kinds of tests are so affected and not others, for Negroes do not perform poorly on all kinds of tests. Jensen (1968b) has shown, for example, that Negro pre-schoolers with a mean IQ nineteen points below white children perform equal to the whites on tests of memory span – when the latter tests are given under the same conditions and by the same examiner as the IQ tests. But a factor analysis showed that the memory tests were not measures of intelligence; they involve another kind of mental ability. In this study, the memory test actually called for more attention and freedom from distraction than did the IQ test. Subsequent studies (Jensen, 1970b, c; 1971a; Jensen & Rohwer, 1970) have consistently found much smaller or non-significant Negro-white differences on tests of immediate memory while at the same time there were differences of more than one standard deviation on intelligence tests administered by the same testers under the same conditions as the memory tests. If motivational factors or testee and tester interactions affect the intelligence score, one would have to explain why these factors do not affect the memory test scores. It appears that, in general, to the degree that a test does not correlate with intelligence or abstract, conceptual, problem-solving ability, it fails to show a mean difference between Negroes and whites. This observation affords a means for assessing motivational differences in test performance more or less uncontaminated by differences involving intellectual ability *per se*. If it is hypothesized that poor test performance results from poor motivation, inhibition of effort, or just not trying as hard as others, it is difficult to pit this hypothesis against one which states that the difference in test performance is due to a lesser cognitive ability for dealing with *g* material, i.e., concepts, relationships, and abstractions, if one and the same test is used to assess motivation and intelligence, for then motivation and mental ability are confounded in the testing situation.

To get around this methodological problem, a motivation-sensitive test involving speed and persistence was devised so as to maximize dependence upon effort and minimize dependence on cognitive ability, particularly of the kind characterized by *g*. This experimental task, called the Making Xs test, is one kind of objective assessment of test-taking motivation. It gives an indication of the subject's willingness to comply with instructions in a group testing situation and to mobilize effort in following these instructions for a brief period of time (see pp. 121-2). It has also shown greater sensitivity to teacher and experimenter differences than is found with intelligence or achievement tests. The Making Xs test was given to all the fourth, fifth, and sixth graders in an urban school system (1,588 whites and 1,242 Negroes). At each grade level, the Negro mean score was equal to or slightly *higher* than the white, and the gain from Part I to Part II was significantly *higher* for Negroes than for whites. Thus, on this non-cognitive, motivation-sensitive test there is no evidence that Negro children perform less well than white children; if anything, just the opposite is true. The same tester, in the same session, also administered a standard verbal and non-verbal intelligence test to all these children. The average white-Negro differences in sigma units (based on the white *SD*) were 1·63 for the verbal IQ and 1·70 for the non-verbal IQ (Jensen & Rohwer, 1970, pp. 55-71). (These differences are equivalent to about 26 and 27 IQ points.)

It is sometimes claimed that lower performance on IQ tests results from poor attention, distractability, carelessness, inability to follow directions, and the like. So a test was devised to measure these factors independently of intellectual ability *per se*. The test makes no demands on knowledge, *g*, or memory. It is called a Listening-Attention Test. It is administered in the classroom by means of a tape recorder. High scores on the Listening-Attention Test indicate that the subject is able to hear and distinguish correctly the numbers spoken by the voice on the tape, and to follow directions, keep pace with the examiner, and mark the answer sheet properly. The procedure is quite simple. The child is provided with a two-page answer booklet containing columns of paired numerals, ten pairs to a column; each column is headed by a capital letter, alphabetically beginning with A. A clear male voice from the recorder says, 'Put the point of your pencil on the letter A. Now, I am going to say one number in each pair, and you should cross out the number I say – cross it out with an X. Ready? 2 – 4 – 8 – 9 – 3 –,' etc. The numbers are spoken at a 2-second rate. At the beginning of each series (ten in all), the subject is told to put his pencil on the letter at the top of the list. This test, too, was given to all fourth, fifth, and sixth graders (1,423 whites, 1,214 Negroes) in an urban school system. There was no significant white-Negro difference in mean scores on this test at any grade level (Jensen & Rohwer, 1970, pp. 58-60).

It might be argued, however, that children perceive whether a test *is* or *is not* really an intelligence test, no matter what the examiner says or how it is labeled, and that this recognition depresses the performance of the Negro pupils. This, too, can be experimentally controlled.

A technique that lends itself ideally to this purpose is the free recall of uncategorized and categorized lists, abbreviated FRU and FRC, respectively. The FRU procedure consists of showing the subject twenty familiar and unrelated objects (e.g., ball, book, brush, toy car, gun) one at a time, and after the whole set has been thus exposed, asking the subject to recall as many of the items as he can remember. The same procedure is repeated for five trials, each time presenting the items in a different random order. The subject's score is the total number of items he recalls correctly on each trial; the items may be recalled in any order that they come to mind. This kind of rote memory, it has been found, shows little or no correlation with IQ. But by a seemingly little change in our set of items, we can turn this procedure into an intelligence test showing a very substantial correlation with standard IQ tests (Glasman, 1968). This is the FRC procedure, which is exactly the same as FRU as regards instructions and requirements of the task. But in FRC the lists are composed of items which can be grouped into several conceptual categories, such as furniture, vehicles, clothing, tableware, etc. The single items, however, are always presented in a random order on each trial without reference to their conceptual categories. The same subjects are never given both FRU and FRC, so there is no basis for any subject's perceiving one test as being different from the other. Subjects are assigned at random to either the FRU or the FRC test. Both groups have the same examiner, the same instructions, and to all outward appearances the two tests do not differ in content, difficulty, purpose, or demands made upon the subject. There is no reason whatsoever that FRU and FRC should elicit different test-taking attitudes or motivational states. However, subjects who do not spontaneously tend to 'cluster' the items of the FRC list into conceptual categories in recalling them, perform no better on FRC than on FRU. The degree to which a subject 'clusters' the items conceptually (a tendency which generally increases from the first to the fifth recall trial) is related to the amount he is able to recall. It is both this amount recalled and especially the conceptual clustering tendency itself which are correlated with IQ. When there is little or no clustering, there is also no appreciable correlation with IQ. It then becomes a test of sheer rote memory, which is psychologically quite different from the *g* factor of intelligence tests.

When the FRU and FRC procedures were given to groups of Negro and white fourth graders, what was found? First, there was a slight but non-significant ($p < 0.162$) difference between Negro and white scores (i.e., totall recall over five trials) in the FRU test (Jensen & Rohwer, 1970, pp. 103-18). On the FRC test, however, the recall score of the white children very significantly

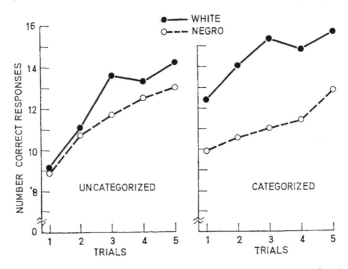

Figure 15.1 Amount of free recall of 20-item uncategorized and categorized lists.

($p < 0.014$) exceeded the Negro mean, by about one standard deviation, as shown in Figure 15.1.

Note that the Negro and white groups' performance in the uncategorized lists are hardly distinguishable. Whites, however, had much better recall on the categorized as compared with the uncategorized lists. The greatest differences, however, were found in the clustering score for the FRC test. This score indicates the degree to which the subject conceptually clusters the items in their order of output in recall. The more items of the same category that are recalled adjacently in sequence, the higher is the clustering score. The clustering measure itself is made to be independent of the *amount* recalled. The Negro-white difference in overall clustering score was great ($p < 0.005$), and while the white group showed a marked regular increase in clustering from trial 1 to 5, there was no increase across trials in the Negro group. It is impossible to account for the lack of a significant Negro-white difference in FRU and the marked difference in FRC in terms of differences in test-taking attitudes, motivation, and the like. The racial difference in this case is clearly attributable to the different cognitive processes involved in these tests.

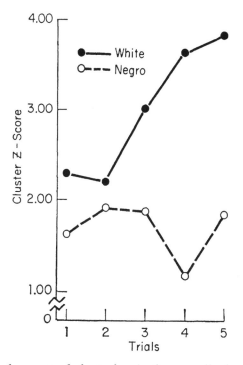

Figure 15.2 Amount of clustering in free recall of categorized lists.

There are other tests which do not look anything like the more usual type of intelligence tests but which in fact correlate with IQ and also show significant Negro-white differences. The Harris-Goodenough 'Draw-a-Man' test is an example. The child is merely led to believe this is a test of his drawing ability and is told to draw a man on a blank sheet of paper. The drawings are scored against age norms for their degree of maturity. We gave this test to classes of Negro and white pupils from kindergarten through sixth grade, removed all identification from the tests, and sent them away for scoring by an expert who knew nothing of the racial composition of the samples. At every grade there were substantial differences

K

(the median difference being 12 IQ points) favoring the white pupils (Jensen & Rohwer, 1970, pp. 86-9). This test, however, is not a very good measure of g (as indicated by correlations of only 0·4 to 0·5 with Raven's matrices) and may be more culturally loaded than some tests of g which show larger Negro-white differences. (A review of other studies of Negro-white differences on the Draw-a-Man test is provided by Shuey, 1966, pp. 24-7; 83-4.)

NOTE

1. Sattler's summary: 'Katz and his co-workers' series of studies show that white testers in comparison with Negro testers do not necessarily impede the performance of Negro college subjects. Negro testers obtained significantly higher scores than white testers when the probability-of-success conditions informed the college subjects that they had little or an equal chance of equaling the white norm; white testers obtained significantly higher scores than Negro testers under certain conditions and with certain groups (e.g., motor instructions and hard digit-symbol task; digit-letter substitution and mild threat; college students with satisfactory high school averages in any pro-bability of success condition)' (p. 143).

16 Language deprivation

The use of dialect and often 'ungrammatical' English in the speech of children called disadvantaged lends plausibility to the popular belief that these children's generally lower IQs and scholastic progress are attributable to environmentally caused verbal and linguistic deficits. We read that

> Children from low socioeconomic groups develop deficits in intellectual functioning because they lack adequate intellectual, particularly verbal, stimulation . . . children in these groups receive less verbal stimulation from parents – through being talked to, read to, taken on trips, etc. – than children in middle-class groups, and the parents are usually not very good examples for children to follow in learning language. (Furfey & Harte, 1970, p. 313)

> It is to be expected that children from homes where certain words are used will do better on a vocabulary test involving those words than will children from homes where the words are never heard . . . most intelligence tests are loaded with middle-class content that is found to be more familiar to white children than to Negro children. (Brown, 1965, p. 186)

Such statements do indeed appear very plausible, even self-evident.

But is linguistic deprivation actually an adequate explanation of intelligence differences? The point is not at issue that learning good English is an advantage to upward social mobility. We are not concerned here with these secondary social consequences of grammar and dialect, but rather with the effect of language on intelligence and intelligence test scores. Several lines of evidence are highly relevant in evaluating the linguistic deprivation hypothesis of intellectual deficit.

In the first place, one would expect that if language differences played the predominant role in the lower intelligence test performance of Negroes, they should obtain their poorest scores on verbal tests and do relatively better on non-verbal and performance tests. In fact, just the opposite is most commonly found. The Wechsler-Bellevue and the Wechsler Adult Intelligence Scale, which are among the best individual tests of intelligence, consist of eleven subtests, six verbal tests and five performance tests, which yield a Verbal IQ and a Non-verbal or Performance IQ. Every study of Negroes tested with the Wechsler scales reported in the literature, except for those involving non-representative samples such as delinquents and prisoners, show higher Verbal IQ than Performance IQ (Shuey, 1966, pp. 295, 359-60, 371). On the Differential Aptitude Tests, Negro children in New York, whether they are middle-class or lower-class, were found to score higher on the verbal ability test than on any of the other tests (Numerical, Reasoning, Spatial) (Lesser, Fifer, & Clark, 1965).

The nationwide Coleman survey used verbal and non-verbal ability tests from grades 1 to 12 and found overall that Negro children did better (0.2σ to 0.3σ) on the verbal than on the non-verbal tests (Coleman, 1966, Supplemental Appendix, Section 9.10). (All other minority groups – Puerto Rican, Indian, Mexican, and Oriental – showed the opposite.[1]) Moreover, the verbal deprivation hypothesis of Negro IQ deficit should predict that the most disadvantaged Negroes with the lowest IQ – those in the rural South – should show a greater verbal deficit relative to their non-verbal test score than would be found in the comparatively more advantaged Negroes with higher IQs in the urban North. But Coleman actually found just the opposite. The largest disparity between verbal and non-verbal scores, in favor of the verbal, showed up in Negroes of the non-metropolitan South (Coleman *et al.*, 1966, pp. 221-71). Urban Negroes of the Northeast, Midwest, and Western regions, in fact, average two or three points *higher* on the non-verbal than the verbal tests beyond grade 3. Here, then, is a massive set of data which goes directly counter to the predictions of the verbal deprivation hypothesis: The presumably most deprived Southern Negroes actually do better on the verbal tests, the comparatively least deprived Northern Negroes do better on the non-verbal tests. (On both verbal and non-verbal tests, the Northern and Urban Negroes excel over the Southern Negroes, but the disparity is *less* on the verbal tests. This appears paradoxical in terms of verbal-environmental deprivation theories of Negro intelligence.)

Do lower-class Negro children fail to understand white or Negro middle-class examiners and teachers, and even their own middle-class schoolmates, because of differences in accent, dialect, and other aspects of language usage? This proposition was examined in an ingenious experiment by Krauss and Rotter (1968). The groups they compared were low SES Negro children in Harlem and middle SES white children in the borough of Queens. Two age levels were used: 7-year-olds and 12-year-olds. Half the children in each group acted as *speakers* and half as *listeners*. The speaker's task was to describe a novel figure presented to him. The listener's task was to pick out this figure from a multiple-choice set of other figures solely on the basis of the speaker's description. The novel figures, drawn on cards, were non-representational and were intentionally made difficult to name, so that they would elicit a wide variety of verbal descriptions. The speakers and listeners were paired so as to have every possible combination of age and race (or SES). (It must be remembered that race and SES are completely confounded in this experiment.) The score obtained by each pair of subjects was the number of figures the listener could correctly identify from the speaker's description. The results: the largest contribution to total variance of scores was the race (or SES) of the listener; the second largest contribution was the age of the listener. In other words, the 7-year-old white (middle SES) children did better as listeners than the 12-year-old Negro (low SES) children. The speaker's age was the third largest source of variance. The race of the *speaker*, although a significant source of variance, was less than one-tenth as great as the race of the *listener*. In both age groups, the rank order of the mean scores for each of the four possible speaker-listener combinations were, from highest to lowest:

> White speaker/White listener
> Negro speaker/White listener
> White speaker/Negro listener
> Negro speaker/Negro listener

The authors conclude: '. . . no support was obtained for the hypothesis that *intra*-status communication is more effective than *inter*-status communication' (Krauss & Rotter, 1968, p. 173). While these results seem paradoxical in terms of the linguistic difference theories, they could be predicted completely on the basis of mental age obtained on a non-verbal intelligence test, such as Raven's matrices. The rank order of the means of all possible race × age combinations of speakers and listeners could be predicted by the simple formula $MA_s + 2MA_L$, where MA is mental age, S is speaker, and L is listener. This is consistent with the hypothesis that it is intelligence rather than language usage *per se* which is the more important factor in communication. The results of several other studies of Negro-white differences based on speaker-listener interactions are consistent with this hypothesis and contradict the verbal deficit hypothesis (Harms, 1961; Peisach, 1965; Eisenberg, Berlin, Dill & Sheldon, 1968; Weener, 1969).

Does the disparity between a white middle-class examiner's standard English and the Negro child's ghetto dialect work to the disadvantage of the Negro child in a verbally administered individual IQ test such as the Stanford-Binet? Quay (1971) attempted to answer this question by having a linguist whose speciality is the Negro dialect translate the Stanford-Binet into the Negro dialect. This form of the test was administered by two Negro male examiners to fifty 4-year-old Negro children in a Head Start program in Philadelphia. Another fifty children, selected at random from the same Head Start classes, were given the test in standard English. The result: no significant difference (Negro dialect form was 0·78 IQ points higher than standard form). The author notes '. . . it is interesting that verbal items were passed with greater frequency than performance items. . . .' 'The analysis of item difficulty raises questions about the existence of either a language "deficit" or a language "difference" for Negro children having the experiences of the present Ss. At least their comprehension of the standard English of the Binet was not impaired.'

Linguists and child psychologists who study the development of language are now finding, contrary to the popular belief, that Negro children, especially lower-class Negro children, are actually somewhat precocious in the most fundamental aspects of language development as compared with middle- and upper-middle-class white children. Baratz (1970), a sociolinguist and student of language development in Negroes, has argued that the Negro child is linguistically advanced compared to the middle-class white child. Entwisle (1970) has carried out a series of studies of the most basic aspects of language development based largely on children's free word associations. Children are asked to give 'the first word you think of' in response to a standard set of stimulus words. The words represent different degrees of rarity and different grammatical form classes – nouns, verbs, adjectives, etc. The nature of the child's associations to the stimulus words follows a regular developmental sequence. It is the *type* of response rather than the specific content of the response that is most important. Younger children, for example, are much more likely to give a *syntactic* phrase completion response to a stimulus word while older children will respond with another word of the same grammatical form class, called a *paradigmatic* association. For example, to the stimulus word *cat* the less mature child may respond with 'drinks milk' or 'nice'; the linguistically more mature child is likely to respond with 'dog' (a noun of the same form) or 'animal' (a noun of a supraordinate category). Or take the stimulus word *begin*. The less mature respond with 'building a house', or 'to cry' or 'to eat', or 'with' – all responses showing a knowledge of how the word is used syntactically. Older children respond to *begin* with 'start', 'end', 'stop', and the like. Children of ages 4 and 5 are also more apt to give so-called klang associations than older children, e.g., *begin* – 'chin' or 'lyn'; *cat* – 'sat' or 'hat'. Although preschoolers, of course, have never been exposed to formal grammar, their word associations and their speech reveal that they have already learned considerable grammar, as indicated by knowledge of pluralization, verb inflections, etc.

Now, what Entwisle (1970) has found in several studies is that in terms of these very basic developmental milestones in children's acquisition of language, low SES Negro children show a more precocious rate of development than middle SES white children. She writes: 'Word associations of black and of white elementary-school children reveal, contrary to expectations, that slum children are apparently more advanced linguistically than suburban children at first grade. . . .' But here is the interesting point:

White [italics added] first-grade slum children of average IQ give paradigmatic responses to about the same extent as gifted

(IQ 130) suburban children, and although inner-city black first-graders of average IQ lag behind inner city white first-graders they give more paradigmatic (i.e., mature) responses than white suburban first-graders of average IQ. Thus, at first grade the white child is slightly ahead of the black child when both are reared in the inner city, but the black slum child exceeds the white suburban child. The superiority is short-lived, however, for by third grade, suburban children – whether blue collar or upper-middle-class – have surpassed the inner city children, whether black or white . . . the temporary advance in linguistic development, and the subsequent decline, appears to be typical of the child in a poverty environment. (Entwisle, 1970)

It may seem surprising that the rate of language development should so markedly decelerate in slum children between the first and third grades in school, where reading and cognitive enrichment are presumably being fostered. The nature of the changes from linguistic precocity to linguistic retardation in these children is interesting. Entwisle observes:

The relative developmental position of blacks and whites does shift with advancing age, however, and both inner-city blacks and whites show a slowed pace of development compared to suburban children by third grade. Again, however, the rate alone tells only a small part of the story, for while the semantic systems of white inner-city children overlap considerably the semantic systems of white suburban children, semantic systems of black children depart significantly from both white groups, especially for more complex words.

The main difference, pointed out in several examples mentioned by Entwisle, is that by fifth grade Negro children's responses in the word association procedure are more restricted to a very specific context, as contrasted with responses reflecting broader meaning, greater generality, conceptual categorizing, supraordination, and the like.

To explain these findings, Entwisle mentions such factors as the greater restriction of television viewing imposed on suburban preschoolers, lack of sufficient reinforcement for learning after school entry afforded to slum children, and a 'lack of environmental forces to encourage semantic development'. However, there is another possible interpretation of these findings which brings them theoretically under the purview of a much broader range of findings in developmental psychology. First, there is a fundamental biological principle, so general that it holds both across species and within a given species, which states that the more prolonged the infancy, the greater in general is the cognitive ability of the species at maturity. Precocity of early motor development, as assessed by infant tests, is *negatively* correlated with IQ at maturity among whites; and low SES white children, who show higher than average motor development scores in the first year of life, obtain below-average IQs as teenagers (Bayley, 1966). At birth and during the first year and a half of life, Negro infants, whether born in Africa or America, are physically and motorically more advanced than white infants; the majority of studies have shown this (Ainsworth, 1963, 1967; Bayley, 1965; Curti *et al.*, 1935; Durham Education Improvement Program, 1966-7a, b; Faladé, 1955, 1960; Géber, 1956, 1958a, b, 1960, 1962; Géber & Dean, 1957a, b, 1958, 1964, 1966; Gilliland, 1951; Kilbride, 1969; Knobloch & Pasamanick, 1953, 1958; Liddicoat, 1969; Liddicoat & Koza, 1963; Massé, 1969; Moreigne & Senecal, 1962; Naylor & Myrianthopoulos, 1967; Nelson & Dean, 1959; Pasamanick, 1949; Ramarosaona, 1959; Scott, Ferguson, Jenkins & Cutler, 1955; Vouilloux, 1959; Walters, 1967; Williams & Scott, 1953). Only three studies, in African samples, have reported findings of no significant differences in infant development (Langton, 1934-5; Theunissen, 1948; Falmagne, 1959).[2] Finally, language development is a species specific characteristic peculiar but universal to humans, which is intimately related to other developmental processes, including motoric behavior. Precocity of language development, as contrasted with the later role of language as a vehicle for abstract, conceptual processes, thus may be viewed as another reflection of generally accelerated sensori-motor development. The generally negative correlation between rapidity of early development and later level of cognitive ability reflected in intelligence tests and other indices of conceptual ability is consistent with the later deceleration of linguistically precocious children – a deceleration that shows up at the age when the child's language begins to reflect more complex, abstract, and conceptual mental processes.[3]

K*

Students of language development recognize that it is largely under the control of innate factors. Lenneberg (1969, p. 638) has reported studies of language acquisition in monozygotic and dizygotic twins, permitting analysis of genetic influences. Individual differences in the age of language acquisition, the rate of development, and the specific types of problems encountered all show a high degree of genetic determination. (Also see Lenneberg, 1967.)

Vocal language, as a species-specific characteristic, does not need to be built up or shaped laboriously through the conditioning and chaining of myriads of behavioral units. Language is learned, to be sure, but learning a species-specific form of behavior is quite different, in terms of individual differences, from the learning of many other kinds of behavioral repertoires. In species-specific behaviors learning capacity for a class of behaviors has been more or less maximized and individual differences minimized; there is relatively little individual genetic variation, but so much genetic determination for the ease of acquisition of certain behaviors that capricious environmental contingencies, within very wide limits, have little effect on the acquisition of the behavior. (We often therefore tend to call it 'development' rather than 'acquisition'.) Houston (1970), a psycholinguist, points out that

> . . . all children learn language merely by being placed in the environment of the language and . . . they do not need any special training or conditioning whatever to achieve this [four references]. Further, all children appear to learn language in about the same length of time, namely, from four to six years. . . . Given the open-ended variation in learning environments previously noted and given the lack of directed reinforcement for language or other behavior in children characteristic of many societies, the argument for a biological basis for language acquisition is convincing. . . . It is now believed by linguists that man has an innate biological capacity for language acquisition, a capacity which has been described as a species-specific and species-uniform language-acquisition device which functions uniquely in the language-acquisition process and the operation of which is constant for all children. Various biological and neurophysiological correlates of the language-learning process have been discovered, so that this position is strengthened. (pp. 949-50)

In these aspects, language acquisition can be likened to the child's learning to walk. All physically normal children learn to do so, given the barest opportunity, and they go through the same sequence from crawling, creeping, and toddling to walking, although showing slight individual differences in rates of acquisition at each stage along the way. Houston points out that '. . . language-acquisition stages seem invariant; it should be additionally noted that all children have rules by which they produce their language at each stage of the acquisition process, irrespective of the particular language or form of language they are acquiring [three references]' (p. 951).

Is the later lag in cognitive development seen in low SES children and especially in low SES Negro children, between grades 1 and 3, due to delayed effects of verbal deprivation during the preschool years or to insufficient verbal stimulation outside school? Does language deficiency *per se* hinder conceptual and abstract thinking? In seeking answers to these questions, it should be instructive to study the most verbally deprived children we know of – children who are born totally deaf. Since the year 1900 there have been some fifty comparative studies of the intelligence of the congenitally deaf; all these studies have been reviewed and summarized in two articles by M. Vernon (1967, 1968). As might be expected if deafness constitutes a severe form of verbal and language deprivation, congenitally deaf children score well below normally hearing children on strictly verbal tests. At age of school entry, when normal children have a vocabulary of 2,000 to 8,000 words and a well-developed syntax, deaf children usually know absolutely no words at all, and it is only after about four years of education, at about ten years of age, that these children can begin to compete with the average first grader in vocabulary and other language skills; about 35 percent of such children never achieve functional literacy, so great is their verbal handicap.

But how do these deaf children score on non-verbal performance tests of intelligence? Vernon summarizes his review of all the literature on this point: '. . . the research of the last fifty years which compares the IQ of the deaf with the hearing and of sub-groups of deaf children indicates that when there are no complicating multiple handicaps, the deaf and hard-of-hearing function at approximately the same IQ level on performance tests as do the hearing' (1968, p. 9),[4] contrary to the popular view that the deaf are retarded, which is correct only as regards verbal tests. But the important thing to note is that the *pattern* of test scores for the deaf is just the opposite to that of Negro children, who do better on the verbal and poorer on the performance tests. Vernon concludes that there is no functional relationship between verbal language and cognition; verbal language is not the mediating symbol of thought, although verbal behavior may serve to mediate and express thought processes in ways I have explicated in detail elsewhere (Jensen, 1971c). Another student of the psychology of the deaf, Hans Furth (1964), has come to similar conclusions:

> In summary, then, the reported investigations [of the cognitive abilities of the deaf] seem to emphasize as legitimate the distinction between intellective and verbal skills. The ability for intellective behavior is seen as largely independent of language and mainly subject to the general experience of living. Various sources of empirical evidence confirm the theoretical position that just as language learning is not closely related to intellectual endowment so intellective performance is not directly dependent on language.

Specifically, Furth concludes,

> Empirical studies of deaf people's performance on non-verbal cognitive tasks were reviewed. Deaf were found to perform similarly to hearing persons on tasks where verbal knowledge could have been assumed *a priori* to benefit the hearing. Such evidence appears to weaken a theoretical position which attributes to language a direct, general, or decisive influence on intellectual development. (p. 145)

Another important difference between low SES children and children who are verbally deprived because of deafness is that while the former begin to lag in linguistic and intellectual development after beginning school, the latter show a gradual catching up to the average level as they progress in school – it merely takes them longer to acquire information because of their severe sensory handicap. But once it is acquired, normal mental development ensues. A study of the developing conceptual capacities of the deaf concluded:

> . . . the differences found between deaf and hearing adolescents were amenable to the effects of age and education and were no

longer found between deaf and hearing adults. Dissociation between words and referents, verbalization adequacy, and (conceptual) level of verbalization were not different for deaf and hearing subjects. Our experiments, then, have shown few differences between deaf and hearing subjects. Those found were shown to fall along a normal developmental line and were amenable to the effects of increased age and experience, and education. (Kates, Kates & Michael, 1962, pp. 31-2)

Thus the language deprivation theory of the Negro-white IQ difference simply does not accord with the facts, and so we must turn to other possible explanations.

NOTES

1. A convenient index for expressing the verbal/non-verbal discrepancy, suggested by Weyl (1969), is 100 × non-verbal/verbal score (expressed in standard score form). Applied to the Coleman data at first grade, before the schools could have had any appreciable cumulative effect, this index for the various subpopulations is Puerto Rican 102·0, Indian 110·9, Mexican 107·7, Oriental 109·7, White 101·6, Negro 95·6.
2. I am indebted to Dr Neil Warren, University of Sussex, for several additions to this list of references, particularly the unpublished studies by Kilbride (1969), Theunissen (1948), and Falmagne (1959). Dr Warren has prepared a valuable review of the literature on this topic ('African Infant Precocity', unpublished manuscript, 1971). His conclusions are summarized in his own abstract of this review:

   Studies of African infant development are reviewed, with reference to the possible phenomenon of African infant precocity, and in an attempt to place these studies within the perspective of a viable strategy of cross-cultural research. Although the majority of studies report precocity, it is held that defects of measurement and design must preclude the conclusion that precocity is an established fact. The better-designed studies do not report precocity. It is also argued that infant differences by social milieu afford the most sensible basis for the necessary introduction of independent variables into this research area, and that improved techniques of assessment should be applied, both in the neonatal period and beyond.

The 'better-designed' studies referred to are the two unpublished studies (Theunissen, 1948; Falmagne, 1959); they report no evidence of infant motor precocity in their African samples (which were from different parts of Africa than those of other studies). I have not had the opportunity to examine these unpublished theses at first hand, but it is interesting that, as the only studies which have not reported advanced development in Negro infants, Warren seems to regard them as the only studies which are methodologically sound. I do not concur in this conclusion. Though many of the other studies surely cannot be held up as methodological paragons of rigorous measurement and statistical inference, the striking magnitude of the differences observed and the great consistency of the many studies by different investigators using various techniques lends a weight to the preponderance of evidence which cannot be dismissed by two studies, whatever their methodological excellence, based on different African subpopulations. In such a case, the difference in results is much more likely due either to sampling differences or to true subpopulation differences, rather than to methodological faults which would have caused all other studies to yield opposite conclusions. One almost wonders if Dr Warren's rather extreme weighting of the evidence toward the weakest possible conclusion is an illustration of Bertrand Russell's remark that 'an intransigent perfectionism is the last refuge of the skeptic'.

It seems apparent that the overall consistency and convergence of many lines of evidence which point in the same direction must have been largely ignored by Dr Warren in summarizing his conclusions. He does not mention studies (e.g., Naylor & Myrianthopoulos, 1967; Harrison, Weiner et al., 1964, p. 347; Nelson & Dean, 1959) which show Negro infants' advanced development in physical characteristics such as rate of bone development (determined from X-rays showing the rate of ossification of cartilage), the earlier eruption (by an average of one year) of the permanent teeth, and the greater maturity of brain wave patterns seen in electro-encephalograms. Nor is there mention of those American studies, with the exception of Bayley's (1965), which are methodologically sound and more sophisticated than most of the African studies (Pasamanick, 1949; Knobloch & Pasamanick, 1953; Williams & Scott, 1953; Durham Education Improvement Program, 1966-7a, b), and all of which report advanced motor development of Negro as compared with white infants.

Of all existing studies, including the unpublished studies referred to by Dr Warren, Bayley's (1965) is based on the largest (1,409 infants) samples of Negroes and whites (and also the most representative of the U.S. Negro and white populations). The standardization and carefulness of testing procedures and the complete adequacy of the presentation of data and the statistical analyses thereof make it probably the best single study available to date. Summarizing the results on the Developmental Motor Quotient (DMQ), derived from her infant tests, Bayley (1965, p. 405) reports: 'The means for the Negroes are higher at every age (from 1 to 15 months) except 15 months. The difference reaches significance at the 0·01 level of confidence at months 3, 4, 5, and 9 and at the 0·05 level at months 7 and 12. After 12 months this difference disappears.' Bayley concludes: 'Although there is considerable overlap of scores among whites and Negroes of the same age, a genetic factor may be operating. That is, Negroes may be inherently more precocious than whites in their motor coordinations' (pp. 408-9). Cravioto (1966, p. 78) has noted similar results in Indian infants of Guatemala and Mexico, commenting that on the Gesell tests of infant behavior 'their development at two or three weeks is similar to that of Western European infants two or three times as old'. It is also interesting that Orientals (Chinese-Americans) who, as school age children, equal or exceed the white population in the most heavily *g* loaded intelligence tests and in the most abstract scholastic subjects, as infants are significantly less motorically reactive than white infants, though they show no significant difference in neuromuscular maturity *per se* (Freedman & Freedman, 1969). Chinese and Caucasian neonates in the nursery of the same hospital were 'tested' shortly after birth. Marked differences in reactivity showed up, for example, when a loosely woven cloth was placed on the face of the supine baby. The typical Caucasian neonate 'immmediately struggled to remove the cloth by swiping his hands and turning his face'; the typical Chinese-American neonate 'lay impassively, exhibiting few overt motor responses'. This behavioral difference was significant beyond the 0·0001 level. 'Similarly, when placed in a prone position, the Chinese infants frequently lay as placed, with face flat against the bedding, whereas the Caucasian infants either turned the face to one side or lifted the head.' Similar studies of Negro neonates suggest that the three racial groups lie on a developmental continuum on which the Caucasian group is more or less intermediate. A related fact is that there is an inverse relationship throughout the phylogenic hierarchy between the tendency for multiple births and the prolongation of immaturity. In the course of evolution there has been genetic suppression of multiple births in all hominids, including man, through natural selection, although twins and other multiple births still occur with low frequencies. As Harrison, Weiner *et al.* (1964, p. 91) have noted, 'Single young is a pre-adaptation for progressively increased maturation time, and in this respect man shows a clear continuity with the pongids' (the phylogenically closest group having the most recent common ancestor with homonids). In terms of 'fitness' in the genetic sense, single births have a selective advantage. Thus the tendency for single births, like the prolongation of immaturity, may be a reflection of evolutionary age. It is interesting therefore that one of the best established differences among the major human races is the large difference in the frequencies of multiple births, particularly dizygotic twinning, being most common in Negroes and least common in Orientals, with Caucasians more or less intermediate (Harrison, Weiner *et al.*, 1964, p. 148; Bulmer, 1970, pp. 83-91).

3. Intellectually gifted children are sometimes reported to have been prococious in various infant behaviors such as walking and talking (e.g., Terman & Oden, 1959, p. 7), on the basis of self-report and/or parental reports. Such after-the-fact retrospective self-reports of individuals (or their parents) who already know they have superior IQs would hardly seem reliable. It is quite well-established, on the other hand, that mental defectives begin talking at a later age than most children and show retarded language development (for a review see McCarthy, 1946, pp. 546-9).

4. Apparently the sensori-motor capability for manipulating objects in the environment also is not crucial for normal cognitive development. The children who are probably the most disadvantaged in this respect are the limbless thalidomide babies, who, despite their severe motor handicap, are reported to show no deficit in cognitive development (Bower, 1971).

17 *Culture-biased tests*

The claim that intelligence tests are culturally biased in favor of white middle-class children and are therefore invalid when applied to minority children (or to lower-class white children) is undoubtedly the commonest argument against studies of subpopulation differences. The SPSSI Council (1969) states:

> We must also recognize the limitations of present-day intelligence tests. Largely developed and standardized on white middle-class children, these tests tend to be biased against black children to an unknown degree. While IQ tests do predict school achievement, we cannot demonstrate that they are accurate as measures of innate endowment. Any generalizations about the ability of black or white children are very much limited by the nature of existing IQ tests.

This view has been the basis for moves to abolish all testing in the public schools. Thus we read in a newspaper: 'The Board of Education voted unanimously last night to appoint a special committee to decide whether all psychological testing of minority children should be stopped. The resolution came after a score of black community leaders pleaded for an immediate moratorium on achievement and intelligence testing of minority children. They said the tests, designed for middle-class whites, were invalid for minority groups' (*San Francisco Chronicle*, 6 May 1970, p. 18). The news report quoted a psychologist as saying, 'Asking a black child the advantages of having a checking account when most black families don't have them is about as fair as asking white children about chitterlings when most white families don't eat them.' The public is left with the clear impression that all intelligence tests are comprised of questions of factual information typical of what children in middle- or upper-class homes are most likely to learn and children from poor homes are least likely to learn. One can always point to some items or some tests which seem to illustrate this point. The next step is to brand intelligence tests as instruments of social injustice, devised and used by the Establishment to maintain the social class structure of the society. Thus an educational sociologist writes: 'In view of the close relationship between IQ scores and social class in Big City, it seems that one very destructive function of the IQ score is that it serves as a kind of cement which fixes students into the social classes of their birth. IQ is the supreme and unchallengeable justification for the social system' (Sexton, 1961, p. 51). This overlooks the fact that more than a third of the population changes social status each generation and that the correlation between SES and IQ is much higher for parents than for their children. Actually, IQ tests, much more so than interviews, teachers' impressions, and school grades, can have a liberalizing influence on the education and upward mobility of lower-class children, since good IQ tests can 'read' through the superficial veneer of cultural factors related to social status. Many intellectually gifted children who might otherwise go undiscovered by their parents, peers and teachers are found by means of intelligence tests. As sociologist Otis Dudley Duncan (1968, p. 11) characterized this position:

> . . . intelligence contributes a large share of variance in achievement (i.e., education, occupation, income) that is *unrelated* to the social class of birth . . . in view of the loose relationship between IQ and social class in the United States, it seems that one very constructive function of the ability measured by intelligence tests is that it serves as a kind of springboard, launching many men into achievements removing them considerable distances from the social class of their birth. IQ, in an achievement-oriented society, is the primary leaven preventing the classes from hardening to castes.

It should also be pointed out that individual differences in the ability measured by IQ tests exist and contribute to educational and occupational achievement and to social mobility, whether or not measured by IQ tests. The doctor will not alter his patient's fever by throwing away the thermometer.

The last refuge of the critics of IQ tests is to argue that there is no such thing as intelligence and that even if there were it could not be measured. A more sophisticated version of this argument is that there are so many different kinds of abilities that it is meaningless to speak of intelligence as a *general* ability or a *g* factor which is relevant to a wide variety of achievements. Readers who wish to see these issues trenchantly spelled out are referred to Quinn McNemar's (1964) presidential address to the American Psychological Association. Philip E. Vernon (1965a, p. 724) has put it most succinctly: 'A general intelligence factor seems unavoidable since substantial positive intercorrelations are found when any cognitive tests are applied to a fairly representative population.' One of the many practical consequences of this fact is noted, as Vernon continues:

> When I visited some military psychological establishments in 1957, I was told more than once that military psychologists could not ignore *g*. Try as they would to find differential tests for different army trades, intercorrelations were so high that recruits appeared to be differentiated more by all-round level of ability than by type of ability, that is to say, by *g* rather than by factor profile.

STANDARDIZATION AND PREDICTIVE VALIDITY

First, let us look at the *standardization* argument, typically expressed as it was in the *New Scientist* (23 July, 1970): 'Is it surprising that Negro children do badly on culturally loaded tests standardized only on white children?'

All that *standardization* means is that the test has been given to some fairly large and representative sample of some population, and the distribution of *raw scores* (i.e., the number of test items the subject gets 'correct') is converted into *standard scores*,[1] so that each age group in the population sample will have the same mean and standard deviation. (On most IQ tests conventionally the mean is set at 100 and the *SD* at 15.) If the raw scores do not conform to the normal or Gaussian bell-shaped distribution, they may be normalized by converting them to percentile scores which are then expressed as deviates of the normal distribution. In essence, standardization is the process of re-scaling raw scores in terms of the mean and standard deviation of the so-called normative population. The normative population may or may not include one or another racial subpopulation. And some normative samples are more representative of one geographical region or its racial composition than another. It is possible to obtain separate norms for whites and Negroes, and it is possible to have norms based on the combined groups each represented proportionally to their frequency in the general population. Various standardized tests have used one or another of these methods. The important point, however, is that it makes absolutely no real difference in terms of the rank order of individuals or of subpopulations on the test, and it has no effect whatsoever on the predictive validity of the test, any more than it lowers a patient's temperature to change from a Fahrenheit to a Centigrade thermometer. We are simply assigning different numbers to the same relative differences. For example, a test standardized exclusively in the white population and given a mean of 100 and an *SD* of 15 will show a mean of approximately 85 and an *SD* of 13 when given to a representative sample of the Negro population. If we standardize the test in a combined sample of whites and Negroes, represented in the proportions of their frequencies in the general population of the United States (approximately 89 percent whites, 11 percent Negroes), the general mean IQ will still be set at 100 and the *SD* at 15. But on this scale the Negro mean will be 87·1 and the white mean will be 101·6, for a difference of 14·5 IQ points. But the percentage of Negroes exceeding the white median (i.e., median overlap) will remain exactly the same, viz., 14·2 percent. (Median overlap has this advantage as a measure of group differences – it is invariant regardless of the scale of measurement.) Thus, it is apparent that re-standardizing or re-scaling IQ tests would make no essential difference in Negro-white comparisons.

Having separate sets of norms for Negro and white populations, each given a mean of 100 and *SD* of 15, could only impair the predictive validity of the tests when they are used in mixed populations. This is because intelligence tests standardized on whites or on Negroes and whites together have the same predictive validity for Negroes as for whites (see Jensen, 1971d and Stanley, 1971, for reviews for this evidence). In other words, the tests themselves are color blind and predict the same scholastic and occupational performance for individuals obtaining the same score, regardless of race. (When prediction discrepancies have been found, they have usually been 'in favor' of Negroes, i.e., the Negroes perform less well on the criterion than was predicted by the test.) Jensen (1971) found in a large elementary school sample ($N = 6,569$) that including 'race' (white, Negro, or Mexican) along with IQ and other psychological tests in a multiple regression equation for predicting scholastic achievement adds no significant increment to the prediction (i.e., R^2). Also, factor analyses of a large battery of mental ability tests yield the same factors in Negro and white samples, although the specific factor loadings on some tests may differ for Negroes and whites. In summary, ability tests behave very much the same in Negro and white populations. This would not be the case if IQs were based on separate norms for the two populations. As it is, a Negro child and a white child with the same IQ can be expected to perform about equally well in school or on the job (in so far as it depends upon intellectual ability). If there were different norms for the two groups, a Negro person and a white person with nominally the same score would not be expected to perform equally in school, etc. In short, in terms of their predictive validity, that is to say their practical usefulness, most standard IQ tests, scholastic aptitude tests, and the like, are not biased against Negroes.[2]

THE CULTURE-BIAS HYPOTHESIS

Though 'culture bias' is the term most commonly used, a better term would be 'status bias', since in making group comparisons within a given culture we are concerned with test content biases that may discriminate according to the differential experiences of persons who have grown up in different social strata. When Negro and white children grow up in the same locality, attend the same schools, watch the same television programs, have the same toys, eat the same food bought in the same stores, wear the same clothes, etc., they have much more in common culturally than not, as judged on a world-wide scale of cultural diversity. Negro and white children growing up, say, in Berkeley, California, surely have much more culturally in common with one another than either group has in common with, say, the Eskimos or the Australian Bushmen. Whatever experiential differences exist are largely social status differences rather than cultural differences in any meaningful sense of the word.

To say that an intelligence test is culturally-biased or status-biased means that the knowledge, skills, and demands of the test sample the specific learning opportunities of one subpopulation (i.e., social class or racial group) more than of another. One can think of many examples of questions that would be easier for children of one subpopulation than of another. The question, for example, 'What are chopsticks made of?' would favor Oriental children; 'What are tortillas?' would favor Mexican children; 'What are chitterlings?' would favor Negro children; 'What is the Talmud?' would favor Jewish children, and so on. One could presumably devise a test composed entirely of specially selected items that would give a marked advantage to any particular subpopulation one might choose. The culture-bias hypothesis claims that this in fact is what has been done: intentionally or unintentionally, standard intelligence tests have been composed of items which favor middle- and upper-class whites and disfavor all other groups, especially Negroes, other minorities, and lower-class whites. How valid is this claim? Since I have discussed these issues at length elsewhere (Jensen, 1968c, 1970b), I will here attempt only a brief summary of the main points.

Surely one can point to 'culture-loaded' items on many standard intelligence tests. Questions about exotic zoo animals, fairy tales, and musical instruments are obvious examples of items that should favor children from well-to-do homes and disfavor children from poor homes which afford little opportunity to learn about such things. In one obvious attempt to discredit IQ tests, five highly 'culture-loaded' items from the Comprehension subtest of the Wechsler Adult Intelligence Scale (WAIS) were selected for display by proponents of the culture-bias hypothesis of Negro-white IQ difference (*Bulletin of the Cambridge Society for Social Responsibility in Science*, 18 July 1970, p. 6). It may therefore seem ironic to discover that, in fact, among the eleven subtests of the WAIS, the one on which Negroes actually differ least from whites is the very Comprehension test that was held up as an example of test items that might seem to be culturally biased against Negroes (e.g., 'Why should people pay taxes?' 'Why does land in the city cost more than land in the country?' 'Why are laws necessary?') (Shuey, 1966, p. 407; Plotkin, 1971, p. 6). Negroes actually score lowest on the Block Design subtest, a non-verbal test requiring the subject to copy patterns of increasing complexity with a set of sixteen colored one-inch blocks. This is probably the least culture-loaded subtest of the WAIS. This is not a result peculiar to the Wechsler tests. In general, Negroes obtain higher scores on tests which by any reasonable criteria appear to be more culture-loaded than on items that are less culture-loaded.

This has been demonstrated most dramatically in a study by McGurk (1953a, 1953b, 1967). He compared the performance of Negro and white 18-year-old high school students on highly culture-loaded as compared with minimally culture-loaded intelligence test items. For this purpose, to quote McGurk (1967, p. 374), 'A special test was constructed, half the questions of which were rated as depending heavily on cultural background (the culture questions) while the other half were rated as depending little on cultural background (the non-cultural questions). Each set of questions yielded a score – either a culture score or a non-culture score.' McGurk found that the 'Negroes performed better (relative to the whites) on the culturally loaded questions' (p. 378). This comparison was based on Negro and white groups selected in such a manner that 'Negroes and whites were paired so that the members of each pair – one Negro and one white – were identical or equivalent for fourteen socio-economic factors' (p. 379).

How can we understand such seemingly paradoxical results, which are the rule and not the exception? In order to find the answer, I have carried out item analyses of many kinds of intelligence tests, seeking those which discriminate the most and the least between Negro and white subjects, as well as between white lower and middle SES subjects. When one brings together large numbers of test items solely on the basis of whether they discriminate minimally or maximally between Negro and white (or low and middle SES) samples, the answer to the paradoxical findings becomes apparent. All intelligence tests are intentionally devised so that the items vary in difficulty, usually beginning with the easiest items and increasing gradually to the most difficult items. Item difficulty is objectively defined simply in terms of the percentage of the normative population that fails to give the correct answer to the item.

Examination and statistical analyses of a wide variety of test items reveal that items are graded in difficulty along two main dimensions (not mutually exclusive). One dimension is *rarity* or infrequency of opportunity to learn the content of the item. Many general information items and vocabulary items vary in difficulty along this rarity dimension, e.g., 'What is the Bible?' *v.* 'What is the Koran?' and define 'physician' *v.* 'philologist'. It happens that the type of items that increase in difficulty along the rarity dimension are those we call the most culture-loaded. Their difficulty depends upon their rarity rather than upon the *complexity* of the mental processes required for arriving at the correct answer. *Complexity* is the other main dimension along which test items increase in difficulty. Items differ in the amount of mental manipulation and transformation of the elements of the question that they require in order to arrive at the correct answer. Thus, the question 'What is the color of fire engines?' is low on both rarity and complexity, while the question 'If a fire engine can go no faster than 50 miles per hour, what is the shortest time it could take it to get to a fire five miles away?' is also low in rarity but considerably higher in complexity. Similarly, digit span memory (repeating a series of numbers after hearing the series spoken once by the examiner) is low on complexity as compared with number series completion, e.g., 'What number should come next in the series: 1, 2, 4, 5, 7, ?'. A Wechsler Information Test item like 'Who wrote *The Republic*?' is difficult because of its rarity. The following Wechsler-type Arithmetic item, on the other hand, may have exactly the same difficulty level, but it is difficult because of its complexity: 'Six men can finish a job in four days. How many men will be needed to finish it in half a day?' Negroes do much better on the Information than on the Arithmetic subtest, despite the fact that the Information items are more culture-loaded. Though it surely is not a necessary condition, it happens that in most intelligence tests there is an inverse relation between items' standing on the rarity dimension and on the complexity dimension. The rarest, most culture-loaded items involve the least complexity, and the most complex items involve the most common contents. And what we find is that the degree to which items discriminate between social classes and between Negroes and whites is much more a function of the item's complexity than of its rarity or culture-loading. This is true whether the complexity involves verbal, numerical, or spatial materials. The degree to which test items call for mental manipulation, transformation, conceptualization, and abstraction – and not so much the rarity or culture-loading of their contents – is what mostly determines the Negro-white discriminability of test items. On the other hand, some subpopulations – American Orientals, for example – show just the reverse; they do relatively better (usually exceeding the white population) on those items most heavily loaded on the complexity dimension. Orientals are somewhat disadvantaged on tests to the extent that cultural items are included as opposed to complexity items, while just the opposite typically is true for Negroes.

When many test items of various types are included in a factor analysis, the degree to which they are loaded on the g factor (i.e., the ability factor which is common to all intelligence tests and mainly accounts for their intercorrelations) is related more to the complexity of the items than to the rarity of their contents, especially if the tests are given to a culturally and socioeconomically heterogeneous sample. That is to say, the items that increase in difficulty along the complexity dimension better represent the g factor of intelligence in a heterogeneous population than do the more culture-loaded items.

By minimizing rarity and maximizing the varieties and degrees of complexity, it is possible to produce tests which are relatively 'culture-fair' or 'culture-reduced'. No one claims that there is any test which is perfectly 'culture-free', and so to attack 'culture-free' tests is to attack a straw man. 'Culture-free' is an idealized and unattainable end-point of an actual continuum along which various tests (or test items) can in fact be rank ordered. To say there is no such thing as a 'culture-free' test does not mean that tests cannot be ordered along a dimension (or a number of dimensions) representing the degree to which they utilize contents having differential rarity in various subpopulations. Just as there are no 'perfectly soft' or 'perfectly hard' gems, it is nevertheless possible to rank gems along a soft-hard continuum.

Numerous attempts have been made to devise culture-reduced tests, the main approaches to which I have reviewed elsewhere (Jensen, 1968c). All approaches have been essentially an attempt to minimize the rarity factor, by using either content that is equally common to all status groups within the culture or non-representational content that is equally unfamiliar to everyone.

Item difficulty then is controlled by the complexity of the mental operations with the equally familiar materials needed to find the answer. One of the pioneering attempts at this, now of historical interest, is the defunct Davis-Eells Games, developed in 1951. The items, represented as games, were cartoons of children doing ordinary things in very familiar settings; in fact, the settings were more typical of a lower-class environment than of a middle-class environment. No reading was required and the tests were untimed – features thought to favor lower SES relative to middle SES children. Practical judgment and commonsense inferences are called for in solving most of the problems. One cartoon, for example, shows three panels, each depicting a boy trying to get over a high backyard fence. One boy is piling up boxes and rubbish cans in a most unstable fashion, one is futilely jumping and one is stacking boxes in a stable fashion. The testee simply marks the picture he thinks shows the best method for getting over the fence. But in order to increase item difficulty with such familiar materials, the problem situations had to be made increasingly complex in the inferences and judgments called for in order to solve them. Logical reasoning was needed, though it always involved only commonplace practical situations. But the test was entirely unsuccessful in the view of those who had hoped it might eliminate social class and racial differences in mean performance. Group differences approximately equal to those found with the ordinary standard IQ tests were found with the Davis-Eells Games. Since they essentially failed in their main purpose and had certain psychometric defects as well, the games were dropped.

Subsequent attempts along the same lines were made by Davis and his co-workers, using items believed to be intrinsically motivating, similar to real-life situations, equally familiar to all social classes, and without time limits. But these tests, too, yielded lower scores for Negroes, lower, in fact, than found for low-status whites. As of the present time, no one yet has succeeded in devising a test that does not discriminate between representative samples of Negroes and whites and which also can be shown to have any *g* loading (which is essentially the complexity factor) or any validity in terms of correlation with any external educational or occupational criteria. If group differences were due to cultural bias in the test and not to true differences in intelligence, it should be possible to devise culturally appropriate tests that eliminate the group difference and yet retain the tests' validity. The fact that no one has yet been able to devise a test, either culture-fair or culture-loaded, on which Negroes perform as well as whites or other minorities, despite many serious attempts to do so, is a strong argument against the culture-bias hypothesis. In this connection, it is interesting to note the kinds of changes that have had to be made in the Wechsler tests to make them have the same reliability, validity, and intercorrelations among subscales in various foreign countries as are found in the normative population of the United States. The necessary changes are surprisingly minimal. None of the Performance tests has to be changed except one involving a picture of the American flag, and the changes required in the Verbal tests are usually no more than translation into the foreign language, with but few exceptions, such as changing two or three Information subtest items involving names of American historical figures and geographical features of the United States commonly taught in our schools. Equivalent items are easy to find for other countries (e.g., 'What is the population of Japan?', 'How far is it from Tokyo to Osaka?' etc.). When so few and such superficial changes can make it possible for persons in foreign lands and different cultures to perform on a par (or exceed) white Americans, it is a wonder why the most diligent efforts have failed to yield an intelligence test on which American Negroes can score on a par with the rest of the population.

The most successful culture-reduced tests have been those employing simple figural materials, requiring subjects to engage in reasoning, inference, generalization, and other basic mental processes in terms of relationships between geometric forms, patterns, etc. Such tests are Raven's Progressive Matrices, Cattell's Culture-Fair Tests of *g*, the Lorge-Thorndike Non-verbal Intelligence Test, the Street Gestalt Test, the Gottschaldt Embedded Figures Test, and others. MacArthur and Elley (1963) set up certain desirable criteria for culture-reduced tests and studied a host of such tests along with conventional IQ tests to determine which of the many tests came closest to meeting their criteria. Raven's *Progressive Matrices* and Cattell's *Culture-Fair Tests of g* proved to be the best in this study, which showed that

(1) Culture-reduced tests sample the general intellectual ability factor [*g*] as well as or better than conventional tests. (2) Most

culture-reduced tests show negligible loadings on verbal and numerical factors. (3) Culture-reduced tests show significantly less relationship with socioeconomic status than do conventional tests. (4) A conventional test (California Test of Mental Maturity) showed a significant increase in relationship with socioeconomic status over four years, whereas the Progressive Matrices showed no change. (5) Verbal items from the CTMM showed greater variation in Item discrimination between social classes than did items from the Progressive Matrices. (p. 118)

The Progressive Matrices Test has been used in numerous truly cross-cultural studies. These studies show mean differences between various ethnic and cultural groups the directions of which are not at all in accord with the popular notion that groups are handicapped on IQ tests directly in relation to their degree of environmental and cultural dissimilarity from that of the white middle- and upper-middle class population of the United States or Western Europe. It would be hard to find an environmentally and culturally more dissimilar group than the Eskimos living in the icy wastes far above the Arctic circle. Yet representative samples of these Eskimos score at or above white Canadian norms on the Progressive Matrices (MacArthur, 1968). Berry (1966) found Eskimo samples scoring near his Scottish samples (one of the highest normative groups) on the Progressive Matrices and the Embedded Figures Tests. Vernon too, has found that on the Matrices and similar tests, such as the Kohs Block Designs and Abstractions, Eskimos and Canadian Indians score much higher than Jamaican Negroes. Vernon seeks an environmental explanation of the marked disparity:

> Now economic conditions are extremely poor in all three groups (Eskimos, Indians, Jamaicans), and there is similar family instability and insecurity. Thus it seems reasonable to attribute the better performance of Eskimo and Indian groups to the greater emphasis on resourcefulness in the upbringing of boys, perhaps combined with their strong masculine identification. True, the traditional hunting-trapping life is rapidly disappearing and the majority of parents are wage earning or on relief, but the children are still brought up permissively and encouraged to explore and hunt. Moreover, a subgroup of the Eskimos who came from the most isolated Arctic communities scored better

on all three of the tests just mentioned (Matrices, Embedded Figures, Abstractions) than did those who lived in closer contact with whites and had become more acculturated. (Vernon, 1965a, p. 732)

(For a comprehensive review of Vernon's cross-cultural studies of abilities see Vernon, 1969.)

In the United States, Negroes generally average about 1 *SD* or more below whites on the Matrices. Figure 12.1 (p. 250) shows

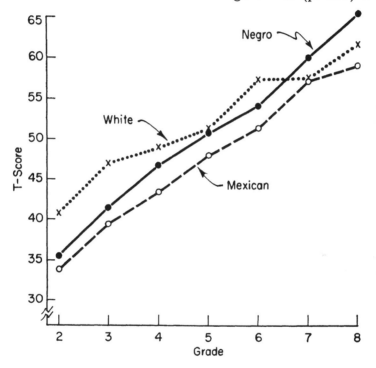

Figure 17.1 Mean *T* scores ($\bar{x} = 50$, $SD = 10$) on composite rote memory tests. (From Jensen, 1971a.)

the Matrices scores of large representative samples of California school children at several grade levels (Jensen, 1971a). The scores are on a *T* scale with the overall mean at 50 and an *SD* of 10 points. The results are particularly interesting in view of the fact that on the Home Index, a measure of environmental and cultural advantages, the Mexican group in this study is as far below the Negro group as the Negro is below the white. Figure 17.1 shows scores of the same three groups on a composite rote memory test which is difficult, requiring sustained attention, concentration, and motivation, but makes no demands on reasoning or abstract conceptual abilities.

One of the most status-fair tests, at least for children who are in school and have had experience with paper and pencil, is the Figure Copying Test (see Figure 3.1, p. 78). The child is asked merely to copy the ten forms, each on a separate page, while they are in full view, without time limit. The children's drawings can be scored with a high degree of reliability for correspondence to the model and for maturity of the drawing. In factor analyses carried out separately in white, Negro, and Mexican samples, this test has a substantial *g* loading in all groups, comparable to that of Raven's Matrices. The test scores of kindergarten children also are prognostic of readiness for the traditional school learning tasks of the primary grades. The high level of motivation elicited by this test is indicated by the fact that the minimum score obtained in each group at each grade level increases systematically. This suggests that all children are making an attempt to perform in accordance with the instructions. Also, virtually 100 percent of the children in every ethnic group at every grade level attempted to copy every figure. The attempts, even when totally unsuccessful, show considerable effort, as indicated by the re-drawing of the figure, erasures and drawing over the figure repeatedly, in order to improve its likeness to the model. It is also noteworthy about this test that normal children are generally not successful in drawing figures beyond their mental age level, and special instruction, coaching and practice in drawing these figures hardly improves the child's performance. Figure 17.2 shows the scores on this test of several ethnic and social class groups totalling nearly ten thousand children in kindergarten to fourth grade in twenty-one California schools. The four ethnic groups are Oriental (O), White (W), Mexican (M), and Negro (N). The letter 'U' represents schools in an urban, relatively upper-status community socioeconomically as compared with the average school district in California; 'L' represents schools in comparatively lower-status rural districts. The groups are ranked on a composite index of socioeconomic status (SES), with SES 1 as the highest, representing largely professional and business-managerial upper-middle-class families. Note that the rank order of SES does not strictly correspond to the rank order of performance in Figure Copying. The Orientals exceed all other groups, and the Mexicans, who are at the bottom in SES, score only slightly below the whites. At fourth grade the range of group mean differences on the test spans more than 2 *SD*s. Negro fourth graders, on the average, match the performance of Oriental children in the first grade. These findings are consistent with results obtained at Yale's Gesell Institute using a battery of similar developmental tests with

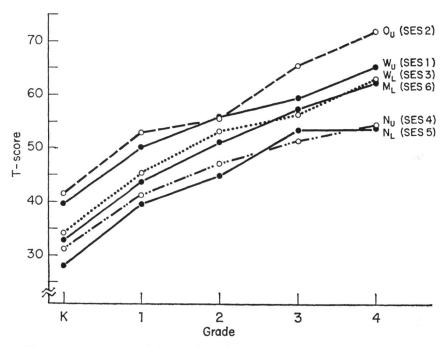

Figure 17.2 Oriental (O), white (W), Mexican (M), and Negro (N) groups from socioeconomically urban, largely middle- to upper-middle class (U) and rural, largely lower- to middle-class (L) communities. The six groups are ranked from highest (SES 1) to lowest (SES 6) on a composite index of socioeconomic status.

Negro and white elementary school children (Ames & Ilg, 1967). Especially for children who have been exposed to three or four years of schooling, such marked differences in performance would seem most difficult to explain in terms of differential experiences, motivation, and the like.

I have suggested previously that tests which are more culture-fair or status-fair can be thought of as having higher heritability in an environmentally heterogeneous population than highly culture- or status-loaded tests (Jensen, 1968c, pp. 81-6). Evidence from kinship correlations on various tests is consistent with this formulation. For example, standard IQ tests show quite low correlations (about 0·25), and consequently large IQ differences, between genetically unrelated (and thus dissimilar) children reared together, and show quite high correlations (about 0·80), and consequently small IQ differences, between genetically identical twins reared apart. On the other hand, certain highly culture-loaded scholastic achievement tests show much less difference, i.e., rather higher correlations (about 0·50) between unrelated children reared together and lower correlations (about 0·70) between identical twins reared apart (Jensen, 1968a, Table 1 and Figure 1).

Now, if we accept this premise that a test's culture-loading is inversely related to its heritability in a given population, let us examine the consequences of comparing the regression of a culture-loaded test upon a hypothetical culture-free test, and vice versa, in each of two hypothetical populations, A and B. If differences are found between groups A and B, one of three hypotheses can be invoked to explain the difference: (1) the groups are genetically equal but differ environmentally; (2) the groups are environmentally equal but differ genetically; or (3) the groups differ both genetically *and* environmentally. The consequences of each hypothesis are shown in Figure 17.3. Our hypothetical perfectly culture-free or environment-free (meaning $h^2 = 1$) test measures the genotype, G: the culture-loaded test measures the phenotype, P. (The phenotypic value, P, is the sum of the genetic and environmental values, i.e., $P = G+E$.) Assume that the heritability of the phenotypic measure, P, is 0·80, so the correlation between genotype and phenotype would be the square root of 0·80, or 0·89. Also assume that the means of the two groups, A and B, differ on the phenotypic measure by 1 *SD*.

Hypothesis 1, then, is the environmental hypothesis. It states that the mean genotypes of the two groups are either equal (which includes the hypothesis that the phenotypically lower group is genetically equal to *or higher* than the phenotypically higher group, i.e., $\bar{G}_A \leqslant \bar{G}_B$) or genotype B is above genotype A, and the average environment of group A is more favorable than that of group B (i.e., $\bar{E}_A > \bar{E}_B$). If this hypothesis is true, and if h^2 is 0·80 in each group, then the regression of P on G and of G on P for groups A and B should appear as shown in Figure 17.3 in the two graphs

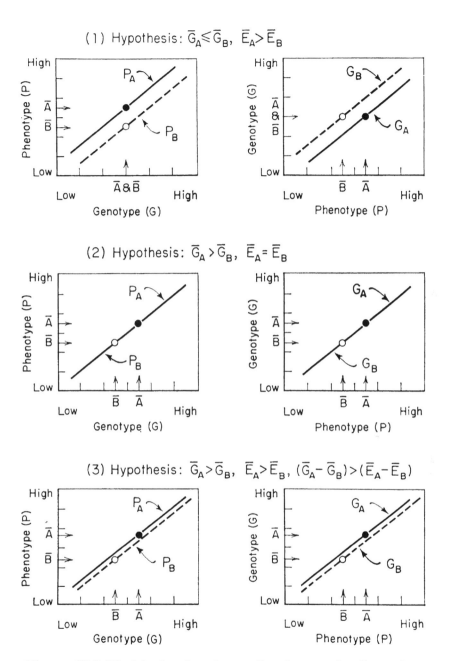

Figure 17.3 Models showing the predicted regression lines of phenotype on genotype (and vice versa) for two groups differing in mean phenotype under three different hypotheses of the cause of the groups' phenotypic difference: (1) environmental, (2) genetic, (3) combined environmental and genetic.

L

at the top.[3] That is to say, for any value of G, the value of P for group A will exceed that of group B by 1 SD. (The dots represent the bivariate means of groups A and B and the solid and dashed lines are the regression of P on G or G on P.)

Hypothesis 2 is a strictly genetic hypothesis; the groups differ in genotype but not in environment ($\bar{G}_A > \bar{G}_B$ and $\bar{E}_A = \bar{E}_B$). Here we see that the regression of P on G (and G on P) is the same line for both groups.

Hypothesis 3 is a combined genetic and environmental hypothesis, with two parts: (i) group A is more advantaged than group B both genetically *and* environmentally ($\bar{G}_A > \bar{G}_B$ and $\bar{E}_A > \bar{E}_B$), and (ii) the genetic difference is greater than the environmental difference ($\bar{G}_A - \bar{G}_B > \bar{E}_A - \bar{E}_B$). Note that in this case the regression line P_A is above P_B, as in the top left graph (Hypothesis 1), but unlike Hypothesis 1, in Hypothesis 3 the regression line G_A remains above G_B.

Now, with the consequences that logically follow from these three clearly formulated hypotheses made explicit, as shown in the regression lines of Figure 17.3, we can perform an empirical test of these hypotheses. Naturally, we can only crudely approximate the idealized hypothetical regressions shown in these graphs since there are no perfectly culture-free tests, i.e., tests with $h^2 = 1.00$. The best we can do at present is to use two tests which differ most conspicuously in culture-loading. (The most culture-loaded test corresponds to P in Figure 17.3 and the least culture-loaded test corresponds to G.) For this purpose we have chosen Raven's Matrices and the Peabody Picture Vocabulary Test (PPVT). We have already pointed out that the Raven is one of the most culture-reduced tests available. The PPVT provides a striking contrast. It is probably the most culture-loaded among all standardized IQ tests currently in use. The test consists of 150 plates each containing four pictures. The examiner says a word that labels one of the four pictures in each set and the testee is asked to point to the appropriate picture. The items increase in difficulty by increasing the rarity of the pictured objects and their corresponding verbal labels. Figure 17.4 shows the mean frequency of these words per every million words of printed English in American books, magazines, and papers. It can be seen that for both equivalent forms of the test (A and B), the commonness of the words decreases systematically from the first, easy items to the last, most difficult items.[4] The PPVT pictures and labels are almost a parody of culture-biased tests: e.g., *kangaroo, caboose, thermos, bronco, kayak, hassock, goblet, binocular, idol, observatory, oasis, walrus, canine.*

The Raven and PPVT were given individually to all white ($N = 638$), Negro ($N = 381$), and Mexican-American ($N = 684$) elementary school children in one small California school district.[5] The raw scores on both tests, within 6-month age intervals, were

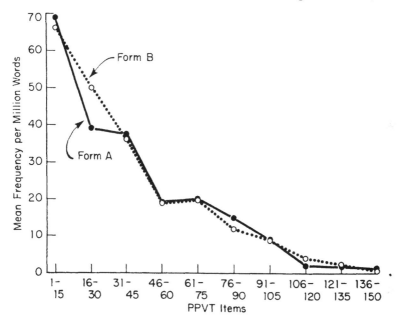

Figure 17.4 Mean Thorndike-Lorge word frequency of Peabody Picture Vocabulary Test items (for Forms A and B) as a function of item difficulty when items are ranked from 1 to 150 in P values (percent passing), based on the normative population.

transformed to z scores, with mean $= 0$, $SD = 1$. The regression of Raven on PPVT and of PPVT on Raven was then plotted separately for each ethnic group. The regression lines are perfectly linear throughout the entire range of test scores in all three groups, as shown in Figure 17.5. The slopes of these regression lines of the three groups do not differ significantly, but the intercepts differ significantly beyond the 0·001 level ($F = 52·38$, $df = 2/1658$). In short, the differences essential to our hypotheses are fully significant. So let us compare these empirical regression lines with the hypothesized ones in Figure 17.3. First consider the white-Negro comparison (corresponding to hypothetical groups *A* and *B*). We see that the top half of Figure 17.5 corresponds to the right-hand graphs in Figure 17.3. Now we see that in both graphs of Figure 17.3 the white regression line is significantly above the Negro regression line. The only hypothesis to which this

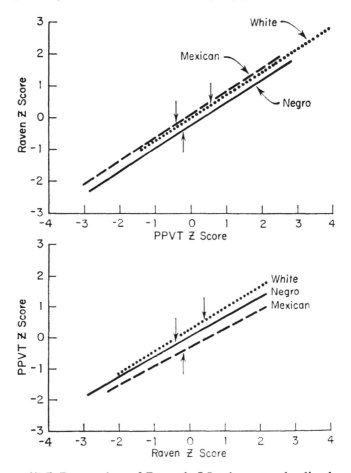

Figure 17.5 Regression of Raven's Matrices standardized scores (*z*) on Peabody Picture Vocabulary Test *z* scores (above), and regression of PPVT scores on Raven scores (below). The vertical arrows indicate the bivariate mean of each group.

situation corresponds is Hypothesis 3 in Figure 17.3. Hypotheses 1 and 2 are both contradicted by the data.

Next, consider the white-Mexican comparison. Here we see that the Mexican regression line is *above* the white regression line for the regression of Raven on PPVT (upper graph in Figure

17.5), and the Mexican regression line is *below* the white regression line for the regression of PPVT on Raven (lower graph in Figure 17.5). This state of affairs is predicted only by Hypothesis 1. Thus we see that the results for the Negro-white comparison are predicted by one hypothesis (Hypothesis 3), and the results for the Mexican-white comparison are predicted by another, although both the Negro and Mexican groups are regarded as disadvantaged and score lower than whites on IQ and scholastic achievement tests. It is most interesting that each of the two sets of ethnic comparisons is consistent with a *different* hypothesis.

Finally, consider the Negro-Mexican comparison. For the regression of Raven on PPVT the Mexican regression line is above the Negro, but just the reverse is true for the regression of PPVT on Raven. This result corresponds to Hypothesis 1 in Figure 17.3, i.e., the hypothesis $\bar{G}_A \leqslant \bar{G}_B$ and $\bar{E}_A > \bar{E}_B$, where A and B represent the Negro and Mexican groups, respectively. That is, the finding is consistent with the hypothesis that the Mexican group is genetically equal to or higher than the Negro, but environmentally or culturally disadvantaged relative to the Negro group. Since the Mexican group was also found equal to or higher than the white group genetically in this analysis, and the white group is genetically higher than the Negro (i.e., Hypothesis 3), it follows that the Mexican group genetically is not equal to but higher than the Negro. (That is, if Mexican $\geq$ white $>$ Negro, then Mexican $>$ Negro.) The results are well comprehended within the framework of these alternative hypotheses. Those who think in terms that are exclusively environmental, however, are usually deeply puzzled by the results shown in Figure 17.5. If (in the lower graph) for any given score on the less culture-loaded test (Raven) whites get the highest score on the more culture-loaded test (PPVT) and Mexicans get the lowest, with Negroes intermediate, it seems to make perfectly good sense from the culture-bias or environmentalist hypothesis. But then when we look at the upper graph in Figure 17.5, we see that for any given score on the culture-loaded test the Mexican gets the highest score on the culture-fair test, and this surely seems to make sense from the environmentalist standpoint. But the Negro group's regression line does not come next – instead it is well below the white group's regression line. In other words, if you match Negro, Mexican, and white children on the culture-loaded test, their scores on the more culture-fair test come out with Mexicans highest, Negroes lowest, and whites intermediate. This seems paradoxical to the environmentalist. It is predictable from the hypothesis formulated in Figure 17.3, which involves hypothesizing group differences in *both* genetic and environmental factors for explaining the Negro-white and Negro-Mexican differences. On the other hand, for these data at least, the hypothesis of only an environmental difference is compatible with the Mexican-white comparison. This methodology is presently being extended to other tests and other subpopulations. In terms of these formulations, it is already apparent from preliminary analyses that California Orientals bear a similar relationship to whites as the Mexicans bear to the Negroes, that is, a higher average genotype and lower average environmental advantages.

PIAGET'S MÉTHODE CLINIQUE

My work has been severely criticized by at least one developmental psychologist on the grounds that my conceptions of intelligence and its measurement were based on standard psychometric tests. Voyat claims that 'IQ tests are simply not adequate to measure processes of thinking' (Voyat, 1970, p. 161). He suggests that, instead of IQ tests, the theory and techniques of Jean Piaget, the noted Swiss child psychologist, should be applied to the problem of comparative mental development: 'Piaget's approach not only allows an understanding of how intelligence functions, but describes it. Since the interest of Piaget's tests lies in describing the mechanism of thinking, they permit an individual, personalized appraisal of further potentialities independent of the culture' (p. 161). 'In contrast, IQ tests, designed by whites for Western culture, have value limited to the culture within which they were designed' (p. 160). In view of these opinions, we must take a more detailed look at the relevance of Piaget's approach, which he calls the *méthode clinique*, to the study of children's mental development.

Briefly, Piaget views the mental development of the child as going through four main stages, which are invariant in sequence for all children: (1) The *sensori-motor* stage (onset from birth to about 1 year) is the first phase of intellectual development, in which knowledge and thought are intimately tied to the content of specific sensory input or motoric activity of the child; it includes conditioning, stimulus-response learning, reward learning, perceptual recognition, and associative or rote learning and memory. (2) The *pre-operational* stage (onset ages 1 to 2 years) is a transitional period between the sensori-motor stage and the next stage and is mainly characterized by symbolic play and cognitive egocentrism, i.e., the child in this stage can view objects and relationships only in terms of his own relation to them. (3) *Concrete operations* (onset 6 to 7 years) is the first stage of what Piaget calls operational thinking, which characterizes his view of intelligence. It involves the capacity for performing mental operations on concrete objects, such as numeration, seriation, and classification or other forms of grouping, and the ability to conceive the invariant structure of classes, relations, and numbers. (4) *Formal operations* (onset 11 to 13 years) is the final level of operational thinking, manifested in logical reasoning (not dependent upon the manipulation of concrete objects), propositional thinking, combinatorial and inferential thinking which involve using hypothetical possibilities, abstractions, and imaginary conditions as well as the mental manipulations of symbols for real or experiential knowledge.

Piaget has devised a large number of ingenious 'test' or clinical-type procedures for assessing the child's mental development as he moves through these stages, each of which has finer gradations or substages marking the course of cognitive development. Most of the techniques have concentrated on the assessment of *concrete operations*, for this is the first stage of operational logical thinking which, in Piaget's view, is the beginning of mature intelligence and most characterizes human intelligence. The child's capacity to grasp and utilize the concepts of conservation of number, weight, and volume, in that order, marks the development of operational thinking. The 7- or 8-year-old child who is well along in concrete operations, for example, tacitly accepts the notion that volume is conserved, that is, the quantity or volume of a ball of clay or a jar of liquid is conceived as invariant regardless of its changing shape (a round ball of clay or the same ball of clay flattened out like a pancake) or the variety of differently shaped flasks into which the liquid can be poured (low, flat bowl or tall, thin cylinder). The pre-operational child does not assume this invariance; to him, when a round ball of clay is flattened out and made to look 'bigger', he actually believes the quantity of clay has been increased; and similarly when he sees liquid poured from a shallow, broad bowl into a tall, slender flask. There are many ways that the concept of conservation shows up: in number, length, area, time, weight, volume, and so on. Piaget has invented means for assessing children's conservation concepts in all these forms, along with many other tests and procedures for studying the sequence of mental development throughout each of its main stages.

Now, what have child psychologists learned from the application of Piaget's tests that is relevant to Voyat's commentary?

First, Voyat is probably correct in his opinion that the Piagetian tests are less culture-bound than conventional IQ tests. For one thing, some groups reared under environmental conditions which are extremely different from those of Western culture have been found to show not only the same sequence of development through Piaget's stages, but are even somewhat more accelerated in this development than white middle-class children. Again, Arctic Eskimos were found to excel over white urban Canadian children in the Piagetian tests, and Canadian Indians do almost as well as the Eskimos (Vernon, 1965b; MacArthur, 1968, p. 48). Obviously it is not necessary to have lived in a Western or middle-class culture in order to perform up to Western middle-class levels on Piagetian tests.

In rank-ordering children of the same chronological age in terms of their rate of mental development, the Piagetian tests are not very different from other culture-reduced tests. Vernon (1965b) factor analyzed a large number of Piagetian tests along with conventional psychometric measures of intelligence and found that the Piagetian tests were heavily loaded on g, the general factor common to all intelligence tests. In fact, the Piagetian tests measured little else than g; the non-g variance seems to be task-specific, i.e., it has nothing in common with other Piagetian tests or with conventional IQ tests. Tuddenham (1970) gave a battery of Piagetian tests, along with Raven's Matrices and the Peabody Picture Vocabulary Test (PPVT), to a large number of elementary school children, and concluded: '. . . the Raven has the higher correlations, ranging from 0·24 to 0·50, as compared with Peabody values of 0·13 to 0·37 for a similar though not identical set of Piagetian items' (p. 68). These are relatively high values for single item correlations within a restricted age range. Tuddenham notes that 'Correlations with Piaget item composites of six and eight items respectively are 0·60 for the Raven *v.* 0·21 for the Peabody'. These are the kinds of correlations one should expect if Piaget's tests are culture-reduced, since among psychometric tests the Peabody and the Raven are probably further apart than any other tests on the continuum going from 'culture-loaded' to 'culture-free'.

Do the Piagetian tests have high heritability? It would be most surprising if they did not, in view of what has just been said, although there have not yet been any heritability studies of these tests. One impressive study, however, strongly supports the idea that Piagetian tests are highly sensitive indicators of genetic factors in mental development. DeLemos (1969) administered a battery of Piagetian tests to Australian Aborigines, ages 8 to 15 years. The Aboriginal children were remarkably retarded as compared with European and American norms. The majority of adolescents were still not up to the level attained by the average European 7-year-old. Even the majority of Aboriginal adults do not reach the level of concrete operations represented by the conservation of quantity and volume, although there are a few exceptions. In the course of this study, DeLemos compared the Piagetian test performances of full-blooded Aborigines with those who were part Aboriginal and part Caucasian. The children's ancestry was known from records kept by the mission in charge of the territory inhabited by these Aborigines. It is unclear whether any intellectually selective factor was involved in the Aborigine-Caucasian matings. The Caucasian ancestors were 'casual', probably being immigrant laborers and sailors, and never lived among the tribe.

> Among the children classified as part-Aborigines the degree of European ancestry was small, the majority being classified as ⅞th Aboriginal [the equivalent of having one Caucasian great-grandparent]. The European ancestry was therefore several generations removed from the present group. There were no apparent differences in the present environment of the part-Aboriginal and full-Aboriginal children. . . . Part-Aborigines and full-Aborigines formed a single integrated community, and the children were brought up under the same mission conditions and attended the same school. (DeLemos, 1969, p. 257)

L*

What DeLemos found was that the part-Aboriginal children were markedly advanced in the Piagetian measures as compared with the full-Aborigines of the same ages. The differences were not small and did not depend upon large samples for their high level of statistical significance. They are remarkably large differences, beyond anything that has ever been produced by direct training on Piagetian tasks and concepts. The results for the six types of Piagetian conservation tests used by DeLemos are shown in Table 17.1. The results appear almost as if the admixture of

Table 17.1 Comparison of the number of part-Aboriginal and full-Aboriginal children showing conservation*

Test	Full Abor. $N = 38$	Part Abor. $N = 34$	χ^2	p
Quantity	4	18	15·21	$<0·001$
Weight	16	25	7·23	$<0·01$
Volume	2	8	3·59	$0·05<p<0·10$
Length	12	20	5·37	$<0·05$
Area	3	10	4·23	$<0·05$
Number	3	9	3·22	$0·05<p<0·10$
Total†	40	90	36·14	$<0·001$

* From DeLemos (1969).
† The chi square test for the Total (given by DeLemos) is statistically inappropriate here, since pooling more than one observation from the same subject violates the requirement of independence of observations upon which the chi square test depends.

Caucasian genes, even so few as one-eighth, introduces mental structures otherwise lacking, that permit the individual to reach higher levels of mental development than normally occurs in the majority of full-Aboriginals. Commenting on this striking finding, DeLemos writes:

> The significance of our results lies in the fact that in this case there were no apparent differences in the environments of the two groups. Both formed an integral part of the same community, being closely related by family and kinship ties, and living under the same mission conditions. The differences cannot therefore be attributed to environmental factors. . . . It would

therefore seem reasonable to attribute the significant differences between the part- and the full-Aborigines in this study to genetic differences between Aborigines and Europeans, resulting in the part-Aboriginal children having a higher probability of inheriting a higher intellectual potential. (p. 268)

Finally, what do the Piagetian tests reveal about the cognitive development of American Negro children? Read Tuddenham (1970) carried out the major study, giving a battery of ten Piagetian tests to some 500 white, Negro, and Oriental children in grades 1 to 3 in three California communities. Negroes did less well than whites on every item. The average percentage of children possessing the concept tested by the particular items was 32·6 for whites *v.* 15·9 for Negroes. Oriental children, on the other hand, were more advanced than white children on seven of the ten items. The Piagetian scale also correlates substantially with SES as indexed by father's occupation, even though, as Tuddenham notes, 'these items tend to involve reasoning about matters universally available to observation, e.g., the horizontality of water levels. It is hard to see how social advantage could be a very large factor in success on some of these items. The genetic selection implicit in occupational level may well have more to do with it' (p. 65).[6]

Gaudia (1972) administered a series of Piagetian conservation tasks to 126 low SES American Indian, Negro, and white children in grades 1 to 3. Overall, these groups, all being of very low SES, averaged about one year behind the age norms on these tests based on samples of the general population. But the Negro children in this study were significantly ($p < 0.001$) delayed in the acquisition of conservation (of area, number, quantity, weight, and mass) as compared with the low SES Indians and whites, who did not differ significantly. The racial disparity was greatest in the older age groups. Expressed as a percentage of the highest possible conservation score, the means of the three age-matched ethnic groups are: white = 51, Indian = 51, Negro = 30.

How much does specific training in attention and classification raise children's performance in these Piagetian tests? To find out, Sigel and Olmsted (1970) gave one month of training on certain skills and concepts intended to promote cognitive development to Negro children enrolled in a Head Start program. A year after the training, these children were compared with a matched control

group on five Piaget tests of logical operations (multiple classification, multiple seriation, and reversibility) and conservation
(number and quantity). The training is reported to have had no
significant effect on performance in any of these tests. The authors
state:

> These results cannot be attributed to a lack of understanding
> of concepts like more, same, or less, since tests for this were
> administered. *All* children passed this test. . . . It is impor-
> tant to point out that the difficulties these first-grade children
> have (both at the beginning and at the end of first grade) in
> not being able to conserve number and/or mass, reveals the
> seriousness of their cognitive deficit, especially if the criterion
> used is our data from middle-class whites. It is worth pointing
> out that among 5-year-old white middle-class children, conser-
> vation of number and mass are soluble. Of the 75 (white)
> children tested . . . approximately 50 percent could conserve
> in these areas without training and after a nine-session training
> program, 68 percent of the previous non-conservers could then
> conserve. (Sigel & Olmsted, 1970, p. 328)

By contrast, of the Negro Head Start children who received the
one month of training, '. . . 81·3 percent could not conserve
numbers and 93·2 percent could not conserve quantity either
before or after training' (p. 328).[7]

NOTES

1. The basic standard score, called a z score, for an individual is simply

$$z = (X - \bar{X})/SD$$

where X is the individual's raw score on the test, $\bar{X}$ is the mean raw
score of the standardization sample (or some precisely defined age
group within the sample), and SD is the standard deviation of the
sample raw scores. This z score can then be transformed to any
convenient scale, with a mean of M and a standard deviation of σ.
   Transformed $z' = \sigma z + M$. A so-called T scale has $M = 100$,
$\sigma = 10$. On the conventional IQ scale, $M = 100$, $\sigma = 15$.
2. For an excellent, though quite technical, discussion of the methodological aspects of this issue, the reader is referred to Einhorn and
Bass (1971).

3. The exact value of h^2 is not a crucial feature in this formulation; I have used 0·80 here because it is the average value of h^2 in studies of the heritability of intelligence in Caucasian populations. Other values would serve as well, although if they differed appreciably for groups A and B, the regression lines would be non-parallel and therefore, of course, would cross, creating more complex hypothetical outcomes. It should be noted that h^2 is the slope of the regression line of phenotypes on genotypes and of genotypes on phenotypes; while h (i.e., the square root of h^2) is the correlation between genotypes and phenotypes.

4. Analyses recently completed in our laboratory show that the rank order of the percent passing (p) each item of the PPVT (as well as of Raven's Progressive Matrices) is virtually the same for very large and representative California school samples of Negroes and whites. The correlations between p values for these tests are above 0·95, and it is interesting that in this respect the two racial groups are even more alike than are boys and girls within each race. In other words, the cultural biases in the test are more apparent with respect to *sex* differences than with respect to *race* differences. (The sexes do not differ appreciably in mean score, however, while the racial groups differ about one standard deviation, or 15 IQ points, on the average.) Moreover, the increments or decrements in the p values of adjacent test items (i.e., p_1-p_2, p_2-p_3, etc.) correlate above 0·90 between the racial groups. In this measure, too, the races differ less than the sexes within each group.

Also it was found that the matrix of item intercorrelations and the factor structure of these tests is not significantly different for white and Negro samples when these are roughly matched for mental age or total score. These properties of the data, for example, do not in the least distinguish between fourth grade white children and sixth grade Negro children. Yet they distinguish between fifth grade and sixth grade Negro children and between fifth grade and sixth grade white children. A culture-bias hypothesis would predict greater Negro-white differences than adjacent grade differences in item intercorrelations. The findings, on the other hand, are more consistent with a development lag hypothesis.

In multiple-choice tests (as the PPVT and Raven are), there is no systematic or significant racial difference in the choice of distractors on those items that are answered 'wrong'. A special scoring key was made up so as to score as correct whatever response was given by the largest number of children in the Negro sample. When the tests were scored by this key, the Negro sample still averaged lower than the white sample.

Scales based on subgroups of items which discriminate either *least* between Negroes and whites or discriminate *most* are correlated with each other over 0·90 (approximately the reliability of the test), showing that the two types of items are measuring the same ability.

The intelligence tests also show essentially the same correlations with scholastic achievement in Negro and white samples. When scholastic achievement is 'predicted' by a multiple regression equation comprised of several intelligence tests, adding race (white *v.* Negro) to the multiple prediction equation does not increase the multiple correlation with scholastic achievement. The predictive validity of the tests is virtually the same for Negroes and whites. Negroes and whites with the same IQ perform about equally well in school.

In short, none of our analyses reveals any racial differences in these tests other than the number of items got right. There seems to be no good reason to believe that these tests behave any differently for Negroes than for whites, except in the mean score.

5. I am indebted to Dr Mabel C. Purl, Director of Research and Evaluation, Riverside Unified Schools, for these data.

6. I did a principal components analysis of the correlation matrix in Tuddenham's Table 3.1 (p. 66), which in addition to the ten Piagetian tests contains the variables age, sex, and father's occupation. On the first principal component (the general factor common to all the tests), father's occupation has a loading of 0·46. The average loading of the ten Piagetian items is 0·51, with a range from 0·22 (lateral reversal) to 0·76 (conservation of volume).

7. If we assume the conservation tests reflect an underlying normal distribution of cognitive development, these percentages correspond to a white-Negro difference of between 1 and 1·5σ, which is the range of difference generally found between low SES Negro and middle SES white children on conventional IQ tests.

18 Sensori-motor differences

There has never been any real disagreement about genetically determined physical differences – biochemical, physiological, and anatomical – between racial groups. It is in the realm of intellectual functions that we see so much *a priori* resistance to rejection of the null hypothesis concerning genetic racial differences. But actually there is a continuum between the physical and the intellectual; there are no discernible discontinuities; and racial differences are found at all points along the continuum going from strictly physical characteristics to behavioral characteristics, including those processes we identify as mental ability. So the point at which one draws the line of resistance to entertaining a genetic hypothesis of racial differences is usually quite arbitrary.

Sensory capacities are intimately related to physical structures and processes and are undoubtedly conditioned by genetic factors. And we find marked racial differences in certain sensory capacities. (An excellent detailed review of much of this evidence is found in Spuhler & Lindzey, 1967). For example, the ability to taste the synthetic chemical substance phenylthiocarbamide (PTC) is known to be genetically determined, probably by a single gene. There are striking race and subpopulation differences in the frequencies of tasters and non-tasters of PTC, going from 0 to 57 percent in the various populations which have been studied (see Spuhler & Lindzey, 1967, pp. 381-4). There are marked racial differences in the incidence of various types of sex-linked color blindness which are completely genetic; and there are differences in ability for color discrimination. Negroes have better visual acuity than whites – only 65 percent of whites in the armed forces pre-induction examination have 20/20 vision, as compared with

82 percent of Negroes (Dreger & Miller, 1968, p. 7); they also show better adaptation to the dark than whites. Negroes show a greater galvanic skin response than whites, and they perceive radiant heat at a lower threshold (Dreger & Miller, 1960, p. 364).

Moving along the behavioral continuum from sheer sensory to more perceptual processes, population differences have been found in degree of susceptibility to various optical illusions (see Dreger & Miller, 1960, 1968; Spuhler & Lindzey, 1967). It is virtually impossible to explain some of these illusions in terms of cultural or experiential differences. Groups whose visual experiences are highly similar may differ greatly in susceptibility to a particular perceptual illusion and groups whose environments differ markedly may show no differences in the illusion. Also, the relationship between race differences and perceptual illusions can be quite complex, as in the case of the black-white radiation size illusion. There is a racial (Negro-white) difference when the illusion stimuli are achromatic but not when they are colored (Pettigrew & Nuttall, 1963).

SPEED OF VISUAL INFORMATION PROCESSING

As we move along the continuum to speed of visual information processing, we come somewhat closer to mental abilities. Intelligence, in fact, is sometimes defined as information processing capacity. So it should be interesting to look at the simplest form of visual information processing, which comes very close to being almost a physiological measure of a basic mental capacity.

Information processing capacity shows up in a most fundamental form in a phenomenon technically known as *meta-contrast* or 'masking'. If a visual stimulus is presented to the observer's view for a standard duration, followed by a 'blank' interval, and then by a second stimulus (equal to or greater in area than the first) of standard duration, the observer either will or will not be able to name the first stimulus (e.g., a letter of the alphabet) depending upon the duration of the 'blank' period between the first and second stimuli (called the 'test signal' and the 'masking stimulus', respectively).[1] Studies have revealed highly reliable individual differences in the shortness of duration of the 'blank' period or interstimulus interval that observers can tolerate without 'losing' the test signal. If the blank interval is too short, the test signal is literally wiped out and the observer's guess as to what it was is no better than chance. The duration of the shortest interval at which the observer can identify the test signal has been called 'information processing rate'.

A meticulous study by Bosco (1970) has shown marked sub-population differences in information processing rate. He compared children in first, third, and sixth grades in urban schools attended by low SES and middle SES children. Race and SES are mixed up in this study (low SES: 28 whites, 62 Negro; middle SES: 88 whites, 2 Negro), so we shall refer to the contrasted groups only as low SES and middle SES. The four test signals were very carefully selected so as to eliminate experiential differences. They consisted of *circle*, *square*, *triangle*, and *five-pointed star*. Bosco comments: 'The stimuli which were used in this study are so pervasive as to rule out any possibility of them not being present within the low SES environment. None of the children in the study had difficulty identifying the four stimuli during the preliminary part of the testing. Even the disadvantaged first graders responded correctly and promptly' (p. 61). Bosco also reported that observations during the testing did not lead him to suspect motivational differences between the two groups. With four stimuli each having equal probability of occurrence, there were only two 'bits'[2] of information transmitted in this procedure, thus making it a very rudimentary but clear-cut measure of information processing capacity.

Bosco found large significant ($p < 0.01$) differences in information processing rate between the low and middle SES groups. The mean SES difference was greater than the mean grade difference. *First*-grade middle SES children had a slightly faster processing rate than low SES children in the *sixth* grade. As one would expect for a processing task involving only two bits of information, the group differences (as well as individual differences) decrease with age. At first grade, low SES children required more than twice as much visual processing time as needed by middle SES children. At sixth grade, the low SES children used about 30 percent more time. Bosco found low correlations (around 0·20) with various scholastic achievement measures. (Unfortunately, these correlations were obtained only in the sixth grade, in which there was relatively little variance in visual processing rate.) Bosco comments, 'The more a variable assesses a basic cognitive variable, the less likely we ought to expect relationship to school success. . . . As it is, there is good reason to think that school achievement is a result of a host of variables in addition to cognitive variables' (p. 51). It seems likely, however, that Bosco underestimates the relevance of his measure of scholastic performance. This could be tested by determining correlations at the first grade, and by increasing the information load of the task at sixth grade in order to yield sufficient variance to permit significant correlations to show up.

REACTION TIME

Reaction time (RT) to a stimulus situation increases as the amount of information transmitted by the stimulus increases. RT increases as a linear function of 'bits' of information, and thus the rate of increase in RT can be taken as a measure of information processing capacity. (It has been reported also that the *slope* of this function is negatively correlated with IQ [Roth, 1964, cited in Eysenck, 1967].) A description of one experimental procedure for demonstrating this measure will help to make it clear. The subject sits in front of a panel on which there is a single light bulb; directly beneath the bulb is a pushbutton. When the light flashes 'on', the subject pushes the button to turn the light 'off'. In this condition, the subject's response time is a measure of simple RT. There is zero information conveyed when there is only one light/button combination. But the subject is required to respond to an increasing number of light/button combinations, simply by having one light go on among an increasing number of potential alternatives. This is called 'choice RT'. The amount of information conveyed increases logarithmically as the number of lights increases.

Fox and Taylor (1967) compared two groups of army recruits on simple RT and choice RT. One group (low AFQT) was selected from recruits having scores between 10 and 21 on the Armed Forces Qualification Test (a composite measure of general intelligence and basic scholastic attainments); the other group (high AFQT) were recruits with scores from 90 to 99. The groups differed significantly in choice RT, but not in simple RT. (A more detailed description of the apparatus, procedure and results of this experiment is presented in Jensen, 1970b, pp. 149-51.) Also, Oswald (1971) found a correlation ($r = -0.41$) between increase in RT with increasing complexity of the stimuli involved in the task (card sorting) and non-verbal intelligence, i.e., information was processed more rapidly by subjects with higher intelligence.

Noble (1969) gave a 4-choice reaction time test to groups of rural Georgia white and Negro children ($N = 106$ in each group) matched for age and sex. Each child was given 160 standard trials. The results, plotted in terms of mean response speed (the reciprocal of RT) for blocks of 20 trials, are shown in Figure 18.1.

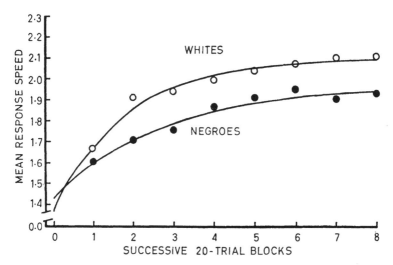

Figure 18.1 Mean response speed in successive 20-trial blocks on choice reaction time. Each curve based on 106 children. (From Noble, 1969.)

The overall white-Negro difference is significant ($p < 0.01$). Note that response speed increases with practice, but soon levels off in both groups. The first trials show no Negro-white difference, and the mean difference in the first block of 20 trials is small as compared with later blocks. If motivational and attitudinal factors were acting to depress the performance of the Negro children, it is hard to see why they should have differed so little at the beginning of practice. Increased practice tends to increase and stabilize the magnitude of the difference between the groups.

MOTOR SKILLS LEARNING

Noble (1968, pp. 230-1; 1969) has reported an exemplary study of motor skill learning in Negro and white rural Georgia school children, ages 9 to 12. From a pool of 500 subjects, all right-handed, 152 were selected so as to form four groups, each with 38 subjects (two Negro and two white groups) matched for age and sex.

The task was pursuit rotor learning. The pursuit rotor is the most widely used instrument in laboratory studies of human motor learning. Hundreds of experiments have been performed with the pursuit rotor and much more is known about experimental parameters of performance on this motor skill than on any other. It is a 'tracking' skill. The apparatus consists of a disc about the size of a phonograph turntable which rotates at a given speed (usually 60 r.p.m.). The disc is made of a smooth non-conductor such as bakelite; flush with the disc's surface and about halfway between the center and the edge is a 'target' – a small silver metal disc, usually about $\frac{3}{4}$ inch in diameter. As the turntable rotates, the subject's task is to learn to keep a metal stylus on the target; the stylus is hinged to its handle in such a way that no pressure can be exerted by the subject as a means of keeping the stylus 'on target'. When 'on target' the stylus completes an electrical circuit, activating a timing device which records the percentage of each consecutive 10-second period that the stylus is on target. Learning, that is, improvement of the skill with practice, is reflected in the increasing average percentage of time on target when the course of practice is divided into a number of periods of equal duration.

Before Noble performed his experiment, a number of relevant factors were already known about pursuit rotor learning. For one thing, this form of learning has not been found to be sensitive to examiner effects; that is, the sex, age, race, and attitude of the experimenter do not significantly affect the subject's performance. Even so, Noble took precautions in his study. He used both male and female Negro and white experimenters, counterbalanced for all groups in the experiment. (He found no statistically significant effects on tracking performance attributable to sex or race of the examiner.) Also, he minimized any possible experimenter influence by leaving the child alone in the testing room after the instructions were given. (Instructions were given largely by means of demonstration by the experimenter.) As a further check, he recorded the subject's pulse rate just before and after the learning period, on the assumption that if there were any differences between the groups it would show up in the pulse rate, which is a sensitive indicator of anxiety. There was no race difference and no pre-post test difference in pulse rate. The children were not anxious but actually enjoyed the task and the fun of taking turns and getting out of their regular class activities to participate in the experiment. Also, there was no prior evidence that pursuit rotor learning has any appreciable correlation with intelligence. In a group of 186 boys, for example, McNemar (1933) found a correlation of only 0·17 between tracking ability and IQ. Obviously, not all kinds of learning ability are as highly related to IQ as is scholastic learning. Finally, it was known that pursuit rotor learning has very high heritability, almost as high as the heritability of height. NcNemar (1933) obtained correlations of 0·95 and 0·51, respectively, for MZ and DZ twins. Using the simplest formula for estimating heritability ($h^2 = 2(r_{MZ} - r_{DZ})$, which assumes no assortative mating for pursuit rotor ability, the value of h^2 obtained from McNemar's data is 0·88. Furthermore, Vandenberg (1962) reports that heritability is much higher for pursuit rotor learning with the right hand (or preferred hand) than with the left. In other words, the tracking task can serve either as a test having very high heritability or as a test having low heritability, depending on whether the subject is required to use his preferred or his non-preferred hand.

With this background in mind, Noble had half of each racial group (all were right-handed) perform with their *right* hand and half of them with their *left* hand. The results are shown in Figure 18.2. The white subject's average left-hand performance was slightly better than the Negro's performance with the right hand. Also, the race difference is much greater for the right-hand performance, with its higher heritability. So striking and interesting were these results that Noble replicated and extended the study on a new group of 268 subjects, and obtained essentially the same results, significant beyond the 0·001 level: 'Whites not only performed at a generally higher level of proficiency than Negroes but also were gaining at a faster rate. Even after fifty practice trials conducted under rigorous controlled conditions, the average Negro *right*-hand ability was still below the average white *left*-hand ability' (Noble, 1969, pp. 22-3).

Noble then went a step further. He divided the Negro group into two groups which we shall call blacks and mulattoes. He used several genetically independent (but phenotypically correlated) objectively measured physical criteria for this classification, and showed that the groups differed significantly on each one: skin pigmentation, nasal width, lip thickness, hair texture, eye color, jaw formation, interpupillary distance, and ability to taste phenylthiocarbamide. The subjects thus classified into three groups showed significantly different mean pursuit rotor scores in the order: whites < mulattoes < blacks. The mean percentage of time

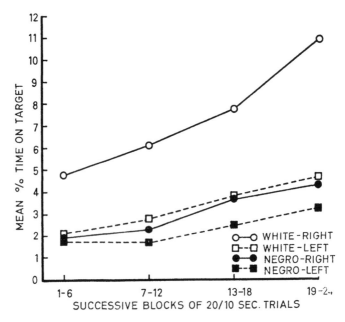

Figure 18.2 Mean percentage of time on target in successive blocks of 20-second *work* and 10-second *rest* trials on the pursuit rotor, for white and Negro children, practising with either the Right or the Left hand. There are 38 subjects in each condition. (From Noble, 1969.)

on target for the three groups were 4·6 percent, 2·6 percent and 2·1 percent, respectively (Noble, 1968, p. 231. It is not clear from Noble's account whether these percentages are for the first trial block of six trials or for all trials.) Noble believed that strictly environmental interpretations of these results in terms of socio-economic and cultural differences would find little evidential support. 'On the contrary', he writes, 'there were numerous observations to suggest that a large part of the interracial behavioral variance is genetically determined' (1969, p. 27). But Noble concludes:

Our data on the learning of psychomotor skills pertain to operationally defined concepts and to statistical aggregates of subjects; nomothetic laws imply nothing about (1) the human worth of a particular individual or (2) their civil liberties. Whether all the living races of mankind are equal in their innate (genotypic) biological potentialities for cultural and scientific achievements in modern civilization is a matter that cannot be determined by single experiments of deliberately limited scope. At the same time, I hold that systematic, theory-oriented, fundamental research on behavior offers our best hope of solving the vexing interracial problems that confront us today. (p. 29)

NOTES

1. Highly precise tachistoscopic equipment is required for this work. For technical details of the phenomenon and its measurement the reader is referred to Holland (1963).
2. For information theory, the 'bit' (an abbreviation for *binary digit*) is the basic unit for quantifying information. One 'bit' is the amount of information necessary to resolve two equally probable alternatives; it is equivalent to the minimum number of binary questions (answerable with Yes or No) needed to reduce the uncertainty to zero. For example, a 'problem' involving no more than making one choice from among one alternative contains zero information; if there are 2 alternatives, there is 1 bit of information, since one must receive the answer to only one binary question in order to know which choice is 'correct'; if there are 4 alternatives, there are 2 bits of information; 8 alternatives = 3 bits. The number of bits (n) can be seen in the following relationship $\sqrt[n]{\text{alternatives}} = 2$. The number of bits can also be described as the logarithm (to the base 2) of the number of alternatives.

19 *Physical environment and mental development*

NUTRITION

In recent years poor nutrition has been frequently mentioned in the literature as if it were established as a major environmental cause of social class and racial differences in intelligence and scholastic performance. Hence we must briefly review what is actually known at present about the effects of nutrition on mental development and weigh its relevance to the issues under discussion in this book.

First of all, the evidence from experimental studies of severe nutritional deprivation in animals leaves no doubt whatsoever that brain functions and their behavioral correlates are influenced by nutritional factors, particularly protein deficiency (Scrimshaw & Gordon, 1968; Eichenwald & Fry, 1969; Dobbing, 1970; Winick, 1970). The authors of animal studies of nutritional deprivation showing effects on brain and behavior usually point out that the deprivation is *severe*, that it has generalized effects on the growth and functioning of other systems, and that larger and more irreversible effects are produced by nutritional deprivation during the periods of most rapid growth of the central nervous system.

The evidence with respect to the psychological effects of malnutrition in humans is much more difficult to evaluate, since it cannot be based on experimental studies but must rely on the occurrence of nutritional deprivation in 'natural' settings. This invariably means that the effects of malnutrition are confounded with a host of other unfavorable factors so frequently associated with poverty and with poor mental development, such as prematurity, low birth weight, poor health care, high incidence of infectious diseases, child neglect, and so on. Also, as Platt (1968, p. 241) points out:

> The effects of maternal undernutrition and those of genetic factors are difficult to separate in disadvantaged populations. Since consequences may be similar and are exhibited even in fetal death, there is often no way to separate these factors in the individual case. Human population and biostatistical studies must be conducted in order for scientists to understand the subtle interactions of genetic endowment and nutrition within, and between, the larger genetic pools of any given geographical or socioeconomic group.

Two or three studies of human malnutrition, however, have involved more or less adequate controls and have yielded sufficiently clear-cut results to warrant the conclusions of one of the leading researchers in this field: 'There can be absolutely no question about the association of significant degrees of malnutrition during the early years of life and concurrent as well as later manifestations of intellectual impairment' (Birch, 1968, p. 57).

I have found a total of only thirteen published studies of the effects of nutrition on mental development. Eleven of these are well summarized by Stein and Kassab (1970), who do not include a study conducted in Peru (Pollitt & Granoff, 1967) or the one published United States study (Harrell, Woodyard & Gates, 1955). It is significant that all but one of the studies showing any mental effects of nutritional deficiency were conducted outside the United States in those parts of Africa, Asia, and Central and South America which suffer the most extreme poverty and protein-calorie deficiency.[1] It is interesting that even in these localities the degree of malnutrition sufficient to depress mental development is not found generally in any appreciable segment of any population; these malnourished cases must be sought out in specific families, and even then usually not all the children in the same family will show signs of malnutrition. The impression that many persons seem to have gained from the popular press, that there are hordes of malnourished children who suffer mental retardation therefrom, is quite at odds with the actual picture given by the total body of scientific literature on this subject. Children in whom mental effects of poor nutrition can be demonstrated have seemed almost as hard for researchers to find as identical twins reared apart. The total number reported in the literature is fewer than a thousand, and in only a fraction of these have psychological effects been adequately demonstrated. The problem, of course, is that malnutrition is most often found in families in which frequently other factors, genetic and environmental, that cause mental retardation are also operative. The mean IQ of children in the general population, or even in that segment of the population in which the undernourished children were found, cannot serve as a proper comparison group because of this close linkage of malnutrition to other adverse familial factors.

Those studies, such as Cravioto's (1968), which have used adequately nourished siblings as controls against which to measure the effects of malnutrition in the affected siblings are the most adequate, and their results leave little doubt that severe protein deficiency in the final months of fetal life and in infancy can depress important cognitive functions that emerge later in childhood. The statistical significance of this finding is not in question, but the magnitude of the effect is difficult to evaluate in terms of any familiar scales of mental measurement. The most adequate studies, carried on in Mexico and Guatemala by Cravioto and his colleagues, make use of special tests measuring 'intersensory integration' (i.e., cross-modal transfer), and from the information given it is impossible to determine how much the significant differences between the nutritionally deprived and their controls would amount to on an IQ scale. I believe, however, that the measures of intersensory integration used by Cravioto *et al.* get at the *g* factor of intelligence at a very basic level (Cravioto & Delicardie, 1970). Thus, although we may conclude that there are significant effects of early malnutrition on cognitive development, little if anything can be said at present about the magnitude of these effects relative to the magnitudes of the social class and racial differences existing in the United States. One study using conventional individual intelligence tests found an average of 20 points IQ deficit in a group of 21 severely malnourished African children as compared with an adequately nourished control group (which was more advantaged in many other respects as well). The degree of chronic malnutrition in these cases was so severe as to actually stunt physical growth and to cause abnormal brain waves; all the children had come to the attention of public health agencies, so their condition could not be regarded as typical even for the slums of South Africa (Stoch & Smythe, 1963).

A number of findings and conclusions are repeated in many of the studies. The degree of malnutrition associated with cognitive deficit is usually severe; in one study in Chile, for example, children during the first year of life were not breast fed but subsisted entirely on a diet of flour and water (Stein & Kassab, 1970, p. 95). The most severe retardation is associated with malnutrition in the last three months of gestation and in the first several months after birth, which is the most active period of brain growth. Retardation is less demonstrable among children who are malnourished after the second year of life, and there is evidence that older children and adults suffer no permanent psychological effects from even severe malnutrition, as existed in concentration camps near the end of World War II. Malnutrition is less often found where children are breast fed in the first year of life; artificial low-protein foods and 'empty calories' in high carbohydrate diets are more often associated with poor nutrition. Early malnutrition hinders general growth and therefore causes an increased correlation between various physical indices and measures of intelligence.[2] Winick (1970) reported that at $2\frac{1}{2}$ to 5 years of age 70 percent of malnourished children had head circumferences below the tenth percentile – a very skewed distribution indeed – as compared with control children, whose head circumferences showed a normal distribution. Among malnourished children there is a significant correlation between head circumference and IQ, but no significant relationship was found in control children whose head size was within normal limits (Stein & Kassab, 1970, p. 101). Similar effects are found for height; malnutrition, particularly protein deficiency, retards the rate of ossification of cartilage in the first months of life (Platt, 1968, p. 243). Malnutrition also retards early motor development. In every study in which infant development tests, such as the Gesell scale, have been used, they show that the malnourished children score below par. Early malnutrition makes for greater inter-sibling differences; siblings within the same family are not equally affected, but in families in which malnutrition is found, there are significantly larger differences between the siblings as compared with adequately nourished families (Cravioto & Delicardie, 1970).

There is also evidence that protein deficiency impairs memory as well as other cognitive functions (Cravioto & Delicardie, 1970).

When a high percentage of low IQs are found among groups of children who themselves have shown no evidence of poor nutrition, it is hypothesized by some investigators that the lower IQs are a result, at least in part, of the children's mother, or even grandmother, having suffered from poor nutrition. There is some evidence for the intergenerational effects of malnutrition (and other environmental factors) on behavior in rats and dogs, but not in humans.[3] Stein and Kassab (1970, p. 109) summarize the present state of knowledge on this point: 'There are no studies in human societies which can be held to support a cumulative generational effect of dietary restriction. Certainly any such effect was not sufficiently widespread, after countless generations of rural poverty, to prevent the emergence during the past century of the technological societies of Europe and North America.'

Since all the studies mentioned so far are based outside the United States, we should look in more detail at the one published study conducted in the United States relating IQ to nutrition, and at another more recent study, as yet unpublished. The first study, by Harrell, Woodyard, and Gates (1955) was carried out in the Cumberland Mountains of Kentucky and in Norfolk, Virginia. The Kentucky subjects were 'poor whites' living in what the authors describe as 'deplorably low' economic conditions. The Norfolk subjects all were mothers on welfare, chosen for their low income status; 80 percent were Negro. There were 1,200 mothers in each group. These women were contacted early in pregnancy through public maternity clinics and given a variety of dietary supplements (one group got vitamins; another group got 'polynutrients', and the control group got a placebo; i.e., a non-nutritive substance). These dietary supplements were taken throughout pregnancy. The children born to these mothers were given two forms of the Stanford-Binet Intelligence Test, at ages 3 and 4. There were 1,414 children tested in all. The Kentucky children showed no significant effects. (For both tests $F < 1$). The Norfolk children did show significant effects, however. At age 3 the vitamin and polynutrient groups averaged 2·5 to 5 IQ points higher than the placebo group. At 4 years of age the average gain over the placebo group was 5·2 IQ points in the vitamin group and 8·1 points in the polynutrient group. However, for both of these groups and the placebo group there was a significant ($P<0.001$) decline of 3·04 IQ points between ages 3 and 4. Thus, while the dietary supplements did raise IQ several points over the placebo group, they did not prevent the lowering of IQ between ages 3 and 4. This rapid decline within a one-year period, in addition to the fact that IQ at age 4 accounts for something less than 50 percent of the IQ variance in late adolescence, makes this study inconclusive as to whether any lasting effects on IQ were derived from the dietary supplements during pregnancy. The IQs of the children at ages 3 and 4 were within the typical range for this population, and the decline in IQ from 3 to 4 is also typical; studies of similar groups have found average declines of about 10 IQ points between 3 and 6 years of age (Shuey, 1966, pp. 6-31).

The second study takes a still different approach, which consisted not of looking for children showing malnutrition and determining their psychological characteristics, but rather of finding children in the poorest families in the poorest slums of a large Southern city, Nashville, Tennessee (Carter, Gilmer, Vanderzwaag & Massey, 1971). The investigators visited community agencies to find out the location of poverty areas and to identify poverty families. These areas were then explored by car, followed by house-to-house canvassing by a social worker to find the most impoverished families with children of certain ages. The groups finally selected came from two housing projects on the East side of Nashville.[4] The criteria for selection included: mother under 35 years of age, the target child should not be farther along in the family than the third child, and younger siblings should be present. Since the medical, nutritional, and psychological assessments were intended to be extremely thorough and elaborate, only 19 families were selected, 10 Negro and 9 white. The target children (singled out for special intensive study and enrolment in an experimental preschool program) were between the ages of 3 years 8 months and 4 years 8 months. The authors describe in general terms the typical backgrounds of the white and Negro families from which their samples were drawn:

> The typical family of a white child . . . is likely to be one in which the natural father is present in the home at least 50 percent of the time. He is usually an unskilled laborer or perhaps

disabled. The average annual income is below the OEO Poverty Guidelines. Half of the mothers were on Welfare or Aid to Dependent Children Programs. . . . [About 40 percent of the white mothers had completed high school.] The typical black family . . . is likely to be one in which the natural father is not at home. If he is, he is usually employed in maintenance work, in the military service, or is a trainee in some OEO program designed to find jobs for the hard-core unemployed. The average annual family income is about the same as that for the urban white families and is well below the OEO Poverty Guidelines. At least 70 percent of the mothers are receiving Welfare, Aid to Dependent Children, or Social Security payments. The average number of children in the family was about the same as in the . . . white families. [20 percent of the Negro mothers had completed high school.]

The medical and nutritional assessments of the nineteen target children were extremely extensive and thorough. More than fifty physical signs were checked in the children's medical histories and examinations at the time of the study. Detailed study was made of the children's diets and was compared with the National Nutrition Survey's standards for dietary intakes of calories, proteins, vitamins, and minerals recommended for healthy four- to six-year-old children.

No appreciable nutritional difference was found between the Negro and white samples, and both groups were well *above* the standards recommended by the National Nutrition Survey. Concerning the results of the medical examinations, the investigators state: 'In general, these children were considered to have physical findings within normal limits' (p. 31). In some ways the health conditions of these children were surely not typical of average American children; about half the subjects in each group, for example, had pin worms. But in both groups extremely thorough examination revealed none of the physical or emotional symptoms associated with poor nutrition and usually seen in the studies conducted in Africa, Asia, Mexico, and South America. With the small samples of this study, the correlations between physical indices and IQ would have too little reliability to be interpretable; they showed no consistent pattern and the authors comment that:

We were not surprised that we failed to turn up anything of particular meaning in correlations between the intelligence test scores of the children, and the various indices of skeletal age, height, weight, bone density, and so on. The number of cases was small and only one index of intellectual ability was used. Perhaps with a larger number of cases and increasingly refined techniques of assessment, such relationships might emerge. (p. 61)

Stanford-Binet IQs were obtained on all the children at the conclusion of the study, after they had spent a school year in an intensive experimental nursery school program aimed at improving these children's educability, with particular emphasis on intellectual and motivational factors. The children by this time (5 to 6 years range) were much at ease among teachers and examiners, and were accustomed to interacting with adults in various cognitive games and experimental learning situations. Thus they would seem to be better prepared for Stanford-Binet testing than the normative population in this age range. The mean IQs of the Negro and white groups, respectively, were 76·1 and 95·3 (SDs = 13·0 and 16·7). Here, then, is a considerable IQ difference (more than 1 SD) without there being any appreciable or consistent differences in nutritional status or in physical development and general health.

If signs of malnutrition were not found in these obviously rather extreme socioeconomically disadvantaged groups, the question naturally arises as to what percent of the United States population, and particularly of the Negro population, suffers from malnutrition to a degree that would affect mental development.[5] Could poor nutrition account for any appreciable fraction of the average white-Negro IQ difference? In order to gain some outer-bound estimate in answer to this question, I asked Dr Herbert Birch, a leading researcher in this field, for a rough estimate of the percentage of our population that might suffer a degree of malnutrition sufficient to affect IQ. He said he would guess 'Not more than about 1 percent' (personal communication, 19 April 1971). So let us take this figure as the basis for an outer-bound estimate. Assume that all of the 1 percent of malnutrition in the U.S. population occurs within the Negro population; this would mean that approximately 9 percent of the Negro population suffers from malnutrition.

Assume further that all 9 percent of this group afflicted by malnutrition has thereby had its IQ lowered by 20 points (which is the difference between severely malnourished and adequately nourished groups in South Africa – the most extreme IQ difference reported in the nutrition literature). Assuming the present Negro mean IQ in the U.S. to be 85, what then would be the mean if the 20 points of IQ were restored to the hypothetical 9 percent who had suffered from intellectually stunting malnutrition? It would be 86·70, or a gain of less than 2 IQ points as an outer-bound estimate. Thus it seems unlikely that nutritional factors could carry much weight in any explanation of the average Negro-white IQ difference. This is not to say that cases of malnutrition do not exist in the U.S., or that all possible means should not be applied to ameliorating poor nutrition wherever it is found. It simply means that a nutritional hypothesis of average Negro-white IQ differences has little or no basis in fact, even as a minor contributory factor.

Actually, no one yet knows what the *net* effect of undernutrition in an entire large population is under natural conditions in which many concomitant factors are free to operate. One might even hypothesize that the *net* effect of extreme nutritional depression in a *population* (not for an individual) might actually be to raise the IQ due to increased fetal loss and infant mortality along with natural selection favoring those who are genetically better endowed physically and mentally. Such a hypothesis could be tested by analysis of physical and mental measurements on individuals conceived and born during the months of severe protein starvation in various European countries, particularly Holland and Poland, toward the end of World War II. Such studies, sponsored by the U.S. Department of Health, Education, and Welfare, are presently underway.

But there are also less speculative reasons for believing that the role of nutrition should not be overrated as a factor in Negro-white IQ differences. For example, children who are malnourished show a long developmental lag, registered in physical as well as psychological characteristics (Cravioto, 1968). No such lag is found in Negro children and what little evidence there is shows no difference between Negroes and whites in the degree of correlation between physical and mental traits. Malnutrition retards the ossification of cartilage; yet representative samples of Negro infants have been found to be advanced over whites in ossification (Naylor & Myrianthopoulos, 1967). Malnutrition results in below-normal performance on infant tests of sensori-motor development, yet Negro babies generally show advanced performance on these tests as compared with the white norms. Malnutrition impairs memory ability as well as other cognitive functions, yet Negro children show little or no deficit in rote memory. One of the most striking and consistent findings in the research of Cravioto and others is that malnutrition markedly increases the differences between siblings (and conversely reduces sibling correlations) within the same family, both in physical and mental characteristics. I have determined the mean absolute difference between all sibling pairs enrolled in the elementary grades of a California school system on a number of physical and mental measurements, all put on the same scale, with a standard

Table 19.1 Mean absolute difference, $|\bar{d}|$, and correlation, r, between all siblings of school age in white and Negro families on eleven measures, standardized within 6-month age groups, with $\sigma = 15$ for every variable in the combined populations

| Variable | White | | | Negro | | |
	N	$|\bar{d}|$	r	N	$|\bar{d}|$	r
Height	1154	12·69	0·44	731	12·84	0·43
Weight	1155	12·63	0·44	731	12·21	0·48
Memory I	573	14·52	0·27	369	14·25	0·29
Memory R	572	13·73	0·34	364	15·05	0·21
Memory D	568	14·46	0·27	358	14·23	0·29
Figure Copying	570	13·88	0·33	395	13·68	0·35
Verbal IQ	1133	13·29	0·39	582	12·83	0·43
Non-verbal IQ	1132	13·11	0·40	600	13·86	0·33
Total IQ	341	12·75	0·43	200	12·81	0·43
Vocabulary	244	12·75	0·43	417	12·73	0·44
Reading Comprehension	251	12·93	0·42	408	13·89	0·33
All Variables		13·34			13·49	

M

deviation of 15, to make them all comparable to the IQ scale. The results, shown in Table 19.1, indicate that there is no appreciable or systematic Negro-white disparity in the magnitudes of the sibling differences and sibling correlations. (The overall Negro-white difference in the value of $|d|$ is 0·15 or 0·01 SD.) A nutritional deprivation hypothesis should predict significantly larger sibling differences (and lower correlations) for Negroes than for whites. This prediction clearly is not borne out by the data. Yet these racial groups differ more than 1 SD in both verbal and non-verbal IQ.

LEAD POISONING

This has been hypothesized increasingly of late as a cause of lower Negro IQs. Physical and mental symptoms of lead poisoning typically depend upon the ingestion of excessive quantities of lead over a period of time. Cases of lead poisoning in children are found almost exclusively in those afflicted by *pica*, a habit of eating non-food substances, occurring most frequently in young children. Nearly all discovered cases of lead poisoning have resulted from children with pica eating the paint peeling off the walls in deteriorating pre-World War II dwellings, usually in urban slums. Almost no post-World War II dwellings have lead paint, and such paint has long been outlawed in the manufacturing of children's toys. Therefore, although the incidence of lead poisoning is not established, it is regarded as a very rare condition as compared with many other health hazards. It has attracted attention largely because of the rather close association that has been found between lead poisoning, pica, and mental retardation. Pica has a much higher incidence among retarded than among normal children, and lead poisoning is highly associated with pica, so the cause-and-effect relationship between lead poisoning and mental retardation remains problematic.

Although the seriousness of lead poisoning, where it occurs, should not be minimized and all possible measures should be taken to prevent its occurrence, the actual known frequencies of the condition appear to be so low that there is no subpopulation whose mean would be shifted appreciably by lead poisoning occurring at such low frequencies. Interest in this problem in New York City in recent years has led to increased efforts to discover cases of lead poisoning, and the apparent increase in reported cases is due to better diagnosis and record keeping. In a population of over 8 million, the annual number of reported cases in the mid 1950s was about 100 (Jacobziner, 1966), and this figure rose to 727 in 1969 and 801 in the first half of 1970 (Guince, 1970). Two deaths were attributed to lead poisoning in 1969. The fact that there are many post-World War housing areas in which leaded paints have never been used and yet in which the majority of children reared in them have IQs a standard deviation or more below the national average suggests that lead poisoning, though undoubtedly serious when it occurs, is an insignificant factor in relation to average racial or social class differences in IQ and educability.

REPRODUCTIVE CASUALTY

The association between social class, race, and lower IQ, and the much higher incidence of mental retardation among low SES groups, have been attributed in varying degrees to brain impairments incurred prenatally and perinatally. There is a continuum of reproductive casualty, going from fetal and neonatal death to behavorial symptoms referred to as 'minimal brain damage'. The prevalence of reproductive casualty, most students of the problem agree, is much higher among Negroes than among other groups of similar socioeconomic status. Reproductive casualty is thus frequently mentioned as a major cause of Negro deficits in IQ and scholastic performance. Typical is the statement by Bronfenbrenner (1967, p. 913):

> Though the Negro infant is not biologically inferior at the moment of conception, he often becomes so shortly thereafter. The inadequate nutrition and prenatal care received by millions of Negro mothers result in complications of pregnancy which take their toll in extraordinarily high rates of prematurity and congenital defect. Many of these abnormalities entail neurological damage resulting in impaired intellectual function and behavioral disturbances, including hyperactivity, distractibility, and low attention span. Of particular relevance is the significant role played by perinatal and prenatal factors in the genesis of childhood reading disorders.

Statements such as this, it turns out, are extremely difficult, if not impossible, to evaluate on the basis of what is at present known about 'reproductive casualty', its causes, its incidence in various subpopulations, and its relationship to mental development. Any reader of the major reviews in this field must be impressed by the chaos and confusion that abounds in this literature and the dearth of consistent and reliable conclusions which can be claimed to have any reasonable degree of generality for any major sub-population (Hardy, 1965; Knobloch & Pasamanick, 1966; Pasamanick & Knobloch, 1966; Dreger & Miller, 1968, pp. 4-6; Amante *et al.*, 1970; Buck, 1970; Graves *et al.*, 1970; McKeown & Record, 1971).

What is quite clear from this literature is that there is some degree of association between prematurity, low birth weight, mother's age (greater risk in early teens and beyond the late thirties), close spacing of pregnancies, and illegitimacy, on the one hand, and higher rates of fetal loss, complications of pregnancy, labor and delivery, infant mortality, neurological difficulties and mental retardation, on the other. It is also clear that both of these sets of conditions have a much higher incidence in the Negro than in the white population. This holds true, in fact, even when Negroes are compared with whites of the lowest SES. The socioeconomically lowest 10 percent of whites in Baltimore, for example, were found to have a 7·6 percent rate of premature births, as compared with 11·4 percent for the full SES range of the Negro population. The same study reported complications of pregnancy in 14·6 percent of the lower fifth in SES among whites, while for the entire Negro population it was 50·6 percent. The authors state:

These higher rates of prematurity and complications of pregnancy among Negroes over even the lowest white socioeconomic groups are so marked that some workers in this field maintain that they must be attributable to some innate racial characteristic. Since average Negro socioeconomic status is generally lower than that in the lowest white groups, it seems more parsimonious to eliminate the postulated racial factor, and to hypothesize that prematurity and pregnancy complication rates increase exponentially below certain socioeconomic thresholds. (Pasamanick & Knobloch, 1966, p. 19)

The authors, however, do not present evidence that the average Negro SES is below the lower tenth or lower fifth of the white population in Baltimore and other studies have found a racial difference in these factors involved in reproductive casualty which are apparently independent of SES (Naylor & Myrianthopoulos, 1967; Amante *et al.*, 1970).

It is when we begin to evaluate the evidence concerning the relationship of reproductive factors to brain damage and mental development that the real ambiguities arise. Again, there is little doubt that high rates of fetal loss, infant mortality, complications of pregnancy, etc., are epidemiologically associated with higher rates of retardation and brain damage; there are correlations among all these poverty-associated factors. But, surprising as it may seem, what does not emerge clearly from this literature is evidence regarding the direction of causality among these variables. It is not at all clear to what extent the conditions of poverty are themselves a cause of reproductive casualty. Other groups subjected to poverty have not shown high casualty rates on any index. Mechanic (1968) and Graves *et al.* (1970) note that Jewish immigrants to America, in spite of their poverty, had even lower rates of infant mortality than any other American group, including the average of the native white population; Orientals are similar in this respect. Something more seems to be involved than just socioeconomic conditions. Amante *et al.* (1970) used a number of signs of CNS dysfunction derived from performance on the Bender Gestalt Test to compare Negro and white children in the two lowest SES groups (on a five-category scale). The only significant main effect in the analysis of variance was Race ($F = 13 \cdot 85, p < 1$); Social Class and the interaction of Race × Social Class were both non-significant ($F < 1$). The authors state:

Rates of brain damage per 100 black children at social class positions IV ($N = 14$) and V ($N = 26$) were, respectively, 50 and 69. . . . That is, 50 percent of the class IV children appeared to be brain damaged according to the set of psychological test parameters analyzed, and 69 percent of the class V children. [The corresponding percentages for the white sample were 25 and 26.] Combining classes IV and V into a total sample size of 40 (which of course is still pathetically small), 58 percent of the black children appear to be neurologically handicapped.

Further, in the case of the black sample, the frequency of maximal brain damage exceeded the frequency of minimal brain damage – constituting, therefore, a direct reversal of the minimal-maximal severity pattern observed in the case of the whites. It is apparent, then, that the black population of children is characterized not only by higher overall rates of brain damage relative to the white population, it is also characterized by more severe cases of brain damage. (Amante *et al.*, 1970, p. 126)

Later in their discussion of the results, the authors state, 'We wish to avoid the implications of racism.' And buried among the several following paragraphs discussing the sociology of racism is put forth what amounts to a major testable hypothesis:

Large groups of white or black *Ss* of varying socioeconomic status are typically uncritically selected and tested with conventional psychometric instruments. Naturally, major differences between the classes and the races are indicated. In all probability the observed differences are largely a function of the fact that the groups so selected contain an unspecified number of neurologically handicapped *Ss*, and these *Ss* pull the group averages down. If the entire group was neurologically screened to begin with, and the neurologically normal or deviant *Ss* appropriately compared with other *Ss* of similar neurological status, and the conventional tests then administered, the supposedly obvious or inevitable IQ differentials between the groups might collapse to zero and/or statistical insignificance. (p. 129)[6]

These investigators seem to be ambivalent, however, since they finally state:

Our final conclusion is that there are interclass and interracial differences in terms of measurable intelligence; both environmental and genetic factors appear to contribute to these IQ differentials. At the present time we are assuming that the major factors contributing to group differences are environmental in nature. (p. 129)[7]

At present there are two lines of evidence that seem incompatible with the hypothesis of such a high incidence of brain damage as suggested by Amante *et al.* and by the many writings of Pasamanick on this subject. The first counterfact is that independently assessed complications of pregnancy are known to be reflected in depressed performance on infant tests of psychomotor development in the first year of life (Honzik, Hutchings & Burnip, 1965). Yet on these very same tests, given at six months to one year of age, large representative samples of Negro infants were found to do as well as, or better than, comparable samples of white infants (Bayley, 1965). Such findings could be compatible with a markedly higher incidence of neurological damage in Negro infants only if it is argued that the Negro infants are normally so very advanced over white infants in psychomotor development that even with a high incidence of brain damage the mean Negro performance is still above the white mean. But this possibility should result in a larger variance of Developmental Quotients for Negroes as compared to whites, and Bayley's data show no significant racial difference in the variance of DQs.

The second item of evidence which is apparently inconsistent with the hypothesis of high rates of brain damage as a principal cause of lower Negro IQ is the heritability of IQ and the intrafamily IQ variance (sibling differences) which are about the same for Negro and white populations. If brain damage is an added external source of environmental variance, it should significantly lower the heritability of IQ and increase sibling differences. Negro and white samples which do not differ significantly on these variables still show an IQ difference of 1 *SD* or more (Scarr-Salapatek, 1971a; and see Table 19.1, p. 339).[8]

These findings seem to accord with the conclusions drawn by McKeown and Record (1971, p. 52) from their recent review of the literature on prenatal environmental influences on mental development:

Prenatal environmental influences appear to contribute little to the variation in intelligence in a general population from which those with recognized defects are excluded. There is little relationship to abnormalities of pregnancy or labour. . . . But the most convincing evidence that prenatal influences have little effect on measured intelligence is the observation that twins separated from their co-twin at or soon after birth have scores which are little lower than those of single births, in spite of

their retarded fetal growth, short period of gestation and increased risks during birth. There are very large variations in
intelligence in a general population of births in relation to
maternal age and birth order (Fig. 1); but *these are due to
differences between rather than within families* [emphasis added],
for there is little variation according to birth rank between sibs.

Thus, it is not yet established that the higher rate of reproductive casualty in Negroes, as reflected in a higher incidence of fetal
loss, prematurity, and infant mortality, causes any substantial
proportion of the IQ deficit. But the question is much too important to be dismissed or allowed to rest ambiguously on the
current inadequate state of the evidence. For we do have some
good statistics on certain population indices of reproductive
casualty, such as fetal loss, and if we make what seems to be a
reasonable assumption that fetal death represents merely a threshold effect on a continuous variable of impaired development, we
have a firm basis for inferring some higher, though quantitatively
undetermined, incidence of physical (including neurological)
impairment in the Negro as compared with the white population.
In 1965, fetal deaths (for gestation periods of twenty weeks or more)
nationwide had almost twice as high a rate among Negroes as
among whites (25·8 *v.* 13·3 per 1,000 live births) (U.S. Department
of Health, Education, and Welfare, 1967, pp. 3-5). Assuming fetal
death to be a threshold effect on a normally distributed variable,
the Negro and white populations can be said to show a mean
difference of $0·46\sigma$ on this variable. This is a large difference by
any standard. But even if this variable (organismic viability, freedom from impairment, or whatever it is) were *perfectly* correlated
with intelligence, it could account for less than half of the Negro-
white IQ difference.

But is the rate of fetal loss in a population entirely a function
of external environmental conditions? It appears not to be. The
recent research on this matter may provide a clue to the hitherto
inexplicably higher rate of fetal loss and other less severe forms
of reproductive casualty among Negroes even as compared with
non-Negro groups of similar or greater environmental disadvantages.

Bresler (1970) has found that the probability of fetal loss is
directly related to the degree of genetic heterogeneity among the

ancestral gene pools of the fetus. In two all-white samples from a New England population, comprising all socioeconomic levels, Bresler established highly significant relationships among three factors: fetal loss, the number of countries in the background of parents, and the distances between birthplaces of parents. The ancestry of each fetus, whether lost or live-born, was determined back as far as the great-grandparental generation. Since there are eight great-grandparents, they could have been born in anywhere from one to eight different countries. Bresler determined percentage of fetal loss as a function of the number of different countries among the birthplaces of the great-grandparental generation. He also determined the percentage of fetal loss as a joint function of number of countries among the great-grandparents *and* the distance apart (in miles) of the birthplaces of the two parents of the fetus. Both of these factors serve as indices of the degree of genetic heterogeneity of the fetus's ancestry. Bresler's summary of his main findings was as follows:

> Data on two white populations show that fetal loss (F_1 generation) in matings of the parental generation (P_1) increases cumulatively by approximately 2·5 percent to 3 percent with each additional country of birth in the great-grandparental generation (P_1). A dependent relation shows that increased fetal loss is also related to greater distances between birthplaces of mates within the P_1 generation. Conversely, low fetal loss is encountered with a small number of countries in the background and shorter distance between birthplaces. It is suggested that a large number of countries of birth represents a larger number of Mendelian gene pools and that with increased mixture of these gene pools, fetal loss increases proportionately. An animal model is cited in support of this contention. (p. 24)

Bresler also found that SES had no significant relationship to percentage of fetal loss in these samples. He specifically excluded from his study all families in which one or more persons had any African background in the family history, and he states, 'No extrapolation of these findings can be made to interracial matings at this time.' So the findings, which are highly reliable, and the genetic theory that explains them, can serve only to suggest an hypothesis that the high rate of fetal loss and the various sublethal aspects of reproductive casualty which are a part of this continuum

M*

are related to the genetic heterogeneity of the ancestral gene pools of the American Negro.

The genetic interpretation of Bresler's findings is highly technical and cannot be examined here, but it has been tested and reliably demonstrated in numerous animal experiments (referenced by Bresler, 1970). Briefly, more distantly related gene pools have greater genetic imbalance between gene loci on the chromosomes; the loci for certain genes do not match up properly, so that if the two alleles required for the production of an enzyme have undergone evolutionary translocations on the chromosomes, the enzyme controlled by a particular gene may not be produced and therefore cannot make its necessary contribution to the normal development of the growing embryo or fetus. Different genes become important at various stages of development, and some genetic imbalances will prove lethal while others will be sublethal but can cause developmental anomalies of varying severity. The effects have been demonstrated, for example, with frogs, all of the same species, but distributed over a wide geographical range. Bresler (1970, p. 24) summarizes some of the findings from these experiments, in which genetic crosses are made between frogs of the same species collected from varying geographic distances:

1. The hybrids between members of adjacent geographical territories tended to be normal in development and morphology.
2. The greater the geographical distance between parental combinations in eastern North America, the more retarded was the rate of development, the greater were the morphological defects in the hybrids, and the fewer were the normal individuals.
3. The greater the geographical distance between parental combinations, the larger was the percentage of eggs which failed to develop properly.
4. The further apart in geographical distance . . . the members were collected from, the earlier in development did reproductive wastage occur.

What about heterosis, or hybrid vigor, which usually results from outcrossings? Heterosis results when there are dominant and recessive genes involved in a characteristic. Outcrossing increases the likelihood of heterozygotes, and if the dominant genes are 'desirable', hybrid vigor (e.g., greater size) is said to result. The effect is quite independent of the effects of loci imbalance involved in the Bresler study; it is a different phenomenon entirely. The two effects can operate simultaneously, in 'opposite' directions; the deleterious effects of genetic imbalance can override desirable effects of heterosis. The opposite of heterosis genetically is inbreeding depression, which shows up most clearly in consanguineous matings, such as cousin marriage. Not all traits show heterosis and inbreeding depression. Height and chest circumference show it, as does IQ (Schull & Neel, 1965), but head shape (cephalic index) and circumference apparently do not (Wolański, Jarosz & Pyżuk, 1970). Too close inbreeding causes depression of some characteristics because of the increased likelihood of the pairing of undesirable mutant alleles, while too much heterogeneity of ancestral gene pools can have undesirable consequences due to genetic imbalance caused by translocations and inversions of loci.

The role of these genetic mechanisms in the causation of reproductive casualty and its differing rates in various subpopulations calls for much further investigation, which hopefully will not be hindered by ideologically motivated insistence that all such effects must be attributable entirely to external environmental factors.

NOTES

1. The locations of these studies: Cape Town, South Africa; Kampala, Uganda; Guatemala; Mexico; Santiago, Chile; Sarajevo, Yugoslavia; Hyderabad, India; Peru.
2. In autopsy studies of stillborn and newborn infants of poor, presumably undernourished mothers in New York City, as compared with infants of non-poor mothers, the magnitude of the effects of 'poorness' (presumably maternal undernutrition) on the growth of various organs and body measurements was determined. Of the eight measurements made on the babies, the brain was least affected, suggesting that it is probably the nutritionally most highly buffered organ in the fetus (Naeye, Diener, Dellinger & Blanc, 1969). The index of relative effect of prenatal undernutrition for the eight infant body measurements and the placenta were: thymus 38, adrenals 25, spleen 23, heart 15, body length 15, liver 21, kidney 10, brain 6, and placenta 4.

3. The closest to anything like this that I have been able to find in the relevant literature on human nutrition and growth is a study, carried out in Aberdeen, Scotland, which showed a correlation between the mother's nutritional status as determined by her height and her infant's birth weight and subsequent growth and development; there were also correlations between mother's height, child's height at age 7, and his performance on achievement tests in school (Birch, Richardson, Baird, Horobin & Illsley, 1970). The possible confounding of genetic and nutritional factors in determining these relationships rules out any definite interpretation.

4. The investigation also conducted parallel studies in two rural samples of poor Appalachian whites in Tennessee. Their nutritional status was higher than that of the urban samples mainly because they raised much of their own food. About 70 percent of the rural samples, as compared with about 50 percent of the urban samples, had pin worms. The IQs of the rural whites averaged about 6 points lower than those of the urban whites.

5. An assistant director of the U.S. Department of Agriculture's human nutrition research division claimed that 50 percent of children with IQs in the range from 70-80 are depressed 10 IQ points due to poor nutrition (*Biomedical News*, November 1971, p. 14). Despite repeated efforts, however, I have not succeeded in obtaining from the official source of this claim any factual evidence that would substantiate it.

6. If we assume a mean IQ of 100 in the white population, 85 in the Negro population, and an *SD* of 15 in each population, and further assume that all brain-damaged persons are of lower IQ than neurologically non-damaged persons, what percentage of the Negro population would have to be screened out as neurologically damaged in order to bear out this prediction by Amante *et al.*? Calculations indicate that at least the lower 62 percent of the Negro population in IQ would have to be screened out for the remaining 38 percent to have a mean IQ of 100. This surprising conclusion would seem to cast some doubt on this hypothesis. Have there been any estimates of the incidence of neurological damage in the Negro population which come anywhere near such a figure and which are also experimentally independent of the IQ determination, i.e., based on criteria that do not include measurement of the dependent variable, viz., IQ? I know of none. The criteria used in the study by Amante *et al.* were derived from signs of the Bender Gestalt Test, which itself has a high *g* loading, making it difficult, if not impossible, to distinguish reliably between signs of neurological impairment and sheer mental immaturity. Among neurologically normal white middle-class elementary school children, Bender-Gestalt perfor-

mance correlates substantially with conventional measures of IQ. The white-Negro difference found by Amante *et al.* on the Bender Gestalt, however, would be roughly equivalent to 11 IQ points, which is slightly larger than the average difference typically found for Negro and white children within the lower social strata.

7. It is interesting to see this conclusion of genetic *inter*class and *inter*-racial IQ differences appearing in a 1970 issue of *Journal of Social Issues*, the official periodical of the Society for the Psychological Study of Social Issues, the Council of which in 1969 publicly censured me for drawing a similar conclusion in my article in the *Harvard Educational Review*. My statement was: 'The preponderance of the evidence is, in my opinion, less consistent with a strictly environmental hypothesis than with a genetic hypothesis, which, of course, does not exclude the influence of environment or its inter-action with genetic factors' (Jensen, 1969a, p. 82).

8. Nichols (1970, p. 65) found the mean absolute difference in 4-year-old Stanford-Binet IQs between full sibs to be 11·82 for whites ($N = 1,100$) and 11·97 for Negroes ($N = 970$). The white and Negro mean Stanford-Binet IQs at age 4 differed by 13 points (p. 70) and mean WISC IQs at 7 years of age differed about 10 points (p. 99) in this sample.

20 *Recapitulation*

The study of ability differences between populations and sub-populations, including cross-cultural studies, remains largely descriptive. It should not be forgotten that *correlations* between various cultural and environmental factors, on the one hand, and abilities, on the other, are merely descriptive, in much the same way that population means and variances are merely descriptive. Inferences concerning the *causes* of ability differences between populations depend upon experimental control and behavior-genetic analysis. The particular hypotheses and the most suitable experimental and genetic methods for testing them may differ markedly depending upon the particular populations and the particular behavioral traits being compared. It is useful to distinguish between cross-cultural studies as contrasted with studies of ability differences among various subpopulations within the same culture. This may involve an arbitrary division of a continuous variable, but at least at the extremes the distinction is obvious. Studying differences between Eskimos and Australian Aborigines seems very cross-cultural. Studying ability differences between Negro and white children born in the same city, attending the same schools, watching the same television programs, speaking the same language, shopping in the same stores, and eating the same foods, does not seem very cross-cultural.

In this monograph I am not concerned with cross-cultural studies in the most obvious sense, but with the average difference in educability of the two largest subpopulations in the United States, Negroes and whites. Neither group should be thought of as homogeneous. Highly significant social-class, regional, and sub-cultural differences exist within each racial group. Also, American Negroes are a hybrid population, having some 20 to 30 percent of its genes from Caucasian ancestors. In some regions the degree of Caucasian admixture is less than 10 percent; in others it is more than 30 percent. Overall, however, the average educability of American Negroes is further below the general average for the United States than is the educability of any other major ethnic or cultural group: Orientals, Mexican-Americans, American Indians, or Puerto Ricans. Although these other groups show more obvious cultural differences and language differences, many of them being recent immigrants from foreign countries, none shows as great a problem in the public schools as the Negro population. Moreover, the educational problems of some minorities seem to be associated with their bilingualism *per se*, and improvement in their scholastic performance is directly related to their improvement in the use of the English language. The educational problems of immigrant, bilingual minorities, therefore, have not posed a major problem to prescriptive remediation.

Much greater concern among educators is aroused by the lower average educability of the Negro population. To those who are not familiar with the educational problems and all their correlates that are associated with approximately one standard deviation difference in average scholastic performance between two sub-populations sharing the same schools and competing in the same world of work, it can be said that the problem is not just another problem on a par with many others in education – it is evolving into a major calamity. So far no hint of a satisfactory solution is in sight. The calamity results, in part, not only from the scholastic achievement difference, but from the fact that the Negro population has its own identity and is highly visible and countable. These facts, combined with the one standard deviation difference and the properties of the normal distribution of abilities and attainments in both populations, result in a situation which has become educational and social dynamite. This state of affairs has troubled America more than any other domestic problem in recent years. In education, as in medicine, effective remedies and constructive solutions to problems depend first of all upon accurate diagnosis of their causes. This can come about only if we formulate hypotheses which are operationally testable. No one should expect that the first hypotheses proposed in what will necessarily be a long series of investigations leading toward a more complete and accurate picture will be 'true' in any final sense. Testable hypotheses are the stepping stones on which we advance toward the kind of knowledge that *works*, in the same sense that our knowledge of physics works when we apply it to the problem of putting a man on the moon. So we must discover not only the *correlates* of differences in educability; we must try to discover their *causes* as well.

EDUCABILITY AND INTELLIGENCE

Educability is defined here as the ability to learn the traditional scholastic subjects, especially the three Rs, under ordinary conditions of classroom instruction. Thus it is apparent that *educability* in this sense is a relative concept. At present it is measured by tests of scholastic achievement. Educability is dependent upon *intelligence*, which is a theoretical construct to account for the consolidation of learning into organized structures which permit its retrieval, broad generalization, and transfer to the solution of new problems and to the facilitation of new learning. A theoretical distinction should be made between *learning per se* and the consolidation of learning into cognitive structures that permit retrieval and transfer. Thus short-term measures of school learning are less highly correlated with intelligence than cumulative long-term measures. The physiological structures underlying intelligence grow from birth to maturity in their capacity to consolidate learning into the kinds of cognitive structures that characterize intelligence. Whatever is learned but not consolidated in this manner is either forgotten or remains a relatively specific response to a specific set of stimulus conditions; operationally it will show up in a factor analysis as an item with large specificity and a negligible loading on a general factor common to a large number and variety of learned facts and skills. The really functional, usable part of traditional school learning is that which gets consolidated into these cognitive structures, and the extent to which this takes place depends upon the person's intelligence. Intelligence is indexed by standard tests, all of which, if valid, share a large common factor, *g*. Intelligence as thus measured correlates more highly with scholastic performance than any other single factor or combination of factors that can be ascertained about a school-age child. Long-term, cumulative educational achievement correlates more highly with intelligence measures than short-range tests of achievement, which reflect also learning ability, time spent in study, motivation, and a host of other factors affecting acquisition of scholastic knowledge. These factors seem to have less effect on the overall rate of consolidation of the learning into cognitive structures. Because short-term achievement measures reflect factors other than intelligence, Negroes and whites differ slightly less on such measures than they differ on intelligence tests. Scholastic achievement scores generally show somewhat smaller differences than intelligence test scores between Negro and white children who have had roughly equal educational opportunities. The problem of Negro-white inequality in educability is thus essentially the problem of Negro-white differences in intelligence.

HERITABILITY OF INTELLIGENCE AND SCHOLASTIC ACHIEVEMENT

The heritability of *individual* differences in intelligence in white populations is now well established. Since heritability (i.e., the proportion of the total variance attributable to genetic factors) is a population parameter, it has no universal or precise value. But the vast majority of studies of the heritability of intelligence indicate that genetic factors are more important than environmental factors as the cause of intelligence differences among individuals. On the average, genetic factors appear to be about twice as important as environmental factors, including prenatal influences.

The available data, which are hardly adequate for strong inference, suggest that the heritability of IQ is about the same in Negroes and whites. In both racial groups, the lowest socioeconomic group shows a somewhat lower heritability of IQ than the higher SES groups. The reasons for this cannot be inferred from the present data.

HERITABILITY AND POPULATION DIFFERENCES

Formally, the heritability of a trait *within* populations cannot tell us the heritability of the difference *between* population means. High heritability *within* populations, however, adds to the *plausibility* of

356 Educability and Group Differences

the hypothesis that genetic factors are involved in the difference *between* populations. High *within*-group heritability *cannot* prove *between*-group heritability, but it does increase the *a priori* likelihood of finding genetic components in the average difference between groups.

Knowledge of the heritability of IQ *within* each of two populations can also place certain constraints on the kinds of hypothesized environmental influences that are invoked to explain population differences. Analyses show, for example, that whatever environmental factors account for the IQ differences between identical twins reared apart have an exceedingly low probability of explaining the one standard deviation IQ difference between the Negro and white populations. If it were established that the heritability of IQ is as high as 0·75 in both the Negro and white populations, then it can be said that as yet no environmental factor or combination of factors has been identified on which the Negro and white populations differ sufficiently to account for the 15 points mean IQ difference solely in terms of non-genetic factors. This makes it necessary, if one wishes to maintain a purely environmentalist theory, to hypothesize the influence of subtle, unmeasured, and perhaps unmeasurable environmental differences which contribute to variance *between* races but not to variance *within* races. If the subtle, hypothetical environmental factors cannot be measured or cannot be shown to bear some relationship to IQ differences within racial groups, then the theory that postulates their existence as an explanation of racial IQ differences is in principle untestable and therefore beyond the pale of science. Such hypotheses will not do as a scientific explanation of population differences. Theories that emphasize genotype × environment interaction as an explanation of racial IQ differences imply a genetic difference, since they are based on the hypothesis that different racial genotypes respond differently to the same environmental influences. There is no evidence as yet for such an interaction between genetic and environmental effects in the determination of IQ differences, either *within* or *between* racial groups.

COMBINING ENVIRONMENTAL EFFECTS

Many environmental differences have been shown to exist between Negro and white populations, and some sizeable proportion of these environmental differences have been shown to have some correlation with IQ *within* each racial group. This creates a subjective impression that all these IQ-related environmental factors taken together can easily account for the 1 *SD* Negro-white IQ difference. However, the proper way of assessing the combined influence of all these variables is in the manner of a multiple regression equation, since the many variables do not each make an independent contribution to the total difference. When environmental measures have been entered into a multiple regression equation to predict IQ or to predict race, the addition of successive variables beyond the first few, especially if these include summary status variables such as socioeconomic level, add vanishingly small increments to the total proportion of explained variance. Multiple correlations thus obtained so far fall extremely short of accounting for the 1 *SD* racial difference, although as yet no single study has entered enough variables into the multiple regression to provide a really stringent test of the environmental hypothesis. The weakness of this correlational approach, of course, is that some of the environmental indices may be correlated with genotypes. Educational level of the parents, for example, is often included as an environmental variable affecting the child's intellectual development. But it almost certainly includes also some genetic component common to both the parents and their children. Despite this bias favoring an environmental hypothesis, no multiple correlations have yet been revealed which account for all of the between-groups variance. If the variables included account for more of the variance *within* groups than the complement of the heritability (i.e., $1 - h^2$) within the groups, then it is virtually certain that the environmental indices are also reflecting correlated genetic factors.

OTHER APPROACHES TO RESEARCH ON THE
NATURE-NURTURE PROBLEM

Although heritability studies can narrow the range of uncertainty about the adequacy of environmental explanations of population differences, there are other potential methodologies which could yield stronger conclusions. The most highly developed methodology now available involves use of the fact that American Negroes are a genetically hybrid population, with some 20 to 30 percent of its genes from Caucasian ancestors. Methods exist for probabilistically estimating the proportion of Caucasian genes in a hybrid Negro population and in *individuals* in such a population, based on a dozen or more genetic polymorphisms (various proteins in the blood) with known frequencies in West African and European populations. If in environmentally homogeneous samples there was a higher correlation between IQ and the proportion of Caucasian ancestry than between IQ and socially visible racial characteristics which can be objectively measured, such as skin color and interpupillary distance, a strictly environmental hypothesis of the IQ difference would not be upheld. If maternal half-siblings were used in such research, even prenatal environmental effects would be controlled. The method used in this way could probably be more definitive than any other method or combination of methods presently available, short of long-term longitudinal studies in which all environmental factors could be rigorously controlled throughout the course of development from the time of conception.

DEFICIENCIES OF MAJOR ENVIRONMENTAL HYPOTHESES

Those environmentalist hypotheses of the Negro-white IQ difference which have been most clearly formulated and are therefore subject to empirical tests are the only ones that can be evaluated within a scientific framework. The most frequently cited environmentalist hypotheses which are sufficiently clear to be put to an empirical test and which already have been tested have not proven adequate to the explanatory function they were intended to serve. A number of lines of such evidence cast serious doubt on purely environmental and cultural theories of the racial IQ difference.

Socioeconomic Differences

Matching or statistically controlling socioeconomic status (SES) of racial samples does not wipe out IQ differences, although on the average it reduces differences by about one-third. The racial difference increases with increasing SES level when the IQs being compared are those of children classified according to their parents' SES. This finding is hard to rationalize along purely environmental lines, but it is predictable from the genetic principle of filial regression toward the population mean. Children of high SES

Negro parents regress toward the lower mean of the Negro population, which makes for a larger regression effect than for white children, who regress toward the white population mean (which is about 1 *SD* higher). High SES Negro parents are more deviant from their population mean than high SES white parents, and therefore, because of regression, the high SES Negro children will resemble their parents less in ability than will the white children. The same thing holds true for siblings of high IQ Negro children.

Criticisms of studies that control for SES argue that SES, as it is usually measured in terms of parental education, occupation, income, etc., is too crude a variable to reflect adequately the important variables of the environment influencing mental development. But SES is crude mainly in the sense that it is non-specific; it summarizes within it many other environmental variables, and adding more refined variables does not markedly increase a multiple correlation with either IQ or with race. SES seems to summarize the larger part of those environmental factors that are most frequently mentioned as the causes of racial IQ differences. Actually, rather than controlling too little of the variance, SES probably controls too much, since within racial groups, at least, there is undoubtedly a correlation between SES and genetic factors. Matching racial groups for SES thus matches them not only for some environmental factors but also to some unknown extent for genetic factors as well. It is interesting also that when such matching is carried out, it is noted that the average skin color of the Negro groups becomes lighter in the higher SES categories, indicating that genetic factors co-vary with SES, for whatever reason. Genetic SES intelligence differences are firmly established within the white population. Matching Negro and white groups on SES, therefore, is certain to minimize genetic as well as environmental differences. For this reason, studies that control for SES are probably biased in favor of the environmentalist hypothesis and can contribute little or nothing to elucidating the nature-nurture problem, except in those instances where the direction of the environmental difference between two groups is opposite to the direction of the IQ difference.

Negative Correlations between Environment and Ability

A number of environmental factors which correlate positively with mental ability *within* various population groups were shown to correlate *negatively* with IQ differences *between* certain groups. On all of the many measurable factors which environmentalists have invoked to explain the Negro-white IQ difference, both American Indians and Mexican-Americans have been found to be much more disadvantaged than Negroes. Yet on non-verbal intelligence tests (which are more fair for bilingual groups such as Mexicans and Indians) and in scholastic performance, Indians and Mexicans significantly outperform Negroes. This finding is neutral with respect to genetic theory, in the sense that no prediction could have been derived from genetic principles; but it contradicts those environmental theories that invoke measurable environmental factors known to correlate with IQ within population groups as the cause of the lower Negro IQ. The only attempts of environ-mentalists to rationalize these findings have invoked highly speculative cultural and attitudinal factors which have not yet been shown to be correlated either with IQ or with race.

Culture-biased Tests

Intelligence tests can be rank-ordered according to certain generally agreed upon criteria of their cultural loading. Within a given culture, tests are better described as differing in *status fairness*. Environmentalists who criticize intelligence tests usually give as examples those tests which are most obviously loaded with what is presumably white, middle-class factual knowledge, vocabulary, and the like, as contrasted with more abstract figural material such as compose Raven's Progressive Matrices and Cattell's Culture-Fair Tests of *g*. Yet it is on the latter type of tests that Negroes perform most poorly, relative to whites and to other minority groups. Disadvantaged minorities, such as American Indians and Mexican-Americans, perform on tests showing different degrees of status bias in accord with the environmentalist hypothesis. Negroes do the opposite. 'Translation' of tests such as the Stanford-Binet into the Negro ghetto dialect also does not improve scores.

The scholastic and occupational predictive validity of IQ tests is the same for Negroes as for whites, and item analyses of tests showing large average group mean differences do not reveal significant differences in rank order of item difficulty or in choice of distractors for error responses. Test-taking attitudes and motivational factors appear unconvincing as an explanation of the group difference in view of the fact that on some tests which make equal demands on attention, persistence, and effort, such as various memory tests, Negroes do perform quite well relative to whites. When various diverse tests and test items are ordered in terms of the degree to which they discriminate between Negroes and whites, the one feature which is common to the most discriminating tests and items is the conceptual and abstract nature of the test material, or the degree to which they accord with the classic definitions of the psychological nature of *g*. Data from other minority groups who are more environmentally disadvantaged than Negroes support an opposite conclusion, in accord with the environmental interpretation.

Language Deprivation

This is an unconvincing explanatory hypothesis in view of the fact that Negroes perform best on the most verbal parts of intelligence tests and poorest on the least verbal materials. All other disadvantaged minority groups within the American population show the opposite trend. Children who are born deaf are the most verbally deprived subjects we can study. They show marked deficits on verbal intelligence tests. Yet they perform at an average level on non-verbal tests, thus showing a pattern of abilities opposite to that of Negroes.

Poor Motivation

There is no consistent evidence that Negroes are less motivated in a test situation than are other groups. Some groups (e.g., Indians) whose general educational aspirations and self-concepts are poorer than those of Negroes actually perform better on tests and in school work. Also, on performance tests specially devised to maximize the influence of motivational factors and to minimize the tests' dependence upon abstract or complex cognitive functions which would involve *g*, Negroes do not perform significantly below whites. The 'expectancy' or 'self-fulfilling prophecy' theory has not been empirically demonstrated, and when put to proper test it has failed to be substantiated.

Non-cognitive Tests

Certain perceptual-motor tests such as choice reaction time and pursuit rotor learning (which has a very high heritability) show large Negro-white differences even under very highly controlled experimental conditions, and the results are independent of the race of the tester. Moreover, the magnitude of the racial difference has been shown to be related to the degree of Caucasian admixture in the Negro sample as assessed by physical indices. If genetic racial differences in behavioral tests other than intelligence tests are admitted, by what principle can one exclude the same possibility for types of tests labeled as measures of intelligence? There is no reason why intelligence tests should be categorically excluded from the possibility of showing genetic race differences when such differences in other physical and behavioral traits can be demonstrated.

Nutritional Deficiencies

The fact that severe malnutrition, especially protein deficiency, during prenatal development and in infancy and childhood can impair mental as well as physical growth is not at issue. Studies from the nutritionally most deprived segments of populations in Africa, Asia, and South America would support this conclusion. There are no data, however, which would support the hypothesis that malnutrition contributes any appreciable fraction to the average Negro-white IQ difference. In Negro communities where there is no evidence of poor nutrition, the average Negro IQ is still about 1 *SD* below the white mean. When groups of Negro children with IQs *below* the general Negro average have been studied for nutritional status, no signs of malnutrition have been found. Physical evidence of malnutrition found to be correlated with lower IQs in studies conducted in Africa, Mexico, and Guatemala have not been found even in the poorest and lowest IQ segments of the American Negro population. On the basis of present evidence, the hypothesis that lower average Negro IQ is due to poor nutrition is not tenable.

The nutritional and health care status of Indian children, as indicated by much higher rates of infant mortality, is much poorer than that of Negroes; yet Indian children in the first grade in school (age 6) have been found to score about 1 *SD* above Negroes on non-verbal ability tests.

Prenatal and Perinatal Disadvantages

The higher rate of fetal loss and infant mortality in the Negro population may indicate disadvantages related to prenatal health care of the mother and undesirable conditions attending birth. These conditions prevail in the poorer segment of the Negro population and probably contribute to the incidence of neurological handicap among Negro children. All of the causes of high fetal loss, however, are not understood, for there are some populations which, even when living under disadvantaged conditions have shown lower rates of fetal loss and infant mortality than are found today in the white majority – Jews and Orientals, for example. There is now some evidence that the degree of genetic heterogeneity of the fetus's ancestors is directly related to the probability of fetal loss, and thus genetic factors may be involved even in this seemingly environmental phenomenon (Bresler, 1970). Disadvantaging forms of birth trauma such as anoxia, low birth weight and prematurity are reflected in subnormal performance on infant tests of perceptual-motor development. But large representative samples of Negro children show no depression of scores on these tests and generally perform at slightly higher levels than middle-class white children. Prenatal and perinatal factors, though differing in Negro and white populations, do not begin to account for such phenomena as the six to eight times higher rate of mental retardation (IQs below 70) in the Negro than in the white population. Unless one hypothesizes the existence of genetic factors, the cause of the mental retardation in the vast majority of cases must be categorized as 'unknown' or 'unidentified'.

SUMMARY

In view of all the most relevant evidence which I have examined, the most tenable hypothesis, in my judgment, is that genetic, as well as environmental, differences are involved in the average disparity between American Negroes and whites in intelligence and educability, as here defined. All the major facts would seem to be comprehended quite well by the hypothesis that something between one-half and three-fourths of the average IQ difference between American Negroes and whites is attributable to genetic factors, and the remainder to environmental factors and their interaction with the genetic differences.

Educational Implications

If this hypothesis stands up under further appropriate scientific investigation, its social implications will be far broader than those that pertain only to education. The educational implications, as I see them at present in terms of what we now know and of what is feasible, would involve three main educational approaches. They are not at all mutually exclusive. (The necessity and desirability of eliminating racial discrimination and of improving the environmental conditions and educational and occupational opportunities of *all* disadvantaged persons in the population are taken for granted.) These approaches have nothing to do with race *per se*, but are concerned with individual differences in those characteristics most relevant to educability. Their success in improving the benefits of education to the majority of Negro children, however, may depend in part upon eventual recognition that racial differences in the distribution of educationally relevant abilities are not mainly the result of discrimination and unequal environmental conditions. None of the approaches that seems to me realistic is based on the expectation of the schools' significantly changing children's basic intelligence.

Seeking Aptitude × Training Interactions. This means that some children may learn better by one method than by another and that the best method may be quite different for different children, depending on their particular aptitudes and other personological characteristics. It implies that the same educational goals can be accomplished to the same degree for children of different abilities provided the right instructional variations are found. This is merely a hope, and the relevant research so far gives little basis for optimism that such aptitude × training interactions will be found which can overcome to any marked degree the importance of IQ level for educability (see Bracht, 1970). But since this type of research has been underway for only a few years, it is much too soon to discount the possibilities that it may turn up – especially if one expects not miracles, but only positive, if modest, benefits from this approach.

Greater Attention to Learning Readiness. The concept of developmental readiness for various kinds of school learning has been too neglected in recent educational trends, which have been dominated by the unproved notion that the earlier something can be taught to a child, the better (Jensen, 1969d). Forced early learning, prior to some satisfactory level of readiness (which will differ markedly from one child to another), could cause learning blocks which later on practically defy remediation. The more or less uniform lock-step sequencing of educational experiences may have to be drastically modified for the benefit of many children, but the recent massive insistence on 'earliness' and uniformity of educational treatment of all children has militated against large-scale research on the implications of readiness for children with below-average educability within the traditional school system.

Greater Diversity of Curricula and Goals. The public schools, in order truly to serve the entire population, must move beyond narrow conceptions of scholastic achievement to find a much greater diversity of ways for children over the entire range of abilities to benefit from schooling – to benefit especially in ways that will be to their advantage after they are out of school. The purely academic goals of schooling have been so strongly ingrained in the thinking and in the values of our society that radical efforts will probably be called for to modify public education in ways whereby it can more effectively benefit large numbers of children who have limited aptitudes for traditional academic achievement. Differences in rates of mental development and in potential for various types of learning will not disappear by being ignored. It is up to biologists and psychologists to discover their causes, and it is up to educators to create a diversity of instructional arrangements best suited to the full range of educational differences that we find in our population. Many environmentally caused differences can be minimized or eliminated, given the resources and the will of society. The differences that remain are a challenge for public education. The challenge will be met by making available more ways and means for children to benefit from schooling. This, I am convinced, can come about only through a greater recognition and understanding of the nature of human differences.

Appendix on Heritability

Heritability, h^2, is a population statistic which expresses the proportion of population variance in a given phenotypic characteristic attributable to genetic factors. The heritability of a trait cannot be determined from study of an individual, since h^2 expresses a proportion of the total variance in some observed or measurable characteristic (phenotype), and variance depends upon differences among two or more individuals. (Variance is the mean of the squared deviations of individuals from the arithmetic mean of the group.) Heritability is seldom if ever obtained for an entire population. It is estimated in a sample of the population, and therefore, like any other sample statistic, is subject to sampling error, the magnitude of which is inversely related to the square root of the sample size. Estimates of heritability are influenced by the amount of genetic and environmental variance in the population sampled, by the nature and reliability of the trait measurements, by the age of the subjects (h^2 for many developmental characteristics generally increases from birth to maturity), and the particular method or formula by which h^2 is estimated. Thus h^2 is clearly not a constant like π or the speed of light. It is more akin to a population statistic, such as the infant mortality rate in a given population, at a given time, in a given place, under a given criterion for tabulating infant deaths.

Heritability can be best understood in terms of the components of variance that enter into it.

$$h^2 = \frac{V_G}{V_P} \qquad (A.1)$$

where
V_G = genetic variance
V_P = phenotypic (total) variance.

The genetic variance, V_G, can be divided into four components,

$$V_G = V_A + V_D + V_{E_p} + V_{AM} \tag{A.2}$$

where

V_A = additive genetic variance

V_D = non-additive genetic variance due to dominance at the same gene loci

V_{E_p} = non-additive genetic variance due to interaction between different gene loci, called *epistasis*

V_{AM} = genetic variance due to assortative mating, i.e., the increment in total variance attributable to degree of genetic resemblance between mates on the characteristic in question.

The phenotypic variance, V_P, is comprised as follows:

$$V_P = V_G + V_E + V_{GE} + \text{Cov}GE + V_e \tag{A.3}$$

where

V_G = genetic variance

V_E = additive environmental variance which is independent of the genotype

V_{GE} = variance due to interaction (i.e., non-additive effects) of genotypes and environments

$\text{Cov}GE$ = covariance of genotypes and environments

V_e = error variance due to unreliability of measurements.

The component, V_{GE}, should not be confused with $\text{Cov}GE$. The statistical interaction, V_{GE}, means that different genotypes may respond differently to the same environmental effect. If a particular change in the environment raises the IQ of every genotype subjected to it by, say, 10 points, the environmental effect is said to be additive, and the variance contributed by such an environmental effect is included in V_E. If, on the other hand, some genotypes gain 20 points, some 10 points, some show no gain at all, and some show a loss, the environmental effect is called non-additive, that is, it does not add the same increment to every individual; the environmental change *interacts* with genotypes to produce different phenotypic effects in different genotypes. This source of variance comprises V_{GE}.

The covariance of genotypes and environments, CovGE, arises when genotypic values and environmental values are *correlated* in the population. An example is children with genotypes for high intelligence who are reared in homes with superior environmental advantages for intellectual development, or a musically talented child who is given music lessons, phonograph records, and taken to concerts more than a child who evinces little or no sensitivity to music. Some part of the covariance is, in a sense, truly created by the genotype, as when an intellectually gifted child spontaneously spends more time in reading or other intellectual activities, or a musically talented child of his own accord spends many hours a day practising a musical instrument. Similarly, in nature, the genotypically larger and stronger animal will get more food in its particular ecological niche and will therefore be favored also nutritionally. This covariance increases the total population variance in the trait (in this case body size). Because the covariance is so closely linked to genotypic characteristics when conditions are such that individuals can choose or create those features of the environment in accord with their genotypic proclivities, some geneticists (e.g., Roberts, 1967, p. 217) include CovGE as part of the total genetic variance rather than as part of the environmental variance, and they define the environmental variance component, V_E, as those environmental effects which are *independent* of the genotype.

Thus heritability can be defined differently for various purposes, depending upon the components that enter into the numerator and denominator.

Heritability in the narrow sense, h_N^2, is the proportion of additive genetic variance, thus:

$$h_N^2 = \frac{V_A}{V_P} \tag{A.4}$$

Heritability in the broad sense, h^2, is:

$$h^2 = \frac{V_A + V_D + V_{E_p} + V_{AM}}{V_P} = \frac{V_G}{V_P} \tag{A.5}$$

Some estimates of heritability in the broad sense include CovGE in the numerator:

$$h^2 = \frac{V_G + \text{CovGE}}{V_P} \tag{A.6}$$

The distinction between the h^2 as defined by Equations A.5 and A.6 is seldom made explicit in the literature and depends upon the method used for estimating h^2. Generally, CovGE is included in h^2 (i.e., formula A.6), either on the assumption that the covariance is due to the genotype and/or because the particular method of estimating h^2 does not permit separation of V_G and CovGE.

BETWEEN- AND WITHIN-FAMILY COMPONENTS

For reasons that will become apparent in the following section, it is useful to partition both the genetic variance, V_G, and the environmental variance, V_E, each into two components, one due to differences *between* families and one due to differences *within* families:

$$V_G = V_{G_B} + V_{G_W} \qquad (A.7)$$

where

V_{G_B} = genetic variance *between* families
V_{G_W} = genetic variance *within* families.

This formula reflects the fact that there are genetic differences between the average value of the trait measurement of different families in the population and also genetic differences among the offsprings within each family.

$$V_E = V_{E_B} + V_{E_W} \qquad (A.8)$$

where

V_{E_B} = environmental variance *between* families
V_{E_W} = environmental variance *within* families.

Formula A.8 reflects the idea that there are systematic environmental differences *between* families which make for differences between families on the trait in question but do not make for differences among offsprings reared together in the same family; this is V_{E_B}. And there are differential environmental influences *within* families which make for differences among offsprings reared together in the same family; this is V_{E_W}. These environmental effects, V_{E_B} and V_{E_W}, can occur at any time after the moment of conception; some are prenatal, some are postnatal; some are associated with biological factors, such as nutrition and disease; some are psychological, social, and cultural.

HOW h^2 IS EMPIRICALLY OBTAINED

Obviously one cannot measure the various components of V_P directly. So they must be estimated indirectly. The indirect estimates are made from correlations (or covariances) among persons of differing degrees of kinship.

The correlation between individuals (who are paired or grouped according to some degree of relationship, such as being reared together, or being twins, or siblings, or cousins, etc.) can be represented in terms of the various components of total variance which the individuals have in common. In general, the correlation, *r*, is

$$r = \frac{\text{Variance Components in Common}}{\text{Total Variance}} \qquad (A.9)$$

Thus, we can theoretically represent the correlations for different degrees of kinship in terms of variance components. For example, the highest degree of relatedness is the case of identical or mono-zygotic (one-egg) twins reared *together* (MZT). The correlation between such twins, r_{MZT}, is:

$$r_{MZT} = \frac{V_G + V_{E_B} + V_{GE} + \text{Cov}GE}{V_P} \qquad (A.10)$$

The correlation between monozygotic twins who are separated and reared *apart* in uncorrelated environments, r_{MZA}, is:

$$r_{MZA} = \frac{V_G}{V_P} \qquad (A.11)$$

To the extent that the genotype influences or selects the environment, some indeterminate part of $\text{Cov}GE$ will be included in the numerator of Equation A.11.

The correlation between fraternal or dizygotic (two-egg) twins or singleton siblings reared together is approximately:

$$r_{DZT} \text{ or } r_{ST} = \frac{V_{G_B} + V_{E_B} + \text{Cov}GE}{V_P} \qquad (A.12)$$

The correlation between dizygotic twins or siblings reared apart is approximately:

$$r_{DZA} \text{ or } r_{SA} = \frac{V_{G_B}}{V_P} \qquad (A.13)$$

if it is assumed that the separated sibs are placed in uncorrelated (i.e., random) environments. Again, as in the case of MZ twins reared apart, Cov*GE* will enter into the numerator to the extent that genotype influences or selects the environment.

But now it must be pointed out that Equations A.12 and A.13 are only rough approximations because they are intentionally over-simplifications made for didactic reasons. In Equations A.12 and A.13, if one is to give a genetically more precise formulation, V_{G_B} should be represented as

$$V_{G_B} = \tfrac{1}{2}V_A + \tfrac{1}{2}V_{AM} + \tfrac{1}{4}V_D + <\tfrac{1}{4}V_{E_p} \qquad (A.14)$$

By thus partitioning V_{GB} into the components shown in Equation A.14, it will be seen that some of these components can be esti-mated from formulas presented later. (The coefficients $\tfrac{1}{2}$ and $\tfrac{1}{4}$, etc. in Equations A.14, A.15, and elsewhere, can be rigorously derived by means of 'Mendelian algebra' applied to a polygenic model of the form $(p\mathbf{A} + q\mathbf{a})^{2n}$, where $p + q = 1$, $\mathbf{A}$ is an allele which adds to the trait, $\mathbf{a}$ subtracts from the trait, and n is the number of gene loci involved in the trait. In the model $\mathbf{A}$ and $\mathbf{a}$ can be assumed to be additive or there can be assumed to be complete or partial dominance. In the case of additivity the value of $\mathbf{Aa}$ is halfway between the values of $\mathbf{AA}$ and $\mathbf{aa}$; when there is complete dominance, the value of $\mathbf{Aa} = \mathbf{AA}$; when there is partial dominance the value of $\mathbf{Aa}$ is closer to $\mathbf{AA}$ than to $\mathbf{aa}$.) The correlation between half-siblings reared apart, r_{HSA}, (same father but different mothers, or same mother but different fathers) is

$$r_{HSA} = \frac{\tfrac{1}{4}V_A + \tfrac{1}{4}V_{AM} + <\tfrac{1}{16}V_{E_p}}{V_P} \qquad (A.15)$$

The correlation between one parent and one offspring who is reared in an environment which is not correlated with the parent's environment is:

$$r_{po} = \frac{\tfrac{1}{2}V_A + \tfrac{1}{2}V_{AM} + <\tfrac{1}{4}E_p}{V_P} \qquad (A.16)$$

The correlation between midparent (i.e., the average of both parents) and one offspring is:

$$r_{\bar{p}o} = \sqrt{r_{po}} \qquad (A.17)$$

The correlation between midparent and midoffspring (i.e., the average of all the offspring) is:

N

$$r_{\bar{p}\bar{o}} = \frac{V_A + V_{AM} + <\frac{1}{2}V_{Ep}}{V_P} \qquad (A.18)$$

The correlation $r_{\bar{p}\bar{o}}$ is equal to the heritability in the narrow sense, h_N^2, when the mean of the offspring is assumed to be the mean of all theoretically possible offspring of the parents, in other words, the mean of an infinite number of offspring. When the number of offspring is fewer than this, as of course must be the case in reality, then $r_{\bar{p}\bar{o}}$ underestimates h_N^2, as can be seen from the following relationship:

$$h_N^2 = \frac{r_{\bar{p}\bar{o}}}{\sqrt{\frac{1}{2}N/[1 + r_{oo}(N-1)]}} \qquad (A.19)$$

where
   N = number of offspring in each family
   r_{oo} = correlation among offspring.

As N increases, the denominator in Equation A.19 approaches 1 and so h_N^2 more closely approximates $r_{\bar{p}\bar{o}}$.

The variance components that various kinships have in common (and their complements, i.e., the components they do not have in common) are given in Table A.1.

The proportion of total variance attributable to various components are estimated from the differences between various kinship correlations which differ in one or more of the variance components they have in common.

For example, if we define broad heritability as $h^2 = V_G/V_P$, we can obtain an estimate of this from the correlation between monozygotic twins reared apart, r_{MZA} (Equation A.11). Another estimate can be obtained from the difference of $r_{MZT} - r_{DZT}$ (Equation A.10 minus Equation A.12), which leaves V_{G_B}/V_P; and under random mating V_{G_B} equals approximately $\frac{1}{2}V_G$, so $2(r_{MZT} - r_{DZT}) \simeq h^2$. If there is positive assortative mating, this value slightly underestimates the true value of h^2, since V_{G_B} is greater than $\frac{1}{2}V_G$ under positive assortative mating. (Assortative mating increases the proportion of V_{G_B} and decreases the proportion of V_{G_W}.)

A better formula for h^2 (in the broad sense) is:

$$h^2 = \frac{r_{MZT} - r_{DZT}}{\rho_{MZT} - \rho_{DZT}} \qquad (A.20)$$

where ρ is the theoretical genetic correlation, which for MZ twins

Table A.1 Variance components in various kinships

Relationship	Reared	Components* in Common				Components Not in Common					
		A	D	Ep	EBF	A	D	Ep	EBF	EWF	e
MZ Twins	Together	1	1	1	1	0	0	0	0	1	1
MZ Twins	Apart	1	1	1	0	0	0	0	1	1	1
DZ Twins (Sibs)	Together	$\frac{1}{2}$	$\frac{1}{4}$	$<\frac{1}{4}$	1	$\frac{1}{2}$	$\frac{3}{4}$	$>\frac{3}{4}$	0	1	1
DZ Twins (Sibs)	Apart	$\frac{1}{2}$	$\frac{1}{4}$	$<\frac{1}{4}$	0	$\frac{1}{2}$	$\frac{3}{4}$	$>\frac{3}{4}$	1	1	1
$\frac{1}{2}$ Sibs	Together	$\frac{1}{4}$	0	$<\frac{1}{16}$	1	$\frac{3}{4}$	1	$>\frac{15}{16}$	0	1	1
$\frac{1}{2}$ Sibs	Apart	$\frac{1}{4}$	0	$<\frac{1}{16}$	0	$\frac{3}{4}$	1	$>\frac{15}{16}$	1	1	1
Parent-Child	'Together'	$\frac{1}{2}$	0	$<\frac{1}{4}$	?>0	$\frac{1}{2}$	1	$>\frac{3}{4}$	?<1	1	1
Parent-Foster Child	'Together'	0	0	0	?>0	1	1	1	?<1	1	1
Unrelated Children	Together	0	0	0	1	1	1	1	0	1	1
Unrelated Children	Apart	0	0	0	0	1	1	1	0	1	1

* A = Additive   D = Dominance   Ep = Epistasis   EBF = Between-Families Environment

EWF = Within-Families Environment   e = Error

is 1 and for DZ twins (or full-sibs) is $\frac{1}{2}$ under random mating. Under assortative mating ρ_{DZ} will be greater than $\frac{1}{2}$. Theoretically, a simplified but close approximation to ρ_{DZ} under assortative mating is given by

$$\rho_{DZ} = \frac{1 + \rho_{pp}}{2 + \rho_{pp}} \qquad (A.21)$$

where ρ_{pp} is the genetic correlation between the parents. It can be estimated by $h_N^2 r_{pp}$, where h_N^2 is narrow heritability and r_{pp} is the phenotypic correlation between parents. A reasonable estimate of ρ_{DZ} based on obtained correlations between parental IQs is 0·55.

Other variance components can similarly be estimated from differences between kinship correlations. For example, the proportion of additive genetic variance, V_A (which includes V_{AM}), is clearly approximated by $r_{\bar{p}\bar{o}}$ if V_{E_p} is very small, as is usually the case. Also, if V_{E_p} is small, an estimate of the proportion of V_A is provided by the correlation of half-sibs reared apart, i.e., $V_A/V_P = 4r_{HSA}$. This is also an estimate of the narrow heritability, since $h_N^2 = V_A/V_P$.

The proportion of dominance variance, V_D, can be estimated from the difference between the correlations of full-sibs reared apart and twice the correlation of half-sibs reared apart, i.e., Equation A.13 (substituting Equation A.14 in the numerator) minus $2 \times$ Equation A.15 $\simeq V_D/V_P$. This assumes the same degree of assortative mating for parents of full-sibs and parents of half-sibs.

The proportion of total environmental variance (including $G \times E$ interaction and CovGE) is estimated by $r_{tt} - r_{MZA}$, where r_{tt} is the test reliability (i.e., proportion of total variance minus error variance). The proportion of between-families environmental variance, V_{E_B}, plus interaction, V_{GE}, and covariance, CovGE, are estimated by $r_{MZT} - r_{MZA}$ (i.e., Equation A.10 $-$ Equation A.11). The proportion of within-families environmental variance is, of course, the total non-error variance minus the total between-families genetic and environmental variance, or $r_{tt} - r_{MZT} = V_{E_W}/V_P$.

Another way of estimating the between-families environmental variance, V_{E_B}, is from the correlation between genetically unrelated children reared together, r_{UT}:

$$r_{UT} = \frac{V_{E_B}}{V_P} \qquad (A.22)$$

If there has been *selective* placement of genetically unrelated children reared together in the same home, r_{UT} would be increased by common genotypic variance and to that extent would over-estimate the proportion of between-families environmental variance.

The presence of statistical interaction between genotypes and environments, which makes for V_{GE}, can be determined by a method proposed by Jinks and Fulker (1970, pp. 314-15), based on MZ twins reared apart. If X_1 and X_2 are the scores of the two twins in each pair, we obtain the mean score for each pair $[\frac{1}{2}(X_1 + X_2)]$ and the absolute difference between the twins in each pair $[|X_1 - X_2|]$. If the rectilinear or curvilinear correlation between the means and the differences is significantly greater than zero, one may infer a significant $G \times E$ interaction. (This method has revealed no evidence of $G \times E$ interaction in any of the studies of IQ of MZ twins reared apart.)

Readers who wish to delve further into the technical aspects of heritability and quantitative genetic analysis are referred to Burt and Howard (1956), Falconer (1960), DeFries (1967), Roberts (1967), Eaves (1969), Jinks and Fulker (1970), Mather and Jinks (1971) and Burt (1972).

References

AINSWORTH, M. D. S. (1963) The development of infant-mother interaction among the Ganda. In B. M. FOSS (ed.), *Determinants of Infant Behaviour*, Vol. 2. London: Methuen.

AINSWORTH, M. D. S. (1967) *Infancy in Uganda*. Baltimore: Johns Hopkins Press.

AMANTE, D., MARGULES, P. H., HARTMAN, DONNA M., STOREY, DOLORES B. & LEWIS, J. W. (1970) The epidemiological distribution of CNS dysfunction. *Journal of Social Issues*, **26**, 105-36.

AMES, LOUISE B. & ILG, FRANCES L. (1967) Search for children showing academic promise in a predominantly Negro school. *Journal of Genetic Psychology*, **110**, 217-31.

ANASTASI, ANNE (1958) Heredity, environment, and the question 'How?' *Psychological Review*, **65**, 197-208.

ANDERSON, J. G. & JOHNSON, W. H. (1971) Stability and change among three generations of Mexican-Americans: Factors affecting achievement. *American Educational Research Journal*, **8**, 285-309.

ANDOR, L. E. (1966) *Aptitudes and Abilities of the Black Man in sub-Saharan Africa 1784-1963: An Annotated Bibliography*. Johannesburg: National Institute for Personnel Research.

BAJEMA, C. J. (1971) The genetic implications of population control. *BioScience*, **21**, 71-5.

BARATZ, JOAN C. (1970) Teaching reading in an urban Negro school system. In F. WILLIAMS (ed.), *Language and Poverty: Perspectives on a Theme*. Chicago: Markham. Pp. 11-24.

BARATZ, S. S. & BARATZ, JOAN C. (1970) Early childhood intervention: The social science based on institutional racism. *Harvard Educational Review*, **40**, 29-50.

BAYLEY, NANCY (1965) Comparisons of mental and motor test scores for ages 1-15 months by sex, birth order, race, geographical location, and education of parents. *Child Development*, **36**, 379-411.

BAYLEY, NANCY (1966) Learning in adulthood: The role of intelligence. In H. J. KLAUSMEIER & C. W. HARRIS (eds.), *Analyses of Concept Learning*. New York: Academic Press. Pp. 117-38.

BEGGS, D. L. & HIERONYMUS, A. N. (1968) Uniformity of growth in the basic skills throughout the school year and during the summer. *Journal of Educational Measurement*, **5**, 91-7.

BEREITER, C. (1970) Genetics and educability: Educational implications of the Jensen debate. In J. HELLMUTH (ed.), *Disadvantaged Child*. Vol. 3, *Compensatory Education: A National Debate*. New York: Brunner-Mazel. Pp. 279-99.

BERRY, J. W. (1966) Temne and Eskimo perceptual skills. *International Journal of Psychology*, **1**, 207-22.

BIESHEUVEL, S. (1972) An examination of Jensen's theory concerning educability, heritability and population differences. *Psychologia Africana*, **14**, 87-94.

BIRCH, H. G. (1968) Problems inherent in population studies of nutrition and mental subnormality. In G. A. JERVIS (ed.), *Expanding Concepts in Mental Retardation*. Springfield, Ill.: Charles C. Thomas.

BIRCH, H. G., RICHARDSON, S. A., BAIRD, S. D., HOROBIN, G. & ILLSLEY, R. (1970) *Mental Subnormality in the Community: A Clinical and Epidemiologic Study*. Baltimore: Williams & Wilkins Co.

BLALOCK, H. M., JR. (1960) *Social Statistics*. New York: McGraw-Hill.

BLOOM, B. S. (1964) *Stability and Change in Human Characteristics*. New York: Wiley.

BLOOM, B. S. (1969) Letter to the editor. *Harvard Educational Review*, **39**, 419-21.

BODMER, W. F. & CAVALLI-SFORZA, L. L. (1970) Intelligence and race. *Scientific American*, **223**, No. 4, 19-29.

BOSCO, J. J. (1970) Social class and the processing of visual information. Final Report, Project No. 9-E-041, Contract No. OEG-5-9-325041-0034(010). Office of Education, U.S. Dept. of Health, Education and Welfare. May.

BOWER, T. G. R. (1971) Early learning and behaviour. The biology of growth—1. *Times Literary Supplement*, 7 May, pp. 523-4.

BOYER, W. H. & WALSH, P. (1968) Are children born unequal? *Saturday Review*, 19 October, pp. 61-9.

BRACHT, G. H. (1970) Experimental factors related to aptitude treatment interactions. *Review of Educational Research*, **40**, 627-45.

BRACHT, G. H. & HOPKINS, K. D. (1972) Stability of educational achievement. In G. H. BRACHT, K. D. HOPKINS & J. C. STANLEY (eds.), *Perspectives in Educational and Psychological Measurement*. Englewood Cliffs, N.J.: Prentice-Hall. Pp. 254-8.

BRESLER, J. (1970) Outcrossings in Caucasians and fetal loss. *Social Biology*, **17**, 17-25.

BRONFENBRENNER, U. (1967) The psychological costs of quality and equality in education. *Child Development*, **38**, 909-25.

BROWN, R. (1965) *Social Psychology*. New York: Free Press.

BUCK, CAROL (1970) Examples of current studies of reproductive casualty. In H. C. HAYWOOD (ed.), *Social-cultural Aspects of Mental Retardation*. New York: Appleton-Century-Crofts.

BULMER, M. G. (1970) *The Biology of Twinning in Man*. Oxford: Clarendon Press.

BURGESS, JOHANNA & JAHODA, MARIE (1970) The interpretation of certain data in 'How Much Can We Boost IQ Score and Scholastic Achievement?', *Bulletin of the British Psychological Society*, **23**, 224-5.

BURKS, B. S. (1928) The relative influence of nature and nurture upon mental development: A comparative study of foster parent – foster child resemblance and true parent – true child resemblance. *Yearbook of the National Society for the Study of Education*, **27** (I), 219-316.

BURT, C. (1943) Ability and income. *British Journal of Educational Psychology*, **13**, 83-98.

BURT, C. (1959) Class differences in general intelligence: III. *British Journal of Statistical Psychology*, **12**, 15-33.

BURT, C. (1961a) The gifted child. *British Journal of Statistical Psychology*, **14**, 123-39.

BURT, C. (1961b) Intelligence and social mobility. *British Journal of Statistical Psychology*, **14**, 3-24.

BURT, C. (1963) Is intelligence distributed normally? *British Journal of Statistical Psychology*, **16**, 175-90.

BURT, C. (1966) The genetic determination of differences in intelligence: A study of monozygotic twins reared together and apart. *British Journal of Psychology*, **57**, 137-53.

BURT, C. (1969) Intelligence and heredity: Some common misconceptions. *Irish Journal of Education*, **3**, 75-94.

BURT, C. (1971) Quantitative genetics in psychology. *British Journal of Mathematical and Statistical Psychology*, **24**, 1-21.

BURT, C. & HOWARD, M. (1956) The multifactorial theory of inheritance and its application to intelligence. *British Journal of Statistical Psychology*, **9**, 95-131.

BURT, C. & WILLIAMS, E. L. (1962) The influence of motivation on the results of intelligence tests. *British Journal of Statistical Psychology*, **15**, 127-36.

BUTCHER, H. J. (1968) *Human Intelligence: Its Nature and Assessment*. London: Methuen.

CARROLL, J. B. (1963) A model of school learning. *Teachers' College Record*, **64**, 723-33.

CARTER, J., GILMER, BARBARA, VANDERZWAAG, R. & MASSEY, KATHERINE (1971) Health and nutrition in disadvantaged children and their relationship with intellectual development. *Collaborative Research Report*. Nashville, Tenn.: Vanderbilt School of Medicine.

CATTELL, R. B. (1950) *Personality*. New York: McGraw-Hill.

CATTELL, R. B. (1971) *Abilities: Their Structure, Growth, and Action*. Boston: Houghton-Mifflin.

CLAIBORN, W. L. (1969) Expectancy effects in the classroom: A failure to replicate. *Journal of Educational Psychology*, **60**, 377-83.

CLARK, K. (1968) The cult of cultural deprivation: A complex social phenomenon. In G. NATCHEZ (ed.), *Children with Reading Problems*. New York: Basic Books.

COLEMAN, J. S. *et al.* (1966) *Equality of Educational Opportunity*. Washington, D.C.: U.S. Office of Education.

COON, C. S. (1962) *The Origin of Races*. New York: Knopf.

COOPER, R. & ZUBEK, J. (1958) Effects of enriched and restricted early environments on the learning ability of bright and dull rats. *Canadian Journal of Psychology*, **12**, 159-64.

Council of the Society for the Psychological Study of Social Issues (SPSSI) (1969) Statement by SPSSI on current IQ controversy: Heredity versus environment. *American Psychologist*, **24**, 1039-40.

CRAVIOTO, J. (1966) Malnutrition and behavioral development in the preschool child. *Pre-School Child Malnutrition*. National Health Science, Public. No. 1282.

CRAVIOTO, J. (1968) Nutritional deficiencies and mental performance in childhood. In GLASS, D. C. (ed.), *Environmental Influences*. New York: Rockefeller University Press.

CRAVIOTO, J. & DELICARDIE, ELSA R. (1970) Mental performance in school age children: Findings after recovery from early severe malnutrition. *American Journal of Diseases of Children*, **120**, 404-10.

CRONBACH, L. J. (1969) Heredity, environment, and educational policy. *Harvard Educational Review*, **39**, 338-47.

CRONBACH, L. J. & SNOW, R. E. (March 1969) *Final Report*: Individual differences in learning ability as a function of instructional variables. Stanford, Calif.: Stanford U.P.

CROW, J. F. (1969) Genetic theories and influences: Comments on the value of diversity. *Harvard Educational Review*, **39**, 301-9.

CROW, J. F. (1970) Do genetic factors contribute to poverty? In V. L. ALLEN (ed.), *Psychological Factor in Poverty*. Chicago: Markham. Pp. 147-60.

CROW, J. F. & FELSENSTEIN, J. (1968) The effect of assortative mating on the genetic composition of a population. *Eugenics Quarterly*, **15**, 85-97.

o

CURTI, M., MARSHALL, F. B., STEGGERDA, M. & HENDERSON, E. M. (1935) The Gesell schedules applied to one-, two-, and three-year-old Negro children of Jamaica, B.W.J. *Journal of Comparative Physiological Psychology*, **20**, 125-56.

DEFRIES, J. C. (1967) Quantitative genetics and behavior: Overview and perspective. In J. HIRSCH (ed.), *Behavior-Genetic Analysis*. New York: McGraw-Hill. Pp. 322-39.

DEFRIES, J. C. (*in press*) Quantitative aspects of genetics and environment in the determination of behavior. In E. CASPARI (ed.), *Future Directions of Behavior Genetics*.

DELEMOS, MARION M. (1969) The development of conservation in aboriginal children. *International Journal of Psychology*, **4**, 255-69.

DEUTSCH, CYNTHIA & DEUTSCH, M. (1968) Theory of early childhood environment programs. In R. HESS and B. BEAR (eds.), *Early Education: Current Theory, Research Action*. Chicago: Aldine Publishing Co.

DEUTSCH, M. (1969) Happenings on the way back to the forum: Social science, IQ, and race differences revisited. *Harvard Educational Review*, **39**, 523-57.

DOBBING, J. (1970) Undernutrition and the developing brain: The relevance of animal models to the human problems. *American Journal of Diseases of Children*, **120**, 411-15.

DREEBEN, R. (1969) Comments on Jensen. *Administrator's Notebook*, Midwest Administration Center, University of Chicago, 18, no. 3.

DREGER, R. M. & MILLER, K. S. (1960) Comparative psychological studies of Negroes and whites in the United States. *Psychological Bulletin*, **57**, 361-402.

DREGER, R. M. & MILLER, K. S. (1968) Comparative psychological studies of Negroes and whites in the United States: 1959-1965. *Psychological Bulletin Monograph Supplement*, **70**, No. 3, Part 2.

DUNCAN, O. D. (1968) Ability and achievement. *Eugenics Quarterly*, **15**, 1-11.

DUNCAN, O. D. (1969) Inequality and opportunity. Presidential address at the annual meeting of the Population Association of America, Atlantic City, N.J., 11 April.

Durham Education Improvement Program, 1966-1967a.

Durham Education Improvement Program, Research, 1966-1967b.

EAVES, L. J. (1969) The genetic analysis of continuous variation: A comparison of experimental designs applicable to human data. *British Journal of Mathematical and Statistical Psychology*, **22**, 131-47.

ECKLAND, B. K. (1967) Genetics and sociology: A reconsideration. *American Sociological Review*, **32**, 173-94.

EICHENWALD, H. F. & FRY, PEGGY C. (1969) Nutrition and learning. *Science*, **163**, 644-8.

EINHORN, H. J. & BASS, A. R. (1971) Methodological considerations relevant to discrimination in employment testing. *Psychological Bulletin*, **75**, 261-9.

EISENBERG, L., BERLIN, C., DILL, ANNE & SHELDON, F. (1968) Class and race effects on the intelligibility of monosyllables. *Child Development*, **39**, 1077-89.

ELASHOFF, JANET D. & SNOW, R. E. (1971) *'Pygmalion' Reconsidered*. Worthington, Ohio: Charles A. Jones Publishing Co.

ELSTER, R. S. & DUNNETTE, M. D. (1971) The robustness of Tilton's measure of overlap. *Educational and Psychological Management*, **31**, 685-97.

ENTWISLE, DORIS R. (1970) Semantic systems of children: Some assessments of social class and ethnic differences. In F. WILLIAMS (ed.), *Language and Poverty: Perspectives on a Theme*. Chicago: Markham Publishing Co. Pp. 123-39.

EVANS, JUDITH L. (1970) *Children in Africa: A Review of Psychological Research*. New York: Teachers' College Press, Columbia University.

EYSENCK, H. J. (1967) Intelligence assessment: A theoretical and experimental approach. *British Journal of Educational Psychology*, **37**, 81-98.

EYSENCK, H. J. (1971) *Race, Intelligence, and Education*. London: Temple Smith. (American edition titled: *The IQ Argument*. Freeport, N.Y.: Library Press, 1971.)

FALADÉ, S. (1955) *Contribution à une étude sur le dévéloppement de l'enfant d'Afrique noire*. Paris: Foulon.

FALADÉ, S. (1960) Le développement psycho-moteur de l'enfant africain du Sénégal. *Concours médical*, **82**, 1005-13.

FALCONER, D. S. (1960) *An Introduction to Quantitative Genetics*. New York: Ronald Press.

FALMAGNE, J. CE (1959) Étude de certains aspects du développement du nourrisson de 0 à 6 mois. Unpublished thesis. Brussels: Université Libre de Bruxelles.

FLAVELL, J. (1963) *The Developmental Psychology of Jean Piaget*. New York: Van Nostrand.

FLEMING, ELYSE S. & ANTTONEN, R. G. (1971) Teacher expectancy or my fair lady. *American Educational Research Journal*, **8**, 241-52.

FOX, W. L. & TAYLOR, J. E. (1967) Adaptation of training to individual differences. Paper presented to the North Atlantic Treaty Organization Conference on 'Manpower Research in the Defence Context', 14-18 August 1967, London. (Hum RRO Division, No. 3, Presidio of Monterey, California.)

FREEDMAN, D. G. & FREEDMAN, NINA CHINN (1969) Behavioral differences between Chinese-American and European-American newborns. *Nature*, **224**, 1227.

382   *Educability and Group Differences*

FREEMAN, H. E., ROSS, J. M., ARMOR, D. & PETTIGREW, T. F. (1966) Color gradation and attitudes among middle income Negroes. *American Sociological Review*, **31**, 365-74.

FURFEY, P. H. & HARTE, T. J. (1970) Reducing the effects of cultural deprivation. *Mental Health Program Reports*-**4.** U.S. Dept. of Health, Education and Welfare. January.

FURTH, H. G. (1964) Research with the deaf: Implications for language and cognition. *Psychological Bulletin*, **62**, 145-64.

GALTON, F. (1870) *Hereditary Genius* (2nd ed.). New York: Appleton-Century-Crofts.

GAUDIA, G. (1972) Race, social class, and age of achievement of conservation on Piaget's tasks. *Developmental Psychology*, **6**, 158-65.

GÉBER, M. (1956) Développement psycho-moteur de l'enfant africain. *Courrier*, **6**, 17-29.

GÉBER, M. (1958a) The psychomotor development of African children in the first year, and the influence of maternal behavior. *Journal of Social Psychology*, **47**, 185-95.

GÉBER, M. (1958b) L'enfant africain occidentalisé et de niveau social supérieur en Ouganda. *Courrier*, **8**, 517-23.

GÉBER, M. (1960) Problèmes posés par le développement du jeune enfant africain en fonction de son milieu social. *Travail Humain,* **1-2**, 97-111.

GÉBER, M. (1962) Longitudinal study and psychomotor development among Baganda children. *Proceedings, Fourteenth International Congress of Applied Psychology*, Vol. 3. Munsgaard: Copenhagen.

GÉBER, M. & DEAN, R. F. A. (1957a) The state of development of newborn African children. *Lancet*, 1216-19.

GÉBER, M. & DEAN, R. F. A. (1957b) Gesell tests on African children. *Pediatrics*, **20**, 1055-65.

GÉBER, M. & DEAN, R. F. A. (1958) Psychomotor development in African children: the effects of social class and the need for improved tests. *Bulletin of the World Health Organization*, **18**, 471-6.

GÉBER, M. & DEAN, R. F. A. (1964) Le développement psycho-moteur et somatique des jeunes enfants africains en Ouganda. *Courrier*, **15**, 425-37.

GÉBER, M. & DEAN, R. F. A. (1966) Precocious development in newborn African infants. In Y. BRACKBILL & G. G. THOMPSON (eds.), *Readings in Infancy and Childhood*. New York: Free Press.

GHISELLI, E. E. (1963) Managerial talent. *American Psychologist*, **18**, 631-42.

GILLILAND, A. R. (1951) Socioeconomic status and race as factors in infant intelligence test scores. *Child Development*, **22**, 271-3.

GITTELL, MARILYN (1971) *New York City School Fact Book*. New York: Institute for Community Studies, Queens College, Flushing, Long Island.

GLASS, B. & LI, C. E. (1953) The dynamics of racial intermixture: An analysis based on the American Negro. *American Journal of Human Genetics*, **5**, 1-20.

GLASMAN, LYNETTE D. (1968) A social-class comparison of conceptual processes in children's free recall. Unpublished doctoral dissertation, University of California.

GOLDHAMMER, H. (1971) Letters. *Science*, **172**, 10.

GORDON, E. W. (1970) Problems in the determination of educability in populations with differential characteristics. In J. HELLMUTH (ed.), *Disadvantaged Child*, Vol. 3. *Compensatory Education: A National Debate*. New York: Brunner-Mazel. Pp. 249-67.

GOTTESMAN, I. I. (1968) Biogenetics of race and class. In M. DEUTSCH, I. KATZ & A. R. JENSEN (eds.), *Social Class, Race, and Psychological Development*. New York: Holt, Rinehart & Winston. Pp. 11-51.

GOUGH, H. G. (1949) A short social status inventory. *Journal of Educational Psychology*, **40**, 52-6.

GOUGH, H. G. (1953) A nonintellectual intelligence test. *Journal of Consulting Psychology*, **17**, 242-6.

GOUGH, H. G. (1971) A cluster analysis of Home Index status items. *Psychological Reports*, **28**, 923-9.

GRAVES, W. L., FREEMAN, M. G. & THOMPSON, J. D. (1970) Culturally-related reproductive factors in mental retardation. In H. C. HAYWOOD (ed.), *Social-Cultural Aspects of Mental Retardation*. New York: Appleton-Century-Crofts.

GROSS, M. (1967) *Learning Readiness in Two Jewish Groups*. New York: Center for Urban Education.

GUINCE, V. F. (1970) Statement on lead poisoning. Presented to Subcommittee on Housing of the House Committee on Banking and Currency, 22 July.

GUTTMAN, L. (1954) The principal components of scalable attitudes. In P. F. LAZARSFELD (ed.), *Mathematical Thinking in the Social Sciences*. Glencoe, Ill.: Free Press. Pp. 216-57.

HALDANE, J. B. S. (1965) The implications of genetics for human society. In S. J. GEERTZ (ed.), *Genetics Today: Proceedings of the XIth International Congress of Genetics*. The Hague, Netherlands, September 1963. New York: Pergamon Press. Pp. xcii-xciii.

HARDY, JANET B. (1965) Perinatal factors and intelligence. In SONIA F. OSLER & R.E. COOKE (eds.), *The Biological Basis of Mental Retardation*. Baltimore, Md.: The Johns Hopkins Press. Pp. 35-60.

HARMS, L. S. (1961) Listener comprehension of speakers of three status groups. *Language and Speech*, **4**, 109-12.

HARRELL, R. F., WOODYARD, E. & GATES, A. I. (1955) *The Effects of Mothers' Diets on the Intelligence of Offspring*. New York: Bureau of Publications, Teachers' College.

HARRIS, A. J. & LOVINGER, R. J. (1968) Longitudinal measures of the intelligence of disadvantaged Negro adolescents. *School Review*, **76**, 60-6.

HARRISON, G. A. (1957) The measurement and inheritance of skin color in men. *Eugenics Review*, **49**, 73-6.

HARRISON, G. A. & OWEN, J. J. T. (1956) The application of spectro-photometry to the study of skin color inheritance. *Acta Genetics*, **4**, 480-5.

HARRISON, G. A. & OWEN, J. J. T. (1964) Studies on the inheritance of human skin color. *Annals of Human Genetics*, **28**, 27-37.

HARRISON, G. A., OWEN, J. J. T., DA ROCHA, F. J. & SALZANO, F. M. (1967) Skin color in Southern Brazilian populations. *Human Biology*, **39**, 21-31.

HARRISON, G. A., WEINER, J. S., TANNER, J. M. & BARNICAT, N. A. (1964) *Human Biology: An Introduction to Human Evolution, Varia-tion, and Growth*. London: Oxford Univ. Press.

HASEMAN, J. K. & ELSTON, R. C. (1970) The estimation of genetic variance from twin data. *Behavior Genetics*, **1**, 11-19.

HAVIGHURST, R. J. (1970) Minority subcultures and the law of effect. *American Psychologist*, **25**, 313-22.

HERSKOVITS, M. J. (1926) On the relation between Negro-white mixture and standing in intelligence tests. *Pedagogical Seminary*, **33**, 30-42.

HESTON, L. L. (1966) Psychiatric disorders in foster home reared children of schizophrenic mothers. *British Journal of Psychiatry*, **112**, 819-25.

HIRSCH, J. (1970) Behavior-genetic analysis and its biosocial conse-quences. *Seminars in Psychiatry*, **2**, 89-105.

HOLLAND, H. C. (1963) 'Visual masking' and the effect of stimulant and depressant drugs. In H. J. EYSENCK (ed.), *Experiments with Drugs*. New York: Pergamon.

HOLZINGER, K. J. (1929) The relative effect of nature and nurture influences on twin differences. *Journal of Educational Psychology*, **20**, 241-8.

HONZIK, M. P. (1957) Developmental studies of parent-child resem-blance in intelligence. *Child Development*, **28**, 215-28.

HONZIK, M. P., HUTCHINGS, J. J. & BURNIP, S. R. (1965) Birth record assessments and test performance at eight months. *American Journal of Diseases of Children*, **109**, 416-26.

HONZIK, M. P., MACFARLANE, JEAN W. & ALLEN, L. (1948) The stability of mental test performance between two and eighteen years. *Journal of Experimental Education*, **17**, 309-24.

HOUSTON, SUSAN H. (1970) A re-examination of some assumptions about the language of the disadvantaged child. *Child Development*, **41**, 947-63.

HUSÉN, T. (1963) Intra-pair similarities in the school achievements of twins. *Scandinavian Journal of Psychology*, **4**, 108-14.

INGLE, D. J. (1967) Editorial: The need to study biological differences among racial groups: Moral issues. *Perspectives in Biology and Medicine*, **10**, 497-9.

JACOBZINER, H. (1966) Lead poisoning in childhood epidemiology, manifestations and prevention. *Clinical Pediatrics*, **5**, 277.

JENCKS, C. (1969) Intelligence and race: What color is IQ? *New Republic*, 13 September, Nos. 10-11, Issues 2854-5, pp. 25-9.

JENSEN, A. R. (1967) Estimation of the limits of heritability of traits by comparison of monozygotic and dizygotic twins. *Proceedings of the National Academy of Sciences*, **58**, 149-56.

JENSEN, A. R. (1968a) Social class, race, and genetics: Implications for education. *American Educational Research Journal*, **5**, 1-42.

JENSEN, A. R. (1968b) Patterns of mental ability and socioeconomic status. *Proceedings of the National Academy of Sciences*, **60**, 1330-7.

JENSEN, A. R. (1968c) Another look at culture-fair tests. In *Western Regional Conference on Testing Problems, Proceedings for 1968*, 'Measurement for Educational Planning'. Berkeley, Calif.: Educational Testing Service, Western Office. Pp. 50-104.

JENSEN, A. R. (1969a) How much can we boost IQ and scholastic achievement? *Harvard Educational Review*, **39**, 1-123.

JENSEN, A. R. (1969b) Reducing the heredity-environment uncertainty. *Harvard Educational Review*, **39**, 449-83.

JENSEN, A. R. (1969c) Criticism or propaganda? *American Psychologist*, **24**, 1040-1.

JENSEN, A. R. (1969d) *Understanding Readiness*. Urbana, Illinois: Univ. of Illinois Press.

JENSEN, A. R. (1970a) IQs of identical twins reared apart. *Behavior Genetics*, **1**, 133-48.

JENSEN, A. R. (1970b) Hierarchical theories of mental ability. In B. DOCKRELL (ed.), *On Intelligence*. Toronto: Ontario Institute for Studies in Education, pp. 119-90 (London, Methuen, 1970).

JENSEN, A. R. (1970c) A theory of primary and secondary familial mental retardation. In N. R. ELLIS (ed.), *International Review of Mental Retardation*, Vol. 4. New York: Academic Press. Pp. 33-105.

JENSEN, A. R. (1970d) Race and the genetics of intelligence: A reply to Lewontin. *Bulletin of the Atomic Scientists*, **26**, 17-23.

JENSEN, A. R. (1971a) Do schools cheat minority children? *Educational Research*, **14**, 3-28.

JENSEN, A. R. (1971b) The race × sex × ability interaction. In R. CANCRO (ed.), *Contributions to Intelligence*. New York: Grune & Stratton.

JENSEN, A. R. (1971c) The role of verbal mediation in mental development. *Journal of Genetic Psychology*, **118**, 39-70.

JENSEN, A. R. (1971d) Selection of minorities in higher education. *Toledo Law Review*, Spring-Summer, Nos. 2 & 3, 403-57.

JENSEN, A. R. (1972) *Genetics and Education*. London: Methuen (New York: Harper & Row).

JENSEN, A. R. & ROHWER, W. D., JR. (1970) *Experimental Analysis of Learning Abilities in Culturally Disadvantaged Children*. Final report on OEO Project No. 2404, U.S. Office of Economic Opportunity.

JINKS, J. L. & FULKER, D. W. (1970) Comparison of the biometrical, genetical, MAVA, and classical approaches to the analysis of human behavior. *Psychological Bulletin*, **73**, 311-49.

JONES, H. E. (1928) A first study of parent-child resemblances in intelligence. *Yearbook of the National Soc. Stud. Educ.*, **27** (I), 61-72.

JUEL-NIELSEN, N. (1965) Individual and environment: a psychiatric-psychological investigation of monozygous twins reared apart. *Acta Psychiatrica et Neurologica Scandinavica* (Monogr. Suppl. **183**).

KAGAN, J. S. (1969) Inadequate evidence and illogical conclusions. *Harvard Educational Review*, **39**, 274-7.

KÁRPINOS, B. D. (1962) *Qualification of American Youths for Military Service*. Washington, D.C.: Medical Statistics Division, Office of the Surgeon General, Department of the Army.

KATES, SOLIS L., KATES, W. W. & MICHAEL, J. (1962) Cognitive processes in deaf and hearing adolescents and adults. *Psychological Monographs*, **76**, whole No. 551.

KATZ, I. (1964) Review of evidence relating to effects of desegregation on the intelligence performance of Negroes. *American Psychologist*, **19**, 381-99.

KATZ, I. (1968) Factors influencing Negro performance in the desegregated school. In M. DEUTSCH, I. KATZ & A. R. JENSEN (eds.), *Social Class, Race, and Psychological Development*. New York: Holt, Rinehart & Winston. Pp. 254-89.

KENNEDY, W. A., VAN DE REIT, V. & WHITE, J. C., JR. (1963) A normative sample of intelligence and achievement of Negro elementary school children in the Southeastern United States. *Monographs of the Society for Research on Child Development*, **28**, No. 6.

KILBRIDE, J. E. (1969) The motor development of rural Ugandan infants. Unpublished Master's dissertation, Pennsylvania State University.

KLINEBERG, O. (1928) An experimental study of speed and other factors in 'racial' differences. *Archives of Psychology*, **15**, No. 93, 111.

KLINEBERG, O. (1935) *Negro Intelligence and Selective Migration*. New York: Columbia University Press.

KLINEBERG, O. (ed.) (1944) *Characteristics of the American Negro.* New York: Harper.

KLINEBERG, O. (1956) Race and psychology. In *The Race Question in Modern Science*, UNESCO.

KLINEBERG, O. (1963) Negro-white differences in intelligence test performance: A new look at an old problem. *American Psychologist*, **18**, 198-203.

KNOBLOCH, HILDA & PASAMANICK, B. (1953) Further observations on the behavioral development of Negro children. *Journal of Genetic Psychology*, **83**, 137-57.

KNOBLOCH, HILDA & PASAMANICK, B. (1958) The relationship of race and socioeconomic status to the development of motor behavior patterns in infancy. *Psychiatric Research Reports*, **10**, 123-33.

KNOBLOCH, HILDA & PASAMANICK, B. (1966) Prospective studies on the epidemiology of reproductive casualty: Methods, findings, and some implications. *Merrill-Palmer Quarterly of Behavior and Development*, **12**, 27-43.

KOHLBERG, L. (1968) Early education: A cognitive-developmental view. *Child Development*, **39**, 1013-62.

KRAUSS, R. M. & ROTTER, G. S. (1968) Communication abilities of children as a function of status and age. *Merrill-Palmer Quarterly of Behavior and Development*, **14**, 161-73.

KUTTNER, R. E. (1968) Use of accentuated environmental inequalities in research on racial differences. *Mankind Quarterly*, **8**, 147-60.

LANGTON, E. A. C. (1934-5) Some observations of infants and young persons in Bunyoro, Uganda. *East African Medical Journal*, **11**, 316-23.

LAUGHLIN, W. S. (1966) Race: A population concept. *Eugenics Quarterly*, **13**, 326-40.

LEAHY, ALICE M. (1935) Nature-nurture and intelligence. *Genetic Psychology Monographs*, **17**, 241-305.

LEDERBERG, J. (1969) Racial alienation and intelligence. *Harvard Educational Review*, **39**, 611-15.

LENNEBERG, E. H. (1967) *Biological Foundations of Language.* New York: Wiley.

LENNEBERG, E. H. (1969) On explaining language. *Science*, **164**, 635-43.

LESSER, G. S., FIFER, G. & CLARK, D. H. (1965) Mental abilities of children from different social-class and cultural groups. *Monographs of the Society for Research in Child Development*, **30**, No. 4.

LEWONTIN, R. C. (1970a) Race and intelligence. *Bulletin of the Atomic Scientists*, **26**, No. 3, 2-8.

LEWONTIN, R. C. (1970b) Further remarks on race and the genetics of intelligence. *Bulletin of the Atomic Scientists*, **26**, No. 5, 23-5.

O*

LI, C. C. A tale of two thermos bottles: Properties of a genetic model for human intelligence. In R. CANCRO (ed.), *Intelligence: Genetic and Environmental Influences*. New York: Grune & Stratton. Pp. 161-81.

LIDDICOAT, R. (1969) Development of Bantu children. *Developmental Medicine and Child Neurology*, **11**, 821.

LIDDICOAT, R. and KOZA, C. (1963) Language development in African infants. *Psychologia Africana*, **10**, 108-16.

LIGHT, R. J. & SMITH, P. V. (1969) Social allocation models of intelligence: A methodological inquiry. *Harvard Educational Review*, **39**, 484-510.

LIGHT, R. J. & SMITH, P. V. (1971) Statistical issues in social allocation models of intelligence: A review and a response. *Review of Educational Research*, **41**, 351-67.

LUSH, J. L. (1968) Genetic unknowns and animal breeding a century after Mendel. *Transactions of the Kansas Academy of Sciences*, **71**, 309-14.

MACARTHUR, R. S. (1968) Some differential abilities of northern Canadian native youth. *International Journal of Psychology*, **3**, 43-51.

MACARTHUR, R. S. (1969) Some cognitive abilities of Eskimo, white and Indian-Metis pupils aged 9 to 12 years. *Canadian Journal of Behavioral Sciences*, **1**, 50-9.

MACARTHUR, R. S. & ELLEY, W. B. (1963) The reduction of socio-economic bias in intelligence testing. *British Journal of Educational Psychology*, **33**, 107-19.

MCCARTHY, DOROTHEA (1946) Language development in children. In L. CARMICHAEL (ed.), *Manual of Child Psychology*. New York: Wiley. Pp. 476-581.

MCCALL, R. B. (1970) Intelligence quotient pattern over age: Comparisons among siblings and parent-child pairs. *Science*, **170**, 644-8.

MCGURK, F. C. J. (1953a) On white and Negro test performance and socioeconomic factors. *Journal of Abnormal and Social Psychology*, **48**, 448-50.

MCGURK, F. C. J. (1953b) Socioeconomic status and culturally weighted test scores of Negro subjects. *Journal of Applied Psychology*, **37**, 276-7.

MCGURK, F. C. J. (1967) The culture hypothesis and psychological tests. In R. E. KUTTNER (ed.), *Race and Modern Science*. New York: Social Science Press. Pp. 367-81.

MCKEOWN, T. & RECORD, R. G. (1971) Early environmental influences on the development of intelligence. *British Medical Bulletin*, **27**, 48-51.

MCNEMAR, Q. (1933) Twin resemblances in motor skills, and the effect of practice thereon. *Journal of Genetic Psychology*, **42**, 70-97.

MCNEMAR, Q. (1940) A critical examination of the University of Iowa studies of environmental influence upon the IQ. *Psychological Bulletin*, **37**, 63-92.

MCNEMAR, Q. (1964) Lost: Our intelligence? Why? *American Psychologist*, **19**, 871-82.

MARTIN, R. & SALLER, K. (1959) *Lehrbuch der Anthropologie*, Vol. II. Stuttgart: Gustav Fischer.

MASSÉ, G. (1969) *Croissance et développement de l'enfant en Dakar.* Paris: Centre Internationale de l'Enfance.

MATHER, K. & JINKS, J. L. (1971) *Biometrical Genetics*, 2nd ed. London: Chapman & Hall.

MECHANIC, D. (1968) *Medical Sociology*. New York: The Free Press.

MILLER, J. O. & PHILLIPS, J. (1966) A preliminary evaluation of the Head Start and other metropolitan Nashville kindergartens. Unpublished manuscript, Nashville, Tenn., Demonstration and Research Center for Early Education, George Peabody College for Teachers.

MOREIGNE, F. & SENECAL, J. (1962) Résultat d'un groupe d'enfants africains au Terman-Merrill. *Revue de psychologie appliquée*, **12**, 15-32.

NAEYE, R. L., DIENER, M. M., DELLINGER, W. S. & BLANC, W. A. (1969) Urban poverty: Effects on prenatal nutrition. *Science*, **166**, 1026.

Nature (1970) Editorial: Fear of enlightenment. *Nature*, **228**, 1013-14.

NAYLOR, A. F. & MYRIANTHOPOULOS, N. C. (1967) The relation of ethnic and selected socioeconomic factors to human birth-weight. *Annals of Human Genetics*, **31**, 71-83.

NELSON, G. K. & DEAN, R. F. A. (1959) *Bull. World Health Organization*, **21**, 779. Cited by J. CRAVIOTO, Malnutrition and behavioral development in the preschool child. *Pre-school Child Malnutrition*. National Health Science, Public. No. 1282, 1966.

NEWMAN, H. H., FREEMAN, F. N. & HOLZINGER, K. J. (1937) *Twins: A Study of Heredity and Environment.* Chicago: Univ. of Chicago Press.

NICHOLS, P. L. (1972) The effects of heredity and environment on intelligence test performance in 4- and 7-year-old white and Negro sibling pairs. Unpublished doctoral dissertation, University of Minnesota (Microfilm).

NICHOLS, R. C. (1965) The National Merit twin study. In S. G. VAN-DENBERG (ed.), *Methods and Goals in Human Behavior Genetics*. New York: Academic Press.

NOBLE, C. E. (1968) The learning of psychomotor skills. *Annual Review of Psychology*, **19**, 203-50.

NOBLE, C. E. (1969) Race, reality, and experimental psychology. *Perspectives in Biology and Medicine*, **13**, 10-30.

Office of the Surgeon General (June 1969) Supplement to health of the Army: Results of the examination of youths for military service, 1968. Washington, D.C.: Medical Statistics Agency, Department of the Army.

OSBORNE, R. T. (1960) Racial differences in mental growth and school achievement: A longitudinal study. *Psychological Reports*, **7**, 233-9.

OSBORNE, R. T. (1970) Population pollution. *Journal of Psychology*, **76**, 187-91.

OSBORNE, R. T. & GREGOR, A. J. (1966) The heritability of visualization, perceptual speed, and spatial orientation. *Perceptual and Motor Skills*, **23**, 379-90.

OSBORNE, R. T. & GREGOR, A. J. (1968) Racial differences in heritability estimates for tests of spatial ability. *Perceptual and Motor Skills*, **27**, 735-9.

OSBORNE, R. T., GREGOR, A. J. & MIELE, F. (1967) Heritability of numerical facility. *Perceptual and Motor Skills*, **24**, 659-66.

OSWALD, W. D. (1971) Über Zusammenhange zwischen Informations-geschwindigkeit, Alter und Intelligenzstruktur beim Kartensortieren. *Psychologische Rundschau*, **22**, 197-202.

PASAMANICK, B. (1949) A comparative study of the behavioral development of Negro infants. *Journal of Genetic Psychology*, **75**, 82-125.

PASAMANICK, B. & KNOBLOCH, HILDA (1966) Retrospective studies on the epidemiology of reproductive casualty: Old and new. *Merrill-Palmer Quarterly of Behavior and Development*, **12**, 7-26.

PAULSON, E. (1942) An approximate normalization of the analysis of variance distribution. *Annals of Mathematical Statistics*, **13**, 233-5.

PEISACH, ESTELLE C. (1965) Children's comprehension of teacher and peer speech. *Child Development*, **36**, 467-80.

PENROSE, L. S. (1951) Genetics of the human race. In L. C. DUNN (ed.), *Genetics in the 20th Century*. New York: Macmillan.

PETERSON, J. & LANIER, L. H. (1929) Studies in the comparative abilities of whites and Negroes. *Mental Measurements Monographs*, No. 5, p. 156.

PETTIGREW, T. F. & NUTTALL, R. L. (1963) Negro American perception of the irradiation illusion. *Perceptual and Motor Skills*, **17**, 98.

PHILLIPS, J. L., JR. (1969) *The Origins of Intellect: Piaget's Theory*. San Francisco: W. H. Freeman.

PIAGET, J. (1960) The general problem of the psychobiological development of the child. In J. M. TANNER & B. INHELDER (eds.), *Discussions on Child Development*, Vol. 4. New York: International Universities Press.

PLATT, B. S. (1968) Nutrition and psychosocial deprivation. In *Perspectives on Human Deprivation: Biological, Psychological and Sociological*. Washington, D.C.: U.S. Department of Health, Education and Welfare. Pp. 241-5.

PLOTKIN, L. (1971) Negro intelligence and the Jensen hypothesis. *The New York Statistician*, 22, 3-7.

POLLITT, E. & GRANOFF, D. (1967) Mental and motor development of Peruvian children treated for severe malnutrition. *Revista Interamericana Psicologia*, 1, 93-102.

QUAY, LORENE C. (1971) Language, dialect, reinforcement, and the intelligence test performance of Negro children. *Child Development*, 42, 5-15.

RACE, R. & SANGER, R. (1968) *Blood Groups in Man*, 5th ed. Philadelphia: Davis.

RAMAROSAONA, A. (1959) Psychomotor development in early childhood in the Tanarariue region. Annex IX in C.S.A. Meeting of Specialists on the Basic Psychology of African and Madagascan Populations, *C.S.A. Publication* No. 51, Tanarariue.

REED, T. E. (1969a) Caucasian genes in American Negroes. *Science*, 165, 762-8.

REED, T. E. (1969b) Letters. *Science*, 165, 1353.

ROBERTS, R. C. (1967) Some concepts and methods in quantitative genetics. In J. HIRSCH (ed.), *Behavior-Genetic Analysis*. New York: McGraw-Hill. Pp. 214-57.

ROSENFELD, M. & HILTON, T. L. (1971) Negro-white differences in adolescent educational growth. *American Educational Research Journal*, 8, 267-83.

ROSENTHAL, R. & JACOBSON, LENORE (1968) *Pygmalion in the Classroom*. New York: Holt, Rinehart & Winston.

ROTH, E. (1964) Die Geschwindigkeit der Verarbeitung von Information und ihr Zusammenhang mit Intelligenz. *Zeitschrift für experimentelle und angewandte Psychologie*, 11, 616-22.

SATTLER, J. M. (1970) Racial 'experimenter effects' in experimentation, testing, interviewing, and psychotherapy. *Psychological Bulletin*, 73, 137-60.

SATTLER, J. M. (1972) Intelligence testing of ethnic minority groups and culturally disadvantaged children. In L. MANN & D. SABATINO (eds.), *The Review of Special Education*. Pennsylvania: Buttonwood Farms.

SCARR-SALAPATEK, SANDRA (1971a) Race, social class, and IQ. *Science*, 174, 1285-95.

SCARR-SALAPATEK, SANDRA (1971b) Unknowns in the IQ equation. *Science*, 174, 1223-8.

SCHULL, W. J. & NEEL, J. V. (1965) *The Effects of Inbreeding on Japanese Children*. New York: Harper & Row.

SCOTT, R. B., FERGUSON, ANGELA B., JENKINS, M. E. & CUTLER, F. E. (1955) Growth and development of Negro infants: V. Neuro-muscular patterns of behavior during the first year of life. *Pediatrics*, **16**, 24-30.

SCRIMSHAW, N. S. & GORDON, J. E. (eds.) (1968) *Malnutrition, Learning, and Behavior.* Cambridge, Mass.: M.I.T. Press.

SCRIVEN, M. (1970) The values of the academy. (Moral issues for American education and educational research arising from the Jensen case.) *Review of Educational Research*, **40**, 541-9.

SEXTON, PATRICIA C. (1961) *Education and Income: Inequalities of Opportunity in our Public Schools.* New York: Viking.

SHIELDS, J. (1962) *Monozygotic Twins Brought Up Apart and Brought Up Together.* London: Oxford University Press.

SHOCKLEY, W. (1966) Possible transfer of metallurgical and astronomical approaches to problem of environment versus ethnic heredity. *Science*, **154**, 428.

SHOCKLEY, W. (1969) Offset analysis description of racial differences. *Proceedings of the National Academy of Sciences*, **64**, 1432.

SHOCKLEY, W. (1970a) 'Cooperative correlation' hypothesis for racial differences in earning power. *Proceedings of the National Academy of Sciences*, **66**, 245.

SHOCKLEY, W. (1970b) New methodology to reduce the environment-heredity uncertainty about dysgenics. Paper presented at the Autumn meeting of the National Academy of Sciences, Rice University, Houston, Texas, 21 October.

SHOCKLEY, W. (1971a) Negro IQ deficit: Failure of a 'Malicious Coincidence' model warrants new research proposals. *Review of Educational Research*, **41**, 227-48.

SHOCKLEY, W. (1971b) Hardy-Weinberg law generalized to estimate hybrid variance for Negro populations and reduce racial aspects of the environment-heredity uncertainty. *Proceedings of the National Academy of Sciences*, **68**, 1390A.

SHOCKLEY, W. (1971c) Models, mathematics, and the moral obligation to diagnose the origin of Negro IQ deficits. *Review of Educational Research*, **41**, 369-77.

SHUEY, AUDREY M. (1966) *The Testing of Negro Intelligence*, 2nd ed. New York: Social Science Press.

SIGEL, J. E. & OLMSTED, PATRICIA (1970) Modification of cognitive skills among lower-class black children. In J. HELLMUTH (ed.), *Disadvantaged Child*, Vol. 3. New York: Brunner-Mazel. Pp. 330-8.

SILBERBERG, N. E. & SILBERBERG, MARGARET C. (1972) A late – but indignant – comment on the arguments raised by Jensen. *The School Psychologist Newsletter*, March, 37-40.

SITGREAVES, ROSEDITH (1971) Comments on the 'Jensen Report'. *The New York Statistician*, **22**, No. 5, pp. 1-2.

SJOGREN, D. D. (1967) Achievement as a function of study time. *American Educational Research Journal*, **4**, 337-43.

SKEELS, H. M. (1966) Adult status of children with contrasting early life experiences: A follow-up study. *Child Development Monograph*, **31**, No. 3, Serial No. 105.

SKEELS, H. M. & DYE, H. B. (1939) A study of the effects of differential stimulation on mentally retarded children. *Proceedings and Addresses of the American Association of Mental Deficiencies*, **44**, 114-36.

SKODAK, MARIE & SKEELS, H. M. (1949) A final follow-up study of one hundred adopted children. *Journal of Genetic Psychology*, **75**, 85-125.

SNOW, R. (1969) Unfinished Pygmalion. *Contemporary Psychology*, **14**, 197-9.

SPSSI Council. See Council of the Society for the Psychological Study of Social Issues.

SPUHLER, J. N. & LINDZEY, G. (1967) Racial differences in behavior. In J. HIRSCH (ed.), *Behavior-genetic Analysis*. New York: McGraw-Hill. Pp. 366-414.

STANLEY, J. C. (1971) Predicting college success of the educationally disadvantaged. *Science*, **171**, 640-7.

STEIN, ZENA A. & KASSAB, H. (1970) Nutrition. In J. WORTIS (ed.), *Mental Retardation: An Annual Review*, Vol. I. New York: Grune & Stratton. Pp. 92-116.

STERN, C. (1970) Model estimates of the number of gene pairs involved in pigmentation variability of the Negro American. *Human Heredity*, **20**, 165-8.

STINCHCOMBE, A. L. (1969) Environment: the cumulation of effects is yet to be understood. *Harvard Educational Review*, **39**, 511-22.

STOCH, M. B. & SMYTHE, P. M. (1963) Does undernutrition during infancy inhibit brain growth and subsequent intellectual development? *Archives of Diseases of Childhood*, **38**, 546-52.

STOUFFER, S. A. *et al.* (1965) *The American Soldier*, Vol. I. New York: Wiley.

TENOPYR, MARY L. (1967) Race and socioeconomic status as moderators in predicting machine-shop training success. Paper presented at the annual meeting of the American Psychological Association, Washington, D.C., 4 September.

TERMAN, L. M. (1926) *Genetic Studies of Genius*. Vol. I. *Mental and Physical Traits of a Thousand Gifted Children*. Stanford, Calif.: Stanford University Press.

TERMAN, L. M. (1940) Personal reactions of the Yearbook Committee. In G. M. WHIPPLE (ed.), *Intelligence: Its Nature and Nurture*, 39th

Yearbook of the National Society for the Study of Education. Part I. Pp. 460-7.

TERMAN, L. M. & ODEN, M. (1959) *The Gifted Group at Mid-life.* Stanford, Calif.: Stanford University Press.

THEUNISSEN, K. B. (1948) A preliminary comparative study of the development of motor behavior in European and Bantu children up to the age of one year. M.A. thesis, Natal University College, Durban.

THODAY, J. M. (1969) Limitations to genetic comparison of populations. *Journal of Biosocial Science, Supplement,* 1, pp. 3-14.

THODAY, J. M. & GIBSON, J. B. (1970) Environmental and genetical contributions to class difference: a model experiment. *Science,* 167, 990-2.

THORNDIKE, E. L. (1940) *Human Nature and the Social Order.* New York: Macmillan.

THORNDIKE, R. L. (1951) Community variables as predictors of intelligence and academic achievement. *Journal of Educational Psychology,* 42, 321-38.

THORNDIKE, R. L. (1966) Intellectual status and intellectual growth. *Journal of Educational Psychology,* 57, 121-7.

THORNDIKE, R. L. (1968) Review of R. Rosenthal and L. Jacobson, 'Pygmalion in the Classroom'. *American Educational Research Journal,* 5, 708-11.

TIBER, N. & KENNEDY, W. A. (1964) The effect of incentives on the intelligence test performance of different social groups. *Journal of Consulting Psychology,* 28, 187.

TUDDENHAM, R. D. (1970) A 'Piagetian' test of cognitive development. In B. DOCKRELL (ed.), *On Intelligence.* Toronto: Ontario Institute for Studies in Education, pp. 49-70 (London, Methuen, 1970).

TULKIN, S. R. (1968) Race, class, family, and school achievement. *Journal of Personality and Social Psychology,* 9, 31-7.

TYLER, LEONA E. (1965) *The Psychology of Human Differences,* 3rd ed. New York: Appleton-Century-Crofts.

U.S. *Department of Health, Education and Welfare* (1967) *Vital Statistics of the United States,* 1965, Vol. II, Mortality, Part A. Washington, D.C.

VANDENBERG, S. G. (1962) The hereditary abilities study: Hereditary components in a psychological test battery. *American Journal of Human Genetics,* 14, 220-37.

VANDENBERG, S. G. (1970) A comparison of heritability estimates of U.S. Negro and white high school students. *Acta Geneticae Medicae et Gemellologiae,* 19, 280-4.

VANE, JULIA R. (1966) Relation of early school achievement to high school achievement when race, intelligence and socioeconomic factors are equated. *Psychology in the Schools,* 3, 124-9.

VERNON, M. (1967) Relationship of language to the thinking process. *Archives of General Psychiatry*, **16**, 325-33.

VERNON, M. (1968) Fifty years of research on the intelligence of deaf and hard-of-hearing children: A review of literature and discussion of implications. *Journal of Rehabilitation of the Deaf*, **1**, 1-12.

VERNON, P. E. (1965a) Ability factors and environmental influences. *American Psychologist*, **20**, 723-33.

VERNON, P. E. (1965b) Environmental handicaps and intellectual development: Part II and Part III. *British Journal of Educational Psychology*, **35**, 1-22.

VERNON, P. E. (1969) *Intelligence and Cultural Environment*. London: Methuen.

VOUILLOUX, — (1959) Étude de la psycho-motricité d'enfants africains au Cameroun: test de Gesell et réflexes archaïques. *Journal de la Société des Africanistes*, **29**, 11-18.

VOYAT, G. (1970) IQ: God-given or man-made? *Saturday Review*, 1969, **52**, 74-5. Reprinted in: J. HELLMUTH (ed.), *Disadvantaged Child*, Vol. 3. New York: Brunner-Mazel. Pp. 158-62.

WALKER, HELEN M. & LEV, J. (1953) *Statistical Inference*. New York: Holt.

WALLER, J. H. (1971a) Differential reproduction: Its relation to IQ test scores, education, and occupation. *Social Biology*, **18**, 122-36.

WALLER, J. H. (1971b) Achievement and social mobility: Relationships among IQ score, education, and occupation in two generations. *Social Biology*, **18**, 252-9.

WALTERS, E. ETTA (1967) Comparative development of Negro and white infants. *Journal of Genetic Psychology*, **110**, 243-51.

WARREN, B. L. (1966) A multiple variable approach to the assortative mating phenomenon. *Eugenics Quarterly*, **13**, 285-90.

WATSON, P. (1970) How race effects IQ. *New Society*, **16**, 103-4.

WECHSLER, D. (1958) *The Measurement and Appraisal of Adult Intelligence*, 4th ed. Baltimore: Williams & Wilkins.

WEENER, P. D. (1969) Social dialect differences and the recall of verbal messages. *Journal of Educational Psychology*, **60**, 194-9.

WEYL, N. (1969) Some comparative performance indexes of American ethnic minorities. *Mankind Quarterly*, **9**, 106-28.

WHITE, S. H. (1965) Evidence for a hierarchical arrangement of learning processes. In L. P. LIPSITT & C. C. SPIKER (eds.), *Advances in Child Development and Behaviour*, Vol. 2. New York: Academic Press. Pp. 187-220.

WILLERMAN, L., NAYLOR, A. F. & MYRIANTHOPOULOS, N. C. (1970) Intellectual development of children from interracial matings. *Science*, **170**, 1329-31.

WILLIAMS, JUDITH R. & SCOTT, R. B. (1953) Growth and development of Negro infants: IV. Motor development and its relationship to child-rearing practices in two groups of Negro infants. *Child Development*, **24**, 103-21.

WILSON, A. B. (1967) Educational consequences of segregation in a California community. *Racial Isolation in the Public Schools*, Appendices, Vol. II, p. 185. U.S. Commission on Civil Rights, Washington.

WINICK, M. (1970) Nutrition, growth, and mental development: Biological correlations. *American Journal of Diseases of Children*, **120**, 416-18.

WOLAŃSKI, N., JAROSZ, EMILIA & PYŻUK, MIRA (1970) Heterosis in man: Growth in offspring and distance between parents' birthplaces. *Social Biology*, **17**, 1-16.

WRIGHT, S. (1931) Statistical methods in biology. *Journal of the American Statistical Association*, **26**, 155-63.

YOUNG, M. & GIBSON, J. B. (1965) Social mobility and fertility. In J. E. MEADE & A. S. PARKES (eds.), *Biological Aspects of Social Problems*. Edinburgh: Oliver and Boyd.

ZEAMAN, D. & HOUSE, BETTY J. (1967) The relation of IQ and learning. In R. M. GAGNÉ (ed.), *Learning and Individual Differences*. Columbus, Ohio: Charles E. Merrill. Pp. 192-212.

ZIRKEL, P. A. & MOSES, E. G. (1971) Self-concept and ethnic group membership among public students. *American Educational Research Journal*, **8**, 253-65.

Author Index

Subject Index